Computing Attitude and Affect in Text: Theory and Applications

THE INFORMATION RETRIEVAL SERIES

Series Editor:
W. Bruce Croft
University of Massachusetts, Amherst

Also in the Series:

INFORMATION RETRIEVAL SYSTEMS: *Theory and Implementation,* by Gerald Kowalski;
   ISBN: 0-7923-9926-9

CROSS-LANGUAGE INFORMATION RETRIEVAL, *edited by Gregory Grefenstette;*
   ISBN: 0-7923-8122-X

TEXT RETRIEVAL AND FILTERING: *Analytic Models of Performance,* by Robert M. Losee;
   ISBN: 0-7923-8177-7

INFORMATION RETRIEVAL: UNCERTAINTY AND LOGICS: *Advanced Models for the Representation and Retrieval of Information,* by Fabio Crestani, Mounia Lalmas, and Cornelis Joost van Rijsbergen; ISBN: 0-7923-8302-8

DOCUMENT COMPUTING: *Technologies for Managing Electronic Document Collections,* by Ross Wilkinson, Timothy Arnold-Moore, Michael Fuller, Ron Sacks-Davis, James Thom, and Justin Zobel; ISBN: 0-7923-8357-5

AUTOMATIC INDEXING AND ABSTRACTING OF DOCUMENT TEXTS, by Marie-Francine Moens;
   ISBN 0-7923-7793-1

ADVANCES IN INFORMATIONAL RETRIEVAL: *Recent Research from the Center for Intelligent Information Retrieval,* by W. Bruce Croft; ISBN 0-7923-7812-1

INFORMATION RETRIEVAL SYSTEMS: *Theory and Implementation,* Second Edition,
   by Gerald J. Kowalski and Mark T. Maybury; ISBN: 0-7923-7924-1

PERSPECTIVES ON CONTENT-BASED MULTIMEDIA SYSTEMS, by Jian Kang Wu;
   Mohan S. Kankanhalli;Joo-Hwee Lim;Dezhong Hong; ISBN: 0-7923-7944-6

MINING THE WORLD WIDE WEB: *An Information Search Approach,* by George Chang, Marcus J. Healey, James A. M. McHugh, Jason T. L. Wang; ISBN: 0-7923-7349-9

INTEGRATED REGION-BASED IMAGE RETRIEVAL, by James Z. Wang;
   ISBN: 0-7923-7350-2

TOPIC DETECTION AND TRACKING: Event-based Information Organization, edited by James Allan;
   ISBN: 0-7923-7664-1

LANGUAGE MODELING FOR INFORMATION RETRIEVAL, edited by W. Bruce Croft; John Lafferty;
   ISBN: 1-4020-1216-0

MACHINE LEARNING AND STATISTICAL MODELING APPROACHES TO IMAGE RETRIEVAL,
   by Yixin Chen, Jia Li and James Z. Wang; ISBN: 1-4020-8034-4

INFORMATION RETRIEVAL: *Algorithms and Heuristics,* by David A. Grossman and Ophir Frieder,
   2nd ed.; ISBN: 1-4020-3003-7; PB: ISBN: 1-4020-3004-5

Computing Attitude and Affect in Text:
Theory and Applications

Edited by

James G. Shanahan

Clairvoyance Cooperation,
Pittsburgh, PA, U.S.A.

Yan Qu

Clairvoyance Cooperation,
Pittsburgh, PA, U.S.A.

and

Janyce Wiebe

University of Pittsburgh,
PA, U.S.A.

 Springer

A C.I.P. Catalogue record for this book is available from the Library of Congress.

ISBN-10 94-007-9257-3 (HB)
ISBN-13 978-94-007-9257-9 (HB)
ISBN-10 1-4020-4102-0 (e-book)
ISBN-13 978-1-4020-4102-0 (e-book)

Published by Springer,
P.O. Box 17, 3300 AA Dordrecht, The Netherlands.

www.springer.com

Printed on acid-free paper

TABLE OF CONTENTS

PREFACE xi

1. CONTEXTUAL VALENCE SHIFTERS

Livia Polanyi, Annie Zaenen 1

1. INTRODUCTION... 1
2. FROM SIMPLE VALENCE TO CONTEXTUALLY DETERMINED VALENCE............................ 2
3. CONTEXTUAL VALENCE SHIFTERS 3
4. CONCLUSION 9

2. CONVEYING ATTITUDE WITH REPORTED SPEECH

Sabine Bergler 11

1. INTRODUCTION... 11
2. EVIDENTIAL ANALYSIS OF REPORTED SPEECH.. 12
3. PROFILE STRUCTURE 14
4. EXTENDED EXAMPLE 16
5. SOURCE LIST ANNOTATION 17
6. EXTENSION TO OTHER ATTRIBUTION 20
7. CONCLUSION 20

3. WHERE ATTITUDINAL EXPRESSIONS GET THEIR ATTITUDE

Jussi Karlgren, Gunnar Eriksson, Kristofer Franzén 23

1. RESEARCH QUESTIONS TO MOTIVATE THE STUDY OF ATTITUDINAL EXPRESSIONS 23
2. STARTING POINTS – PROTOTYPICAL ATTITUDINAL EXPRESSIONS.................................. 24
3. TEXT TOPICALITY: PLAYERS 24
4. TEXT TOPICALITY: MOVES.. 25
5. IDENTIFYING PLAYERS 25
6. THE CASE FOR ANIMACY: ADJECTIVAL ATTRIBUTES AND GENITIVE ATTRIBUTES 25
7. THE CASE FOR SYNTACTIC STRUCTURE: SITUATIONAL REFERENCE 26
8. USING SYNTACTIC PATTERNS MORE SYSTEMATICALLY.. 28
9. GENERALIZING FROM SYNTACTIC PATTERNS TO THE LEXICON.................................... 29
10. CONCLUSIONS 29

4. ANALYSIS OF LINGUISTIC FEATURES ASSOCIATED WITH POINT OF VIEW FOR GENERATING STYLISTICALLY APPROPRIATE TEXT

Nancy L. Green... 33

1. INTRODUCTION... 33
2. PERSPECTIVES IN CORPUS 34
3. ASSOCIATED FEATURES 36

4. IMPLICATIONS FOR NATURAL LANGUAGE GENERATION AND AUTOMATIC RECOGNITION OF
POINT OF VIEW 38

5. THE SUBJECTIVITY OF LEXICAL COHESION IN TEXT

Jane Morris, Graeme Hirst 41

1. INTRODUCTION.. 41
2. THEORETICAL BACKGROUND... 42
3. EXPERIMENTAL STUDY 43
4. DISCUSSION... 45

6. A WEIGHTED REFERENTIAL ACTIVITY DICTIONARY

Wilma Bucci, Bernard Maskit.. 49

1. INTRODUCTION.. 50
2. METHODS 52
3. RESULTS.. 58

7. CERTAINTY IDENTIFICATION IN TEXTS: CATEGORIZATION MODEL AND
   MANUAL TAGGING RESULTS

Victoria L. Rubin, Elizabeth D. Liddy, Noriko Kando 61

1. ANALYTICAL FRAMEWORK 62
2. PROPOSED CERTAINTY CATEGORIZATION MODEL 65
3. EMPIRICAL STUDY.. 68
4. APPLICATIONS... 74
5. CONCLUSIONS AND FUTURE WORK... 74

8. EVALUATING AN OPINION ANNOTATION SCHEME USING A NEW MULTI-
   PERSPECTIVE QUESTION AND ANSWER CORPUS

Veselin Stoyanov, Claire Cardie, Diane Litman, Janyce Wiebe.. 77

1. INTRODUCTION.. 77
2. LOW-LEVEL PERSPECTIVE INFORMATION 78
3. THE MPQA NRRC CORPUS.. 80
4. MULTI-PERSPECTIVE QUESTION AND ANSWER CORPUS CREATION 80
5. EVALUATION OF PERSPECTIVE ANNOTATIONS FOR MPQA....................................... 83
6. CONCLUSIONS AND FUTURE WORK... 89

9. VALIDATING THE COVERAGE OF LEXICAL RESOURCES FOR AFFECT
   ANALYSIS AND AUTOMATICALLY CLASSIFYING NEW WORDS ALONG
   SEMANTIC AXES

Gregory Grefenstette, Yan Qu, David A. Evans, James G. Shanahan 93

1. INTRODUCTION.. 94
2. THE CURRENT CLAIRVOYANCE AFFECT LEXICON 95
3. EMOTIVE PATTERNS... 97
4. SCORING THE INTENSITY OF CANDIDATE AFFECT WORDS....................................... 101
5. FUTURE WORK 105
6. CONCLUSIONS 106

10. A COMPUTATIONAL SEMANTIC LEXICON OF FRENCH VERBS OF EMOTION

Yvette Yannick Mathieu **109**

1. INTRODUCTION.. 109
2. SEMANTIC LEXICON DESCRIPTION 109
3. *FEELING* SYSTEM 116
4. EVALUATION.. 122
5. RELATED WORK... 123
6. CONCLUSION.. 123

11. EXTRACTING OPINION PROPOSITIONS AND OPINION HOLDERS USING SYNTACTIC AND LEXICAL CUES

Steven Bethard, Hong Yu, Ashley Thornton, Vasileios Hatzivassiloglou, Dan Jurafsky 125

1. INTRODUCTION.. 125
2. DATA.. 127
3. OPINION-ORIENTED WORDS... 130
4. IDENTIFYING OPINION PROPOSITIONS 132
5. RESULTS.. 136
6. ERROR ANALYSIS.. 138
7. DISCUSSION.. 139

12. APPROACHES FOR AUTOMATICALLY TAGGING AFFECT

Nathanael Chambers, Joel Tetreault, James Allen **143**

1. INTRODUCTION.. 143
2. BACKGROUND 144
3. ROCHESTER MARRIAGE-COUNSELING CORPUS...................................... 145
4. APPROACHES TO TAGGING 146
5. EVALUATIONS 153
6. DISCUSSION.. 154
7. CATS TOOL 156
8. RELATED WORK... 157
9. CONCLUSION.. 157

13. ARGUMENTATIVE ZONING FOR IMPROVED CITATION INDEXING

Simone Teufel **159**

1. CITATION INDEXING AND CITATION MAPS.. 159
2. ARGUMENTATIVE ZONING AND AUTHOR AFFECT 161
3. META-DISCOURSE 163
4. HUMAN ANNOTATION OF AUTHOR AFFECT 165
5. FEATURES FOR AUTHOR AFFECT.. 167
6. EVALUATION.. 167
7. CONCLUSION.. 168

14. POLITENESS AND BIAS IN DIALOGUE SUMMARIZATION: TWO EXPLORATORY STUDIES

Norton Trevisan Roman, Paul Piwek, Ariadne Maria Brito Rizzoni Carvalho 171

1. INTRODUCTION.. 172
2. FIRST STUDY: POLITENESS AND BIAS IN UNCONSTRAINED DIALOGUE SUMMARIZATION 174
3. SECOND STUDY: POLITENESS AND BIAS IN CONSTRAINED DIALOGUE SUMMARIZATION 178
4. COMPARISON... 180
5. CONCLUSION AND OUTLOOK... 181

15. GENERATING MORE-POSITIVE AND MORE-NEGATIVE TEXT

Diana Zaiu Inkpen, Ol'ga Feiguina, Graeme Hirst... 187

1. NEAR-SYNONYMS AND ATTITUDINAL NUANCES 187
2. RELATED WORK... 189
3. ESTIMATING THE RELATIVE SEMANTIC ORIENTATION OF TEXT............................... 189
4. WORD SENSE DISAMBIGUATION 190
5. ANALYSIS... 190
6. GENERATION 191
7. EXPERIMENTS... 192
8. EVALUATION 195
9. CONCLUSION 196

16. IDENTIFYING INTERPERSONAL DISTANCE USING SYSTEMIC FEATURES

Casey Whitelaw, Jon Patrick, Maria Herke-Couchman....................................... 199

1. INTRODUCTION... 200
2. SYSTEMIC FUNCTIONAL LINGUISTICS 200
3. REPRESENTING SYSTEM NETWORKS 204
4. IDENTIFYING REGISTERS 209
5. CONCLUSION 212

17. CORPUS-BASED STUDY OF SCIENTIFIC METHODOLOGY: COMPARING THE HISTORICAL AND EXPERIMENTAL SCIENCES

Shlomo Argamon, Jeff Dodick 215

1. INTRODUCTION... 216
2. BACKGROUND 216
3. SYSTEMIC INDICATORS AS TEXTUAL FEATURES 219
4. EXPERIMENTAL STUDY 222
5. EXAMPLE TEXTS 227
6. CONCLUSIONS 228

18. ARGUMENTATIVE ZONING APPLIED TO CRITIQUING NOVICES' SCIENTIFIC ABSTRACTS

Valéria D. Feltrim, Simone Teufel, Maria das Graças V. Nunes, Sandra M. Aluísio 233

1. INTRODUCTION.. 234

2. THE SCIPO SYSTEM.. 234
3. ARGUMENTATIVE ZONING FOR PORTUGUESE TEXTS 237
4. EVALUATION OF SCIPO'S CRITIQUING TOOL... 242
5. CONCLUSIONS 244

19. USING HEDGES TO CLASSIFY CITATIONS IN SCIENTIFIC ARTICLES

Chrysanne Di Marco, Frederick W. Kroon, Robert E. Mercer **247**

1. SCIENTIFIC WRITING, THE NEED FOR AFFECT, AND ITS ROLE IN CITATION ANALYSIS 247
2. HEDGING IN SCIENTIFIC WRITING 248
3. CLASSIFYING CITATIONS IN SCIENTIFIC WRITING 250
4. DETERMINING THE IMPORTANCE OF HEDGES IN CITATION CONTEXTS........................ 252
5. A CITATION INDEXING TOOL FOR BIOMEDICAL LITERATURE ANALYSIS 256
6. CONCLUSIONS AND FUTURE WORK... 261

20. TOWARDS A ROBUST METRIC OF POLARITY

Kamal Nigam, Matthew Hurst.. **265**

1. INTRODUCTION.. 265
2. RELATED WORK.. 266
3. CLASSES OF POLAR EXPRESSION... 268
4. RECOGNIZING POLAR LANGUAGE 269
5. TOPIC DETECTION IN ONLINE MESSAGES... 270
6. THE INTERSECTION OF TOPIC AND POLARITY... 272
7. EMPIRICAL ANALYSIS 273
8. METRICS FOR TOPIC AND POLARITY 275
9. CONCLUSIONS AND FUTURE WORK... 277

**21. CHARACTERIZING BUZZ AND SENTIMENT IN INTERNET SOURCES:
LINGUISTIC SUMMARIES AND PREDICTIVE BEHAVIORS**

Richard M. Tong, Ronald R. Yager... **281**

1. INTRODUCTION AND MOTIVATION 281
2. LINGUISTIC SUMMARIES.. 282
3. EXAMPLE APPLICATIONS 289
4. TRENDS-2™ INFRASTRUCTURE 292
5. PREVIOUS AND RELATED WORK 293
6. OPEN R&D AND APPLICATION ISSUES 293

22. GOOD NEWS OR BAD NEWS? LET THE MARKET DECIDE

Moshe Koppel, Itai Shtrimberg.. **297**

1. INTRODUCTION.. 297
2. EXPERIMENTS... 298
3. RESULTS... 299
4. CONCLUSIONS 300

23. OPINION POLARITY IDENTIFICATION OF MOVIE REVIEWS

Franco Salvetti, Christoph Reichenbach, Stephen Lewis 303

1. INTRODUCTION 303
2. RELATED RESEARCH 304
3. PROBABILISTIC APPROACHES TO POLARITY IDENTIFICATION 305
4. FEATURES FOR ANALYSIS 306
5. PART OF SPEECH FEATURE SELECTION 307
6. EXPERIMENTS 308
7. SYNONYMY AND HYPERNYMY FEATURE GENERALIZATION 312
8. SELECTION BY RANKING 314
9. DISCUSSION 314
10. CONCLUSION 315

24. MULTI-DOCUMENT VIEWPOINT SUMMARIZATION FOCUSED ON FACTS, OPINION AND KNOWLEDGE

Yohei Seki, Koji Eguchi, Noriko Kando 317

1. INTRODUCTION 318
2. EXPERIMENT OVERVIEW: MULTI-DOCUMENT VIEWPOINT SUMMARIZATION WITH SUMMARY TYPES 319
3. SENTENCE-TYPE ANNOTATION 323
4. GENRE CLASSIFICATION 325
5. EXPERIMENT RESULTS 328
6. CONCLUSION 333

INDEX 337

Preface

Human Language Technology (HLT) and Natural Language Processing (NLP) systems have typically focused on the "factual" aspect of content analysis. Other aspects, including pragmatics, opinion, and style, have received much less attention. However, to achieve an adequate understanding of a text, these aspects cannot be ignored.

The chapters in this book address the aspect of subjective opinion, which includes identifying different points of view, identifying different emotive dimensions, and classifying text by opinion. Various conceptual models and computational methods are presented. The models explored in this book include the following: distinguishing attitudes from simple factual assertions; distinguishing between the author's reports from reports of other people's opinions; and distinguishing between explicitly and implicitly stated attitudes. In addition, many applications are described that promise to benefit from the ability to understand attitudes and affect, including indexing and retrieval of documents by opinion; automatic question answering about opinions; analysis of sentiment in the media and in discussion groups about consumer products, political issues, etc.; brand and reputation management; discovering and predicting consumer and voting trends; analyzing client discourse in therapy and counseling; determining relations between scientific texts by finding reasons for citations; generating more appropriate texts and making agents more believable; and creating writers' aids. The studies reported here are carried out on different languages such as English, French, Japanese, and Portuguese.

Difficult challenges remain, however. It can be argued that analyzing attitude and affect in text is an "NLP"-complete problem. The interpretation of attitude and affect depends on audience, context, and world knowledge. In addition, there is much yet to learn about the psychological and biological relationships between emotion and language.

To continue to progress in this area in NLP, more comprehensive theories of emotion, attitude and opinion are needed, as are lexicons of affective terms and knowledge of how such terms are used in context, and annotated corpora for training and evaluation.

This book is a first foray into this area; it grew out of a symposium on this topic that took place at Stanford University in March, 2004, under support from American Association for Artificial Intelligence (AAAI). Several of the presentations were extended into the chapters that appear here. The chapters in this collection reflect the majors themes of the workshop, corresponding to a balance among conceptual models, computational methods, and applications. The chapters in this book are organized along these themes into three broad, overlapping parts.

Linguistic and Cognitive Models

The chapters in the first part of this book explore linguistic and cognitive models which could support developing richer computational models of attitude and affect. This section begins with Polanyi and Zaenen's fascinating study of attitudinal valence (or polarity) as it is expressed in context. While individual words often suggest a negative or positive attitude, such as "horrible" and "great", respectively, the context of a word may change its base valence. Polanyi and Zaenen describe and illustrate a number of such contextual valence shifters, both intra-sentential (e.g., negatives and modals) and inter-sentential (e.g., discourse connectives and multi-entity evaluation).

The next chapter, by Bergler, also explores linguistic devices for conveying attitudes in text, namely reported speech expressions which convey attitudes. Bergler argues that reported speech serves to segment information into discourse segments called profiles. Each profile involves such things as degree of credibility of the source of the information, and the role the source has in the argumentative structure of the text. Bergler performs a detailed profile analysis of an extended story, and discusses extending this type of analysis to other attributes than reported speech.

Like Polaryi and Zaenen, and Bergler, Karlgren et al. focus on contextual aspects of linguistic expressions of attitudes. Their particular objects of study are attitude expressions which are internally structured. They argue that simple lists of attitudinal terms are not sufficient for recognizing attitudes in texts: it is often only in particular lexical and syntactic patterns that words convey attitudes. They present interesting results of a corpus study suggesting that certain syntactic contexts are more likely to be loci of attitudes, and that this is realized in stylistic differences between opinionated text types such as editorials and more objective text types such as reporting news articles.

The second set of chapters in this section address cognitive as well as linguistic issues in understanding attitude and affect in text. Green's chapter presents the results of a qualitative analysis of letters written by genetic counselors to their clients. The goal is to find stylistic features that would be salient for natural generation systems in this genre. Her study suggests that perspective must be taken into account to generate stylistically appropriate text. Green identifies a number of perspectives in this genre, including specific agents such as the author and client, as well as abstract perspectives such as education and research. As a generation system assumes different perspectives while generating such a letter, it should choose forms of reference, tenses, types of evidential language, and so forth to reflect that perspective.

Morris and Hirst's chapter addresses readers' perceptions of lexical semantic relations, in particular the perceived subjectivity of such relations. They perform a study to assess the degree of individual differences in readers' interpretations of lexical chains, which are groups of related words that create lexical cohesion. The results showed that subjects identified a common core of groups of related words in text, but also exhibited individual differences. Such knowledge could help NLP systems recognize which types of text meaning can be expected to be shared by most readers, and understand and generate text appropriately.

Bucci and Maskit's presentation of a "Weighted Referential Activity Dictionary" is the most psychologically oriented chapter in the collection. Bucci and Maskit use their dictionary in computer modeling of a psycholinguistic variable which they call Referential Activity (RA). RA ratings measure the degree to which language connects to nonverbal experiences such as bodily and emotional experience. In Bucci and Maskit's model, RA is mainly indicated by domain-independent stylistic attributes of language, aspects of which are included in their dictionary. The chapter presents compelling RA analyses of literary passages, and describes a method for assigning RA weights to dictionary entries. Their study reveals differential linguistic roles of particular lexical items in producing vivid versus abstract texts. They plan to investigate the psychological significance of these differences in future work.

The final two chapters in this part of the book present annotation schemes, i.e., schemes for manually labeling texts to create data for training and evaluating NLP systems. The chapter by Rubin et al. presents a framework for coding the writer's certainty in text. They categorize a set of linguistic certainty markers (such as "probably"and "allegedly") along four dimensions – level (degree of certainty), perspective (whose certainty is being encoded), focus (abstract versus factual information), and time (past, present, or future). They perform an empirical study of their framework in which they applied their annotation scheme to 32 newspaper articles. Among their findings are that editorials contain more explicit certainty markers than news articles, and that a few specific combinations of dimension values dominate in editorials. The framework and empirical results will be informative for developing automatic certainty identification systems.

The chapter by Stoyanov et al. addresses annotations for Multi-Perspective Question Answering (MPQA), whereby an NLP system answers opinion-oriented questions. To be successful, an MPQA system will presumably need to recognize and organize the opinions expressed in one or more documents. An annotation scheme for encoding such opinions has been developed and evaluated in previous work. This chapter investigates the utility of that annotation scheme for MPQA processing. It first describes a new corpus of multi-perspective questions and answers. It then presents the results of a study investigating the usefulness of the earlier opinion annotations for multi-perspective versus fact-based question answering. Their findings are that opinion annotations can be useful for MPQA if used appropriately.

Lexical Resources and Attitude/Affect Recognition and Generation
The first two chapters in this part of the book focus on lexical resources that could support recognition and generation of attitude and affect. Lexicons of words of emotion-conveying potential have been used in much work for identifying and generating affect. The chapter by Grefenstette et al. addresses the problems of automatically extracting affect words for expanding the coverage of existing affect lexicons, and of automatically assigning the affect words along multiple semantic axes. Emotive patterns are used as seeds to extract affect words from the Web. Through evaluation of the precision and recall of the extracted words, the authors show that it is possible to identify lexical patterns for finding emotion-bearing affect words with high precision. Once the affect words are extracted, the authors discuss ways to automatically assign the words along the different semantic axes using measures similar to point-wise mutual information. The measures show promise for finding degrees of belongingness to the semantic classes while at the same time assigning degrees of intensity to the affect words.

In the following chapter, Mathieu first presents a manually constructed lexicon of French verbs of emotion with positive, negative, or neutral affect. Thirty-three semantic classes are proposed and the classes are arranged in graphical structures through links of intensity and antonyms. French verbs of each class are described by simple attribute-pair type properties such as whether a verb accepts a non-agentive subject or not. The lexicon is evaluated for identifying positive, negative, or neutral affect of sentences from French Letters to the Editors texts. The evaluation shows that taking into account the intensity of verbs of emotion produces better classification results.

The next three chapters present computational methods for recognizing attitude and affect in text. The first chapter by Bethard et al. addresses the tasks of detecting propositional opinions and detecting holders of these opinions. Unlike a variety of previous work on separating facts from opinions at the document or sentence level, this paper focuses on determining the opinion status of a smaller piece of text. Propositional opinions are opinions that are generally found as the sentential complements of a predicate. The authors use supervised statistical classification methods for proposition detection and opinion-holder detection, incorporating semantic constituent labeling, opinion-oriented words, and syntactic features such as the presence of complex adjective phrases.

The next chapter by Chambers et al. presents approaches for automatically tagging the attitude of the speakers in transcribed dialogues. The authors explore several n-gram- and vector-based approaches and present results in a marriage-counseling domain and the Switchboard Corpus. In the marriage-counseling domain, each transcript is broken into thought units that are manually annotated with tags classifying the attribute and emotional commitment of the participants to a particular topic of discussion. The Switchboard corpus consists of conversations of random topics and has a richer tagging scheme. The performance results over both corpora are comparable, and the simple n-gram based approaches outperform or perform as well as the vector-based approaches. The authors also describe a Java tool for tagging attitude and affect which integrates the automatic classification capability.

The chapter by Teufel addresses the problem of automatically classifying academic citations in scientific articles according to author affect. The two rhetorical roles for citation analysis that are associated with affect in text include Contrast (comparison with, criticism of, or contract to other work) and Basis (agreement with or continuation of other work). Teufel examines discourse features such as section structure, history to classify author affect, in addition to other features such as semantic class of main verb, indicator phrases, etc. Such analysis aims at improving citation indexing through better detection of subjectivity in scientific text.

The last two chapters in this part of the book explore attitude and affect in text generation and summarization. Roman et al. explore the influence of affect and attitude on summarizing dialogues. In particular, they address the question of whether politeness should be reported in dialogue summaries and, if so, how politeness is reported. The chapter presents empirical studies designed to gather information about how people summarize dialogues. In these studies, a collection of four dialogues, involving a customer and vendor about buying a car, was used. Each dialogue was generated by an automated system with the politeness of the dialogue participants manipulated. Subjects were asked to summarize the dialogues from a particular dialogue participant's point of view. The studies showed that the percentage of summaries reporting some behavior information was higher when the dialogues were more impolite. This result is independent of the point of view and summary size. The studies also indicated that the point of view adopted by the summarizer biases the reporting of behaviors in their summaries. In particular, negative reporting of behavior information depends on the point of view of the summarizer rather than on the actual dialogue behavior. Tentative evidence showed that positive reporting is less subject to such bias.

While Roman et al. study how people's points of view influence human generation of text and summaries, Inkpen et al. explore a way of producing text with different attitudinal nuances by varying word choices. In particular, they examine nuances that differentiate near-synonyms relating to expressed attitude and text, and propose to transform the semantic orientation of a text automatically by choosing near-synonyms accordingly. The transformation of semantic orientation involves first representing text as an inter-lingual representation and a set of lexical nuances, and then replacing the words with attitudinal nuances in the original text by their near-synonyms according to the desired nuances.

Applications
The third part of this book focuses on applications of attitude and affect. The first two chapters in this section explore the categorization of text based on the manner in which a document is written rather than its content. In particular, both chapters use a computational model based on different aspects of systemic functional linguistic (SFL) theory. Whitelaw et al. present a study that

demonstrates that the pronominal and determination systems of SFL are indeed powerful ways of characterizing interpersonal distance (between author and reader). They show empirically that this characterization of text is a robust means of recognizing financial scam email from regular email with a performance accuracy of 98% using a variety of machine learning algorithms. In contrast, Argamon and Dodick focus on conjunction, modality, and comment subsystems of SFL for genre-based text categorization of scientific articles in the historical and experimental sciences. Using a support vector machine trained on a systemic functional feature set (with no domain specific terms), they achieved over 83% accuracy for classifying articles according to field. The most highly-weighted features for each were consistent with hypothesized methodological differences between historical and experimental sciences.

The next two chapters in this section deal with applications that analyze the rhetorical structures of scientific papers. The first chapter by Feltrim et al. describes a system that uses argumentative zoning, a technique for identifying the rhetorical structure of text, as a thesis writing aid for graduate students working in Portuguese. Argumentative zoning techniques assign a label (drawn from possible rhetorical role labels such as background, purpose, results, and conclusion) to each sentence, indicating its argumentative role in a portion of text. The argumentative zoning algorithm (realized through a Naïve Bayes classier) is used to label each sentence as being a background, gap, purpose, methodology, result, conclusion, or outline. These rhetorical labels are then used by a rule-based system to identify problems in scientific text abstracts. A reported user study highlights the value of such a system for masters-level students. The work represents a successful adaptation of the argumentative zoning technique to the Portuguese language. In contrast, Di Marco et al., in their chapter, empirically validate a hypothesis that the use of hedges (words that make text more or less vague) is highly correlated with sentences that contain or surround citations. This study is based upon 985 peer-reviewed recent biology journal articles from the BioMed Central corpus. In addition, Di Marco et al. describe a system for classifying citations into 35 categories using a hand-built decision tree over cue-words, polarity switching words, and knowledge of the discourse structure of the article, among other features. Citation categories vary depending on the function of the citation, e.g., support or contrast.

The next two chapters in this section focus on aggregation of opinion from multiple sources. Nigam and Hurst describe an interesting polarity classifier which uses shallow NLP techniques and a topic-based classifier. They propose using a Bayesian statistical approach to aggregate the opinions expressed about a specific topic in Internet forums. Tong and Yager explore aggregating and characterizing opinion over time. They first create a time series of the subjects, opinions, and attitudes expressed in Internet sources. Subsequently, they generate linguistic summaries, using fuzzy set theory, which provide perspicuous overviews of the opinions expressed towards an event over a period of time.

The final three chapters of this section focus on empirical studies of deploying opinion-based systems. Koppel and Shtrimberg examine the use of sentiment analysis as a means of predicting future stock prices. Though their findings highlight that this is not a useful investment strategy, one potentially useful outcome of their work is a method for collecting labeled data for sentiment analysis, where data is labeled based upon the direction of relative large changes in stock price.

Salvetti, Reichenbach and Lewis describe an approach to opinion classification of movie reviews based upon feature selection (using part of speech tags), feature generalization (in terms of synonymy and hypernymy), and probabilistic classifiers (namely Naïve Bayes and Markov

Models). They note that using a simple thresholding of the log odds ratio of the positive and negative posterior probabilities can dramatically improve performance.

The final chapter, by Seki, Eguchi and Kando, focuses on multi-document summarization based on a topic/query and investigates the impact of using sentence and document-level genre information on building three types of summaries: summaries that concentrate on facts (events), opinions, or knowledge (definitions), respectively. The topic, characterized as a query, is used to retrieve/select documents from a collection of documents. The retrieved documents are then summarized using a clustering-based approach, where clusters and sentences within clusters are ranked and selected based upon similarity to the topic. The user is further allowed to select the type of summary required. The reported results on Japanese newswire articles show significant improvement in summary coverage and precision when combining sentence-level typing and genre classification information over baseline multi-document summarization techniques.

Target Audience
The book is intended for advanced undergraduate and graduate students, as well as a broad audience of professionals and researchers in computer science, engineering, information science, and content analysis who have an interest in the subjective aspects of text. The subject matter in this book is far ranging, including conceptual models, computational models, and applications.

Acknowledgements
We thank Helen Perilioux, Jesse Montogomery, and Debbie Moran for their help in editing this book.

James G. Shanahan
Yan Qu
Janyce Wiebe
Pittsburgh, June 2005

Chapter 1

Contextual Valence Shifters

Livia Polanyi
FXPAL
3400 Hillview Ave, Bldg. 4
Palo Alto CA 94304
E-mail: polanyi@fxpal.com

Annie Zaenen
PARC,
3333 Coyote Hill Road,
Palo Alto, CA 94304 USA
E-mail: zaenen@parc.com

Abstract
In addition to describing facts and events, texts often communicate information about the attitude of the writer or various participants towards material being described. The most salient clues about attitude are provided by the lexical choice of the writer but, as discussed below, the organization of the text also contributes information relevant to assessing attitude. We argue that the current work in this area that concentrates mainly on the negative or positive attitude communicated by individual terms (Edmonds and Hirst, 2002; Hatzivassiloglou and McKeown, 1997; Turney and Littman, 2002; Wiebe et al., 2001) is incomplete and often gives the wrong results when implemented directly. We then describe how the base attitudinal valence of a lexical item is modified by lexical and discourse context and propose a simple, "proof of concept" implementation for some contextual shifters.

Keywords: attitude, discourse, valence shifters, genre structure, multiple constraints, calculating valence.

1. Introduction

In addition to describing facts and events, texts often communicate information about the attitude of the writer or various participants towards an event being described. Salient clues about attitude are provided by the lexical choice of the writer but, as discussed below, the organization of the text also contributes critical information for attitude assessment. We start from the current work in this area that concentrates mainly on the negative or positive attitude communicated by individual terms (Edmonds and Hirst, 2002; Hatzivassiloglou and McKeown, 1997; Turney and Littman, 2002; Wiebe et al. 2001). We argue that this approach is incomplete and often gives the wrong results when implemented directly. We describe how the base attitudinal valence of a lexical item can be modified by context and propose a simple "proof of concept" implementation for some contextual shifters.

2. From Simple Valence to Contextually Determined Valence

2.1 Simple Lexical Valence

Examples of lexical items that communicate a negative or positively attitude (*valence*) can be found in all open word classes and as multi-word collocations such as *freedom fighter*. Below we have listed some examples of English words which can be readily characterized as positively or negatively valenced[1].

PART OF SPEECH	Positive Valence	Negative Valence
Verbs	Boost, Embrace, Ensure, Encourage, Delight, Manage, Ease	Conspire, Meddle, Discourage, Fiddle, Fail, Haggle
Nouns	Approval, Benefit, Chance, Approval Benefit, Credit, Favor, Freedom, Hope	Backlash, Backlog, Bankruptcy, Beating, Catastrophe
Adjectives	Attractive, Better, Brave, Bright, Creative, Dynamic,	Annoying, Awry, Arbitrary, Bad, Botched,
Adverbs	Attractively, …	Annoyingly, …

Table 1. Examples of words with non-neutral valence.

2.2 Lexical Valence in Texts

To illustrate how lexical valence influences interpretation, let us look briefly at three short texts.[2] While all of the texts communicate the same denotative information, the connotative force of each version is different. In the first text, the protagonist is an unremarkable young man, in the second text, he is a much friendlier, warmer sort of chap while he emerges in the third text as a juvenile delinquent[3]:

Text 1. *The **eighteen year old walked** through the **part of town where he lived**. He **stopped for a while** to **talk** with people on the street and then **went** to a **store** for some **food** to bring to the **small apartment** where he **lived** with some **people he knew**.*

---

[1] Not all terms can be characterized along this dimension: many terms are essentially neutral.

[2] Space constraints and the difficulty of finding short texts that exemplify important complex cases while presenting few other distractions oblige us to construct our example.

[3] Notation: Relevant terms are bold; positive terms are marked with a +; negative terms are marked with a -; comparable neutral terms are underlined.

Text 2. *The **young man⁺ strolled⁺** through **his neighborhood⁺**. He **lingered⁺** to **chat⁺** with people on the street and then **dropped into⁺** a **shop⁺** for some **goodies⁺** to bring **home⁺** to the **cozy⁺** place which he **shared⁺** with some **friends⁺**.*

Text 3. *The **teenaged male⁻ strutted⁻** through his **turf**. He **loitered⁻** to **shoot the bull⁻** with people on the street and then **ducked⁻** into a **dive⁻** for some **grub⁻** to bring to the **cramped hole-in-the-wall⁻** where he **crashed⁻** with some **cronies⁻**.*

The difference in perlocutionary force among these texts emerges solely from the combined effects of the choice of synonyms (or near synonyms) chosen to depict the persons, events and situation involved.

Observations such as these have led researchers to classify terms as positive or negative. The simple computation of the attitude expressed in a text would then consist of counting the negative and positive instances and decide on the basis of the highest number.
To see that the simple counting will not work for many texts, consider the following example (from *The Economist*):

*Of course, that would not stop deregulation of the power industry altogether. The **blunderbuss⁻** of state initiatives will see to that. However, by prolonging **uncertainty⁻**, it would **needlessly⁻ delay⁻** the arrival of the **bonanza⁺** of **benefits⁺** that consumers **deserve⁺**, and give them **legitimate⁺** grounds for their **cynicism⁻**.*

While there are six negative lexical items (marked with -) and only four positive items (marked with +) in this text, readers do not conclude that the author is negative about "deregulation". In fact, the writer views deregulation positively. Clearly, then, the full story of how lexical items reflect attitudes is more complex than simply counting the valences of terms would suggest. In the reminder of this paper, we will propose a number of ways in which the basic valence of individual lexical items may be strengthened or weakened by context provided by (1) the presence of other lexical items, (2) the genre type and discourse structure of the text and (3) cultural factors.

In looking at texts, it is clear that lexical items can be strongly positive or negative or somewhat strong or weak or "hint" at a positive or negative connotation. Therefore, characterizing terms in binary terms as either positive or negative as we have done so far is too crude. Believing that it would be desirable to have a more fine-grained classification, we have adopted a slightly more sensitive scale with three positive and three negative values. In the notation we adopt in this paper, therefore, we assume that words like *clever* and *successful* are marked +2 in the lexicon. Negatively valenced items are marked -2. It should be kept in mind, however, that this scheme falls far short of an adequate solution to this problem.

3. Contextual Valence Shifters

3.1 Sentence Based Contextual Valence Shifters

While some terms in a text may seem to be inherently positive or negative, we shall show how others change base valence according to context – receiving their perlocutionary force either from the domain of discourse or from other lexical items nearby in the document. In the remainder of this paper we will discuss a number of interacting factors that make the determination of the point of view that an author expresses in a document difficult. We will begin with a survey of several lexical phenomena that can cause the valence of a lexical item to shift from one pole to the other or, less forcefully, to modify the valence towards a more neutral position.

3.1.1 Negatives and Intensifiers

The most obvious shifters are negatives.[4] How *not* can flip the valence of a term has been discussed in the computational literature (Das and Chen, 2001; Pang, Lee and Vaithyanathan 2002). However, in addition to *not*, negatives can belong to various word classes. Simple negatives include *never, none, nobody, nowhere, nothing*, and *neither*. For example:

John is clever versus *John is **not** clever.*
John is successful at tennis versus *John is **never** successful at tennis.*
Each of them is successful versus ***None** of them is successful.*

Combining positively valenced words with a negation such as *not* flips the positive valence to a negative valence. For example[5]:

clever +2 combined with *not* ⇒ *not clever* -2
successful +2 combined with *not* ⇒ *not successful* -2

The combination of a positive evaluator with a negation turns the evaluation as a whole into a negative one. Inversely the combination of a negative evaluator with negation turns the whole into a positive evaluation (e.g., "*He is **not** stupid*").

Not all modifiers switch the valence. Intensifiers such as the *rather* in *rather efficient* and the *deeply* in *deeply suspicious* act to weaken or strengthen the base valence of the term modified. *Rather* weakens the force of a term and *deeply* enhances it (Riloff and Wiebe, 2003). We can calculate their effect by adding or subtracting a 'point' to/from the base valence of a term.

Suspicious -2 ⇒ *deeply suspicious* -3
Efficient +2 ⇒ *rather efficient* +1

As with the negative shifters, intensifiers can belong to all open lexical classes. In addition to adverbs, quantifiers such as *few, most*, and nouns such as *lack (of)* also exist.

3.1.2 Modals

Language makes a distinction between events or situations which are asserted to have happened, are happening or will happen (*realis* events) and those which *might, could, should, ought to*, or *possibly* occurred or will occur (*irrealis* events). **Modal operators** set up a context of possibility or necessity and in texts they initiate a context in which valenced terms express an attitude towards entities which do not necessarily reflect the author's attitude towards those entities in an actual situation under discussion. Therefore, in computing an evaluation of the author's attitude, terms in a modal context should not be treated precisely as terms in a realis context.

Assume the realis sentences: *Mary is a terrible person. She is mean to her dogs. Terrible* and *mean* are negatively valenced terms. The score for each of the sentences is -1. However, the sentence *If Mary were a terrible person, she would be mean to her dogs*, asserts neither that *Mary*

---

[4] Of course for a shift in attitude to take place there has to an attitude expressed in the first place. A simple sentence such as "*John is home*" might express a simple fact without betraying an attitude (i.e. the attitude score is 0). When negated, as in "*John is not home*", there is no shift in attitude (i.e. the negation of 0 is 0).

[5] While it is a simplification to take the scope of a negative as always a whole clause, we will assume this here.

is a terrible person nor *that she is mean to her dogs.* On the contrary, the force of *would* suggests that *she is not mean to her dogs* while the *If* sets up a context in which *Mary is* not necessarily *a terrible person.* In fact, we tend to believe that she is not *terrible* at all. Therefore, the modal operators neutralize the base valence of *terrible* and *mean,* resulting in a re-computed value of 0 for the modal version.

3.1.3 Presuppositional Items

Often words shift the valence of evaluative terms through their presuppositions. This is typical for adverbs like *barely* as shown by comparing "It is sufficient" with "It is *barely sufficient.*" "Sufficient" is a positive term, "barely sufficient" is not: it presupposes that better was expected. These terms can introduce a negative or a positive evaluation even when there are no other evaluative terms around, as in *He got into Foothill College* versus *He barely got into Foothill College* or *He got into Harvard* and *He even got into Harvard.* Words like *barely* and *even* will be marked in the lexicon as evaluation words that interact with other terms. For instance, in the sentence *It was barely sufficient,* the evaluation of the combination is negative. Examples of nouns that act like shifters are *failure* and *neglect.* In the phrase *'failure to succeed',* for example, the force of the meaning of *failure* transforms the positive valence of *succeed* into a negative property. The expression as a whole counts as negative.

The same observations can be made with respect to verbs like *fail, omit, neglect….* They not only convey the information that something did not happen but also that the author was expecting it to happen and that this not borne out expectation has negative consequences as illustrated by *He stayed around* versus *He failed to leave.*[6]

3.1.4 Irony

Sometimes the contributions made by various lexical items combine in ways that cannot be accounted for in the ways described above. For example, in the ironic sentence *The very brilliant organizer failed to solve the problem*[7], the extremely positive connotation of *very brilliant* is turned against itself by the meaning of the sentence. We account for this phenomena by assuming that in the lexicon *brilliant* will be marked as +2, *very* will increase the base valence of the expression to +3; *fail* will be marked as negative and the expression *solve the problem* will be marked positive. Evaluative terms under the scope of *fail,* such as *solve the problem* will be marked 0; entities whose existence is not denied by the use of *fail* but to whom failure is ascribed will turn negative. In this case, the base score was 0, however, very brilliant goes from positive to negative and *solve the problem* is neutralized, while *fail* remains negative. The adjusted score is: -4.

---

[6] Often the use of *fail* leads to an indirect negative evaluation of the person to whom the failure is attributed. This can be exploited in irony (see below).

[7] Note that when we add *even,* the situation changes again. The sentence is not necessarily ironic. Items under the scope of words like *even* are neutralized. So the sentence *Even the* brilliant *organizer failed to* solve the problem. is scored -1 for *fail* only.

brilliant	+2		Original valence is adjusted by very
very brilliant	+3	-3	adjusted because of fail
failed	-1	-1	
solve the problem	+1	0	neutralized by fail
total score:		-4	

Table 2. Valence calculation for "The very brilliant organizer failed to solve the problem."

3.2 Discourse Based Contextual Valence Shifters

3.2.1 Connectors

Connectors such as *although, however, but, on the contrary, notwithstanding* etc. can both introduce information, and act on information elsewhere in the text to mitigate the force of that information[8]. For example, take the sentence *Although Boris is **brilliant** at math, he is a **horrible** teacher*. While the statement *Boris is brilliant at math* positively assesses Boris' math skills, the force of *although* combined with the negative assessment in the sentence's main clause *he is a* **horrible** *teacher* effectively negates the positive force of the evaluation as applied to Boris. In computing the author's attitude towards Boris, therefore, the effect of *although* is to neutralize the effect of the positive assessment, resulting in a negative assessment score for the sentence. Let's follow that along step-by-step to make the claim clear:

Although Boris is brilliant at math, he is a horrible teacher.			
Base valence of terms:		Adjusted computation:	
brilliant	+2	**(Although) brilliant**	0
horrible	-2	**horrible**	-2
total score:	0	total score:	-2

Table 3. Example of valence adjustment based on discourse connective.

In this example we also see how the micro organization of the discourse makes a difference: the positive effect of **brilliant** is encapsulated in the embedded clause and does not contribute to the evaluation of the larger unit.

3.2.2 Discourse Structure and Attitude Assessment

A third discourse level valence adjuster included in this paper concerns *discourse structure* itself. There are two basic discourse relations of interest to us here: *lists* and *elaborations*. Some discourse constituents are linked to others in a list in which each constituent encodes a similar relationship to some more general concept and other constituents that give more detailed information of some sort about material encoded in constituents preceding them in the linear organization of the text. These earlier constituents structurally dominate the elaborating constituents (Grosz and Sidner, 1986; Mann and Thompson, 1988; Polanyi and Scha, 1984). Of

---

[8] As was noticed by Hatzivassiloglou and McKeown (1997), the construction *Adj1 but Adj2* can be used to determine the valency of one adjective if the valency of the other one is known.

interest to us here is how base lexical valence scores are modified by their position in a hierarchical discourse structure.

In an Elaboration, a constituent gives more detail about another constituent which is in a structurally accessible position in a discourse stack. For instance in *John walks a lot. Last month he walked 25 miles on Tuesdays,* the second sentence illustrates the concept expressed in the dominating sentence. When valence information is introduced in a dominating sentence, the elaborations reinforce its effects. For example, lexical valence information is introduced by the use of *terrific* in the dominating sentence in the following passage:

John is a **terrific**$^+$ *athlete. Last week he walked 25 miles on Tuesdays. Wednesdays he walked another 25 miles. Every weekend he hikes at least 50 miles a day.*

Each of the dominated constituents is itself neutrally valenced. However, in this text, each is an example of John's terrific athleticism. Therefore, the positive valence of *terrific* is inherited by each subsequent new example. Effectively, the force for this one instance of the positively valenced term *terrific* as applied to *John* is greatly strengthened when the sentence is treated in its discourse context rather than as an independent expression.

3.2.3 Multi-entity Evaluation

Up to now we have looked at the effects that context can have on the evaluation of one single entity. But in most complex documents a wide variety of entities are discussed – some of which might be evaluated positively and others negatively. For example, a product reviewer discusses one negative aspect of a product extensively in a review which was otherwise very positive about many other features. In this case, it would be incorrect to assume that the reviewer was negative towards the product because of having described one negative feature in some detail. In such a case, simple methods of comparing the number of positive terms versus the number of negative terms could result in a faulty assessment of the reviewer's attitude towards the product. No simple correlation need obtain between the length at which a particular aspect of situation is discussed and the weight that discussion plays in an overall assessment.

3.2.4 Genre and Attitude Assessment

The assessment of author attitude may be complexly related to the genre of the communication in which valence marked terms occur. For example, any use of evaluative language in a document in which such assessments seldom occur will carry more weight than would otherwise be the case. Similarly, the presence of valence carrying items in a text by an author or found in a text type associated with the use of highly evaluative language may carry less weight. As we show below, assessing attitude in a document in which there are various participants "speaking" in a text can be at issue as well.

3.2.5 Reported Speech

Take the sentence *Mary was a slob*. The base valence of this sentence is –1, since **slob** is a negatively valenced term. Now, consider, *John said that Mary was a slob*. Here the author asserts that John said something unflattering about Mary, not that the author accepts John's assessment. However, information later in the text could force its inclusion as in *John said that Mary was a slob and he is right*. In this case, the negative valence attached to *slob* will be counted along with the positive valence of *right*. To illustrate consider this text:

The utilities argue that they performed well⁺. But the public still remembers those miserable⁻ rotten⁻ nights.

Both *argue* and *remembers* are Reported Speech and Thought operators. Therefore, the valence of the reported material is not ascribed to the author (Wiebe, Wilson and Bell, 2001; Wiebe, Wilson, Bruce, Bell and Martin, 2004) but to the utilities and the public respectively. The positive and the negative valences do not cancel each other out. The text is not neutral; it is positive in relation to utilities and and negative in relation to public. We need two different counters one for the utilities and one for the public.

Notice also that the weight of both valences is not equal for the larger unit composed of both sentences. By using *But* the author chooses to give more weight to the second point of view reported as this point in the text. A sensitive weighing scheme could be devised to reflect these complex facts (Riloff and Wiebe, 2003).

3.2.6 Subtopics

Sometimes it is possible to split a longer document into subtopics. The point of view of the author can then be made relative to each subtopic. Take for instance the following artificially constructed short text.

Our yearly overview of the situation in Ubitopia.
The economic situation is more than satisfactory⁺. The leading indicators show a rosy⁺ picture. The manufacturing sector is booming⁺. Exports have exceeded⁺ the wildest expectations⁺.
When one looks at the human rights picture, one is struck by the increase in arbitrary⁻ arrests, by needless⁻ persecution⁻ of helpless⁻ citizens and increase of police brutality⁻.

In a text like this, one could link the positive and the negative attitudes to the two subtopics, the economy and the human rights situation. In most cases, this will not be as easy as is the case here, and, even if the text can be clearly divided into subtopics, it is not necessarily the case that all subtopics contribute equally to the overall impression that a text makes. One factor that will influence their contribution is genre, which we discuss next.

3.2.7 Genre Constraints

Movie reviews have been a focus of attention in the document classification community for some time. These texts are known to be notoriously difficult to work with using existing techniques (Pang, Lee and Vaithyanathan, 2002). Problems arise because these texts are composed of two types of information: information about the events and situations in the story and information about the film which has been created to tell the story. Since the question one is interested in primarily interested in having answered by a movie review is *Is this a good movie?* and since the review is prepared by the reviewer to answer this question, it is necessary to separate the description of the entities pertaining to the story from the description of the entities pertaining to the production. Only the valence scores of the entities pertaining to the production should be considered in ascertaining if the review is positive or negative.

Reviews of films loosely follow a set of genre conventions that can be mined for factors which can influence basic valence assignment. For example, movie reviews are often constructed as a quasi-interaction between author and reader. Comments in or about the first or second person reflect information about the film since neither reader nor author are characters in the film. Positional information can also be important: comments at the very beginning or very end of a review are accorded more weight than remarks in less prominent positions.

Let's consider an artificially constructed example based on an excerpt from a movie review taken from MRDb website used in Pang, Lee and Vaithyanathan (2002)[9]:

*This film should be **brilliant**[+]. The characters are **appealing**[+]. ... Stallone plays a **happy**[+], **wonderful**[+] man. His **sweet**[+] wife is **beautiful**[+] and **adores**[+] him. He has a **fascinating**[+] **gift**[+] for living life fully[+]. It sounds like a **great**[+] plot, however, the film is a **failure**[-]*

	Adjusted Score	
*This film should be **brilliant**[+].*	0	*brilliant* within scope of *should* is 0
*The characters are **appealing**[+].*	0	*appealing* elaboration under *should* 0
*Stallone plays a **happy**[+], **wonderful**[+] man. His **sweet**. wife is **beautiful**[+] and **adores** him. He has a **fascinating**[+] **gift**[+] for living life fully[+].*	0	*Happy, wonderful, sweet* etc. all refer to storyworld entities and thus are not counted.
*It sounds like a **great**[+] story,*	-1	*However* reverses + valence of *great*
*however, the film is a **failure**[-]*	-1	*failure* is –1
Total Score:	-2	

Table 4. Valence calculation for the movie review.

The adjusted score is –2. The review is negative.

In some cases, we should be able to exploit genre constraints in determining the attitude of authors towards the entities created in the documents. But to do this computationally, the structure that genres impose on documents needs to be determined automatically. This is not yet possible.

4. Conclusion

We have shown that even when the author attention is restricted to one topic/entity/fact, lexical items in a discourse context will interact with one another. An author's attitude cannot be calculated based on individual items. We proposed a calculation of local interactions that improves upon the results of current approaches based on simple counts. We also argued that valence calculation is critically affected by discourse structure. In addition, we discussed cases in which a document describes more than one entity/topic/fact. We showed that, in these cases, the calculation of point of view must be done with respect to each entity separately and must take into account higher order factors such as genre that influence document structure

Taken together, these considerations argue strongly that calculating author attitude must be based on a finer grained analysis of the text on all levels than has been previously proposed.

---

[9] The authors explain that their context insensitive evaluative lexical methods fail on texts in which the author sets up a deliberate contrast to an expected position. They cannot deal with the mismatch between the base valence of the term and the author's usage.

5. Bibliography

Das, S. and Chen, M. (2001) *Yahoo! For Amazon: extracting market sentiment from stock message boards*. Paper presented in the *8th Asia Pacific Finance Association Annual Conference*, Bankok, Thailand.

Edmonds, P. and Hirst, G. (2002) *Near-synonymy and lexical choice*. Computational Linguistics, 28 (2), 105–144.

Grosz, B. and Sidner, C. (1986) *Attention, Intention, and the Structure of Discourse*. Computational Linguistics, 12 (3), 175–204.

Hatzivassiloglou, V. and McKeown K. (1997) *Predicting the Semantic Orientation of Adjectives*. Computational Linguistics, 174–181.

Hatzivassiloglou, V. and Wiebe, J. (2000) Effects of Adjective Orientation and Gradability on Sentence Subjectivity. Paper presented at Coling 2000. Saarbrucken.

Mann, W. and Thompson, S. (1988) *Rhetorical Structure Theory: Toward a functional theory of text organization*. Text 8 (3), 243–281.

Pang, B. Lee, L. and Vaithyanathan, V. (2002) *Thumbs up? Sentiment Classification using Machine Learning Techniques*. In *Proceedings of the 2002 Conference on Empirical Methods on Natural Language Processing*. 79–86.

Polanyi, L. and Scha, R. (1984) *A Syntactic Approach to Discourse Semantics*. Paper presented at *6th International Conference on Computational Linguistics*, Stanford, CA.

Riloff, E. and Wiebe, J. (2003) *Learning Extraction Patterns for Subjective Expressions*. In *Proceedings of the 2003 Conference on Empirical Methods in Natural Language Processing*. 105–112.

Tong, R. (2001) *An operational system for detecting and tracking opinions in on-line discussion*. Paper presented at the *SIGIR Workshop on Operational Text Classification*.

Turney, P. and Littman, M. (2002) *Unsupervised Learning of Semantic Orientation from a Hundred-Billion-Word Corpus*. Technical Report, National Research Council Canada, Institute for Information Technology, ERB-1094, NRC-44929.

Wiebe, J., Wilson, T., and Bell, M. (2001) *Identifying Collocations for Recognizing Opinions*. Paper presented at the *ACL/EACL '01 Workshop on Collocation*, Toulouse, France, July 2001.

Wiebe, J., Wilson, T., Bruce, R., Bell, M., and Martin, M. (2004) *Learning subjective language*. Computational Linguistics 30 (3).

Chapter 2

Conveying Attitude with Reported Speech

Sabine Bergler
Concordia University
Department of Computer Science and Software Engineering
1455 de Maisonneuve Blvd. West
Montreal, Quebec, H3G 1M8, Canada
Email: bergler@encs.concordia.ca

Abstract

Attribution is a phenomenon of great interest and a principled treatment is important beyond the realm of newspaper articles. The way natural language has evolved to reflect our understanding of attribution in the form of reported speech can guide investigations into principled representations forming the basis for shallow text mining as well as belief revision or maintenance.

Keywords: attribution, reported speech, reliability of information, argumentative structure, profile structure, potential belief space.

1. Introduction

Society has developed a multitude of mechanisms that serve to authenticate items, and in particular information. Signatures authenticate letters, paintings, and seal contracts. Imprints on money, seals, and forms make them official. Insignia establish membership in certain groups, as do uniforms and religious symbols. Information, likewise, has well established mechanisms of authentication, which vary slightly from society to society. The Native American language Pawnee has four different prefixes that obligatorily have to mark statements for their reliability (hearsay, reasonably certain but not witnessed directly, leaving room for doubt, or mere inference) (Mithun, 1999). And while the number and type of such evidential markers differ in different languages, hearsay is maybe the most widespread one.

English and most European languages do not have a system of evidential morphology, but mark hearsay and other evidentiality at the syntactic level. Reported speech, both in form of direct quotation (*... and then she said "I have to go."*) or indirect paraphrases (*... and then she said that she had to go.*), is the most formalized register. Reported speech is most prominent in newspaper articles, where it can occur in up to 90% of the sentences of an article. Computational linguistic treatments of newspaper articles usually ignore reported speech, either by omitting the material entirely, or by ignoring its evidential status. This paper argues that reported speech segments information into coherent subunits, called *profiles* after (Bergler, 1992). Different profiles can imply different credibility of the source of the information, different roles of the source in an argumentative structure, or a different context (temporal or other). An extended example illustrates profiling on a product review article. This paper concludes that the mechanism of profiling (and its proper analysis) should be extended beyond reported speech to all explicit attributions, such as newsgroup messages, etc.

2. Evidential Analysis of Reported Speech

Reported speech is characterized by its syntactic structure: a matrix clause, containing at least the source as subject NP and a reporting verb, embeds the information conveyed in a complement clause. The complement is optionally introduced by "that" for indirect reported speech, and it is surrounded by quotation marks for direct reported speech. As argued in (Bergler, 1992), the complement usually conveys the *primary information* in newspaper articles and most other genres. In fact, the case where the matrix clause bears the major information, namely that something had been uttered by somebody under certain circumstances without the utterance itself being of importance, is rare (but see (Clark and Gerrig, 1990) for examples). The syntactic dominance of the matrix clause shows the semantic importance of the contained *circumstantial information* (Bergler, 1992), the who, when, where, and how. But the natural propositional encoding of the complement clause as embedded in the matrix clause is not suitable. Rather, the information of the matrix clause should be seen as a meta-annotation for interpreting the primary information differently in different contexts and for different purposes. Thus the a priori trust a Republican reader has in utterances by Cheney is different from a Democrat's. And a text will be interpreted differently at the time of the events unfolding and after additional information is known. This variability of the pragmatic force of the matrix clause also suggests that it cannot be "resolved" at the time of first text analysis, but has to remain attached in a form close to the original for further analysis. (Bergler, 1992) gives a general linguistic treatment of reported speech. This paper presents, in contrast, one particular implementation of the general representation for further automatic analysis. The underlying assumption is that the further processing will be by an information extraction or mining system that works with shallow, possibly statistical techniques. But the representation does not preclude the deeper linguistic analysis outlined in (Bergler, 1992).

Politics & Policy: Democrats Plan Tactic to Block Tax-Cut Vote
Threat of Senate Filibuster Could Indefinitely Delay Capital-Gains Package

(S_1) Democratic leaders have bottled up President Bush's capital-gains tax cut in the Senate and may be able to prevent a vote on the issue indefinitely.

(S_2) Yesterday, Sen. Packwood acknowledged, "We don't have the votes for cloture today."

(S_3) The Republicans contend that they can garner a majority in the 100-member Senate for a capital-gains tax cut.

(S_4) They accuse the Democrats of unfairly using Senate rules to erect a 60-vote hurdle.

(S_5) Democrats asserted that the proposal, which also would create a new type of individual retirement account, was fraught with budget gimmickry that would lose billions of dollars in the long run.

Figure 1. Adapted from Jeffrey H. Birnbaum, The Wall Street Journal, 10/27/89.

As Figure 1 demonstrates, the role of reported speech is attribution: the statement does not assert as 'true' what amounts to the information content of the sentence, but a situation in which this content was proffered by some source. This device can be used both to bolster a claim made in the text already, and to distance the author from the attributed material, implicitly lowering its credibility (Anick and Bergler, 1992). Thus the credibility or reliability of the attributed information is always in question for reported speech and other attributions. If the attribution is used to bolster a claim already made by citing a particularly strong source for endorsement, ignoring the fact that an explicit attribution was made will do no great harm. This is in fact a frequent case in the type of newspaper articles typically used for large-scale system development and testing (as in MUC, TREC, DUC, etc.) and this is why ignoring attribution has been tolerable. But when a text is argumentative (opposing two or more points of view on a topic), speculative (when the final outcome of an event is not yet decided and the text uses different sources as predictors), or presents a personal opinion or experience, text meaning depends on proper attribution recognition (Bergler, 1995a). Argumentative or speculative text structure is not limited to newspaper articles. Scientific articles, too, use reported speech for this purpose, but in a different rhetorical style. And multi-participant political analysis segments on newscasts form the same phenomenon: different opinions are identified with different individuals and contrasted, even though we might term it broadcast speech, rather than reported speech. Interestingly, broadcast speech retains the required elements of reported speech, in that it is always anchored by the identity of the source and the circumstances of the utterance (date, occasion, place, etc.) as they are relevant to its analysis. The reported material is always literal and quoted, of course, but has still undergone an editing process, extracting the broadcast speech from a larger interview and potentially juxtaposing material that the source did not intend to. Thus the simple fact that no paraphrasing is involved does not make broadcast speech necessarily truer to the original than reported speech.

Reported speech in newspaper articles can be detected and analyzed without a complete syntactic analysis, using shallow means and standard tools. In a feasibility study, Doandes (2003) presents a knowledge-poor system that identifies sentences that contain reported speech in Wall Street Journal texts and analyzes them into structures inspired by (Bergler, 1992) and illustrated in Figure 2.

The system works in a shallow environment: Built on top of ERS (Witte and Bergler, 2003), it has access to slightly modified versions of the Annie tools distributed with GATE (Cunningham, 2002) and an in-house NP chunker and coreference resolution module. The NP chunker relies on the Hepple tagger (Hepple, 2000) and Annie Gazetteer, the coreference module has access to WordNet (Fellbaum, 1998).

BP	basic profile
OTHERCIRC	circumstantial information other than source and reporting verb
PARAPHRASE	paraphrased material, usually complement clause in case of indirect reported speech
REPSOURCE	source, in active voice the matrix clause subject
REPORTEDSPEECH	complement clause
REPVERB	reporting verb, main verb in matrix clause
QUOTEDSPEECH	material in quotation marks

Figure 2. Template for representing reported speech sentences in (Doandes, 2003).

Doandes uses part-of-speech tags to identify main verb candidates. In a detailed analysis of verb clusters, she determines main verbs and compares them against a list of likely reported speech verbs. In case a reported speech verb is found, the sentence pattern (with complete part-of-speech annotations, annotations for NPs, and annotations for verb groups) is compared to the possible patterns for reported speech constructions as described in (Quirk et al., 1985). Figure 3 gives the resulting *basic profile* for the sentence: *Yesterday, Sen. Packwood acknowledged, "We don't have the votes for cloture today."*

```
BP
OTHERCIRC Yesterday,
PARAPHRASE
REPSOURCE Sen. Packwood
REPORTEDSPEECH, "We don't have the votes for cloture today."
REPVERB acknowledged
QUOTEDSPEECH "We don't have the votes for cloture today."
```
Figure 3. Example representation in (Doandes, 2003).

The development corpus consisted of 65,739 sentences from the Wall Street Journal, the test corpus of 2,404 sentences taken mainly from the Wall Street Journal, with a few articles from the DUC 2003 corpus of newspaper articles (DUC, 2003). 513 occurrences of reported speech were found and precision is 98.65%, recall is 63%. The analysis into basic profiles incurred some mistakes (such as retaining only part of the subject NP in the SOURCE slot). Using a strict notion of correctness for the entire basic profile, the performance drops to 87% precision and 55% recall.

Many recall problems are linked to limitations of the particular implementation, such as tagging errors, the NP chunking process (the NP chunker splits heavy NPs into several smaller chunks, thus occasionally obfuscating the reported speech pattern), and an incomplete list of reported speech verbs. (Doandes, 2003) works from a simple list of candidate reported speech verbs with no attempt at word sense disambiguation. The results seem satisfactory for the evaluation corpus, but will not necessarily hold outside the newspaper genre. (Wiebe et al., 1997) report on the difficulty of distinguishing *private state, direct speech, mixed direct and indirect speech, other speech event, other state or event*. Most of these categories describe attributions and thus do not need to be distinguished for profile structure at the level described here, even though their distinction would refine the use of the profile for subsequent processing.

3. Profile Structure

Figure 1 is typical for newspaper articles: information from two different points of view, here Democrats and Republicans, is interleaved. Ideally, an automatic system would group S_1 and S_5 into one profile, and S_2, S_3, and S_4 into another, effectively grouping Democrats versus Republicans. This is, however, not possible with shallow techniques. S_1 is not a reported speech sentence and thus does not generate a profile. World knowledge is required to infer that *Sen. Packwood* speaks for the *Republicans* in this article, but pronoun resolution techniques allow *they* to be resolved to *Republicans*, creating a merged profile from S_3 and S_4, enabling interpretation of *a 60-vote hurdle* in the context of S_3.

Profile structure is complementary to both rhetorical structure (cf. Marcu, 1997) and text structure (cf. Polanyi et al., 2004). It creates another type of context, which is coherent with respect to underlying processing assumptions, such as reliability of the source, or, as seen above, inferential assumptions (*60-vote hurdle*). For a more detailed discussion, see (Bergler, 1995a). The profile structure for the text in Figure 1 is given in Figure 4.

The use of profiles is simple: profiles provide a partition of the text according to the source of the information transmitted. This local context can be used for different reasoning. As seen above, a follow-up statement (*60-vote hurdle*) may make (more) sense when interpreted in the context of the previous utterance of the same source (*100-member senate*), even if other text had interfered.

> BP
> OTHERCIRC Yesterday,
> PARAPHRASE
> REPSOURCE Sen. Packwood
> REPORTEDSPEECH, "We don't have the votes for cloture today."
> REPVERB acknowledged
> QUOTEDSPEECH "We don't have the votes for cloture today."

MERGED-PROFILE:

> BP
> OTHERCIRC
> PARAPHRASE they can garner a majority in the 100-member Senate for a capital - gains tax cut.
> REPSOURCE The Republicans
> REPORTEDSPEECH they can garner a majority in the 100-member Senate for a capital - gains tax cut.
> REPVERB contend
> QUOTEDSPEECH

> BP
> OTHERCIRC
> PARAPHRASE the Democrats of unfairly using Senate rules to erect a 60-vote hurdle.
> REPSOURCE They
> REPORTEDSPEECH the Democrats of unfairly using Senate rules to erect a 60-vote hurdle.
> REPVERB accuse
> QUOTEDSPEECH

BP
OTHERCIRC
PARAPHRASE the proposal, which also would create a new type of individual retirement account, was fraught with budget gimmickry that would lose billions of dollars in the long run.
REPSOURCE Democrats
REPORTEDSPEECH the proposal, which also would create a new type of individual retirement account, was fraught with budget gimmickry that would lose billions of dollars in the long run.
REPVERB asserted
QUOTEDSPEECH

Figure 4. Profile structure for the text in Figure 3.

Statements from different sources cannot necessarily be assumed to be coherent in the same way, since beliefs and assumptions may differ. Secondly, profile structure facilitates evaluation of the reliability or credibility of several attributions together and in context. Moreover, different sources in a text can influence the evaluation of their respective credibilities: compare the status of *Police Officer XYZ* first to *the thief* (status: high reliability) and then to *disciplinary commission* (status:

neutral). Thus the basic frames representing a single utterance should be grouped by coreference resolution on the source into merged profiles. Different sources may be aligned for the sake of the argument in one article, as are *Sen. Packwood* and *Republicans* in Figure 1. This is called *supporting group structure* in (Bergler, 1992). The respective lexicalizations of the sources indicate in part the reliability or credibility of the primary information (from the point of view of the reporter).

4. Extended Example

As mentioned in the introduction, reported speech is not limited to newspaper articles and occurs also in other genres. This section demonstrates the usefulness of the proposed representations and processing strategies on an extended example from an online product review found on ConsumerSearch.

---

ge amount of consumer mail complaining about the Kenmore Calypsos problems with lint, Consumer Reports ran a s year. Editors washed a load of white towels and black T-shirts to test four competing models for lint left behind wet clothing. Editors say they are considering testing all washers for lint in the future. The limited test here does to have been a factor in Consumer Reports overall ratings. Some models, which performed poorly in the lint test, ratings chart.

ed our own mail from consumers regarding washers, and most of it concerns reliability factors involving the latest models, such as the Kenmore Calypso. The Calypso is a top-loading machine with a unique agitating technology. Instead of twisting clothes around, it bounces them up and down and showers them with water. One owner wrote to us about a lengthy ordeal involving four repair visits. Repair issues with the Kenmore Calypso (also sold as the Whirlpool Calypso) are born out in over 150 postings in ThatHomeSite.coms appliance forum as well as on Epinions. Owners report clothing working its way below the basket (one user reports a handkerchief made it all the way to the sump pump), and others have problems with electronic error messages and clothing that comes out too wet or lint-covered.

Interestingly, theres a class-action lawsuit in the works regarding problems with the Calypso. Mark Tamblyn, a lawyer with Kershaw, Cutter, Ratinoff and York, LLP of Sacramento told us that the main issues appear to be with the control board and U-joint, along with water leakage and drainage problems (the first case and request for class-action status was filed in late June in Illinois state court). In the last version of our report, we featured the Kenmore/Whirlpool Calypso as a high-efficiency top-loader. In some tests, it still outperforms other models. However, given the number of consumer complaints we read on Epinions and ThatHomeSite.com, were not placing it in ConsumerSearch Fast Answers for this version of our report.

We contacted Stephen Duthie, Manager of Global Communications for Whirlpool. Duthie told us by e-mail that We have no knowledge about a suit, pending or otherwise, and no reason to believe there will be a suit.Duthie offered no further comments on the Calypsos repair record.

Figure 5. ConsumerSearch
http://www.consumersearch.com/www/house_and_home/washing_machines/ fullstory.html.

The abbreviated text in Figure 5 is a screenshot of Doandes' system, highlighting the reported speech occurrences it found. The reported speech clearly segments the text into topical areas. Here, the profile structure contains a much smaller proportion of the text than it did for the text in Figure 1. The automatic system missed two instances of reported speech in the last sentence of the second paragraph (introduced by the reporting verb *report*, which was not in the list of reporting verbs). More interestingly, the text contains an instance of explicitly reported material that does not follow the reported speech pattern in *In the last version of our report, we featured the Kenmore/Whirlpool Calypso as a high-efficiency top-loader.* These functionally equivalent constructions have to be represented and analyzed in the same manner and the prototype has extended the treatment already to *according to.*

We know from the genre of text that in fact it contains only secondary information, taken from other sources. The explicit reported speech sentences, however, appear to ground an entire paragraph. We see the reported speech here playing two distinct roles: in the first paragraph, rather than openly criticizing that the tests for lint had not been done for all washers, anonymous editors are reported as stating that *they are considering testing all washers for lint in the future.*

In the second paragraph, the reported speech (both the detected and the undetected instances) serves to ground a general point in a particular experience (*four repair visits*). In the third paragraph, detailed statements about problematic parts are attributed to a lawyer involved in preparing a class-action lawsuit. Both explicit attributions shift the (legal) responsibility from the editors to the cited sources, but at the same time serve to increase their credibility.

The basic profiles for this text are straightforward, but they do not fall into an interesting profile structure (each reported speech occurrence stands alone, not connected to the others in profile structure). The basic profiles are more interesting here as goalposts in the rhetorical and text structure: each reported speech occurrence has a privileged relationship to the rest of the information within the same paragraph. It is beyond the scope of this paper to show how to integrate text structure and profile structure. The role the profile structure should play in follow-up analysis of the text, however, can be sketched in isolation in the next section.

5. Source List Annotation

In a nutshell, (Bergler, 1992, 1995) advocates using the primary information for further processing (such as information extraction or summarization), but to keep an annotation attached that reports the evidential chain, or in this case, the list of sources and the other circumstantial information encoded in the matrix clause. This information can then be interpreted as needed in the context of the ultimate use of the information. This is a most important point: reporters use reported speech not because they couldn't make the necessary inferences themselves and write down the interpretation of what was said, but because this interpretation depends on the context and the 'user'. The text in Figure 5 indicates this very phenomenon: the ranking of a certain washing machine was lowered from the year before, because of information gained about repair issues and consumer complaints, not because of different test results.

The source list annotation is the product of a percolation process over the embedded structures formed by the successive attribution of the material. For instance, the basic profile of Figure 3 shows one level of embeddedness: if we call the primary information $\emptyset$ = "*We don't have the votes for cloture today.*", then the basic profile encodes one level of embedding, $C(\emptyset)$, where C stands for the circumstantial information provided regarding $\emptyset$. But the description of the circumstantial information and the selection of the material has as its source the reporter R, in this case *Jeffrey H. Birnbaum,* leading to another level of embedding R(C(Ø)). And the newspaper where the reporter published the story has its own influence on style and credibility, leading to a third level of embedding, P(R(C(Ø))). And for an automated reasoner or agent, this would be embedded in the context of the agent's beliefs, A(P(R(C(Ø)))). This now properly represents that the agent A read in the paper P an article written by reporter R indicating that under the circumstances C (which include the source S) Ø was asserted. These levels of embedding have to be chosen for each agent, since some agent may not consider different newspapers differently and can thus drop one level of embedding. For agent A, Ø has been asserted under (P',R',C'), where P' is agent A's assessment of paper P's credibility, R' is the agent's assessment of the reporter's credibility, and C' is the agent's assessment of the source S's credibility combined with the pragmatic force of the reported speech verb and other circumstantial information. (P',R',C') is called the *source list* of Ø.

(Gerard, 2000) implemented a proof of concept system called *Percolator*, based on the process of percolation introduced by (Wilks and Ballim, 1991). Percolator assumes a particular agent's interpretation and constructs the representation of Figure 6 for the text of Figure 1.

System believes
   Reader believes
      Reporter Jeffrey H. Birnbaum believes
         Sen. Packwood said
            [``We don't have the votes for cloture today.''
            Source-list(Sen. Packwood, h, n, n, n)]
         Republicans said
            [Republicans can garner a majority in the 100-member Senate for a
            capital-gains tax cut.
            Source-list(Republicans, n, n, n, n)]
            [the Democrats are unfairly using Senate rules to erect a 60-vote hurdle.
            Source-list(Republicans, n, h, n, n)]
         Democrats said
            [the proposal, which also would create a new type of individual retirement
            account, was fraught with budget gimmickry that would lose billions of
            dollars in the long run.
            Source-list(Democrats, n, n, n, n)]

Figure 6. Percolator's representation of profile structure for Figure 1 with source lists.

In this representation, each reported speech complement is indexed by its *Source-list*. The Source-list (which is a particular implementation of the more general concept of a source list elaborated above) holds the description of the source (as given in the subject noun phrase of the matrix clause) and four evaluation features, which represent in turn: the reporter's confidence in the source(s) as expressed by the lexicalization of the matrix clause's subject NP, the reporters confidence in the reported information as expressed by the lexicalization of the reporting verb, the reader's confidence in the source (potentially from prior knowledge or beliefs), and the reader's confidence in the reported information (again, potentially from previous knowledge or beliefs). Important here is the translation of a strength feature encoded in the lexical entries of reporting verbs (Bergler, 1995b) into a credibility rating of the reported information: *acknowledge* as a reporting verb here carries an implication that the information of the complement clause is negative for the subject. If a source is reported to *acknowledge* information this has to be rated as information of high reliability (possible values for the prototype were high, neutral, and low), because sources will not falsely make detrimental statements.

The Source-list pairs the reporter's apparent evaluation of the source and the reported information from lexical semantics with the reader's evaluation of the source and the reported information. This reflects a reader's ability to immediately discount the reporter's apparent evaluation based on previous knowledge or on previous beliefs (about the reporter, the source, or the information). But a reader with no relevant previous beliefs has to rely solely on the intrinsic evaluation of the reporter.

For any specific agent, previous beliefs about the reporter, the source, or the topic are already encoded (or absent, as in Figure 7). Gerard assumes one such agent's strategy to further process the Source-list annotated representation in Figure 6 into the belief-space annotation of Figure 7, loosely modelled on the nested belief environments in (Wilks and Ballim, 1991). Figure 7 illustrates an evolved source list in a flattened-out embedding structure. By *percolating* out of the embedding for the source and the reporter (i.e. deleting it) the lost information is transformed in additional information in the evolving source list, which has now an additional source, namely the reporter. Gerard showed on several examples that an extension of Wilks' and Ballim's percolation mechanism allows to properly combine subjective evaluations of each level of attribution.

Note that Figure 7 does not model a traditional belief space, because there is not enough evidence to transform this information into a belief. Rather, it introduces the notion of a *potential* belief, defined as information that might or might not turn into a *held* belief given further evidence. This reflects a reader's ability to accommodate contradictory information: having read an article that presents two contradictory theories, one can argue both ways if one has no own opinion on the matter until there is evidence that "settles" the issue. This representational device permits to delay the decision as to whether information is believed until a certain threshold of comfort is reached. (Gerard, 2000) explores ideas on when to transform potential beliefs into held beliefs.

```
System believes
    Reader believes
        NIL
    Reader potentially believes
        ["We don't have the votes for cloture today."
        Source-list(Sen. Packwood, Reporter Jeffrey H. Birnbaum, h, n, n, n)]
        [Republicans can garner a majority in the 100-member Senate for a capital-gains
        tax cut.
        Source-list(Republicans, Reporter Jeffrey H. Birnbaum, n, n, n, n)]
        [the Democrats are unfairly using Senate rules to erect a 60-vote hurdle.
        Source-list(Republicans, Reporter Jeffrey H. Birnbaum, n, h, n, n)]
        [the proposal, which also would create a new type of individual retirement
        account, was fraught with budget gimmickry that would lose billions of dollars
        in the long run.
        Source-list(Democrats, Reporter Jeffrey H. Birnbaum, n, n, n, n)]
```

Figure 7. Potential belief spaces for the text of Figure 1 for an agent with no prior knowledge or beliefs.

Note that this work has important differences with traditional work on *belief* reports. Utility texts such as newspaper articles expressly avoid using belief reports because they represent an evaluation by the reporter which the reader might not share. Instead, newspaper articles offer *evidence* reports which only give rise to beliefs through an additional interpretation step. (Gerard, 2000) presents one possible way to transform these evidence reports into first potential, and eventually held beliefs. The focus of this paper is on the extraction of a proper representation of the evidence reports that will enable the intricate reasoning about beliefs discussed in the literature (see for instance (Rapaport et al., 1997, Rapaport, 1986)).

6. Extension to Other Attribution

Reported speech is an important issue in its own right, but it can moreover serve as a model for attribution in different registers, as well. Reported speech is a culturally determined vehicle for evidential annotation of hearsay. It requires at least a description of the source and the minimal pragmatic characterization of the speech act (encoded in the reporting verb). This then is a minimal requirement for all attribution in this cultural context and we can see it borne out in email and chat groups, where the sender is always identified (at least by their email aliases) and the "speech act" is implicit in the vehicle (email). The importance of this authentication vehicle for information is also felt when one hits on a Web page with interesting content but no hint or link as to its author and purpose: this is a highly unsettling situation and may well lead to dismissing the page for further use. It incurs the same stigma as anonymous messages by phone or traditional mail.

Like reported speech, information of any kind should have a source list annotation detailing the path it took from the original source to the current user, in addition to other circumstantial information that impacts its interpretation. Moreover, it is convenient, especially when compiling many sources into a comprehensive overview over different opinions (like in product reviews), to compile structures akin to profile structures, that group sources with similar points of view into larger supporting groups, for easier structuring of the information and coherence of interpretation. Because information may be easier to interpret in the pertinent context, profile structures restore this original context. Finally, a reasoner that has to make sense of many differing accounts must have a reasoning zone like potential beliefs, where contradictory information is stored together with its authenticating information (akin to the source list) until enough evidence is accumulated to adopt one side as the predominant one, which can be transformed into actually held beliefs.

Reported speech as the most widely used example of evidential coding can thus serve as the guiding model for the treatment of second hand information in general.

7. Conclusion

Attribution is a phenomenon of great interest and a principled treatment is important beyond the realm of newspaper articles. The way natural language has evolved to reflect our understanding of attribution in the form of reported speech can guide investigations into representations forming the basis for shallow text mining as well as belief revision or maintenance systems.

This paper has shown the importance of a two step process in interpreting reported speech and other explicit attributions: interpreting first the shallow semantics of reported speech, then interpreting it in the pragmatic and semantic context. The first step can be achieved with acceptable performance using shallow techniques as has been demonstrated in a proof of concept system. The importance of analyzing the profile structure even for shallow further analysis lies in the contexts it constructs: interpretation of material in different profiles may differ (this point has also been raised by Polanyi and Zaenen (this volume) discussing reported speech, among others, as a conceptual valence shifter).

The second step is largely dependent on the particular use for the system and can thus not be described in general. Yet, the general principle of a potential belief space that can accommodate conflicting information without disabling the underlying reasoning system should be part of any particular system that deals with attitudes and affect in text.

8. Acknowledgements

Monia Doandes' help is gratefully acknowledged, as are the valuable comments from Jan Wiebe and anonymous reviewers. This work was funded in part by the National Science and Engineering Research Council of Canada and the Fonds nature et technologies of Quebec.

9. Bibliography

Anick, P. and Bergler, S. (1992) Lexical Structures for Linguistic Inference, In *Pustejovsky, J. and Bergler, S. (Eds.), Lexical Semantics and Knowledge Representation,* Springer, Berlin.

Bergler, S. (1992) *The Evidential Analysis of Reported Speech.* PhD Dissertation, Brandeis University, Massachusetts.

Bergler, S. (1995a) From Lexical Semantics to Text Analysis, in Saint-Dizier, P. and Viegas, E. (Eds.), *Computational Lexical Semantics,* Cambridge University Press, Cambridge.

Bergler, S. (1995b) Generative Lexicon Principles for Machine Translation: A Case for Meta-lexical Structure, *Journal of Machine Translation 9(3).*

Clark, H. and Gerrig, R. (1990) Quotations as Demonstrations. *Language 66(4),* 764-805.

Cunningham, H. (2002) Gate, a General Architecture for Text Engineering. *Computers and the Humanities, 36,* 223-254.

Doandes, M. (2003) *Profiling for Belief Acquisition from Reported Speech.* Master's thesis, Concordia University. Montreal.

DUC (2003) Document Understanding Conference. NIST. http://www-nlpir.nist.gov/projects/duc/index.html

Fellbaum, C. (Ed.) (1998) *WordNet: An Electronic Lexical Database.* MIT Press.

Gerard, C. (2000) *Modelling Readers of News Articles Using Nested Beliefs.* Master's thesis, Concordia University. Montreal.

Hepple, M. (2000) Independence and Commitment: Assumptions for Rapid Training and Execution of Rule-based Part-of-Speech Taggers. In *Proceedings of the 38th Annual Meeting of the Association for Computational Linguistics (ACL-2000).* 278-285. Hong Kong.

Marcu, D. (1997) The Rhetorical Parsing of Natural Language Texts. In *Proceedings of the 35th Annual Meeting of the Association for Computational Linguistics and the 8th Conference of the European Chapter of the Association for Computational Linguistics.* 96-103. Madrid.

Mithun, M. (1999) *The Languages of Native North America*. Cambridge University Press, Cambridge.

Polanyi, L., Culy, C., van den Berg, M., Thione, G.L., and Ahn, D. (2004) A Rule Based Approach to Discourse Parsing. In *Proceedings of the 5th SIGdial Workshop on Discourse and Dialogue*. Cambridge.

Polanyi, L. and Zaenen, A. (2004) Contextual Valence Shifters. In Qu, Y., Shanahan, J.G., Wiebe, J. (Eds.) *Exploring Attitude and Affect in Text: Theories and Applications AAAI-EAAT 2004*, AAAI Press Report SS-04-07.

Quirk, R., Greenbaum, S., Leech, G., and Svartvik, J. (1985) *A Comprehensive Grammar of the English Language*. Longman, London.

Rapaport, W. J. (1986) Logical Foundations for Belief Representation, *Cognitive Science 10*. 371-422.

Rapaport, W.J., Shapiro, S.C., and Wiebe, J. (1997) Quasi-Indexicals and Knowledge Reports, *Cognitive Science 21(1)*. 63-107.

Wiebe, J., Bruce, R., and Duan, L. (1997) Probabilistic Event Categorization, In *Recent Advances in Natural Language Processing (RANLP-97)*. 163-170. Tsigov Chark.

Wilks, Y. and Ballim, A. (1991) *Artificial Believers*. Erlbaum, Norwood.

Witte, R., and Bergler, S. (2003) Fuzzy Coreference Resolution for Summarization. In *Proceedings of the International Symposium on Reference Resolution and Its Applications on Question Answering and Summarization (ARQAS 2003)*. 43-50. Venice.

Chapter 3

Where Attitudinal Expressions Get their Attitude

Jussi Karlgren, Gunnar Eriksson, and Kristofer Franzén
Swedish Institute of Computer Science
Box 1263
164 29 Kista
Sweden
Email: {jussi | guer | franzen}@sics.se

Abstract
    A number of attitudinal expressions are identified and analyzed using dependency based syntactic analysis. A claim is made that attitudinal loading of lexical items is dynamic rather than lexical and that attitudinal loading of individual lexical items is acquired through their use in attitudinally loaded structures.

Keywords: Attitude extraction, attitudinal expressions, dynamic attitudinal loading, emotion, perspective.

1. Research Questions to Motivate the Study of Attitudinal Expressions

The new field of attitude extraction is motivated primarily as an application area – as an area which will provide innovation to future generations of information access services. The study of attitude, expression, emotion, and perspective in text and discourse is interesting for other reasons as well. The link between form of expression, topical content, and referential processing is exceptionally clearly present in the examples discussed in this volume. In this paper we explore text to find attitudinal expressions, to find what characterizes such expressions, and to eventually understand them in the sense of being able to note what attitudes are held by whom as regards to what.

As a starting point, we use the notions of animacy and transitivity to formulate a methodology to probe the interface joining the formally defined but practically indivisible linguistic functions of syntax, semantics, and pragmatics. To do so reliably we need powerful tools for automatic linguistic analysis – we have recourse to quite competent morphological and syntactic analysis, but make do with simple algorithms for reference resolution and other higher level dependencies. Our aim is not to build a knowledge base, a lexical resource, or an ontology for the purposes of natural language processing. Our purpose is to understand how much information is couched in the form of linguistic expression and to explore and possibly expand the limits of processing that can be done using algorithmic rather than knowledge intensive methods.

2. Starting Points – Prototypical Attitudinal Expressions

A prototypical attitudinal expression has three constituents: an attitude, a target for the attitude, and an expressor. Someone has an attitude as regards something. This someone is always an animate agent. The object of the attitude is typically topical for the text. The attitudinal expression conforms in most cases to expectations for such expressions: the attitude is expressed through attitudinally loaded terms, using syntax which accommodates some of the three constituents and relates them to the topical frame of the narration or discussion at hand. Our claim in this paper is that attitude is not conveyed by lexical choice alone. We claim that attitude is largely expressed through the form of the utterance – with no requirement for any one lexical item in the utterance to be prototypically attitudinal. Lexical items are initially attitudinally loaded by virtue of their distributional history (see, e.g., Sahlgren (2002) or Sahlgren and Karlgren (2003) for a discussion on distributional semantics) but can be coerced to be more or less attitudinally loaded through their syntactic context. Similarly, experiments by Riloff and Wiebe (2003) make use of syntactic patterns to find subjective expressions, because lexical resources by necessity are incomplete and static in the face of the variety of emotional expression available to authors.

The experiments and examples given below focus on clauses with predicative complements. We believe that they are more often than other constructions loci for attitudinal expression. Our aim is to be able to find attitudinally loaded patterns with constituents identified and categorized from prototypical macro-patterns, specified on the syntactic and informational level.

> It is W-ly X to Y.
> Z believes that Y is very X.
> The X really Y'd Z off.
> An X seems quite often Y.

3. Text Topicality: Players

We model text topicality by *players* or *discourse referents*. Discourse referents – a theoretical concept since Coling 1969 (Karttunen, 1969), but hitherto not directly applied to information access technology – introduce a representation of text on a higher level of abstraction than terms are able to, and are text-internally and syntactically detectable, independent of text-external domain-specific knowledge bases. Identifying potential players in text (as opposed to entities that are mentioned non-topically, in passing) will need syntactic analysis, at least some initial steps towards anaphora resolution, a theory of topicality in text, and some statistical finesse. For our purposes in these experiments, we are interested in animate players with emotive potential, on the one hand and in topical players, on the other, as targets of attitudinal expression. The former have a central role in the attitudinal expression itself but need not be textually as important as the latter can be presumed to be.

We do not aim to push the envelope as regards identification of discourse referents themselves – the literature on how to identify and formalise discourse referents is plentiful albeit unproven in large scale processing experiments such as the ones we envision (e.g., Grosz et al., 1995; Sidner, 1979, 1986; Rich and LuperFoy, 1988; Fraurud, 1988). In the experiments presented in this paper we use a commercially available dependency based syntactic analysis tool to identify player candidates and filter the candidate set using text global term frequency calculations. Simpler syntactic analysis – adjacency based patterns, e.g. – would not, even for a fixed word order language such as English, give us enough information to identify, e.g., the subject of a matrix clause with any reliability.

4. Text Topicality: Moves

Players, in our model of text topicality, engage in *moves*. Moves are primarily encoded in *transitive clauses* – briefly put, in clauses that describe action, with animate agents and well anchored in the discourse space (Halliday, 1967, 1968; Hopper and Thompson, 1980). Expressing attitude is one form of action, and a move in our model.

5. Identifying Players

Candidate players are found in a text using a combination of lexical and syntactic criteria. Our claim is that there are players of different kinds in a text, and that their different informational roles will have them occupying different syntactic functions. To exemplify, we run an experiment on a longish review or column of Michael Moore's recent movie "Fahrenheit 9/11", published in Slate in June 2004. In Figure 1, results from different combinations of criteria are displayed, ordered by descending frequency and truncated at the lowest frequencies.

The subject position, unrestricted, displays a large variety of nouns and names. Note that [Michael] *Moore* and [Richard] *Clarke*, George W. Bush's former chief of counterterrorism, are subjects much more frequently than is *Bush*. The object position shows the reverse. "*Film*", an ordinarily inanimate noun, follows the pattern of *Moore* in most of the sets.

Moving to predicate clauses, which we claim to be a prototypical locus of attitudinal expression, we find, in the third column, subjects to verbs of belief to be a much more clearly restricted set of players. The example article is a very opinionated text, with author as the main source of attitude; Michael Moore does not appear in this position. The fourth column, subjects of predicative clauses with adjectival complements, is a position we claim is indicative of the target of the attitudes. Here, we find *Moore*, *Osama*, *Laden* and *Iraq* – but no Bush, who is a side topic of the text! This shows how players can be usefully distinguished with respect to their syntactic function – or rather, their *moves* – in ways that are relevant to their attitudinal role.

6. The Case for Animacy: Adjectival Attributes and Genitive Attributes

The examples discussed in the previous section show how syntax mirrors the attitudinal role of the player. This is no coincidence. Certain types of player will occur more typically in certain syntactic positions. This is by virtue of their informational position and by their ontological status: strongly animate agents, typically human, active, and that stand out, are more likely to be in focus, both as regards attitudes expressed by the players in question or about them by other players or the author. In the following example, with data shown in Figure 2, we have selected a lexical item "*Clinton*", which can be expected to engender attitudinal expression and extracted adjectival attributes attached to it. By simple examination it is evident that the adjectives in the second column, derived in this fashion, have more pronounced attitudinal loading than the baseline adjectives shown in the first column.

Similarly, constructions that are marked for animate agents can be expected to hold attitudinal expressions more often than others. The third column shows adjective-noun constructions with a genitival modifier – the position marked X is reserved for animate agents. The fourth column shows the same extraction pattern, but with an agent selected for high topical focus – as above, "*Clinton*". The adjectives in the fourth column are mostly and typically highly attitudinal. This demonstrates how the status of the referent is a useful selector for attitudinal items.

Subject nouns	Object nouns	Subjects of verbs of belief with predicative complements	Subjects to predicatives with adjectival complements	Noun heads of predicative complements	Noun heads of predicative complements with adjective attributes
		We believe it is difficult	*Iraq would still be the personal property of...*	*... is a pacifist*	*... is a brave man*
Moore	film	we	it	fact	man
film	Bush	here	this	Moore	edifice
Clarke	army	there	there	film	cowardice
war	way	I	that	Afghanistan	book
shot	vote		Moore	war	army
Saudi	troop		Laden	time	
Saddam	removal		point	point	
regime	president		Osama	Iraq	
people	Orwell		meeting	way	
meeting	Moore		Iraq	sort	
Laden	line		he	pacifist	
Iraq	life		describe	man	
half	courage		company	word	
Fahrenheit	coalition		capital	United States	
civilian	chance			right	
Bush				interview	
Baghdad				family	
attack				exercise	
Afghanistan				day	
administration				course	
				Baghdad	
				audience	
				airport	

Figure 1. Examples of player candidates and filtered sets of players.

7. The Case for Syntactic Structure: Situational Reference

Texts abound with self reference, clause reference, situational reference and other types of meta-level references. Examples of such references are the pronoun *It* in: "*I kissed the ticket collector on the train yesterday. It was nice.*" and the pronoun *That* in "*Sometimes there is no correlate. That is an annoying problem.*" Most practically oriented studies on referential expressions gather such cases under the heading "situation reference". Resolving what the pronoun in the example above is referring to is at present problematic or near-impossible, but for the present purpose, collecting the attitude expressed towards them is not. In the examples above, we know that the author regards something as *nice* and something as *annoying*, even if we are unable to identify that entity.

Figure 2 gives in the first column the most frequent of all adjectives found in three months of Los Angeles Times newsprint; in the second column, the most frequent of adjectives that function as predicative complements; in the third, the most frequent of adjectives that are predicative complements to the three frequently situational pronouns *it, this,* and *that.*

Adjectives, all	Adjective attributes to "*Clinton*"	Adjective-noun constructions with any genitive attribute	Adjective-noun constructions with genitive attribute "*Clinton*"
New	early	X's executive director	Clinton's white house
good	encouraging	X's general fund	Clinton's strong commitment
high	former	X's good friend	Clinton's proposed alliance
big	standard	X's general manager	Clinton's tough talk
federal	actual	X's central bank	Clinton's proposed reform
american	agitated	X's young brother	Clinton's prominent role
orange	entire	X's general plan	Clinton's political quagmire
public	frequent	X's technical program	Clinton's federal budget
great	gregarious	X's national championship	Clinton's vehement response
own	high-ranking	X's valuable player	Clinton's strong defense
long	leaving	X's close friend	
national	longtime	X's advisory council	
former	now-famous	X's winless streak	
large	opportunistic	X's Vietnamese community	
local	outraged	X's super bowl	
small	proposed	X's short story	
same	real	X's Greek row	
old	regular	X's good player	
free	staunch	X's athletic director	
southern	underfunded		
major			
young			
white			
political			
late			
real			

Figure 2. Animate and focused heads accommodate more typically attitudinal adjectives. Data from one month of Los Angeles Times newsprint, first column sorted in descending frequency and truncated to fit.

Even from a cursory glance it is evident that the third column has more prototypical attitudinal adjectives than the first; the difference between the second and third is more open to discussion. Whatever the added value of the more stringent filtering criterion, it is clear that the position in predicative complement seems to be well established for attitudinal lexical items. Our first claim is that a predicative complement, especially in a situational reference setting, is a locus for attitude in text.

Further inspection of the second and third columns shows that, even in the top ten list of adjectives, there are items that are non-typical attitudinal items: *ready, likely, available, possible* are all examples of non-attitudinal lexical items. Our second claim is that the clauses and contexts they participate in may well be attitudinal in any case ("*Now comes the big one, and we're ready!"*; *"Others simply are not ready to..."*; *"She's always fully available to help."*), in support of our contention that attitude is not simply a lexical question: no simple list of attitudinal terms will select attitudes from texts; no simple algorithm will allow us to draw up such a list, even provisionally.

All adjectives	Adjectives as predicative complement	Adjectives as predicative complement under *it*, *this*, and *that*
new	good	Hard
good	able	good
high	available	easy
big	hard	difficult
orange	sure	important
long	important	true
public	easy	bad
federal	ready	possible
own	likely	great
great	bad	nice
N = 35 000	N = 7 500	N = 2 500

Figure 3. Examples of how certain syntactic constructions are repositories of attitudinal expression.

8. Using Syntactic Patterns more Systematically

The earlier experiments showed that animacy and clausal structures, evaluated informally, seem to carry weight. To investigate this more formally, we formulated a number of progressively more restrictive criteria for identifying attitudinal expressions which we searched for in two sets of texts taken from the Wall Street Journal. One set (N=3398) is composed of editorials, opinion pieces, and letters to the editor; the other (N=3500) of reporting news articles, our assumption being that there are more overt expressions of attitude in the former set. The number of times the respective criteria matched in each text were calculated, normalized by number of clauses and are shown in detail in Figure 4. All reported results are statistically significant.

The first criterion we looked for was number of adjectives per clause, under the relatively weak assumption that attitudinal expression often finds its realization in adjectival form. For the second criterion we looked for occurrences of *"good"* or *"bad"* per clause – assuming these two most prototypical attitudinal adjectives would be noticeable. The third criterion adds syntactic constraints, looking for adjectives in a predicative complement – constructions such as *"It is good"* or *"... is a wonderful feeling"*. The fourth criterion further looks to see if the complement is an object to another verb in constructions such as *"... believe this is a serious question"*.

While the two evaluation sets admittedly are rather crudely fashioned, the results are unequivocal: there are clear stylistic differences between the two categories of text and this difference is better modeled using a syntactic distinguishing criterion. The most stringent object criterion does not seem to carry as strong a distinguishing power between the two sets as does the simpler predicative complement one, but is still clearly statistically significant.

Criterion	Opinion texts	Reporting texts	Rank sum
Adjectives per clause	1.75	1.64	12452777.5
"good" or "bad" per clause	0.0333	0.0131	12866718.5
Adjectives in predicative complement	0.354	0.183	14453290
Adjectives in predicative complement which is in object relation to other verb	0.0432	0.0368	12105678

Figure 4. Average number of occurrences of a attitudinal item or syntactic construction, for a collection of opinion pieces and reporting newspring, respectively. All differences significant (p > 0.95) by Mann Whitney U rank sum test, criterion level 11857416.2673481.

9. Generalizing from Syntactic Patterns to the Lexicon

A further examination of differences between the two sets defined above show how the sets of adjectives differ between sets and between the different contexts examined. The top ten adjectives in each condition are shown in Figure 5. The two document sets have slightly differing ranking of adjectives used – but six out of the top ten are shared between the document sets. In the most stringent criterion the overlap is slightly lower – only five out of the top ten are shared. The top ten adjective lists give the same impression as the lists in Figure 2: the more restrictive contexts seem to be loci for attitudinal expression, and the expressions found give purchase to our claim that adjectives gain their attitudinal loading from being used in certain expressions. This would also seem to point at the potential for mining attitudinally loaded items from expressions, if some statistical finesse is observed.

10. Conclusions

Our conclusion at this juncture is fairly abstract, but well supported by the data in our preliminary experiments reported here. The expression of attitude is done through a combination of syntactic and lexical means – most lexical items and constructions that participate in attitudinal expressions are typically also found in non-attitudinal expressions. Our further claim is consistent with the data but as of yet unproven – that lexical items gain attitudinal loading from the contexts they participate in. On a more theoretical note, we conclude that to explore the expression of attitude in text, it is necessary to explore the interaction of syntax and pragmatics – lexical resources by themselves will not be sufficient, be they static or dynamic.

	Opinion texts	Reporting texts
Adjectives	new	new
	good	high
	political	federal
	american	big
	public	large
	economic	good
	federal	american
	national	national
	own	low
	high	major
Adjectives in	good	high
predicative	able	good
complement	true	likely
	political	able
	important	big
	new	new
	likely	low
	high	large
	bad	strong
	wrong	bad
Adjectives in	good	good
predicative	able	likely
complement which is	bad	high
in object relation to	wrong	able
another verb	important	strong
	necessary	big
	willing	bad
	only	new
	new	low
	easy	willing

Figure 5. Examples of adjectives in predicative complements, with and without object verb criterion.

11. Bibliography

Fraurud, K. (1988) Pronoun Resolution in Unrestricted Text. *Nordic Journal of Linguistics*. 11, 47-68.

Grosz, B., Joshi, A., and Weinstein., S. (1995) Centering: a Framework for Modelling the Local Coherence of Discourse. *Computational Linguistics*, 21 (2), 44-50.

Halliday, M. A. K. (1967) Notes on Transitivity and Theme in English I. *Journal of Linguistics*, 3(1), 37-81.

Halliday, M. A. K. (1967) Notes on Transitivity and Theme in English II. *Journal of Linguistics*, 3(2), 199-244.

Halliday, M. A. K. (1968) Notes on Transitivity and Theme in English III. *Journal of Linguistics*, 4 (2), 179-215.

Hopper, P., and Thompson., S. (1980) Transitivity in Grammar and Discourse. *Language* 56, 251-99.

Karlgren, J., and Sahlgren, M. (2001) From Words to Understanding. In Uesaka, Y., Kanerva, P. & Asoh, H. (Eds.): *Foundations of Real-World Intelligence*, 294-308, Stanford: CSLI Publications.

Karttunen, L. (1969) Discourse Referents. *Proceedings of the Third International Conference on Computational Linguistics* (COLING). International Committee on Computational Linguistics and KVAL research group on quantitative linguistics.

Rich, E., and LuperFoy, S. (1988) An architecture for anaphora resolution. *Proceedings of the Second Conference on Applied Natural Language Processing (ANLP-2)*, 18-24.

Riloff, E., and Wiebe, J. (2003) Learning Extraction Patterns for Subjective Expressions. *Proceedings of the Conference on Empirical Methods in Natural Language Processing (EMNLP-03)*, 105-112.

Sahlgren, M. (2002) Towards a Flexible Model of Word Meaning. In Karlgren, J. (Ed.) Papers from *Acquiring (and Using) Linguistic (and World) Knowledge for Information Access*, AAAI Spring Symposium 2002, Technical Report SS-02-09. AAAI Press.

Sidner, C. L. (1979) Towards a Computational Theory of Definite Anaphora Comprehension in English Discourse. Technical Report No. 537. M.I.T., Artificial Intelligence Laboratory.

Sidner, C. L. (1986) Focusing in the Comprehension of Definite Anaphora. In Grosz, B., Sparck Jones, K., and Webber, B. (Eds.) *Readings in Natural Language Processing.*, Morgan Kaufmann Publishers.

Chapter 4

Analysis of Linguistic Features Associated with Point of View for Generating Stylistically Appropriate Text

Nancy L. Green
University of North Carolina at Greensboro
Dept. of Mathematical Sciences
University of North Carolina at Greensboro
Greensboro, NC 27402-6170 USA
Email: nlgreen@uncg.edu

Abstract
We describe a qualitative analysis of a corpus of clinical genetics patient letters. In this genre, a single letter is intended to serve multiple functions and is designed for multiple audiences. The goal of the analysis was to identify stylistically-related features for a natural language generation system. We found that, perhaps because of the multiple intended functions and audiences, within a single letter more than one writing style (set of realization choices) can be observed, and the sets of features are associated with different perspectives. Thus, an NLG system must take perspective into account to generate stylistically appropriate text in this application. The paper outlines the perspectives and the features associated with each that were identified in the corpus.

Keywords: clinical genetics, patient letters, style analysis, natural language generation, perspective, point of view.

1. Introduction

We are studying a corpus of clinical genetics patient letters written by genetic counselors to their clients. According to Baker et al. (2002), the typical patient letter, one to two pages in length, summarizes the counselor's meeting with the client. At a meeting the counselor may provide information on the client's case (e.g., test results, diagnosis of a genetic disorder, prediction of genetic risks), counseling to cope with the potential emotional effects of the information, as well as explanations of genetics concepts relevant to the client's case. While the client is the addressee of the letter, intended secondary audiences include family members and (in case the client is the parent or guardian of a pediatric patient) staff members at the patient's school or daycare. In addition, the letter is intended to provide medical documentation for healthcare providers. These audiences differ in background (e.g., expert or layperson), in information needs (e.g., a description of patient symptoms to support a medical diagnosis or to provide information for caregivers), and in their emotional relationship to the patient (e.g., a parent or someone not personally involved with the patient). The motivation for our study of the corpus, unlike most of the other papers in this volume, is generation rather than interpretation. We wish to identify stylistically-related features to guide linguistic realization and content selection in a natural language generation (NLG) system for genetic counselors. The system will generate the first draft of a patient letter using general information about clinical genetics and specific information about the patient's case.

Previous NLG research on stylistic variation has viewed style as a constant property within a document and as defining a genre (Hovy, 1990; DiMarco and Hirst, 1993). After informal review of letters in the corpus, we noted that, perhaps because of the multiple intended functions and audiences, within a single letter (and in some cases within a single sentence) more than one writing style can be observed. Our hypothesis is that each style (i.e., coherent set of realization choices) is associated with a different perspective assumed by the writer, e.g., a counseling perspective addressing the client's emotional state or a medical perspective serving a documentation function. For example, in sentence (2) below the writer uses the referring doctor's perspective in reporting the reason for the referral to the author's clinic. (The number in parentheses identifies the sentence; the letter's identifier, *VCF*, is given in parentheses at the end of the excerpt. In the corpus, capitalized words in brackets have been substituted for original text to maintain client confidentiality but convey the gist of the original text. In this domain, *proband* refers to the person who is the focus of a genetic study, i.e., the patient.)

> (2) [DOCTOR] asked us to evaluate [PROBAND] to determine if [HIS/HER] delays in development and [SPECIFIC TYPES OF BIRTH DEFECT] were due to a recognizable genetic condition. (letter VCF)

When speaking from the referring doctor's perspective, the writer's description of the patient's symptoms is precise and uses words that may have negative connotations to the addressee (the patient's parent), e.g., a description of the specific types of birth defects and use of the term *delays*. In contrast, when the writer assumes the genetic counselor's perspective, the wording is designed to mitigate the possible negative effect of the information on the addressee. A key stylistic choice expressing the voice of the counselor in sentence (14) below is use of the value-free or nonstigmatizing phrase *altered form* instead of *mutation* (Baker et al., 2002).

> (14) [PROBAND] could have inherited an altered form of a gene from both you and [HIS/HER] father that caused [HIS/HER] birth defects and learning problems. (letter VCF)

In summary, we claim that in addition to a representation of what must be said, our NLG system must take perspective into account in order to be able to generate stylistically appropriate text in this application. This paper justifies the claim by outlining a set of perspectives and some of the features potentially associated with each that we have identified by qualitative analysis of the corpus.

2. Perspectives in Corpus

Based upon a review of letters in the corpus and information on genetic counseling, e.g., (Wilson, 2000), we have identified the following perspectives:
- author: the letter writer, i.e., a genetic counselor writing on behalf of a genetics clinic. This voice can be distinguished from the voices that we call *genetic counselor* and *clinic*. For

example, in the author's voice, formulaic expressions are used (e.g., *We hope this information is helpful*), which are not used in parts of a letter representing those other perspectives.

- client: the person(s) who met with the counselor and who is (are) the principal addressee(s) of the letter, usually the patient or some member(s) of the patient's family. This perspective is taken to document discussion initiated by the client at the meeting (e.g., *You expressed concern that ...*) as well as to enable the writer to include information for the medical record although it is already known to the client (e.g., *As you know, [DOCTOR] first saw [PROBAND] at eight months...*).

- referring doctor: the doctor who referred the patient to the clinic (e.g., *[DOCTOR] asked us to evaluate ...*). This perspective is used to document the referring doctor's findings and tentative diagnosis, with which the clinic need not agree.

- clinic: genetics clinic with which the genetic counselor is affiliated and that was visited by the client. This voice is used to document what was done to a patient (e.g., *We obtained a blood sample ...*), or told to the client (e.g., *We have recommended ...*) during the visit.

- genetic counselor: the genetic counselor who met with the client(s), who is also the letter writer. This perspective is used in discussing patient-specific information such as the diagnosis or a family member's inheritance risks in terms that the client can understand and that mitigate the potential negative effect of the information (e.g., *It is important to remember that [PROBAND'S] problems could still be caused by genetic alteration...*).

- education: basic background knowledge about human genetics. For example, this perspective is used to explain the role of genes in health and how genes are inherited (e.g., *In autosomal dominant inheritance, only one altered gene is needed for the person to have the condition. This gene can come from either the mother or the father...*).

- research: information from the clinical genetics research literature (e.g., *Most children [with osteogenesis imperfecta] have fragile bones, blue sclera, ...*).

Although originally developed for the automated analysis of narrative (Wiebe, 1994), and later applied to analysis of attitude in newspaper articles (Wilson and Wiebe, 2003), the model of psychological point of view (POV) provides a framework for our own study. That model defines a private-state relation whose components include an *experiencer*, an *attitude*, and the *object* of the private state. For example in sentence (2, VCF) repeated below, the experiencer, identified as [DOCTOR], is the referring doctor, the attitude could be interpreted as *believes it likely that*, and the object corresponds to what is expressed as *the proband's delays in development and [SPECIFIC TYPES OF BIRTH DEFECT] were due to a recognizable genetic condition.*

(2) [DOCTOR] asked us to evaluate [PROBAND] to determine if [HIS/HER] delays in development and [SPECIFIC TYPES OF BIRTH DEFECT] were due to a recognizable genetic condition.

(3) During your appointment on [DATE], we obtained a blood sample from [PROBAND].

(4a) In addition to the routine chromosome study,

(4b) in which a microscopic study of the 46 chromosomes is done,

(4c) a special analysis of the long arm of chromosome 22 (22q11)

(4d) by a technique called fluorescence in situ hybridization (FISH)

(4e) was done to test for Velocardiofacial syndrome (VCF).

(5) Individuals with VCF often have [SPECIFIC TYPES OF BIRTH DEFECT] and learning problems. (letter VCF)

This excerpt illustrates several other points. As noted in (Wiebe, 1994), experiencer and attitude need not be stated explicitly. In (3), the experiencer, signaled by *we*, is the clinic and the attitude could be interpreted as *knowledge shared by experiencer and addressee*. In (4a), the experiencer could be interpreted as the clinic again, although it was not explicitly signaled; (4a) *continues* (Wiebe, 1994) the experiencer of the current POV. However, we claim that the explanatory information provided in (4b) and (4d) is the voice of the genetic counselor and the attitude for those phrases could be interpreted as *knowledge that the experiencer believes the addressee does not share with the experiencer*. This change in attitude is associated with a shift in tense; the explanatory information in (4b) and (4d) is presented in the present tense while the rest of (2) through (4), a narration of the patient's referral, history and clinic visit, is presented in the past tense. Finally, the experiencer in (5) is the research perspective. This change in experiencer is marked also by a shift to the present tense.

3. Associated Features

Table 1 shows, for each perspective defined above, some associated features that we have identified by manual inspection of the corpus. The second column lists the typical forms used for referring to each type of experiencer. Note that according to the table, first person plural pronoun forms such as *we* are used to refer to several categories of experiencer. The third column lists typical forms for referring to individuals other than the experiencer. For example, the education and research perspectives are characterized by reference to generic individuals instead of to members of the client's family. According to Baker et al. (2002) the strategy of conveying information about a patient indirectly by using general terms (e.g., *Children with this condition tend to lose their hearing*, instead of *Nisha is likely to lose her hearing*) can be used by the writer to mitigate the negative impact of the information on the client. The fourth column lists verb tenses characteristic of each perspective. The fifth column lists forms for conveying probability, and is discussed below. The last column lists other associated features, including characteristic open-class words and word patterns. For example, several perspectives can be distinguished on the basis of use of *expert* biomedical terminology in contrast to use of more *layperson-oriented* terminology, e.g., use of the geneticist's term *allele* instead of the layperson-oriented *copy*. In addition to this distinction, some perspectives can be characterized by use of value-free or non-stigmatizing language.

Experi-encer	Reference to experiencer	Reference to others	Tense	Probability	Other cues
author	pronoun (1p-plural), self-reference to letter (e.g., *this letter*)	reference to family members by name or pronoun (2p, 3p)	present or past (time of clinic visit)		formulaic language (e.g., *it was a pleasure*), position near beginning and end of letter
client	reference to family members by name or pronoun (2p, 3p)		past (time of clinic visit)		client's knowledge or questions (e.g., *you asked whether, as you know*)
referring doctor	doctor's name	reference to family members by name or pronoun (2p, 3p)	past (before clinic visit)	implicit (e.g., *due to*)	referral verbs (e.g., *referred by*), expert biomedical terminology, non-value-free words
genetics clinic	pronoun (1p-plural)	reference to family members by name or pronoun (2p, 3p)	past (time of clinic visit)		clinic's actions (e.g., *we gave you, we obtained*), expert biomedical terminology
genetic counselor	pronoun (1p-plural)	reference to family members by name or pronoun (2p, 3p)	present or future	qualitative (e.g., *could, it appears that*), Mendelian ratio (e.g., *a 50% chance*)	emphasis (*still, it is important*), value-free words (e.g., *alteration* instead of *mutation*), layperson-oriented biomedical terminology
education	agentless passive (e.g., *it is believed that*)	reference to population (e.g., *the parents, the mother*) or universal (e.g., *we, everyone*)	habit-ual present or future	qualitative, Mendelian ratio	layperson-oriented biomedical terminology, *called* (e.g., *a gene called GJB2*)
research	agentless passive (e.g., *has been reported*)	reference to population (e.g., *individuals*)	habit-ual present	qualitative, quantitative	expert biomedical terminology

Table 1. Types of features characterizing each perspective.

In a previous study of this corpus (Green, 2003), we manually tagged both qualitative and quantitative indicators of probability. Examples of qualitative indicators are modal verbs (e.g., *can, could*), frequency adverbs (e.g., *often*), and quantifiers (e.g., *many*). Quantitative indicators are phrases containing numeric expressions (e.g., rates, odds, percentages), possibly with qualifiers (e.g., *approximately 80%.*). That study determined that the ratio of probability cues to the number of sentences was high, which is not surprising due to the inherent uncertainty in human genetics. Column five of Table 1 shows the types of probability cues associated with each perspective. Qualitative cues are used in all perspectives characterized by explicit use of probability terms. The cues that we call *Mendelian ratios*, i.e., the idealized ratios of a Mendelian inheritance model (e.g., 0%, 25%, 50%, 75%, and 100%) are characteristic of the education perspective (in explanations of inheritance patterns) and in the genetic counselor perspective (in explaining inheritance patterns that occur in the client's family). Presence of a quantitative, non-Mendelian probability value (e.g., *6%*), seems to be a good indicator of the research perspective, since the original source of information would have been from empirical studies published in the research literature.

4. Implications for Natural Language Generation and Automatic Recognition of Point of View

An NLG system for a domain such as this must take perspective into account in order to be able to generate stylistically appropriate text, regardless of whether perspective is considered in generating text from "first principles", or whether it is "compiled into" quasi-textual building blocks. Otherwise, for example, information needed for medical documentation purposes might be realized in layperson-oriented terminology that is unsuitable for its intended function, or information intended for a parent might be realized in obscure-sounding medical terminology that fails to consider the emotional impact on the parent. Even when a generator uses precompiled "building blocks" (Hirst et al., 1997), if the generator is not informed of the perspective represented by each building block, then subsequent transformations such as text aggregation or referring expression construction could produce phrasing that mixes perspective infelicitously.

In contrast to our work, most of the other projects described in this volume have goals related to automatic recognition of point of view in text. Despite the difference in motivation, our qualitative analysis can be seen as a possible step towards automatic recognition of point of view in clinical genetics-related documents. It seems likely one could build a classifier to predict perspective based on features like those that we have identified. The classifier might be used, for example, in a question-answering system with access to a heterogeneous collection of text, e.g., patient medical records and general patient education material on genetic disorders.

5. Acknowledgments

This work is supported by the National Science Foundation under CAREER Award No. 0132821.

6. Bibliography

Baker, D.L., Eash, T., Schuette, J.L., and Uhlmann, W.R. (2002) Guidelines for Writing Letters to Patients. *Journal of Genetic Counseling, 11 (5)*, 399-418.

DiMarco, C. and Hirst, G. (1993) A Computational Theory of Goal-Directed Style in Syntax. *Computational Linguistics, 19 (3)*, 451-500.

Green, N. (2003) Towards an Empirical Model of Argumentation in Medical Genetics. In *Proceedings of IJCAI 2003 Workshop on Computational Models of Natural Argument (CMNA-03)*. 39-44.

Hirst, G., DiMarco, C., Hovy, E., and Parsons, K. (1997) Authoring and Generating Health-education Documents that are Tailored to the Needs of the Individual Patient. In *Proceedings of User Modeling 1997*.

Hovy, E. (1990) Pragmatics and Natural Language Generation. *Artificial Intelligence 43*, 153-197.

Wiebe, J. M. (1994) Tracking Point of View in Narrative. *Computational Linguistics 20 (2)*, 233-288.

Wilson, T. and Wiebe, J. (2003) Annotating Opinions in the World Press. In *Proceedings of the 4th SIGDial Workshop*.

Wilson, G.N. (2000) *Clinical Genetics: A Short Course*. Wiley-Liss.

Chapter 5

The Subjectivity of Lexical Cohesion in Text

Jane Morris
University of Toronto
Faculty of Information Studies,
University of Toronto, Toronto,
ON, Canada, M5S 3G6
Email: morris@fis.utoronto.ca

Graeme Hirst
University of Toronto,
Dept. of Computer Science,
University of Toronto, Toronto,
ON, Canada, M5S 3G4
Email: gh@cs.toronto.edu

Abstract
    A reader's perception of even an "objective" text is to some degree subjective. We present the results of a pilot study in which we looked at the degree of subjectivity in readers' perceptions of lexical semantic relations, which are the building blocks of the lexical chains used in many applications in natural language processing. An example is presented in which the subjectivity reflects the reader's attitude.

Keywords: Lexical cohesion, lexical semantic relations, subjectivity, inter-subject agreement.

1. Introduction

How much of a reader's understanding of a text is idiosyncratic and how much is common to that of most other readers of the same text of a similar age and education? What is the degree of individual difference or subjectivity in text understanding? The answers to these questions are likely to vary with text type. In this paper, the focus will be on general-interest articles (from *Reader's Digest*), and on readers' perceptions and interpretations of lexical cohesive relations in the text. Perceptions of these relations contribute to a reader's perception of the structure of the text.

There are two fundamentally different approaches to text structure: Some methods, such as Rhetorical Structure Theory (Mann and Thompson, 1988), aim to identify pre-defined structures in a text. Other methods are *associationist*; they focus on building up text-specific structures, for example through the creation of ad-hoc categories such as those proposed by Barsalou (1989) or groups of related words within the text such as *lexical chains* (Halliday and Hasan, 1976; Morris and Hirst, 1991). There is much to be gained by accepting the contributions of each approach, and in discovering how they interact. In a sense, the work of Morris and Hirst attempted this by relating associationist lexical chains to the predefined intentional structure of discourse that was proposed by Grosz and Sidner (1986). However, that particular model of discourse structure was itself rather associationist in that the "intentional structure" of a text is quite ad hoc and text-specific.

The present work is an examination of the degree of subjectivity of two aspects of the *lexical cohesion* (Halliday and Hasan, 1976) perceived by readers of text: the word groups (lexical chains) that are formed and the *lexical semantic relations* that are perceived between the words. We know of no prior research on readers' perceptions of lexical cohesion or the associated lexical semantic relations in text. Furthermore, most of the research on lexical semantic relations has not been done in the context of text. Instead, most researchers have just looked at word pairs and the four "*classical*" lexical relations: synonymy, antonymy, hyponymy, and meronymy (Fellbaum, 1998; Cruse, 1986; Halliday and Hasan, 1989). The classical relations themselves form predetermined structures consisting of hierarchies that have been studied and widely applied since Aristotle. The *non-classical* relations (all of the rest) have tended to remain unnamed and unstructured, as in the relations implicit in *Roget's Thesaurus*, in the "associative" relations or Related Terms used in Library and Information Science (Neelameghan, 2001; Milstead, 2001), in the "associative" relations widely assumed in psychology, and in the relations between members of Lakoff's (1987) non-classical categories.

Consider, for example, this (constructed) text: "How can we figure out what a text means? One could argue that the meaning is in the mind of the reader, but some people think that the meaning lies within the text itself." In what ways do readers see the relations in this text? One reader reports two lexical chains or word groups: 'understanding', which contains the words *figure out, means, meaning, mind, think, meaning*, and 'text', which contains the words *text, reader, text*. In the 'understanding' word group, related word pairs and the non-classical relations that this reader reports are these: *figure out, means*: *means* is the likely result of the action *figure out*: *mind, figure out*; *mind* is where the *figure out* action happens; *think, meaning*: *meaning* is a result of the action of *think*ing. The reader's description of the word group is 'words to do with human understanding'[1].

We have carried out a study of the degree of subjectivity of the word groups and lexical semantic relations perceived by readers of a text. The results will be presented below.

2. Theoretical Background

The linguistic study of the contribution made by inter-sentence groups of related words to text understanding started with the concept of lexical cohesion (Halliday and Hasan, 1976) and has been extended by Hasan (1984; Halliday and Hasan, 1989) to include the concept of *cohesive harmony*. Cohesive harmony adds lexico-grammatical structure to word groups (lexical chains) by first dividing them into two types — *identify-of-reference chains*, which combine reference and lexical cohesion, and *similarity chains* (using only classical relations) — and then by linking these chains together into a more tightly-knit unit with grammatical intra-sentence relations similar to the case relations of Fillmore (1968), such as agent–verb and verb–object. Cruse (1986) briefly discusses a

---

[1] These are the chains and relations that were reported by reader 'JM'. Another reader, 'GH', also reported two chains, but grouped *means* and *meaning* with *text* and *reader*.

related concept of "patterns of lexical affinities", where similar intra-sentence patterns called "syntagmatic affinities" can create more-general inter-sentence patterns (relations) called "paradigmatic affinities". Cohesive harmony and the concept of patterns of lexical affinities make the important contribution of linking lexical (and grammatical, in the case of reference cohesion) inter-sentence cohesion with grammatical intra-sentence cohesion. But no analysis of these concepts has been done using readers of text. It is therefore not known how subjective the process is.

Lexical semantic relations are the building blocks of lexical cohesion, cohesive harmony, and the concept of patterns of lexical affinity. The original view of them by Halliday and Hasan (1976) was very broad and general; the only criterion was that there had to be a recognizable relation between two words. Many of these relations were found in *Roget's Thesaurus* by Morris and Hirst (1991) in an application of the theory. The more-recent view of Hasan (1984; Halliday and Hasan, 1989) is to only use classical relations, since the rest are "too intersubjective", and both Hasan and Cruse (1986) indicate that they focus on classical relations because of prior historical focus. In psychology, the focus has been mostly on classical relations; however, there have been recent calls to broaden the focus and include non-classical relations as well (McRae and Boisvert, 1998; Hodgson, 1991). Some researchers have always included some non-classical relations, such as Evens et al. (1983), Chaffin and Herrmann (1984), and researchers in Library and Information Science. However, as noted earlier, the research on lexical semantic relations has been done out of the context of text, and then assumed to be relevant within it; and in lexical cohesion research, lexical semantic relations were analyzed by experienced linguists with particular theoretical points of view, not by ordinary readers.

3. Experimental Study

We are interested in analyzing readers' perceptions and interpretations of the lexical cohesion in text for individual differences. To this end, a pilot study was conducted with five participants as readers of the first 1.5 pages of a general-interest article from the *Reader's Digest* on the topic of movie actors and movie characters as possibly inappropriate role models for children.

Subjects were instructed to first read the article and mark the word groups that they perceived, using a different color of pencil for each different group. Once this task was completed, they transferred each separate word group to a new data sheet, and then, for each word group, indicated which pairs of words they perceived as related and what the relation was. Finally, they described the meaning of each word group in the text.

This data was analyzed to determine the degree of individual differences in the responses. For each of these groups, we computed the subjects' agreement on membership of the group in following manner: We took all possible pairs of subjects, and for each pair computed the number of words on which they agreed as a percentage of the total number of words they used. Averaged over all possible pairs of subjects, the agreement was 63%. Next, we looked at agreement on the word pairs that were identified as directly related (within the groups that were identified by a majority of subjects). We restricted this analysis to *core* words, which we defined to be those marked by a majority of subjects. We counted all distinct instances of word pairs that were marked by at least 50% of the subjects, and divided this by the total number of distinct word pairs marked. We found that 13% of the word pairs were marked by at least 50% of the subjects. For the set of word pairs used by at least two subjects, we then computed agreement on what the relation between the pair was deemed to be. We found that the subjects agreed in 70% of the cases.

Gloss of word group	Average pairwise agreement (%)
Movies	71
Communications[a]	69
Smoking	73
Groups and causes	63
Bad behaviors	41

[a] Only three subjects used this group.

Table 1. Word group similarity among readers: Average agreement between pairs of readers.

Table 1 summarizes the results for the major word groups found in the text by the readers. Individual differences showed up as different non-core words within a group, or as a different focus for the same group. As an example of the latter case, one reader added idiosyncratic attitude-bearing choices to the 'bad behaviours' word group, reflecting a law-and-order focus on bad behaviours. This is shown in Table 2, where the readers largely agree on the core words of the group, but one reader adds a group of seven "law-and-order" words that no other reader includes. (The number of readers who used each word is shown in the left column of the table.)

Table 1 shows a "trend" of 60–70% agreement (average of 63%) on word groups (though the sample of five readers and one text is small). The outlier group of 'bad behaviors' was much lower at 41% and seems to reflect the fact that judgment of bad behavior is an inherently value-laden human endeavor. For example, two out of five readers included *witchcraft*, two out of five did not include smoking-related words, and, as noted, one reader included a law-and-order focus while the other four did not.

Agreement on which word pairs within a group are related is much lower at around 13% (Table 3). This could be a reflection of the following two factors:

- This is a much more indirect task than identifying word groups. It is also cumbersome (as reported by some subjects) in that the potential number of pairs of related words is large. They were asked to be exhaustive (*i.e.*, give all word pairs that they perceived as related), but complained and were not. In contrast to forming word groups, this process was not intuitive for the readers.

Core words (chosen by ≥ 3 readers)		"Law/order/authority" outliers (all chosen by only 1 reader)	
5	shooting	1	Police
4	sex	1	Caught
4	drinking	1	British Intelligence Service
4	dangerous	1	gun control lobby
3	drag racing	1	Department of Role Model Development
3	irresponsible [behaviors]	1	M.A.D.D. [Mothers Against Drunk Driving]
		1	Spies

Table 2. 'Bad behaviors' word group: an example of subjectivity reflecting reader attitude.

Gloss of word group	Word pairs agreed on (%)	Relation agreement (%)
Movies	10	75
Communications[a]	12	20
Smoking	13	85
Groups and causes	18	69
Bad behaviors	12	100

[a]*Only three subjects used this group.*

Table 3. Lexical semantic relation similarity among readers: Average agreement on related word pairs and on the nature of the relation in agreed-on pairs.

- The word groups might be comprehended as gestalts or wholes, and words entering the category or group are, in some way, all related. That is, the relations are not perceived as binary, but holistically. In fact many of the relation descriptions were context specific. For example, one subject said that the relation in the word pair *sex–smoking* is that "both are undesirable activities for kids in the article".

In cases where subjects identified identical word pairs as related, they also showed a marked tendency (at an average of 70% agreement) to agree on what the relation was. In fact, they showed a notable ability and ease at being able to explain how words are related in context. This contrasts sharply with the commonly known fact, noted by Cruse (1986), that people find words hard to define out of context. This high level of reader agreement on what the relations were is a reflection of the importance of considering aspects of text understanding such as lexical semantic relations as being situated within their surrounding context. In other words, while explaining or perceiving linguistic meaning out of context is hard, doing so within text seems here not to be, and is therefore likely a rich and meaningful area for further study.

4. Discussion

The subjects in this small study identified a common "core" of groups of related words in the text, as well as exhibiting subjectivity or individual differences. It might be objected that our subjects simply showed "a low kappa" (or "a *bad* kappa"), and all this shows is that we asked them "the wrong question". We disagree. Rather, we believe that these preliminary results indicate that lexical cohesion is useful both as a theory and as a practical tool for determining both the commonly agreed on and the subjective aspects of text understanding. In fact, the kappa statistic doesn't apply here, as the words in a word group are not independent, and so agreement by chance cannot be computed.

Our work here does not investigate cases where the author of a text either implicitly or explicitly marks the text as being a subjective point of view taken by a particular person. Rather, we focus on the overall subjectivity in readers' perceptions of a text's meaning (i.e., aspects that are inherent in the word groups and lexical semantic relations). We consider this subjectivity to be a crucial aspect of text understanding in that it builds on research that views meaning as something created by the reader or processor of text, as opposed to meaning as something that somehow exists in text alone, separate from the reader/processor (Olson, 1994). For automation purposes it will be useful to have a clear understanding of what aspects of text meaning do exist "in the text", and what aspects can be expected to contribute to individual differences in comprehension.

Our next step will be the larger study for which this was a pilot; we will use three different texts and at least ten readers per text. We will look for overall patterns in the types of words and relations that form part of the core group and those that do not. We intend to focus on aspects of word pairs and relations such as whether they are classical or non-classical and text-general or text-specific. We also intend to analyze the relations to determine whether a common set of relation types is being used by readers. These non-classical relation types could be used to augment future or existing lexical resources.

An obvious area for future research is the effect of different types of texts and readers. We are interested in how text-specific the word groups and relations are, since non-text-specific information can be added to existing resources, but text-specific knowledge will require further complex interaction with the rest of the text. We also intend to investigate the potential linkages between the word groups in the texts for evidence of cohesive harmony or any other relations to other theories of pre-determined mechanisms of text understanding.

5. Acknowledgements

This research was supported by the Natural Sciences and Engineering Research Council of Canada. We are grateful to Clare Beghtol for helpful discussions.

6. Bibliography

Barsalou, L. (1989) Intra-concept similarity and its implications for inter-concept similarity. In Vosniadou, S. and Ortony, A. (Eds.) *Similarity and analogical reasoning.* 6–121. Cambridge University Press.

Chaffin, R. and Herrmann, D. (1984) The similarity and diversity of semantic relations. *Memory and Cognition, 12(2)*, 134–141.

Cruse, D. (1986) *Lexical semantics.* Cambridge University Press.

Evens, M., Markowitz, J., Smith, R., and Werner, O. (Eds.) (1983) *Lexical semantic relations: A comparative survey.* Linguistic Research Inc., Edmonton, Canada.

Fellbaum, C. (1998) *WordNet: An electronic lexical database.* The MIT Press, Cambridge, Mass.

Fillmore, C. (1968) The Case for Case. In Bach, E. and Harms, R. (Eds.) *Universals in linguistic theory.* 1–88. Holt, Rinehart and Winston, New York.

Grosz, B.J. and Sidner, C.L. (1986) Attention, intentions, and the structure of discourse. *Computational Linguistics, 12(3)*, 175–204.

Halliday, M.A.K. and Hasan, R. (1976) *Cohesion in English.* Longman, London.

Halliday, M.A.K. and Hasan, R. (1989) *Language, context, and text: aspects of language in a social-semiotic perspective*, 2nd edition. Oxford University Press.

Hasan, R. (1984) Coherence and cohesive harmony. In Flood, J. (Ed.) *Understanding reading comprehension: Cognition, language and the structure of prose.* 181–219. International Reading Association, Newark, Delaware.

Hodgson, J. (1991) Informational constraints on pre-lexical priming. *Language and Cognitive Processes, 6(3),* 169–205.

Lakoff, G. (1987) *Women, fire and dangerous things.* University of Chicago Press.

Mann, W.C. and Thomson, S.A. (1988) Rhetorical structure theory. *Text, 8,* 243–281.

McRae, K. and Boisvert, S. (1998) Automatic semantic similarity priming. *Journal of Experimental Psychology: Learning, Memory and Cognition, 24(3),* 558–572.

Milstead, J.L. (2001) Standards for relationships between subject indexing terms. In C.A. Bean and R. Green (Eds.) *Relationships in the Organization of Knowledge.* 53–66. Kluwer Academic Publishers.

Morris, J. and Hirst, G. (1991) Lexical cohesion computed by thesaural relations as an indicator of the structure of text. *Computational Linguistics, 17(1),* 21–48.

Neelameghan, A. (2001) Lateral relationships in multicultural, multilingual databases in the spiritual and religious domains: The OM Information Service. In C. Bean and R. Green (Eds.), *Relationships in the Organization of Knowledge.* 185–198. Kluwer Academic Publishers.

Olson, D. (1994) *The World on Paper.* Cambridge University Press.

Roget, P. M. *Roget's International Thesaurus.* Many editions and publishers.

Chapter 6

A Weighted Referential Activity Dictionary

Wilma Bucci
Adelphi University
Derner Institute,
Garden City NY 11530
Email:bucci@panther.adelphi.edu

Bernard Maskit
Stony Brook University
Mathematics Department,
Stony Brook NY 11794-3651
Email:bernie@math.sunysb.edu

Abstract

The Weighted Referential Activity Dictionary (WRAD) is a dictionary (word list) containing 696 items, with weights ranging between -1 and +1, used for computer modeling of a psycholinguistic variable, Referential Activity (RA), in spoken and written language. The RA dimension concerns the degree to which language reflects connection to nonverbal experience, including imagery, and bodily and emotional experience, and evokes corresponding experience in the listener or reader. RA is primarily indicated by attributes of language style independent of content. High RA language is vivid and evocative; low RA language may be abstract, general, vague or diffuse. RA ratings have been widely used in psycholinguistic and clinical research. RA was initially measured using scales scored by judges; the CRA (Mergenthaler and Bucci, 1999), a binary dictionary, was the first computerized RA measure developed to model judges' RA ratings. The WRAD, a weighted dictionary, shows higher correlations with RA ratings in all text types tested. The development of the WRAD and its applications are made possible by the authors' Discourse Attributes Analysis Program (DAAP), which uses smooth local weighted averaging to capture the ebb and flow of RA and similar variables.

Keywords: referential activity, weighted dictionary, multiple code theory, narrative analysis, expression of affect, linguistic style.

1. Introduction

Computerized text analysis procedures have largely emphasized aspects of content rather than style. Our new procedure has several innovative features: it assesses a psychological variable, Referential Activity (RA), that is primarily indicated by attributes of linguistic style; both RA as scored by judges, and its computerized measure are independent of specific content. We use empirical, rather than conceptual, procedures for selecting and weighting items.

The RA dimension concerns the degree to which spoken or written language reflects connection to nonverbal experience, including imagery, and emotional and bodily experience, and evokes corresponding nonverbal experience in the listener or reader. High RA language is vivid and evocative; see, for example, the following passage:

> In the late summer of that year we lived in a house in a village that looked across the river and the plain to the mountains. In the bed of the river there were pebbles and boulders, dry and white in the sun, and the water was clear and swiftly moving and blue in the channels. Troops went by the house and down the road and the dust they raised powdered the leaves of the trees. The trunks of the trees too were dusty and the leaves fell early that year and we saw the troops marching along the road and the dust rising and leaves, stirred by the breeze, falling and the soldiers marching and afterward the road bare and white except for the leaves.

As illustrated in this opening paragraph from Hemingway's "Farewell to Arms", the effective verbal communication of nonverbal experience often takes place in narrative mode (Bucci, 1995, 1997).

Speech and written language have somewhat different characteristics, which are often not well understood. Here is an example of high RA speech from JSI, one of our data sets; these are described below.

> Other than my finger? Uh, I don't remember how old I was but my grandmother came to live with us. Her husband had died and we had been in a two bedroom apartment and moved to a three bedroom but my sister and I still had to share a room. Grandmother got her own room and just at the time she came to live with us, she started to develop arthritis in her hands. And there was a decanter and glasses set I was very fond of. The decanter was all trimmed in gold and it was a beautiful shape and the glasses were very delicate all trimmed in the same gold. And she picked it up one night. She was having an argument with my parents. She used to fight with my father. This was my mother's mother and between her being upset and the fight, and what they told me was it was her arthritis, but now I wonder if she threw it. She broke this set, and it had always been my favorite. If I were home sick, my mother would fill up the glasses and I would have my juice out of the glasses and on special occasions the decanter would be on the table and I was very angry at her that it was broken and they kept saying it was her arthritis, her hand had a spasm. And I wasn't allowed to be angry at her about this.

In the other direction, low RA language may be dominated by abstract ideas, as in the opening paragraph of Bertrand Russell's "A History of Western Civilization":

> The conceptions of life and the world which we call "philosophical" are a product of two factors: one, inherited religious and ethical conceptions; the other, the sort of investigation which may be called "scientific," using this word in its broadest sense. Individual philosophers have differed widely in regard to the proportions in which these two factors entered into their systems, but it is the presence of both, in some degree, that characterizes philosophy.

Low RA may also be expressed in spoken language that is vague and diffuse, as in this passage from an interview with a hospitalized depressed patient:

> I love people and I like to be with people. And right now I feel very bad because I can't be with them and do the things I would like to do. But I'm looking forward to a happier and healthier future and - I don't know what else to say. What else can I talk about? Well - I've had a very eventful life, I think. I've worked practically all my life and I love people.

Any type of content may be expressed in low or high RA ways; contrast the passage spoken by the psychiatric patient, which refers to emotion, with the manifestly neutral contents of the Hemingway passage, which is nevertheless far more evocative.

RA can be reliably scored by trained judges, using scales derived conceptually from the psychological features of the referential process as defined by Bucci (1997, 2002). The linguistic attributes that are associated with RA and that form the basis for the RA scales are Specificity (quantity of detail), Imagery (degree to which language evokes imagery), Clarity (organization and focus), and Concreteness (degree of reference to sensory and other bodily experience). These scales are described more fully in the RA scoring manual (Bucci et al. 1992). Measures of RA have been widely used in clinical and psycholinguistic research. The RA dimension has been shown to be operative in functions such as bodily and emotional self-regulation; interpersonal communication; and the capacity to synthesize cognitive, linguistic and emotional experience. Details concerning the applications of the RA measures and their reliability and validity can be found in Bucci (1997, 2002).

The development of a computerized RA measure has both practical and theoretical significance. On the applied level, while the scales are reliably and easily scored after brief training, computerized procedures are needed to permit assessment of RA in large sample and longitudinal studies, and to permit reliable micro-analytic tracking of fluctuation in RA within various forms of communicative discourse. From a theoretical, psycholinguistic perspective it is of considerable interest to distinguish the types of lexical items that figure in texts that are expressive and evocative, as opposed to texts that are vague, general or abstract.

The first method for computerized scoring of RA was the Computerized Referential Activity (CRA) measure of Mergenthaler and Bucci (1999). This is based on two dictionaries, comprising a total of 181 types. The CRA measure includes a set of items that are characteristic of high RA speech, the High CRA dictionary, and a set of items characteristic of low CRA speech, the Low CRA dictionary. (The definitions and selection procedures for "characteristic" vocabularies are not specifically described in that paper.)

CRA has generally been applied using one of two text analysis systems, the UNIX based TAS/C (Mergenthaler, 1985) and the Windows based CM (Mergenthaler 1998). Neither permits use of weighted dictionaries, and both track fluctuations using either arbitrary segmentation into units of fixed size, or labor intensive operator scored segmentation. A new Windows based computer methodology, the Discourse Attributes Analysis Program (DAAP), which automatically produces a continuous measure without use of segmentation into arbitrary units, has been developed (Maskit, Bucci and Roussos, in preparation). The DAAP produces a mathematically smooth local averaging that starts anew with each change of speaker, and was specifically designed to permit use of weighted as well as unweighted dictionaries. The availability of the DAAP system was a necessary condition for the application of our new Weighted Referential Activity Dictionary (WRAD) that was built to model the RA scores.

To the authors' knowledge, all dictionaries thus far produced for computerized text analysis are unweighted; that is, an item either is in the dictionary or it is not. Weighted rather than binary dictionaries are particularly important for assessment of stylistic variables, which tend to vary in degree, in contrast to content features, which can usually be defined as present or absent. We anticipate that weighted dictionaries for other psychological and linguistic variables that are more closely related to style than to content can also be produced using this technique. A preliminary version of an Italian WRAD was developed using these techniques, and is now available; a Spanish WRAD is currently being developed, using the same general techniques.

This brief presentation is concerned primarily with the method for producing a weighted dictionary that measures stylistic features of speech rather than content categories. A longer paper, including discussions of linguistic and psychological implications of the results presented here, as well as an explication of several other dictionaries and measures derived from these dictionaries, is in preparation (Bucci and Maskit, In preparation). Our procedure used a principle of modeling RA scale scores as rated by judges, similar to that introduced by Mergenthaler and Bucci (1999); but we used new techniques specifically designed to produce weighted dictionaries.

2. Methods

2.1 The Data Sets

We combined four distinct sets of spoken language texts for the initial construction of the WRAD. This Combined Data Set has a total of 763 texts, comprised of 5,542 lexical items and 130,138 tokens. The average length was 170 items per text, with a range from 19 to 950 items.

The first data set of the Combined Data Set, JSI, consists of 141 directed monologues, with a total of 2,609 items, and 32,316 tokens. For this data set, the speaker was asked to tell about an early memory, or a memory involving some particular emotion, such as shame or guilt. The data were collected over ten years ago, from 50 middle class women who were students at a graduate teachers training institution in an eastern U.S. city.

The second data set, JST, consists of 201 responses to Thematic Apperception Test (TAT) picture cards, with a total of 2,712 items and 46,711 tokens, from the same sample as in JSI.

The third data set, EKM, has 133 texts, with a total of 2,258 items and 22,053 tokens. This data set consists of segmented interviews, carried out over ten years ago with 41 working class men and women in a middle western U.S. city; only interviewee speech was used for this analysis.

The fourth data set, MSC, has 288 texts, with a total of 1,777 items and 29,058 tokens. This data set was derived from a set of psychoanalytic sessions, all with the same patient and analyst, that had been segmented into idea units, and then scored for RA. Sessions were collected more than twenty years ago, but were scored within the past several years.

The Combined Data Set consists of the four previously described data sets, JSI, JST, EKM and MSC.

The fifth data set, TSI, was used for the penultimate step in the construction of the WRAD. This data set consists of 64 texts, with a total of 16,301 tokens. The data set was derived from a set of directed monologues, including early memories, as in JSI, responses to TAT cards, as in JST, and undirected monologues, where the speaker was asked to speak on any topic for five minutes. This sample is less than five years old, and comes from a population of college students.

The sixth data set, MPJ, which was used only to test the final dictionary, and to compare it with CRA, consists of 72 responses, from 36 interviewees, to questions such as in JSI, asking for early memories and recent memories. The interviews were conducted in 2003 with a varied general population. These 72 responses were further divided by judges into 113 idea units, each of which was then scored for RA using the scales. There were a total of 14,495 tokens in this data set.

The basic information for the texts in these data sets is summarized in Table 1.

NAME	No. of Texts	No. of Types	No. of Tokens	Mean Text Length	Max. Text Length	Min. Text Length
JSI	141	2,609	32,316	229	950	62
JST	201	2,712	46,711	232	619	63
EKM	133	2,258	22,053	166	620	19
MSC	288	1,777	29,058	101	682	20
Combined	763	5,542	130,138	171	950	19
TS	64	1,582	16,301	254	1,138	43
MPJ	113	1,881	14,495	128	273	36

Table 1. Basic data set information.

2.2 RA Scoring

All the texts were scored for the four RA scales by at least two trained raters, who followed the RA scoring manual of Bucci et al. (1992), and who had achieved reliability of at least .80 measured as Cronbach's alpha, or .75 measured as the single measure intraclass correlation coefficient. Each rater scored each text on a scale of 0 to 10, on each of the four scales. The final RA score for each rater is the average of the four scales, and the final RA score used in our computations is the average of the RA scores of the raters. (The MPJ data set, however, which is used only for testing the final dictionary, has thus far been scored for RA by only one rater, who had achieved excellent reliability in previous work.)

Table 2 shows RA data for the sets of texts used in the construction and testing of the WRAD.

Data Set	RA Mean	RA Maximum	RA Minimum	Standard Dev.	RA/Text Length Correlation
JSI	5.62	10	1	2.217	0.397
JST	4.53	10	.25	2.109	0.298
EKM	4.32	8.75	.625	1.789	0.522
MSC	3.72	7	1.0625	1.167	0.212
Combined	4.39	10	.25	1.898	0.428
TS	4.09	8.25	1.25	1.698	0.329
MPJ	5.37	8.125	2	1.147	0.363

Table 2. RA scoring data.

2.3 Transcription Modifications

A set of text preparation transcription rules (Maskit et al., in preparation) has been developed for applications of dictionaries, such as WRAD, within the DAAP system. Special rules for WRAD and related dictionaries include disambiguations of some frequently used words with multiple meanings such as "like", "kind", "know" and "mean". Transcribers modify the data sets by introducing new lexical items with distinguishing suffixes. For example, the item **likeC** represents the word "like", when used as a comparative, as in, "This looks likeC a good paper."; **likeV** is the word "like", when used as a verb, as in, "I likeV to go to the movies", and the word **like** itself is reserved for the filler use of the word, as in "So then, like, we like went to the mall". Specific rules are provided for events and sounds other than words. Transcribers use the item "MM" to represent all meaningless, neutral sounds generally characterized as filled pauses, such as "hm", "mm", "um". Items such as "oh", or "ah", judged by the transcriber to have intended communicative meanings, are transcribed as separate items. In order to maintain consistency, specific rules are also provided for transcription of incomplete or unclear words, contractions and colloquial forms, punctuation and other linguistic and paralinguistic features. The transcriber also uses special markings to indicate each change of speaker.

2.4 The RA Divisions

RA scores are assigned by judges on a continuous scale from 0 to 10. The final averaged RA score for each text was rounded to the nearest $1/8^{th}$ (.125), yielding 81 score divisions, counting both 0 and 10. The total number of tokens in the Combined Data Set, in each of these 81 divisions, was counted, and the 81 scores were then divided to form six categories which were as close to equal as possible in number of tokens. Table 3 describes these six *range categories*.

RA Range Category	Range of RA scores	Number of Tokens
Very Low	0 - 2.75	22,804
Moderately Low	875 - 3.75	22,354
Mildly Low	3.875 - 4.75	22,242
Mildly High	4.875 - 5.75	21,236
Moderately High	5.875 - 7.125	20,218
Very High	7.25 - 10.00	21,284
Total	0 - 10.00	130,138

Table 3. The RA range categories.

2.5 The Main Matrix

Using the Combined Data Set, a first matrix with 5,542 rows and 8 columns was produced. In each row, the first column contains the item, and the next 6 columns contain the total number of tokens for that item in each RA range category. The main matrix (see Table 4) was then derived from the first matrix using the following procedures: First, any item for which the total number of tokens was less than 13 (approximately one in 10,000) was eliminated; this eliminated most specific content words and reduced the number of rows in the main matrix to 737. Second, since the total numbers of tokens in each RA range category were only approximately equal, the entries presented as numbers of tokens in the six range columns were changed to proportions, i.e., the number of tokens for a given item in each range category, divided by the total number of tokens in that range (given in the third column of Table 3.) The eighth column in the main matrix shows the number of tokens in the Combined Data Set for each item.

For illustrative purposes, the first twenty rows of the main matrix, arranged in order of frequency in the Combined Data Set, are shown in Table 4. The last column in Table 4 is the dictionary weight for these items in the WRAD; this will be explained below. We note that, of these twenty most frequent items in our sample of spoken language, eight are pronouns; three are prepositions; two are copulative verbs; two are conjunctions; two are articles; and there are the three special items "MM", "s" and "t". We also note that none of these are content words.

Item	Range 1 Very Low	Range 2 Mod. Low	Range 3 Mildly Low	Range 4 Mildly High	Range 5 Mod. High	Range 6 Very High	Num. Of Tokens	Dictionary Weight
			Proportion of total tokens in range					
I	0.0563	0.0569	0.0491	0.0512	0.0451	0.0468	6642	-.75
and	0.0327	0.0382	0.0384	0.0461	0.0494	0.0573	5652	1.0
the	0.0247	0.0307	0.0286	0.0323	0.0343	0.0408	4135	1.0
to	0.0293	0.0293	0.0290	0.0306	0.0256	0.0271	3713	.25
it	0.0247	0.0245	0.0229	0.0206	0.0216	0.0196	2912	-.875
s	0.0247	0.0217	0.0236	0.0202	0.0233	0.0178	2852	-1.0
she	0.0216	0.0168	0.0205	0.0198	0.0220	0.0248	2718	1.0
that	0.0230	0.0229	0.0208	0.0180	0.0170	0.0165	2574	-.875
a	0.0166	0.0146	0.0196	0.0205	0.0227	0.0198	2457	.625
was	0.0097	0.0130	0.0143	0.0182	0.0204	0.0230	2120	1.0
t	0.0185	0.0198	0.0167	0.0170	0.0129	0.0120	2115	-.625
of	0.0167	0.0167	0.0164	0.0153	0.0157	0.0144	2066	-.625
in	0.0102	0.0110	0.0131	0.0130	0.0141	0.0151	1654	1.0
MM	0.0144	0.0161	0.0143	0.0111	0.0101	0.0066	1587	-.625
he	0.0107	0.0098	0.0120	0.0122	0.0151	0.0115	1542	.625
you	0.0109	0.0142	0.0102	0.0095	0.0077	0.0070	1298	-.625
her	0.0096	0.0073	0.0084	0.0100	0.0076	0.0116	1180	1.0
my	0.0063	0.0051	0.0069	0.0087	0.0125	0.0120	1104	.625
but	0.0095	0.0095	0.0098	0.0085	0.0069	0.0063	1102	NA
is	0.0100	0.0079	0.0076	0.0073	0.0064	0.0063	991	-1.0

Table 4. The first twenty rows of the main matrix.

2.6 Constructing a Single Weighted Dictionary Depending on a Parameter

For each item in the main matrix, one of the six proportions is necessarily larger than the other five; we call the category with the largest proportion the dominant category. We introduce the *weight parameter* P, which provides a measure of *how much larger* this largest proportion is than the other five. The assignment of a weight to each lexical item depends on the level of P that is chosen as the criterion of dominance. The following procedures are used to determine this assignment. First, the range category with the maximum proportion is identified for each generalized type. Call this maximum proportion M, and the range category in which it occurs C. We then compute P*M using the selected value of the parameter P. If the entries in the other five columns are all less than P*M, then the item will be included in the dictionary with the weight assigned to that range category according to the scheme given in Table 5; the weights range in value from -1 to +1, representing the six range categories varying from Very Low to Very High.

C	Weight
1	-1.0
2	-.625
3	-.25
4	.25
5	.625
6	1.0

Table 5. First step in construction of weights.

If the first step fails for a given entry, that is, there are one or more of the five cells in this row other than C, where the value in that cell is greater than P*M, then we look at all such cells. If one of these cells (i.e., cells whose entry is greater than P*M) is **not** adjacent to C, then this item is viewed as having bimodal features and it is dropped from the dictionary. If there are two such cells, both adjacent to the cell containing M, one on either side, then this item is put in the dictionary, with the same weight as above. If there is only one such cell, and it is adjacent to the cell containing M, then this item is put in the dictionary, with weight as given in table 6.

Column where M occurs	Column of next highest value	Weight
1	2	-0.875
2	1	-0.750
2	3	-0.500
3	2	-0.375
3	4	-0.125
4	3	0.125
4	5	0.375
5	4	0.500
5	6	0.750
6	5	0.875

Table 6. Second step in construction of weights.

2.7 Selecting the Weighting Parameter

The fifth data set, TS, which was not used for the selection of the dictionary items, or for computing the weights assigned to them, was then used to find the best value of the weight parameter, P. We can construct a weighted dictionary, WRAD(P), for each parameter value P, using the above procedure. For each WRAD(P), we can obtain a WRAD(P) score for each text of any of our data sets, as the sum of the dictionary weights of each of the items in the text that match an item in the dictionary. To obtain this score, each item in the text is compared with the items in the dictionary; if the item matches an item in the dictionary, then the WRAD(P) score for the text is increased (decreased) by the positive (negative) weight assigned to that item; if the text item does not match an item in the dictionary, the score for the text is neither increased nor decreased. After all the words in the text have been compared, the total score for the text is the sum of these weights. As previously shown in Table 2, there is a fairly strong correlation between the RA scale scores and text length for some data sets; this problem may be handled in several different ways. The method selected here was to correct the WRAD(P) scores for text length; that is, we introduce the mean WRAD(P) score (MWRAD(P)); this is the WRAD(P) score divided by the number of words in the segment. We report both the WRAD(P) and MWRAD(P) scores here. There are several natural questions concerning the linguistic and psychogical differences between these two measures, one corrected for text length and the other left uncorrected, for this as well as for our other dictionaries. Investigations along these lines will be pursued in future work.

Using the procedure described above for computing the WRAD(P) and MWRAD(P) scores, we compared the relative validity of the WRAD(P) dictionaries for different values of P as follows. We computed, for each value of P, the (Pearson) correlation between the WRAD(P), or MWRAD(P), scores for the texts in a data set with the corresponding RA scale scores. We computed these correlations for the TS data set, which was not used to construct these dictionaries, using P values from P=.80 to P=.985, in steps of .005. We observed that the correlation increased from P=.80 to P=.975, and then decreased from P=.975 to P=.985; i.e., the maximum correlation with judges' scores occurred at P=.975. Our almost final dictionary was then WRAD(.975), which has 699 items.

2.8 Final Adjustments and Comparisons

The items in this almost final dictionary were reviewed, and the following anomalies were found and corrected. Proper names including names of days of the week were removed. (Interestingly, the days of the week occurred with widely different weights in the WRAD; such anomalies need to be further explored.) Several numbers between one and ten appeared in the dictionary with positive but somewhat different weights. Since the modal weight for these numbers was +1, all integers from one to ten were put in the dictionary with weight +1. After the above modifications were carried out, we obtained the final WRAD with 696 items.

The final step in the process was to test the WRAD on the new data set, MPJ; that is, we obtained WRAD scores, which are uncorrected for text length, and the MWRAD scores, which are corrected for text length, for each text, and then computed the correlations with the RA scale scores.

3. Results

3.1 Description of the WRAD

The final WRAD is a list of 696 item types, of which 674 are ordinary words. Of the other 22, 12 are beginnings of contractions, such as "couldn" or "didn"; 7 are ends of contractions, such as "s" or "t"; two are artificial words used for disambiguation, "knowD" and "likeV", as described above. One item is the neutral sound often written as "mm", "um" or "hm"; all of these are written, following our transcription rules, as "MM".

3.2 Correlations with Scale Scores

Table 7 shows the correlations of both the WRAD scores, and the mean WRAD scores, with the overall RA scores based on the scales as scored by judges, and the proportion of text covered by the dictionaries, for each of the seven data sets described above. These are compared to the corresponding correlations for the first generation Computerized RA dictionary, the CRA.

As the table indicates, with one exception (the mean WRAD score for EKM compared with the mean CRA score), the correlation of WRAD with the RA scales is higher than the RA-CRA correlation for both measures in every data set. This advantage holds for the three data sets (JSI, JST and EKM) that were also used to produce the CRA dictionary, as well as for the new data sets. The TSI data were not used to generate the word list, but only to find the best value of the parameter P, and the MPJ is a new data set used for test purposes only. The data indicate that the WRAD is robust across demographic groups and across a time span of several decades, and is generally robust across text type, with the exception of the WRAD/RA correlation for the MSC data set, the psychoanalytic sessions. We believe this data set was affected by being restricted to one patient-analyst dyad; the assessment of correlations for therapy text material will be expanded substantially in subsequent work.

As table 7 also shows, the coverage of the WRAD list is very high; the 696 types account for a total of between .83 and .87 of all tokens in the 6 data sets. This contrasts with coverage ranging from .50 to .56 for CRA. The greater coverage is made possible primarily by the weighting procedure; without weighting, as in the construction of CRA, only items associated with RA extremes could be included; the weighting procedures permit inclusion of mid-range items with appropriate weights.

Data Set	WRAD/RA Correlation	MeanWRAD/RA Correlation	WRAD Cover	CRA/RA Corr.	MeanCRA/RA Correlation	CRA Cover
JSI	0.61	0.60	0.85	0.47	.50	0.53
JST	0.58	0.54	0.87	0.37	0.33	0.52
EKM	0.62	0.51	0.83	0.55	0.53	0.51
MSC	0.23	0.49	0.87	0.11	0.39	0.56
Combined	0.60	0.54	0.86	0.40	0.44	0.53
TSI	0.57	0.57	0.86	0.30	0.39	0.51
MPJ	0.47	0.38	0.83	0.31	0.33	0.50

Table 7. Correlation of RA scale scores with computerized procedures.

3.3 Summary Data for WRAD

The mean of the mean WRAD (MWRAD) scores for the Combined Data Set, which was used to build the WRAD, with a total of 763 texts, is -0.03, where the MWRAD scores of course lie between -1 and +1. This would be equivalent to a RA scale score of 5, the mid-point of the RA range. The maximum MWRAD score for the combined data set was .37; and the minimum was -.61; this minimum can be found in the therapy material. We can now place our excerpts in the context of these summary data. As shown in Table 8, the Hemingway excerpt gets an MWRAD score of 0.41, higher than the maximum of our Combined Data Set; the segment about the decanter has an MWRAD score of 0.374, which is the maximum of the MWRAD in the Combined Data Set; the Russell excerpt a score of .15; and the psychiatric material a score of -.24.

3.4 Linguistic Implications

The nature of the WRAD list is suggested by the items previously shown in the illustrative matrix in Table 4. Of the twenty most frequent items in our sample data set of spoken language, only one, "but" is bimodal, and not in the dictionary, and only one, the item "to", has relatively low weight. The remaining 18 items account for approximately 35% of all items in our data set. In order to show the importance of these words, we formed a new small dictionary, the 18WRAD, consisting of just these 18 items. The results of using both the full WRAD, and this 18WRAD on the four vastly different samples of language we used in our introduction appear in Table 8. The first column identifies the sample; the second column is the mean WRAD score for this segment; the third column is the mean 18WRAD score for this segment; the fourth column is coverage of the WRAD, and the fifth column is the coverage of the 18WRAD. We note that the 18WRAD shows the same relationship among the sample segments as the WRAD, but also shows lower variability as well as lower coverage. While we do not expect this small dictionary to be useful for making fine distinctions, it can be used for widely varying texts. We also note the difference in coverage between spoken and written language, and expect to explore this further.

Text	Mean WRAD	Mean 18WRAD	WRAD Cover	18WRAD Cover
Hemingway	0.4097	0.355	0.675	0.413
Decanter	0.374	0.208	0.842	0.389
Russell	0.154	0.113	0.575	0.26
Depressed	-0.281	-0.017	0.888	0.3

Table 8. The value of small words.

3.5 Other Languages

The RA scoring manual (Bucci et al. 1992) has been translated into Italian and Spanish, and substantial corpora of texts have been scored for RA in these languages. There are currently two projects underway, one in each language, involving teams of researchers, including native language speakers, in a project to construct a weighted referential activity dictionary in each of these languages. Preliminary indications suggest that, while spoken Italian and Spanish are linguistically similar, there are strong differences between these languages as spoken, and spoken (American) English. We will report on these similarities and differences in a future publication.

3.6 The Mystery of Simple Words

In discussing the Hemingway paragraph quoted above, Joan Didion (1998) notes that it contains 126 words, of which 24 are "the" and 15 are "and"; and says that the arrangement of these simple words "remains as mysterious and thrilling to me now as it did when I first read them, at twelve or thirteen". We hope that our RA and WRAD studies will help to unravel at least some of these linguistic and psychological mysteries. The differential linguistic role of particular lexical items in producing vivid and evocative vs. abstract and general texts, and the psychological significance of these differences, merit further study.

4. Bibliography

Bucci, W. (1995) The power of the narrative; A multiple code account. In Pennebaker, J. (Ed.) *Emotion, Disclosure and Health*. 93-122. American Psychological Association Books, Washington, D.C.

Bucci, W. (1997) *Psychoanalysis and Cognitive Science: A multiple code theory*. Guilford Press, New York.

Bucci, W. (2002) Referential Activity (RA): Scales and computer procedures. In Fonagy et al. (Eds.) *An Open Door Review of Outcome Studies in Psychoanalysis; Second Edition*. 192-195. International Psychoanalytical Association, London.

Bucci, W., Kabasakalian, R., and the Referential Activity Research Group. (1992) *Instructions for scoring Referential Activity (RA) in transcripts of spoken narrative texts*. Ulmer Textbank, Ulm, Germany.

Bucci, W. and Maskit, B. (In preparation) Linking words and things: Measurement and linguistic features of Referential Activity.

Didion, J. (1998) Last Words. *The New Yorker*, November 9. 74-80.

Maskit, B., Bucci, W. and Roussos, A.J. (In preparation) Capturing the flow of verbal interaction – the Discourse Attributes Analysis Program.

Mergenthaler, E. (1985) *Textbank Systems: Computer science applied in the field of psychoanalysis*. Springer, Heidelberg & New York.

Mergenthaler, E. (1998) CM – the Cycles Model software. (Version 1.0) Universität Ulm, Germany.

Mergenthaler, E. and Bucci, W. (1999) Linking verbal and nonverbal representations: Computer analysis of Referential Activity. *British Journal of Medical Psychology, 72*, 339-354.

Chapter 7

Certainty Identification in Texts: Categorization Model and Manual Tagging Results

Victoria L. Rubin and Elizabeth D. Liddy
Syracuse University
School of Information Studies
Center for Natural Language Processing
Syracuse University
Syracuse, NY 13244-1190, U.S.A
Email: {vlrubin, liddy}@syr.edu

Noriko Kando
National Institute of Informatics
2-1-2 Hitotsubashi, Chiyoda-ku
Tokyo 101-8430, Japan
Email: kando@nii.ac.jp

Abstract

This chapter presents a theoretical framework and preliminary results for manual categorization of explicit certainty information in 32 English newspaper articles. Our contribution is in a proposed categorization model and analytical framework for certainty identification. Certainty is presented as a type of subjective information available in texts. Statements with explicit certainty markers were identified and categorized according to four hypothesized dimensions – level, perspective, focus, and time of certainty. The preliminary results reveal an overall promising picture of the presence of certainty information in texts, and establish its susceptibility to manual identification within the proposed four-dimensional certainty categorization analytical framework. Our findings are that the editorial sample group had a significantly higher frequency of markers per sentence than did the sample group of the news stories. For editorials, high level of certainty, writer's point of view, and future and present time were the most populated categories. For news stories, the most common categories were high and moderate levels, directly involved third party's point of view, and past time. These patterns have positive practical implications for automation.

Keywords: Subjectivity, manual tagging, natural language processing, uncertainty, epistemic comments, evidentials, hedges, certainty expressions; point of view, annotating opinions.

1. Analytical Framework

1.1 Introduction: What is Certainty Identification and Why is it Important?

The fields of Information Extraction (IE) and Natural Language Processing (NLP) have not yet addressed the task of certainty identification. It presents an ongoing theoretical and implementation challenge. Even though the linguistics literature has abundant intellectual investigations of closely related concepts, it has not yet provided NLP with a holistic certainty identification approach that would include clear definitions, theoretical underpinnings, validated analysis results, and a vision for practical applications. Unravelling the potential and demonstrating the usefulness of certainty analysis in an information-seeking situation is the driving force behind this preliminary research effort.

Certainty identification is defined here as an automated process of extracting information from certainty-qualified texts or individual statements along four hypothesized dimensions of certainty, namely:
- what degree of certainty is indicated (LEVEL),
- whose certainty is involved (PERSPECTIVE),
- what the object of certainty is (FOCUS), and
- what time the certainty is expressed (TIME).

Some writers consciously strive to produce a particular effect of certainty due to training or overt instructions. Others may do it inadvertently. A writer's certainty level may remain constant in a text and be unnoticed by the reader, or it may fluctuate from statement to statement and blatantly attract readers' attention. There may be evident traces of such writers' behavior that may become apparent upon a closer examination with a systematic theoretical framework. The difficulty is to discern such traces at the discourse, syntactic, semantic, and lexical levels, wherever such explicit information is available and to be able to recognize these explicit markers with a series of NLP algorithms.

The importance of assessing how certain writers are about their statements is evident, especially in the stream of constantly updated news reports. Readers want to know, for instance, how sure writers or experts might be about public policy changes, about a possibility of a political or a financial turmoil, about what the government's intentions are regarding interest rates or about chances of coup d'etats versus peaceful transfers of power.

Recognizing such certainty assessments would traditionally be considered a task for humans. While humans may rely to some extent on the big picture as obtained from world knowledge and prior experience, much certainty information comes from linguistic coding in texts and may be accessible to a systematic analysis with the help of NLP algorithms. Combined with the capabilities of an IE system, the task of linguistic de-coding of certainty information could then be handled successfully automatically, and the results could be presented to users for confirmation and possible modifications.

1.2 Certainty, Explicit Certainty Markers, and Closely Related Concepts

A typical dictionary definition of certainty is "the quality or state of mind of being free from doubt, especially on the basis of evidence" (Merriam-Webster 2004). The notion of certainty in the context of this chapter incorporates a full spectrum of certainty states ranging from doubt to complete conviction in the truth of a statement. There are several related concepts that have been previously addressed in NLP and linguistics literature: subjectivity, modality, evidentiality, and hedging. This section reports on how these closely related linguistic concepts are interpreted to define certainty, and concludes with a list of terms that are considered to be explicit certainty markers.

1.2.1 Subjectivity

This study departs from the notion of subjectivity. Uncertainty, or certainty in terms of this chapter, is the speculative type of subjectivity (Wiebe 2000) that is analogous to the other types of subjectivity for which manual and automated tagging has proven to be a feasible NLP task (Wiebe et al. 2001). Subjectivity has been defined in NLP as "aspects of language used to express opinions and evaluations" (Wiebe 1994, 2000, Wiebe et al. 2001). Cognitive Grammar describes subjectivity as "a part of the conceptual structure of information that lies behind linguistic 'packaging'" (Mushin 2001).

Subjectivity tagging is considered particularly relevant for the news report genre (Wiebe et al. 2001). When developing news report schemata components for an automated text structurer, Liddy et al. (1993) noted that subjectivity, or objectivity, as an attribute in texts, deserved special attention. They observed that binary distinctions of statements (e.g., "+ subjective" or "-subjective") may not be sufficient to adequately represent micro-level similarities and distinctions in texts. In addition, discourse components may have multiple dimensions embedded in each of the concept labels (Liddy et al. 1995). This study further explores identifiable dimensions of certainty in written news reports and editorials.

1.2.2 Epistemic Comments and Modality

Certainty can also be seen as a variety of epistemic modality expressed through epistemic comments. One type of epistemic comment is certainty expressions (e.g., *probably, perhaps, undoubtedly*) that provide clues to the writer's certainty or assessment of the truth of a statement and qualify a writer's attitude towards expressed knowledge. Epistemic comments reflect epistemic modality, which is described in Functional Linguistics as a writer's assumptions or assessments of possibilities expressed in statements, specifically regarding confidence in the truth of the expressed propositions (Coates 1983). Writer's confidence in the truth is synonymous with certainty. In other words, certainty is a writer's assessment of the truth of the statement.

1.2.3 Evidentials and other Reportive Means

Certainty, in particular in languages other than English, can be expressed by means of evidentials that reveal a degree of reliability of expressed information. English resorts to other reportive means, such as attributive adverbials (e.g., *supposedly, allegedly*) and reporting verbs (e.g., *claim, suggest*).

Evidentials were originally narrowly described as "suffixes expressing subjective relations... those expressing subjective knowledge" (Mushin 2001) and later understood as a semantic category that specifies the type of the reported information source. Based on her comparison of Macedonian, Japanese and English corpora, Mushin (2001) concluded that English lacks clear grammatical markers of evidentiality, and that most types of English discourse are "faceless" in the sense of lacking epistemic evaluation in a grammatical inventory of reportive suffixes or other purely grammatical manifestations. However, she comes to a promising conclusion that English compensates for such lack of reportive means by other identifiable means by which speakers express, for instance, that the story they are telling was the product of someone else's telling. In particular, she notes that English does have a rich inventory of adverbials of "propositional attitude" (Mushin 2001).

The choice of reporting verbs depends on how strongly the writer wants to be aligned with the reported source (Hyland 1998). Bergler et al. (2004) also hypothesize that the description of the source and the choice of the attributive or reporting verbs can, in fact, express the writer's level of confidence in the attributed material. Such verbs can be used "both, to bolster a claim made in the text already, or to distance the author from the attributed material, implicitly lowering its credibility" (Anick and Bergler, 1992, cited in Bergler et al., 2004).

In the same line of Evidential Semantics research, Chafe (1986) suggested a model that addresses reliability of knowledge expressed through evidentials. Knowledge was broadly defined as "the basic information whose status is qualified in one way or another by markers of evidentiality," where the notion of evidentiality extends beyond evidence and can be as inclusive as any "attitude toward knowledge" (Chafe 1986). In other words, he suggests different statuses that reveal the reliability of the expressed information: "People are aware, though not necessarily consciously aware, that some things they know are *surer bets for being true than others,* that not all knowledge is equally reliable." This is what is called "certainty" in this chapter. Chafe continues: "Thus, one way in which knowledge may be qualified is with an expression indicating the speaker's assessment of its *degree of reliability,* the likelihood of its being a fact." Chafe's degrees of reliability can be expressed in English through propositional attitude adverbials (in Mushin's terms), which are the same as epistemic comments (in Coates' terms), or explicit certainty markers in this chapter's terms.

1.2.4 Hedges and Other Terminology for Explicit Certainty Markers

The term traditionally associated with linguistic uncertainty, especially in scientific writing, is hedging. Hedging was introduced by Lackoff (1972) and has generally been defined as "words whose job is to make things more or less fuzzy." In Hyland (1998), hedging refers to "any linguistic means used to indicate either a) a lack of commitment to the truth value of an accompanying proposition, or b) a desire not to express that commitment categorically." In research articles, hedges are "a crucial means of presenting new claims for ratification and are among the primary features which shape the research article as the principle vehicle for new knowledge" (Hyland 1998).

Hyland (1998) identifies several categories of how hedges can be expressed in everyday speech and scientific writing. The following surface lexical markers are used to attenuate strength of utterance: epistemic adjectives, epistemic adverbs, lexical verbs, auxiliary verbs, prosody, tag questions, and verbal fillers. Syntactic markers include *if*-clauses of condition and concessions, contrastive markers (e.g., *nevertheless*), and passivization (e.g., *it can be questioned*). Several other devices are classified as hedges particular to scientific writing only: hedging quantities for purposeful imprecision, admitting to lack of knowledge, citing a source, and referring to limitations (of the model, experimental conditions, or methods) (Hyland 1998).

Thus, hedging is a device that indicates a lack of commitment to the statement, reveals scepticism, expresses caution, or displays an open mind about a proposition. In this study hedges classify statements into low or moderate levels of certainty. Several other linguistic means of a writer's assessment of knowledge such as shields, approximators (Lackoff 1972), understatements, and tentatives; as well as intensifiers (Cappon 2000), emphatics (Holmes 1990), boosters and assertives (Searle 1979) are considered to be explicit certainty markers of varying certainty levels.

In summary, certainty is viewed as a type of subjective information available in texts and a form of epistemic modality expressed through explicitly-coded linguistic means. Such devices as subjectivity expressions, epistemic comments, evidentials, reporting verbs, attitudinal adverbials, hedges, shields, approximators, understatements, tentatives, intensifiers, emphatics, boosters, and assertives, often overlap in their definitions, classifications, and lexical representations in English. In essence, they perform the same role for the purpose of this study. They explicitly signal the presence of certainty information that covers a full continuum of a writer's confidence, ranging from uncertain possibility and withholding full commitment to statements to a confident necessity, reassurance, and emphasizing of the full commitment to statements. For the purpose of this study, these devices are all called explicit certainty markers.

In the remainder of the paper, we develop a certainty categorization model, report on preliminary results, and conclude with outlined challenges and applications.

2. Proposed Certainty Categorization Model

Expressing some degree of certainty in language is inevitable, just as one is bound to have a spatial angle of vision. By analogy with subjectivity, certainty is generally understood to be a pragmatic position rather than a grammatical feature. Banfield (1982) observed that subjectivity, a closely related concept, is a spatial notion by nature, and in language, it is taken to be located in a speaker. While it is questionable whether truly objective statements may exist, it seems even less likely that a statement may exist without a degree of certainty in the presented information. Each statement should potentially reveal a particular pragmatic position, or a level of certainty, but not all of them are explicitly marked. The commonly used declarative mood of stating facts and opinions may have an implied certainty level without any explicit indication that would be considered identifiable for Information Extraction purposes. Statements with implicit certainty levels are not discussed under the current categorization model, they are grouped into a separate pool of no identifiable explicit certainty information.

The proposed certainty categorization model distinguishes 4 dimensions for explicitly identifiable certainty. The certainty level is the first and most important dimension. The other three are perspective, focus, and time (Figure 1). Each dimension is subdivided into several categories creating 72 possible dimension-category combinations (4 levels by 3 perspectives by 2 foci by 3 times).

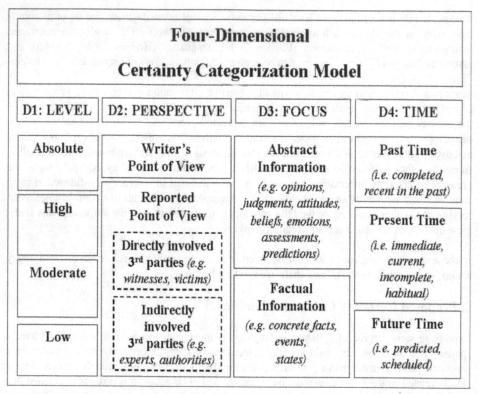

Figure 1. Four-Dimensional Certainty Categorization Model with the Four Hypothesized Dimensions (across) and Their Categories (down).

2.1 First Dimension: Certainty Level

The concept of certainty seems to fall inherently into levels. We suggest the division of the certainty level dimension into four categories - absolute, high, moderate, and low. The excerpts below exemplify a decreasing degree of certainty from absolute certainty in the first example to low certainty in the last one. The explicit certainty markers are highlighted in bold.

*(1) An enduring lesson of the Reagan years, **of course**, is that **it really does take smoke and mirrors to** produce tax cuts, spending initiatives and a balanced budget at the same time. (ID=e3.28)*

*(2) ... but **clearly** an opportunity is at hand for the rest of the world to pressure both sides to devise a lasting peace based on democratic values and respect for human rights. (ID=e22.6)*

*(3) That fear **now seems** exaggerated, but it was not entirely fanciful. (ID=e4.8)*

*(4) So far the presidential candidates are more interested in talking about what a surplus **might buy** than in the painful choices that lie ahead. (ID=e3.7)*

Having an explicit certainty marker that places a statement into one of the levels of certainty is what distinguishes a certainty-qualified statement from a non-marked one. Each certainty-qualified statement is further hypothesized to contain some information regarding a perspective, a focus, and a time of certainty.

2.2 Second Dimension: Perspective

The second dimension in Figure 1, the certainty perspective, separates the certainty point of view into the writer's and the reported points of view. The writer's certainty refers to the experiencer of certainty at the time of writing a statement as exemplified below.

> *(5) More evenhanded coverage of the presidential race would help enhance the legitimacy of the eventual winner, which **now appears likely to be** Putin. (ID=e8.14)*

The certainty is clearly attributed to the writer in the example above. A practical question is whether third party voices can be isolated from the author's since they are presented through the author's prism.

Reported point of view can refer to either individuals or organizations. It is divided into two sub-categories. First, those of directly involved third parties, such as victims, witnesses, and survivors, are direct event participants, who are either present at the described event or whose life is directly affected by the events. Second, those of indirectly involved third parties, such as experts, authorities, and analysts, are tangentially related to the event in professional or other capacities.

> *(6) The Dutch recruited settlers with an advertisement that **promised** to provide them with slaves who "**would accomplish** more work for their masters, ..." (ID=e27.13)*

> *(7) The historian Ira Berlin, author of "Many Thousands Gone," **estimates** that one slave perished for every one who survived capture in the African interior... (ID=e27.8)*

In the first example the writer reports on the certainty of the group of direct participants, the Dutch; and in the second example, the writer refers to the expert historian's opinion.

The writer's certainty as expressed in text should not be confused with the reader's certainty that the text is believable. The writer's certainty about his or her own and others' assertions is captured in texts. The reader's certainty is related to numerous factors that inform his or her own subjectivity, or point of view. The former is accessible for analysis since it has a written record, but the latter is less tangible and may reflect high inter-personal variability. Thus, the reader's certainty is out of scope for this study, as this inquiry focuses on the writer's certainty model and its multi-dimensional complexity in the newspaper context.

2.3 Third Dimension: Certainty Focus

The third dimension, the certainty focus, is divided into abstract and factual information in the narrative. The term focus is used in van Dijk's (1981) localized selection sense as the referent, or the object, subject, or topic of conversation that is being talked about, or predicated upon, in a particular localized syntactic unit, such as a sentence or a clause.

Abstract information may include judgments, opinions, attitudes, beliefs, moral principles, and emotions. Usually such statements, as in the example below, reflect an idea that does not represent an external reality, but rather a hypothesized world, existing only in someone's mind, and separated from embodiment or object of nature.

>*(8) In Iraq, the first steps **must be taken** to put a hard-won new security council resolution on arms inspections into effect. (ID=e8.12)*

Factual information contains reports of states or events, evidence, and known facts. It is usually based on facts that have an actual existence in the world of events.

>*(9) The settlement **may not fully compensate** survivors for the delay in justice, ... (ID=e14.19)*

2.4 Fourth Dimension: Time

The fourth dimension accounts for the relevance of time (past, present and future) to the moment when the statement was written. The past naturally includes completed or recent states or events; the present consists of current, immediate, and incomplete states of affairs; and the future contains predictions, plans, warnings, and suggested actions. The time dimension is relevant since certainty of predictions into the future, for instance, may alter an action plan for someone who is reviewing certainty analysis information in a systematic way, as business or intelligence analysts may do.

3. Empirical Study

In order to obtain a preliminary sense of the nature and frequency of certainty markers in text, we conducted a pilot study.

3.1 Research Questions

The goals of the study were to empirically determine:

1.   if the sample data support the hypothesized four dimensional categorization model,
2.   if so, which categories are most and least frequent for a sample of English news articles,
3.   if the data do not support the model, how the categorization might be enhanced,
4.   whether there are differences in certainty distributions between editorials and news stories, overall and per hypothesized category,
5.   how many perceived categories of certainty can be distinguished within each dimension.

3.2 Data

We manually analyzed 32 articles published in *The New York Times* during the first week of January 2000 (from the AQUAINT Corpus of English Texts). This constitutes a total of 685 sentences, excluding headlines. The topics of the sample articles varied – the editorials included discussions of political leaders, presidential and state government campaigns, the economic and financial situations in US, Croatia, and Angola, recent historical discoveries, pharmaceutical consumer alerts, and the role of the Internet and computers in everyday lives. The news included reports on the misnumbering of *The New York Times* issues, on the controversy around the millennium and Y2K bug, and on women's basketball.

3.3 Analysis Methods

The data were analyzed manually at the sentence-level by one coder, the first author. If a sentence contained explicit certainty information markers, it was decomposed along each certainty dimension by answering questions such as "What is the certainty level?" and "Whose perspective is being presented?" The number of occurrences of markers per article were totalled and adjusted for article sentence length, resulting in one frequency score per article. The length of explicit certainty markers was not pre-determined.

First, we were interested in an overall frequency of occurrence of explicit certainty markers across all of the data. Second, we identified whether the two sample groups, editorials and news stories, had significantly different means. Third, we looked at the overall distribution of frequency scores (in markers per sentence) per category within each dimension. For instance, were there more occurrences of high or low levels of certainty on average? Fourth, for the editorial sample, we identified the least and most frequent combinations out of 72 possible dimension-category combinations. And last, we assessed whether the data easily fell into the hypothesized categories.

3.4 Results and Discussion

3.4.1 Certainty Markers Frequency Distributions in Two Sample Groups

In the total set of 32 articles (685 sentences), an average of 0.53 explicit certainty markers per sentence were identified. Identified certainty markers included but were not limited to *it was not even clear that, remains to be seen, don't believe they will, not necessarily, we thought, estimated, seems exaggerated, would probably have to, is expected to,* and *will almost certainly have to.*

The sample group of 28 editorials (564 sentences) contained more explicit certainty markers per sentence (M=0.6, SD=0.26) than the sample group of 4 news stories (121 sentences; M=0.46, SD=0.04 markers per sentence). This difference was statistically significant, $p = 0.0056$, two-tailed heteroscedastic t-test.

Within three dimensions, level, perspective, and time, average frequencies of occurrence of explicit certainty markers per sentence differed from category to category, as well as between sample groups.

3.4.2 Certainty Frequency Distributions in the Level Dimension

Table 1 shows that, of all possible level categories, the high certainty level contained most markers per sentence (0.33). Here is an example sentence from an editorial that falls into the category of high certainty:

> (10) The crowd cheering the opening of the Erie Canal in 1824 **knew** that the city **would forever be** transformed, Wallace notes. (ID=e28.19, certainty level = high)

In an automated implementation, the Information Extraction frame would receive a value of "high" in the certainty level slot, as shown above. The explicit certainty markers are in bold as in the rest of the data samples throughout the chapter.

	Editorials Sample Group		News Stories Sample Group	
LEVEL	Mean, markers per sentence	St. dev., markers per sentence	Mean, markers per sentence	St. dev., markers per sentence
Absolute	0.07	0.09	0.03	0.05
High	**0.33**	0.17	**0.19**	0.09
Moderate	0.17	0.14	**0.20**	0.15
Low	0.04	0.06	0.04	0.05

Table 1. Distribution of Markers Per Sentence in the Four Level Categories.

In news stories, both high and moderate levels of certainty were the two most prominent levels (approximately 0.2 markers per sentence). An example of the moderate level of certainty follows:

> *(11) But as midnight closed in, the streets teemed with people and **there seemed to be** little left of the anxiety over terrorist attacks that prompted the mayor of Seattle last week to cancel a major outdoor celebration around the city's famed Space Needle. (ID=n3.9, certainty level = moderate)*

3.4.3 Certainty Frequency Distributions in the Perspective Dimension

Table 2 demonstrates that in editorials certainty from the writers' points of view is expressed more commonly (0.43 mean markers per sentence) than certainty of third parties (0.13 and 0.04), as is expected.

	Editorials Sample Group		News Stories Sample Group	
PERSPECTIVE	Mean, markers per sentence	St. dev., markers per sentence	Mean, markers per sentence	St. dev., markers per sentence
Writer's	**0.43**	0.23	0.16	0.10
3rd directly involved party's	0.13	0.13	**0.24**	0.11
3rd indirectly Involved party's	0.04	0.06	0.05	0.06

Table 2. Distribution of Markers Per Sentence in the Three Perspective Categories.

Consider that even though this example sentence talks about a third party, the expressed certainty actually belongs to the writer:

> *(12) He also **ought to** urge France and Russia to persuade Saddam Hussein to accept the resolution. (ID=e8.14, perspective = writer's point of view)*

We also observed that in news stories attention shifts to the certainty of the directly involved third parties (0.24) such as presidential candidates, political leaders, a Cuban orphan and his family, and just a person waiting for a flight at the airport whose direct words are cited below:

> *(13) "I think it will probably be OK..." (ID=n4.23, perspective = directly involved third party's point of view)*

The indirectly involved third parties are rather rare and usually occur in the form of experts' opinions, sometimes cited as well. For instance, the economists' points of view rendered below reflect their certainty, and the writer may or may not be sure about that statement:

> *(14) **Most** economists **believe** Alan Greenspan is more responsible for the economy's spectacular performance than Congress, Presidents Bush and Clinton or any other*

identifiable factor. (ID=e9.1, perspective = indirectly involved third party's point of view)

The difficulty for automation will likely be in correctly interpreting the writer's intended use of the experts' opinions. Sometimes the reference to the source is vague but it is quite clear that the expressed certainty is the writer's:

(15) *Although* **some research suggests** *that* **some** *supplements* **can** *produce positive health effects, there have also been cases where people have been made ill by supplements, or their conditions have become worse... (ID=e28.3,* perspective = writer's point of view)

3.4.4 Certainty Frequency Distributions in the Focus and Time Dimensions

Table 3 demonstrates that abstract and factual foci of certainty were approximately evenly distributed in editorials (0.33 and 0.27) and in news stories (0.23), even though the editorial sample group had a larger deviation from the mean compared to the news stories.

FOCUS	Editorials Sample Group		News Stories Sample Group	
	Mean, markers per sentence	St. dev., markers per sentence	Mean, markers per sentence	St. dev., markers per sentence
Abstract	0.33	0.20	0.23	0.05
Factual	0.27	0.19	0.23	0.09

Table 3. Distribution of Markers Per Sentence in the Two Focus Categories.

As for the time dimension, it is not surprising that certainty analysis captures the news stories' tendency to report events in the past (0.20, as opposed to 0.11 and 0.14, as seen in Table 4).

TIME	Editorials Sample Group		News Stories Sample Group	
	Mean, markers per sentence	St. dev., markers per sentence	Mean, markers per sentence	St. dev., markers per sentence
Past	0.14	0.12	**0.20**	0.11
Present	**0.24**	0.18	0.11	0.05
Future	**0.22**	0.16	0.14	0.09

Table 4. Distribution of Markers Per Sentence in the Three Time Categories.

The editorials' tendency to state opinions about current and predicted events also becomes apparent. An example from a news story about millennium flight cancellations refers to a piece of factual information with certainty expressed by the experts in the past:

(16) *The failure lasted only about 30 minutes and had no operational effect, the FAA said, adding that* **it was not even clear that** *the problem was caused by the date change.* (ID=n4.19, time = past)

An example from editorials demonstrates an abstract writer's assessment in the present:

(17) **Whatever happens next,** *these candidates have shown that one-on-one debates* **really can** *give voters a choice on issues and on leadership temperament as well.* (ID=e16.18, time = present)

Also, many editorials had a closing statement in the last paragraph that contained some certainty markers that either urged action or expressed an overall opinion statement in the form of a prediction, such as shown below:

(18) *There will be problems along the way, but the Internet* **will likely** *change the way America does business far beyond the habits of holiday shoppers. (ID=e2.22,* time = future)

On the whole, the presence of data in each category suggests that the categorization model is viable when applied manually. Now a gold standard and a codebook of rules can be created for an inter-coder agreement study and further automation of the process. High frequency of explicit certainty markers in some categories emphasizes where linguistic analysis should be concentrated to cover the majority of certainty expression cases.

3.4.5 Certainty Marker Occurrences in Dimension-Category Combinations

Table 5 shows the distribution of occurrences of explicit certainty markers in dimension-category combinations for editorials, the larger of the two sample groups. The table is to be read by cross-referencing the two dimensions in columns (focus and level) with the two dimensions in rows (perspective and time). For instance, the absolute level of a writer's certainty about abstract information in the past only happened once, while in the present it occurred 18 times. The table forms 72 possible combinations (4 levels by 3 perspectives by 2 foci by 3 times), plus an additional group ('None') that recorded the occurrence of statements containing no explicit certainty information (289 sentences). In total, there were 624 occurrences of certainty-qualified sentences and non-qualified sentences, while the editorial sample group contained 564 sentences. This means that 335 certainty markers were assigned to 275 sentences. The difference of 60 occurrences is explained by a special treatment of complex sentences. The unit of analysis was generally a sentence; but complex sentences were split into two or more simple sentences, if each simple sentence expressed a different idea qualified by a distinct certainty marker.

FOCUS		Abstract Information				Factual Information				
		LEVEL								
PERSPECTIVE	**TIME**	Abs.	High	Mod.	Low	Abs.	High	Mod.	Low	
										Total
Writer's	Past	1	8	10	1		12	11		43
	Present	18	**29**	16	8		13	10	1	95
	Future	13	**25**	12	2	2	**27**	12	3	96
3rd Indirectly Involved Arty	Past		8	4		1	11	2		26
	Present	2	3	2		1	7	5	1	21
	Future	1	8	1		1	11	2	2	26
3rd Directly Involved Party	Past		3	1	2		4			10
	Present	2	4				4	2	1	13
	Future						5			5
NONE										289
Total		35	86	50	13	5	94	44	8	624

Table 5. Certainty Markers Count of Occurrences in the Editorials Sample Group.

Of the 72 possible combinations, 15 combinations were rather typical in editorials. Three had an unusually high representation in editorials. These combinations are writer's high level of certainty about abstract information in the present or future, such as predictions and current assessments, which had 29 and 25 occurrences respectively. There were also 27 occurrences of a writer's future high level certainty factual predictions, stating with high certainty what will happen in the future. Twelve combinations accounted for the majority of occurrences (between 10 and 18).

Additionally, 35 combinations were found to be rare in editorials, with ≤ 8 occurrences in our data; for instance, the low level of a writer's certainty about present or future factual information had 1 and 3 occurrences respectively. The remaining 22 combinations did not have any representation in our data. For instance, directly involved third parties' low level of certainty about abstract information in either past, present or future were never found.

The observed distribution is consistent with the goal of editorials to state opinions, inevitably with different levels of certainty. It directs us to the combinations that cover the majority of explicit certainty markers and provide guidance in automating the categorization.

3.4.6 Challenges

One criterion for deciding whether the sample data support the hypothesized model is "ease-of-fit" experienced by the coders when analyzing the data, in other words, whether the data landed naturally or had to be forced into the allotted categories within each dimension. Our coder found the easiest dimension for categorization to be time. The only adjustment that had to be made was an expansion of the notion of present time to include regular or habitual actions. It was also noted that certainty level categorization may include an additional fifth category of uncertainty in the model refinements. Currently, we have made no distinction between low certainty and uncertainty.

The dimension of perspective, on the other hand, is sufficiently granular and, depending on the application, could even be collapsed into two main categories: the writer's and third party's point of view. The benefit of distinguishing a rather rare category of third indirectly involved party's perspective is for when we are particularly interested in, let's say, experts' certainty. The experts could also be sub-divided into groups of political, economic, media-related, religious expertise and influence that can be identified with NLP and IE tools.

The distinction of focus into factual and abstract information presented the most difficulties for annotation due to fuzzy boundaries between known facts and opinions. The focus was considered factual when an event or state of affairs was clearly mentioned. Otherwise, the focus was considered abstract and further sub-categorized into a type of opinion, judgment, or emotion, such as fear, a warning, an assessment, or a conviction, the details of which are not herein reported.

As concluded in most pilot studies, the annotation could be improved with a clearer set of guidelines and definitions. All of the hypothesized categories in the model are not final and are open to further refinement, as the data analysis proceeds and the theoretical framework stabilizes. In addition, the uneven sizes of the two sample groups (editorials and news reports) presented a statistical challenge. In the future, we will distribute our manual tagging efforts evenly. The first author will incorporate some of the above-mentioned refinements into her doctoral thesis.

The proposed model makes several assumptions and raises several philosophical and practical issues. For instance, we are assuming that uncertainty is expressed due to doubt on the basis of evidence (by our definition), thus we do not make a distinction between truly being uncertain and appearing to be uncertain. There may be other desired reasons for appearing to be uncertain, such as the psychological effect of non-aggression, the social politeness effect, the humbling effect of hedged speech, and practical concerns for avoiding liabilities. Identifying these pragmatic functions of uncertainty is currently out of the scope of the study, but poses a challenge for future automated identification. Another problem is literal interpretation of the identified clues. For instance, the word "certain" itself has an alternate meaning of "definite but not specified." Our model does not include this meaning, but the issue of contextual disambiguation still persists.

4. Applications

The categorization, and the resulting linguistic clues and patterns for most frequent categories, will serve as a starting point for a certainty identification module in an intelligence analyst's question and answering system. This model will be applied to identifying and extracting perceived certainty of specified writers or reported third parties relative to the analyst's topics of interest.

The nature of government or business analysts' work requires time and effort to look through enormous amounts of raw textual information such as news reports or editorials in order to find answers to their questions. Traditional search systems can normally alleviate the analysts' load by retrieving texts by key words or phrases. State-of-the-art QA systems can usually localize the best answers and provide them in the form of short answers, best paragraphs, or best-fit full documents. But none of these current methods incorporate certainty of the text.

Certainty analysis, in addition to the QA-application, will add an extra level of sophistication that may assist analysts by alerting them in advance of, or at the time of, retrieval of the certainty of the information in the responses. For instance, data can be analyzed by a set of user-specified parameters from the refined and validated certainty model. An implemented system could be capable of providing users with alerts that warn the user of extreme levels of certainty, multiple levels of certainty in the same texts, absence or presence of certainty-qualified statements, and change of certainty levels. A cross-document summary could trace changes in certainty over time. The goal is to make raw data searchable by natural language certainty-oriented questions such as *"How certain were President Bush's statements about presence of weapons of mass destruction in Iraq in 2003 compared to 2004?"* The answers can be provided in QA system answer style – a flexible number of either best short answers, or most relevant paragraphs, or most relevant documents.

In addition, the collection of certainty expressions may become input data to machine learning algorithms for certainty identification and extraction. It also may suggest a new way of automating genre identification based on differences in markers per sentence frequencies and category distributions. Also, the study results capture current trends in newspaper writing, and are potentially useful as a set of suggestions on how to convey a desired level of certainty.

5. Conclusions and Future Work

Our contribution is in a proposed categorization model and analytical framework for certainty identification. The results of this pilot study reveal an overall promising picture of the presence of certainty information in texts, and establish the ability to manually identify and categorize individual statements according to the proposed certainty model.

Generally, our findings are that editorials had a significantly higher frequency of markers per sentence than did news stories. For editorials, high level of certainty, writer's point of view, and future and present time were the most populated categories. For news stories, the most common were high and moderate levels, directly involved third party's point of view, and past time. We are interested in conducting further data analysis per genre within newspaper articles since we have established that the frequency distribution differs depending on genre. This may have implications for automated genre identification. We will use insights from previous work on genre classification (Liddy et al. 1995, Kando 1996).

For editorials, of the possible 72 combinations, the high level of certainty from the writer's point of view expressed abstractly in the present and the future, and expressed factually in the future were most common; 12 combinations were typical; 35 were rather rare; and 22 never occurred. These results shed light on where the majority of lexical, semantic and syntactic patterns can be expected during linguistic analysis of editorials for automating categorization.

The sample data fit relatively well into the pre-defined categories. Some categories, such as the certainty level, can still be further refined with finer distinctions. The focus dimension will require further research. The study yielded a collection of explicit certainty markers which will be further grouped and analyzed in terms of lexical, semantic and syntactic patterns.

We also plan to conduct a full-scale inter-coder reliability study with multiple annotators by adapting our online data collection facility, developed for a concurrent study of emotional subjective content (Rubin et al. 2004).

6. Acknowledgements

This research was made possible by the National Science Foundation East Asia Summer Institutes for U.S. Graduate Students Research Grant No. 0309745. The first author extends her gratitude to her host researchers, Dr. Kando and Dr. Adachi, for welcoming this effort at the National Institute of Informatics, Tokyo, Japan. We are also grateful to the colleagues at Dr. Nakagawa's Language Informatics Laboratory, Information Technology Center at the University of Tokyo, and the researchers at Dr. Isahara's Computational Linguistics Group at the Communications Research Laboratory in Kyoto, Japan, for their comments and suggestions during the early stages of the research. We would especially like to thank Dr. Wiebe for her input in personal interactions at the 41st Annual Meeting of the Association for Computational Linguistics in Sapporo, Japan in 2003.

7. Bibliography

Anick, P. and Bergler, S. (1992) *Lexical structures for linguistic inference.* In Pustejovsky, J. and Bergler, S. (Eds.) Lexical Semantics and Knowledge Representation. Berlin, Springer Verlag: 121-135.

Banfield, A. (1982) *Unspeakable Sentences.* Routledge and Kegan Paul, Boston.

Bergler, S., Doandes, M., Gerard, C., and Witte, R. (2004) *Attributions.* In Qu, Y., Shanahan, J. G., Wiebe, J. (Eds.) Proceedings of AAAI Spring Symposium: Exploring Attitude and Affect in Text: Theories and Applications, Stanford, CA. AAAI Press.

Cappon, R. J. (2000) *The Associated Press Guide to News Writing.* Foster City, CA, IDG Books Worldwide Inc.

Chafe, W. (1986) *Evidentiality in English Conversation and Academic Writing.* In Chafe, W. and Nichols, J. (Eds.) Evidentiality: The Linguistic Coding of Epistemology. Norwood, New Jersey, Ablex Publishing Corporation. 20: 261-273.

Coates, J. (1983) *The Semantics of the Modal Auxiliaries.* London & Canberra, Croom Helm.

Holmes, J. (1990) *Hedges and boosters in women's and men's speech.* Language and communication 10 (3): 185-205.

Hyland, K. (1998) *Hedging in Scientific Research Articles.* Amsterdam, Philadelphia, John Benjamin Publishing Company.

Kando, N. (1996) *Text structure analysis based on human recognition: Cases of Japanese newspaper and English newspaper.* Bulletin of National Center for Science Information Systems, No. 8, pp.107-126 (Japanese)

Lackoff, G. (1972) *Hedges: a study of meaning criteria and the logic of fuzzy concepts.* Chicago Linguistic Society Papers.

Liddy, E.D., McVearry, K., Paik, W., Yu, E.S., and McKenna, M. (1993) *Development, implementation & Testing of a Discourse Model for Newspaper Texts.* Proceedings of the ARPA Workshop on Human Language Technology, Princeton, NJ, March 21-24, 1993.

Liddy, E.D., Paik, W., and McKenna, M. (1995) *Development and Implementation of a discourse model for newspaper texts.* Proceedings of the AAAI Symposium on Empirical Methods in Discourse Interpretation and Generation. Stanford, CA.

Merriam-Webster Online Dictionary, http://www.m-w.com/. Accessed on January 30, 2004.

Mushin, I. (2001) *Evidentiality and Epistemological Stance: Narrative Retelling.* Amsterdam, John Benjamins Publishing Co.

Rubin, V. L., Stanton, J. M., and Liddy E. D. (2004) *Discerning Emotions in Texts.* AAAI Spring Symposium: Exploring Attitude and Affect in Text: Theories and Applications, Stanford, CA.

Searle, J. R. (1979) *Expression and Meaning : Studies in the Theory of Speech Acts.* Cambridge, London, New York, Melbourne, Cambridge University Press.

van Dijk, T. A. (1981) *Studies in the Pragmatics of Discourse*, Mouton Publishers, The Hague, The Netherlands

Wiebe, J. M. (1994) *Tracking Point of View in Narrative.* Computational Linguistics 20 (2): 233-287.

Wiebe, J. M. (2000) *Learning Subjective Adjectives from Corpora.* Proceedings of the 17th National Conference on Artificial Intelligence (AAAI-2000). Austin, Texas, July 2000.

Wiebe, J., Bruce, R., Bell, M., Martin, M., and Wilson, T. (2001) *A Corpus Study of Evaluative and Speculative Language.* Proceedings of the 2nd ACL SIGdial Workshop on Discourse and Dialogue. Aalborg, Denmark, September, 2001.

Chapter 8

Evaluating an Opinion Annotation Scheme Using a New Multi-Perspective Question and Answer Corpus

Veselin Stoyanov and Claire Cardie
Cornell University
Dept. of Computer Science
4130 Upson Hall
Ithaca, NY 14850, U.S.A.
Email: {ves, cardie}@cs.cornell.edu

Diane Litman and Janyce Wiebe
University of Pittsburgh
Dept. of Computer Science
6135 Sennott Square
210 S. Bouquet St.
Pittsburgh, PA 15260 U.S.A.
Email: {litman, wiebe}@cs.pitt.edu

Abstract

In recent work, Wiebe et al. (2003) propose a semantic representation for encoding the opinions and perspectives expressed at any given point in a text. This paper evaluates the opinion annotation scheme for multi-perspective vs. fact-based question answering using a new question and answer corpus.

Keywords: multi-perspective question answering, sentiment analysis, opinions, question and answer corpus.

1. Introduction

In recent work, Wiebe et al. (2003; Wilson and Wiebe 2003) propose a semantic representation for encoding the opinions and perspectives expressed at any given point in a text. In addition, they develop the NRRC[1] corpus --- a collection of 252 articles that are manually annotated according to

---

[1] The corpus was created in support of the Northeast Regional Research Center (NRRC) which is sponsored by the Advanced Research and Development Activity in Information Technology (ARDA), a U.S.

this opinion representation scheme (Wiebe 2002). Cardie et al. (2003) further hypothesize that such representations will be useful for practical natural language processing (NLP) applications like multi-perspective question answering. In multi-perspective question answering (MPQA), for example, the goal of the NLP system is to answer opinion-oriented questions (e.g. "What is the sentiment in the Middle East towards war on Iraq?" or "What is Kofi Annan's opinion of the UN resolution on Iraq?") rather than fact-based questions (e.g. "Who is the current president of the United States?" or "What is the primary substance used in producing chocolate?"). To be successful, such MPQA systems will presumably require the ability to recognize and organize the opinions expressed throughout one or more documents. To date, however, the proposed opinion annotation scheme has not been directly studied in this question-answering context.

The goals of this paper are two-fold. First, we present a new corpus of multi-perspective questions and answers. This question and answer (Q&A) corpus contains 15 opinion-oriented questions and 15 fact-oriented questions along with all text spans that constitute the answers to these questions for a subset of the documents in the above-mentioned NRRC corpus. Second, we present the results of two experiments that employ the new Q&A corpus to investigate the usefulness of the Wiebe et al. (2003) opinion annotation scheme for multi-perspective vs. fact-based question answering. We find ultimately that low-level perspective information can be useful in MPQA if used judiciously.

The paper is organized as follows. The next section provides a brief overview of Wiebe et al.'s opinion annotation framework and the NRRC opinion-annotated corpus. We then present the question and answer (Q&A) corpus, followed by a section that describes our evaluation using the new corpus and discusses the results.

2. Low-Level Perspective Information

The framework suggested by Wiebe et al. (2003) provides a basis for annotating opinions, beliefs, emotions, sentiment, and other private states expressed in text. *Private state* is a general term used to refer to mental and emotional states that cannot be directly observed or verified (Quirk et al. 1985).

There are two principal ways in which private states are expressed in language: they could be explicitly stated, or they could be expressed indirectly by the selection of words and the style of language that the speaker or writer uses. For instance, in the sentence "John is afraid that Sue might fall," "afraid" is an explicitly mentioned private state. On the other hand, the sentence "It is about time that we end Saddam's oppression," does not mention explicitly the opinion of the author, but the private state of disapproval of Saddam is expressed by the words and style of the language used: the phrases "it is about time" and "oppression" are examples of what Wiebe et al. (2003) call *expressive subjective elements*.

An important aspect of a private state is its *source*. The source of a private state is the experiencer of that state, that is, the person or entity whose opinion or emotion is being conveyed in the text. Trivially, the overall source is the author of the article, but the writer may write about the private states of other people, leading to multiple sources in a single text segment. For example, in the sentence "Mary believes that Sue is afraid of the dark," the private state of Sue being afraid is expressed through Mary's private state (of "believing") and Mary's private state is expressed

Government entity which sponsors and promotes research of import to the Intelligence Community which includes but is not limited to the CIA, DIA, NSA, NIMA, and NRO.

through the implicit private state of the author of the sentence. This presents a natural *nesting of sources* in a text segment. Nesting of sources may become quite deep and complex, and expressive subjective elements may also have nested sources.

The perspective annotation framework includes annotations to describe expressive subjective elements as well as explicitly-mentioned private states and speech events.

Annotations for private states and speech events are comprised of what Wiebe et al. (2003) refers to as the *on* --- the text span that constitutes the private state or speech event phrase itself --- as well as the *inside* of the speech event, which is the text segment inside the scope of the private state or speech event phrase. For instance, in the sentence "Tom believes that Ken is an outstanding individual," the *on* is "believes" and the *inside* is "Ken is an outstanding individual." Similarly, in the sentence "Critics say that the new system will fail," the *on* is "say" and the *inside* is "the new system will fail."

An important aspect of each private state and speech event annotation is encoded in its *onlyfactive* attribute. This attribute indicates whether the associated text segment is presented as factual (i.e. *onlyfactive=yes*), or indeed expresses the emotion, opinion, or other private state of the source (i.e. *onlyfactive=no*). For example, all expressions that are explicit private states such as "think" and "believe" as well as private states mixed with speech such as "praise" and "correct" by definition are *onlyfactive=no*, whereas neutral speech events such as "said" and "mentioned" may be either *onlyfactive=no* or *onlyfactive=yes*, depending on the context.

In contrast, the text span associated with expressive subject element annotations is simply that of the subjective phrase itself. The attributes that can be assigned to each of the two annotation types are summarized in Table 1.

Explicit private state
onlyfactive: *yes, no*
nested-source
overall-strength: *low, medium, high, extreme*
on-strength: *neutral, low, medium, high, extreme*
attitude-type: *positive, negative, both*
attitude-toward
is-implicit
minor
Expressive subjective elements
nested-source
strength: *low, medium, high, extreme*
attitude-type: *positive, negative, both*

Table 1. Attributes for the two main annotation types. For annotations that can take values from a fixed set, all values are given.

This investigation considers both *explicit private state* and *expressive subjective element* annotations. Furthermore, the investigation makes use of the *onlyfactive* attribute of the *explicit private state* annotations as an indicator of whether the annotation should be considered factive or expressing opinion.[2] In particular, we will use the term **fact annotation** to refer to an *explicit private state* annotation with its *onlyfactive* attribute set to *yes* and **opinion annotation** to refer to either an explicit private state annotation with its *onlyfactive* attribute set to *no* or an expressive subjective element.

3. The MPQA NRRC Corpus

Using the perspective annotation framework, Wiebe et al. (2003) have manually annotated a considerable number of documents (over 100 reported in Wiebe et al. (2003) and 252 reported in Wilson and Wiebe (2003)) to form the NRRC corpus. The annotated documents are part of a larger data collection of over 270,000 documents that appeared in the world press over an 11-month period, between June 2001 and May 2002. The source of almost all of the documents in the larger collection is the U.S. foreign broadcast information service (FBIS).

Note that documents in the NRRC corpus have not been annotated with *insides* for all private states and speech events. The only private state annotations that include *insides* are those that span entire sentences.[3]

Wiebe et al. have performed interannotator studies to validate the annotation scheme by assessing the consistency of human annotators. In particular, they report an interannotator agreement of 85% on direct expressions of perspective information (*explicit private states*), about 50% on indirect expressions of subjective information (*expressive subjectivity*), and up to 80% kappa agreement on the rhetorical use of perspective information (Wiebe et al. 2003). In a subsequent study, the average of the reported values for agreement between groups was 82% for *on* agreement and 72% for *expressive-subjective* agreement (Wilson and Wiebe 2003). Values for both studies were reported using measure $agr(a||b)$ for annotator groups a and b calculated as the proportion of a's annotations that were found by b. For every two groups a and b a value was calculated as the mean of $agr(a||b)$ and $agr(b||a)$, since the measure is directional.

Wiebe et al. (2003) concluded that the good agreement results indicate that annotating opinions is a feasible task, and suggest ways for further improving the annotations.

4. Multi-Perspective Question and Answer Corpus Creation

This section describes the creation of the question and answer question and answer (Q&A) corpus used to evaluate the low-level perspective annotations in the context of opinion-oriented (*opinion*) and fact-based (*fact*) question answering.

The Q&A corpus consists of 98 documents from the opinion-annotated NRRC corpus. Each document addresses one of four general topics:

- **kyoto** - concerns President Bush's alternative to the Kyoto protocol
- **mugabe** - concerns the 2002 elections in Zimbabwe and Mugabe's reelection
- **humanrights** - discusses the US annual human rights report
- **venezuela** - describes the 2002 coup d'etat in Venezuela

---

[2] Using other attributes of the annotation would require specific processing adapted for the MPQA task and goes beyond the scope of the current investigation.
[3] These have been identified automatically and added to the corpus.

The documents were automatically selected from the larger set of over 270,000 documents as being relevant to one of the four topics using the SMART (Salton 1971) information retrieval system. The Q&A corpus contains between 19 and 33 documents for each topic.

Kyoto	
1 f	What is the Kyoto Protocol about?
2 f	When was the Kyoto Protocol adopted?
3 f	Who is the president of the Kiko Network?
4 f	What is the Kiko Network?
5 o	Does the president of the Kiko Network approve of the US action concerning the Kyoto Protocol?
6 o	Are the Japanese unanimous in their opinion of Bush's position on the Kyoto Protocol?
7 o	How is Bush's decision not to ratify the Kyoto Protocol looked upon by Japan and other US allies?
8 o	How do European Union countries feel about the US opposition to the Kyoto protocol?
Human Rights	
1 f	What is the murder rate in the United States?
2 f	What country issues an annual report on human rights in the United States?
3 o	How do the Chinese regard the human rights record of the United States?
4 f	Who is Andrew Welsdan?
5 o	What factors influence the way in which the US regards the human rights records of other nations?
6 o	Is the US Annual Human Rights Report received with universal approval around the world?
Venezuela	
1 f	When did Hugo Chavez become President?
2 f	Did any prominent Americans plan to visit Venezuela immediately following the 2002 coup?
3 o	Did anything surprising happen when Hugo Chavez regained power in Venezuela after he
4 o	was removed by a coup?
	Did most Venezuelans support the 2002 coup?
5 f	Which governmental institutions in Venezuela were dissolved by the leaders of the 2002 coup?
6 o	How did ordinary Venezuelans feel about the 2002 coup and subsequent events?
7 o	Did America support the Venezuelan foreign policy followed by Chavez?
8 f	Who is Vice-President of Venezuela?
Mugabe	
1 o	What was the American and British reaction to the reelection of Mugabe?
2 f	Where did Mugabe vote in the 2002 presidential election?
3 f	At which primary school had Mugabe been expected to vote in the 2002 presidential election?
4 f	How long has Mugabe headed his country?
5 f	Who was expecting Mugabe at Mhofu School for the 2002 election?
6 o	What is the basis for the European Union and US critical attitude and adversarial action toward Mugabe?
7 o	What did South Africa want Mugabe to do after the 2002 election?
8 o	What is Mugabe's opinion about the West's attitude and actions towards the 2002 Zimbabwe election?

Table 2. Questions in the Q&A collection by topic.

Fact and opinion questions for each topic were added to the Q&A corpus by a volunteer not associated with the current project. He was given two randomly selected documents on each topic along with a set of instructions for creating fact vs. opinion questions.[4] The complete set of 30 questions is shown in Table 2. The set contains an equal number of opinion (o) and fact (f) questions for each topic.

Once the documents and questions were obtained, answers for the questions in the supporting documents had to be identified. In particular, we manually added *answer* annotations for every text segment in the Q&A corpus that constituted, or contributed to, an answer to any question. The *answer* annotations include attributes to indicate the **topic** of the associated question, the **question number** within that topic, and the annotator's **confidence** that the segment actually answered the question. Annotators did not have access to the low-level perspective annotations during answer annotation.

Documents were annotated by the first two authors of the paper, with each annotator handling 61 documents.[5] Out of the 98 documents in the collection, 24 were selected at random and annotated by both annotators. The remaining 74 documents were split equally between the two annotators using a random draw. The 24 documents that were annotated by both annotators were used to study the interannotator agreement. Using Wiebe et al.'s (2003) *agr* measure, we determined that the agreement between the two annotators was 85% on average with values of 78% and 93% for the two annotators. The good interannotator agreement indicates that, despite the difficulties, annotating the answers is a feasible task and can be performed consistently in the presence of robust annotation instructions.

4.1 Difficulties in Corpus Creation

This section summarizes some of the difficulties encountered during creation of the Q&A corpus.

4.1.1 Question Creation

In spite of the question creation instructions, it appears that a few questions were reverse-engineered from the available documents. These questions are answered in only one or two of the documents, which presents some challenges when using the collection for evaluation. Nevertheless, the setting is not unrealistic since the situation in which questions find support in only a few documents is often present in real-world QA systems.

In addition, the classification associated with each question --- fact or opinion --- did not always seem appropriate. In particular, **mugabe** opinion question #6 --- "What is the basis for the European Union and US critical attitude and adversarial action toward Mugabe?" --- could arguably be classified as fact-based, since the question is in essence not asking about the European Union and US's opinion, but rather about the basis for it. Similarly, **venezuela** factual question #2 --- "Did any prominent Americans plan to visit Venezuela immediately following the 2002 coup?" --- could be judged as asking about the opinion of prominent Americans.

---

[4] The instructions are available from www.cs.cornell.edu/home/cardie/.

[5] These instructions are also available at www.cs.cornell.edu/home/cardie/.

4.1.2 Annotating Answers

The most frequently encountered problem in answer annotation is a well-known problem from fact-based QA; namely, the difficulty of deciding what constitutes an answer to a question. The problem was further amplified by the presence of opinion questions. For instance, the question "Did most Venezuelans support the 2002 coup?" had potential answers such as "Protesters...failed to gain the support of the army" and "... thousands of citizens rallied the streets in support of Chavez." Both segments hint that most Venezuelans did not support the coup that forced Chavez to resign. Both passages, however, state it in a very indirect way. It is hard even for humans to conclude whether the above two passages constitute answers to the question.

A related issue is that opinionated documents often express answers to the questions only very indirectly, by using word selection and style of language (*expressive subjectivity*), which is often hard to judge. An indication of the difficulties associated with judging the subjectivity expressed indirectly is contained in the interannotator studies reported by Wiebe et al. (2003), which showed that annotators agree less often on *expressive subjectivity* (50% of the time) than on direct expressions of opinions (80% of the time).

An additional problem is that opinion questions often ask about the opinions of certain collective entities, such as countries, governments, and popular opinions. It was hard for human annotators to judge what can be considered an expression of the opinion of collective entities (e.g. what sources represent "ordinary Venezuelans" or "the Japanese"' or "Japan"?), and often the conjecture required a significant amount of background information (e.g. knowing what countries are "EU" countries or "U.S. allies").

5. Evaluation of Perspective Annotations for MPQA

We designed two different experiments to evaluate the usefulness of the perspective annotations in the context of fact- and especially opinion-based QA. The first experiment, *answer probability*:

1. visits each answering text segment (as denoted by the manual answer annotations),
2. categorizes it as either OPINION or FACT based on the associated perspective annotations (using one of the criteria described below), and
3. counts how many FACT/OPINION segments answer fact/opinion questions.

That is, we compute the probabilities $P(\textit{FACT/OPINION answer} \mid \textit{fact/opinion question})$ for all combinations of fact and opinion questions and answers.

The second experiment, *answer rank*, implements the first step of most contemporary QA systems: given a question from the Q&A corpus as the query, it performs sentence-based information retrieval (IR) on all documents in the collection. We then study the effect of considering only retrieved sentences classified as FACT vs. OPINION (using the criteria below) for fact and opinion questions, respectively, on the performance of the information retrieval component.

For both experiments, we consider multiple criteria to determine whether a text segment (or sentence) should be considered FACT or OPINION based on the underlying perspective annotations. First, we use two *association criteria* to determine which perspective annotations should be considered associated with an arbitrary text segment.

- For the *overlap* criterion, a perspective annotation is considered associated with the segment if its span includes any part of the segment.
- For the *cover* criterion, a perspective annotation is considered associated with the segment if its span contains the entire text segment.[6]

Once we determine the set of perspective annotations associated with a text segment, we use four *classification criteria* to categorize the segment as one of FACT or OPINION:

- **most nested (m nested):** a segment is considered OPINION if the **most nested** annotation from the set of associated perspective annotations is an opinion; the segment is considered FACT otherwise. Note that nested sources can have nested perspective annotations. Overlapping non-nested annotations are not possible if the annotation instructions are followed (Wiebe 2002).
- **all:** a segment is considered OPINION if **all** associated perspective annotations are opinion; FACT otherwise.
- **any:** a segment is considered OPINION if **any** of the associated perspective annotations is opinion; FACT otherwise.
- **most:** a segment is considered OPINION if **the number** of associated perspective annotations that are opinion is **greater than** the number of associated perspective annotations that are fact. A segment is considered FACT otherwise.

The above criteria exhibit a bias towards opinion annotations. Criteria were designed in this way because we expected opinion annotations to be more discriminative. For instance, if a fact annotation is embedded inside an opinion annotation, the fact expressed in the internal annotation will be expressed from the perspective of the outer source.

5.1 Results: Answer Probability

As mentioned above, this experiment counts the number of answer segments classified as FACT and OPINION, respectively that answer each question. We hypothesize that opinion questions will be answered more often in answer segments classified as OPINION, and that fact questions will be answered more often in text segments classified as FACT. For this experiment we consider every text segment annotated as an answer and examine the perspective annotations associated with the text segment.

The results of this experiment are summarized in Table 3 below. Table 3 has eight rows, one for each combination of association (total of two) and classification (total of four) criteria. For each of the eight criteria, Table 3 shows the total number of fact and opinion questions answered in text segments classified as FACT and OPINION. Overall, there were 120 answers annotated for fact questions and 415 answers annotated for opinion questions. The first row of the table, for example, indicates that 84 of the answers to fact questions were classified as FACT using the *overlap m nested* criterion. This represents 70% of all fact questions. Similarly, 375 of the answers to opinion questions (90.36% of the total) were classified as OPINION using the same *overlap m nested* criterion.

---

[6] As mentioned earlier, the only *insides* annotated in the Q&A corpus are those that cover entire sentences. This affects both criteria, but especially *cover*, since it is only these sentence-length *inside* annotations that will ever be considered associated with an answer segment that spans more than a single *on*.

	Answer type	Question type			
		Fact	Pct of total	Opinion	Pct of total
overlap, m nested	fact	84	70.00%	40	9.64%
	opinion	36	30.00%	375	90.36%
cover, m nested	fact	94	78.33%	238	57.35%
	opinion	26	21.67%	177	42.65%
overlap, any	fact	84	70.00%	34	8.19%
	opinion	36	30.00%	381	91.81%
cover, any	fact	94	78.33%	238	57.35%
	opinion	26	21.67%	177	42.65%
overlap, all	fact	94	78.33%	307	73.98%
	opinion	26	21.67%	108	26.02%
cover, all	fact	94	78.33%	301	72.53%
	opinion	26	21.67%	114	27.47%
overlap, most	fact	93	77.50%	223	53.73%
	opinion	27	22.50%	192	46.27%
cover, most	fact	94	78.33%	305	73.49%
	opinion	26	21.67%	110	26.51%

Table 3. Number of fact/opinion questions answered in FACT/OPINION segments based on each of the 6 criteria.

Several observations can be made from Table 3. First, for each of the eight criteria, the percentage of fact questions answered in FACT text segments is significantly greater than the percentage of fact questions answered in OPINION segments (e.g. 70.00% vs. 30.00% for *overlap m nested*). Furthermore, for two of the eight criteria, namely *overlap m nested* and *overlap any*, the percentage of opinion questions answered in OPINION segments is greater than the percentage of opinion questions answered in FACT segments (e.g. 90.36% vs. 9.64% for *overlap m nested*). Additionally, for five of the eight criteria, excluding *overlap all, cover all*, and *cover most*, *P(FACT answer | fact question)* is significantly greater than *P(FACT answer | opinion question)* (and symmetrically for opinion answers) (e.g. 70.00% vs. 9.64% for *overlap m nested*).

The most discriminative runs for fact questions appear to be *cover*, with any of the four classification criteria. Using any of the *cover* criteria, 78.33% of the fact questions are answered in FACT segments and only 21.67% are answered in OPINION segments. As for opinion questions, the most accurate criterion is *overlap any*, for which 91.81% of the opinion questions are answered in OPINION segments and only 8.19% in FACT segments. Considering the characteristics of the data, the above results can be expected, since *cover* is more likely to classify segments as FACT than OPINION, with *cover all* being the most restrictive criterion in terms of classifying segments as OPINION. At the same time, *overlap any* is the most liberal criterion, in that it is likely to classify the most segments as OPINION. Two of the four *overlap* criteria, namely *overlap m nested* and *overlap any* appear to exhibit a good balance between classifying answers to fact questions as FACT and at the same time classifying opinion question answers as OPINION. These two criteria show the two best performances on opinion questions, while diverging from the best performance on fact questions only slightly. The best predictor for the classification of the answer, however, appears to be a combined measure that relies on *overlap any* for opinion questions and on any of the four *cover* criteria for the fact questions. For such a combined criterion, 78.33% of the answers to fact question appear in segments classified as FACT and 91.81% of the answers to opinion questions appear in segments classified as OPINION.

A somewhat surprising fact is that all four variations of the *cover* criterion exhibit identical performance on fact questions. This is due to the fact that in most cases the only perspective annotation segments that cover answer text segments spanning more than a single *on* are perspective annotations that span the entire sentence, as described in the experimental setup section.

5.2 Results: Answer Rank

The second experiment is designed to resemble the operation of a traditional QA system. More precisely, we attempt to determine whether information from the perspective annotations can assist in the IR phase of traditional QA approaches. The hypothesis is that perspective annotations can be useful in ranking the retrieved text segments. More precisely, we hypothesize that low-level perspective information can be used to promote the correct answer segments in the ranking.

For this experiment, we divide each document into a set of text segments at sentence borders. We then run an IR algorithm (the standard tf.idf retrieval implemented in the Lemur IR kit, available from http://www.cs.cmu.edu/~lemur/) on the set of all sentences from all documents in the Q&A collection, treating each question, in turn, as the query. We then refine the ranked list of sentences returned by Lemur for each particular question. We optionally apply one of two filters, each of which removes OPINION answers for fact questions and vice versa. The two filters constitute the two best performing criteria from the *answer probability* experiment for opinion and fact questions --- the *overlap any* criterion (which performed best for opinion questions) and *cover all* (which performed best for fact questions). From the modified ranked list of answers, we determine the rank of the first retrieved sentence that correctly answers the question. A sentence is considered a correct answer if any part of it is annotated as an answer to the question in the Q&A corpus.

After the ranking from the IR system is refined we obtain for each question the rank of the first sentence containing a correct answer to the question (1) without using the perspective annotations (*unfilt* ranking), and (2) using one of the two filters. If our hypothesis is supported, we would expect to see a higher ranking for the first correct answer for each question in runs that make use of the perspective-based filters.

Table 4 (below) summarizes the results from the answer rank experiment. It shows the rank of the first answering sentence for every question in the collection. Table 4 has four columns, one for the baseline *unfiltered* results, one for each of the *overlap any* and *cover any* perspective-based filters, and one for a filter that combines the two filters (*mixed*). The *mixed* filter combines the *overlap* and *cover* filters, using *overlap* to filter answer sentences for opinion questions, and *cover* to filter answers for fact questions. The construction of the *mixed* filter was motivated by observing from the data in Table 3 that *overlap any* discriminates well answers to opinion questions, while *cover any* discriminates well answers to fact questions.

Table 4 computes two cumulative measures as well, the Mean Reciprocal Rank (MRR) of the first correct answer, which is a standard evaluation measure in QA, and the mean rank of the first correct answer (MRFA). MRR is computed as the average of the reciprocals of the ranks of the first correct answer (i.e. if the first correct answer to a question is ranked 4, the contribution of the

Topic	Question	Rank of first answer			
		unfiltered	filtered (overlap)	filtered(cover)	filtered (mixed)
Kyoto	1 (fact)	10	4	6	6
	2 (fact)	1	1	1	1
	3 (fact)	3		3	3
	4 (fact)	2	2	2	2
	5 (opinion)	1	1		1
	6 (opinion)	5	4	2	4
	7 (opinion)	1	1	1	1
	8 (opinion)	1	1	2	1
Hum. Rights	1 (fact)	1	1	1	1
	2 (fact)	1	14	1	1
	3 (opinion)	1	1	10	1
	4 (fact)	1		1	1
	5 (opinion)	10	7	24	7
	6 (opinion)	1	1	1	1
Venezuela	1 (fact)	50	9	32	32
	2 (fact)	13		9	9
	3 (opinion)	106	93	44	93
	4 (opinion)	3	3	7	3
	5 (fact)	2		1	1
	6 (opinion)	1	1	1	1
	7 (opinion)	3	3	2	3
	8 (fact)	1	1	1	1
Mugabe	1 (opinion)	2	2	39	2
	2 (fact)	64	89	55	55
	3 (fact)	2		2	2
	4 (fact)	16	15	16	16
	5 (fact)	1	117	1	1
	6 (opinion)	7	6	111	6
	7 (opinion)	447	356		356
	8 (opinion)	331	260		260
MRR:		0.52	0.39	0.45	0.55
Mean rank of first answer:		36.27	39.72	13.93	29.07
Fact questions only:					
MRR:		0.54	0.27	0.58	0.58
Mean rank of first answer:		11.20	25.30	8.80	8.80
Opinion questions only:					
MRR:		0.51	0.52	0.32	0.52
Mean rank of first answer:		61.33	49.33	20.33	49.33

Table 4. Results for IR module evaluation.

question to the mean will be 1/4). The two cumulative measures are computed across all of the questions and also for fact and opinion questions separately for each of the four rankings.

Table 4 shows that in the ranking using the *overlap* filter the first OPINION answer for each of the 15 opinion questions in the collection is at least as highly ranked as in the unfiltered ranking. As a result, the MRR for overlap is higher than the MRR for *unfiltered* for opinion questions. Similarly, in the *cover* ranking the first FACT answer for each of the 15 fact questions in the collection is at least as highly ranked as in the *unfiltered* ranking. Thus, the MRR for *cover* for fact questions is higher than MRR for *unfiltered* for fact questions. At the same time, for five of the fact questions, *overlap* filters all answering segments, returning no sentence answering the question. Similarly, *cover* fails to return answering sentences for three of the opinion questions.

Since *overlap* always outperforms *unfiltered* for opinion questions and *cover* always outperforms *unfiltered* for fact questions, it is not surprising that *mixed* performs at least as well as *unfiltered* on every question in the collection. As a result, *mixed* exhibits an overall MRR of .55 as opposed to *unfiltered*'s MRR of .52. The mean rank of the first correct answer for *mixed* is 29.07 as opposed to 36.27 for *unfiltered*.

5.3 Discussion

Results of the first experiment support the hypothesis that low-level perspective information can be useful for multi-perspective question answering. The discriminative abilities of the criteria show that perspective information can be a reliable predictor of whether a given segment of a document answers an opinion/fact question. More specifically, an MPQA system might use the low-level perspective information in one of two ways: the system can combine the two top-performing criteria on fact and opinion questions, or can use one of the two highly performing *overlap* criteria, *overlap all* and *overlap any*. The low-level perspective information may be used to re-rank potential answers by using the knowledge that the probability that a fact answer appears in an OPINION segment, and vice versa, is very low.

An interesting observation concerns the performance of the eight criteria on the two questions that were identified as problematic in their fact/opinion classification during corpus creation. Such questions are discussed in the corpus creation section. The performance of all eight criteria on the problematic questions was worse than the performance on the rest of the questions in the collection. For instance, one of the questions given as an example in the corpus creation section, "What is the basis for the European Union and US critical attitude and adversarial action toward Mugabe?" (**mugabe**, question #6), is answered at least as often from FACT text segments as from OPINION segments for all of the eight criteria, despite being classified as opinion. An MPQA system that can classify questions as fact or opinion and assign a confidence to the assignment might be able to recognize such situations and rely less on the low-level perspective information for "borderline" questions.

The second experiment provides further evidence in support of the hypothesis that low-level perspective information can be useful in MPQA. An IR subsystem has been an important part of almost all existing effective QA systems (Cardie et al. 2000; Moldovan et al. 1999; 2002; Harabagiu et al. 2001; Pasca and Harabagiu 2000; Voorhees 2000; 2001; 2002; Voorhees and Tice 1999). Our results suggest that, if used properly, low-level perspective information can improve the ranking of potential answer segments returned by the IR subsystem. Our experiments show that the most effective criterion that can be used for re-ranking is *mixed*. Using filters, however, can sometimes cause all answering segments for a particular question to be discarded.

Based on the results of *answer ranking*, we can conclude that while being good predictor for re-ranking of the results from the IR subsystem, low-level perspective information should not be used as an absolute indicator of the relevance of a potential answer segment. In particular, low-level perspective information helps improve the ranking, but in doing so at least some answering summaries are discarded, which can prove costly if the system uses a limited set of supporting documents. The number of discarded entities is smaller for *mixed*, which provides the most conservative estimation.

In summary, both the *answer probability* and the *answer rank* experiments show that low-level perspective information can be a generally useful predictor of whether a text segment answers a question given the type of the question. It is unrealistic, however, to use the FACT/OPINION segment classification as an absolute indicator of whether the segment can answer fact/opinion questions. Completely disregarding potential answer segments of the incorrect type can cause an MPQA system to eliminate all answer to a question in the supporting collection. This is less of a concern for systems that rely on a larger supporting set of documents (e.g. the World Wide Web), but a valid limitation to systems built to use restricted support document sets.

6. Conclusions and Future Work

The current investigation addressed two main tasks: constructing a data collection for MPQA and evaluating the hypothesis that low-level perspective information can be useful for MPQA. Both tasks provided insights into potential difficulties of the task of MPQA and the usefulness of the low-level perspective information.

As a result of the first task, a small data collection for MPQA was constructed. The current collection consists of 98 manually annotated documents and a total of 30 questions divided into four topics. As part of future work, the collection can be improved using questions from a real-world question logs.

During the collection construction phase some of the potential difficulties associated with the tasks of MPQA where identified. The main problems identified consist of the problem of deciding what constitutes answer, the presence of indirect answers (*expressive subjectivity*), the difficulty of judging what constitutes an opinion of a collective entity, and the fact that most answers to opinion questions are not stated explicitly in the text, but have to be deduced.

The investigation showed that low-level perspective information can be an effective predictor of whether a text segment contains an answer to a question, given the type of the question. The results, however, suggest that low-level perspective information should not be used as an absolute indicator of whether a segment answers a particular question, especially in the setting where each question is expected to be answered in a limited number of documents.

7. Acknowledgements

This material is based in part upon work supported by the Advanced Research and Development Activity (ARDA) under Contract # NBCHC040014, NSF Grant IIS–0208028, and an NSF Graduate Research Fellowship to the first author.

8. Bibliography

Cardie, C., Ng, V., Pierce, D., and Buckley, C. (2000) Examining the role of statistical and linguistic knowledge sources in a general-knowledge question-answering system. In *Proceedings of the Sixth Applied Natural Language Processing Conference.* 180–187.

Cardie, C., Wiebe, J., Wilson, T., and Litman, D. (2003) Combining low-level and summary representations of opinions for multi-perspective question answering. *Working Notes of the 2003 AAAI Spring Symposium on New Directions in Question Answering.*

Harabagiu, S., Moldovan, D., Pasca, M., Surdeanu, M., Mihalcea, R., Girju, R., Rus, V., Lacatusu, F., Morarescu, P., and Bunescu, R. (2001) Answering complex, list and context questions with lcc's question-answering server. In Voorhees, E., and Harman, D. K., (Eds.) *Proceedings of the Tenth Text Retrieval Conference (TREC 2001).* 355–362.

Moldovan, D., Harabagiu, S., Pasca, M., Mihalcea, R., Girju, R., Goodrum, R. and Rus, V. (1999) Lasso: A tool for surfing the answer net. In Voorhees, E., and Harman, D. K., (Eds.) *Proceedings of the Eighth Text Retrieval Conference (TREC-8).*

Moldovan, D., Harabagiu, S., Girju, R., Morarescu, P., Lacatusu, F., Novischi, A.., Badulescu, A., and Bolohan, O. (2002) Lcc tools for question answering. In Voorhees, E., and Buckland, L. P., (Eds.) *Proceedings of the Eleventh Text REtrieval Conference (TREC 2002).* 79–89.

Pasca, M. and Harabagiu, S. (2000) High performance question/answering. In *Proceedings of the 38th annual meeting of the association for computational linguistics (ACL-2000).* 563–570.

Quirk, R., Greenbaum, S., Leech, G., and Svartvik, J. (1985) A comprehensive grammar of the English language. New York. Longman.

Salton, G. (Ed.) (1971) The SMART Retrieval System — Experiments in Automatic Document Processing. Englewood Cliffs, NJ. Prentice Hall Inc.

Voorhees, E. and Tice, D. (1999) The TREC-8 question answering track evaluation. In Voorhees, E. and Harman, D. K., (Eds.) *Proceedings of the Eighth Text Retrieval Conference (TREC-8).* 83–105.

Voorhees, E. (2000) The TREC-9 question answering track evaluation. In Voorhees, E. and Harman, D. K., (Eds.) *Proceedings of the Ninth Text REtrieval Conference (TREC-9).* 71–81.

Voorhees, E. (2001) Overview of the TREC 2001 question answering track. In Voorhees, E. and Harman, D. K., (Eds.) *Proceedings of the Tenth Text Retrieval Conference (TREC 2001).* 42–52.

Voorhees, E. (2002) Overview of the TREC 2002 question answering track. In Voorhees, E. and Buckland, L. P. (Eds.) *Proceedings of the Eleventh Text REtrieval Conference (TREC 2002).* 53–75.

Wiebe, J., Breck, E., Buckley, C., Cardie, C., Davis, P., Fraser, B., Litman, D., Pierce, D., Riloff, E., Wilson, T., Day, D., and Maybury, M. (2003) Recognizing and organizing opinions expressed in the world press. *Working Notes of the 2003 AAAI Spring Symposium on New Directions in Question Answering.*

Wiebe, J. (2002) Instructions for annotating opinions in newspaper articles. *Department of Computer Science TR-02-101.* University of Pittsburgh, Pittsburgh, PA.

Wilson, T. and Wiebe, J. (2003) Annotating opinions in the world press. *4th SIGdial Workshop on Discourse and Dialogue (SIGdial-03).*

Chapter 9

Validating the Coverage of Lexical Resources for Affect Analysis and Automatically Classifying New Words along Semantic Axes

Gregory Grefenstette[1]
CEA/LIST/DTSI/SCRI/LIC2M
Commissariat à l'Energie Atomique, Centre de Fontenay-aux-Roses, B.P. 6
92265 Fontenay-aux-Roses Cedex, France
Email: Gregory.Grefenstette@cea.fr

Yan Qu and David A. Evans
Clairvoyance Corporation, 5001 Baum Boulevard, Suite 700
Pittsburgh, PA 15213-1854 USA
Email: {yqu,dae,jimi}@clairvoyancecorp.com

James G. Shanahan[1]
Turn Inc
1400 Fashion Island Blvd, Suite 510
San Mateo, CA 94404, U.S.A.
Email: James Shanahan@turn.com

Abstract

In addition to factual content, many texts contain an emotional dimension. This emotive, or affect, dimension has not received a great amount of attention in computational linguistics until recently. However, now that messages (including spam) have become more prevalent than edited texts (such as newswire), recognizing this emotive dimension of written text is becoming more important. One resource needed for identifying affect in text is a lexicon of words with emotion-conveying potential. Starting from an existing affect lexicon and lexical patterns that invoke affect, we gathered a large quantity of text to measure the coverage of our existing lexicon. This chapter reports on our methods for identifying new candidate affect words and on our evaluation of our current affect lexicons. We describe how our affect lexicon can be extended based on results from these experiments.

Keywords: affect lexicon, emotion, lexicon discovery, semantic axes.

---

[1] This work was done while the first author was an employee of Clairvoyance Corporation.

1. Introduction

The emotive, or affective, component of text has received revived attention in computational linguistics recently. As messages (e-mail including spam, short messages, electronically submitted user opinion) become more prevalent on the Internet than edited text (such as newswire), recognizing the emotion contained in a text is becoming important as a filtering tool. All language users know that the same message content can be delivered with a wide variety of affective nuances. For example, one can present the same event as a glorious or horrible thing through judicious word choice. While the facts concerning the event may remain the same (*who, what, when, how*), different lexical selections, grammatical choices, and different focus can change the affect register of a text. Recognizing affect completely in a text would require at least recognizing rhetorical structures and emotion-bearing words. Automatic recognition of rhetorical structure is still in its infancy (Teufel and Moens, 2002), but work on the emotive content of words has a long history in linguistics[2].

1.1 Early Work on Affect Labelling

In psychological research in the early 1960s, Deese (1964) postulated that words were stored internally along semantic axes, and elaborated experiments in free association that were used to predict which words were found along axes such as "big-small", "hot-cold", etc. These ideas entered the field of linguistics as a "linguistic scale," defined by Levinson (1983) as set of alternate or contrastive expressions that can be arranged on an axis by degree of semantic strength along that dimension, and also somewhat in the idea of semantic fields (Berlin and Kay, 1969; Lehrer, 1974) which correspond to a group of words that cover and divide up some semantic dimension, such as "colors."

In addition to these lines of research interested in placing terms along semantic axes, other researchers such as Stone and Lasswell began building lexicons in which words were explicitly labeled with affect. For example, in the Lasswell Value Dictionary (Lasswell and Namenwirth, 1969), the word *admire* was tagged with a positive value along the dimension *RESPECT*. This dictionary marked words with binary values along eight basic value dimensions (WEALTH, POWER, RECTITUDE, RESPECT, ENLIGHTENMENT, SKILL, AFFECTION, and WELLBEING). Stone's work on the General Inquirer dictionary (Stone et al., 1966) has continued to this day (see http://www.wjh.harvard.edu/~inquirer/inqdict.txt for an online version). Currently (in mid 2004) the dictionary contains 1,915 words marked as generally positive and 2,291 words marked as negative. In addition to these two general classes, a wide variety of other affect classes are used to label entries, e.g., Active, Passive, Strong, Weak, Pleasure, Pain, Feeling (other than pleasure or pain), Arousal, Virtue, Vice, Overstated, Understated. The dictionary also includes an open-ended of set of semantic labels, e.g., *Human, Animate, …, Region, Route,…, Object, Vehicle,…, Fetch, Stay,…* (see http://www.wjh.harvard.edu/~inquirer/homecat.htm for an explanation of these labels). In these dictionaries, all labels are binary. For example, in the General Inquirer, the word *admire* has the labels (among others) corresponding to *Positive* and *Pleasure*. Words either possess the attribute or not; there is no question of degree.

---

[2] Computer recognition of emotion in human faces is a possibly related and now dynamic line of research. For one reference, see Brave and Nass (2002).

1.2 Recent Work

In addition to these manually labeled lexicons of affect words, recent experiments have attempted to find labels such as *positive* and *negative* automatically via statistical corpus analysis. Hatzivassiloglou and McKeown (1997) took a number of frequently occurring adjectives that they decided had an orientation and then used statistics on whether two adjectives appeared together in a corpus in the pattern *X and Y* to automatically classify adjectives as having positive or negative orientation. Essentially, words that co-occurred with each other in that pattern were considered as having the same polarity, and the bigger class of words was considered as having negative polarity (since there are more negative words than positive words in English). They achieved 92% accuracy over a set of 236 adjectives that they classified as positive or negative. Wiebe (2000) used a seed set of "subjective" adjectives and a thesaurus generation method (Hindle, 1990) to find more subjective adjectives. Turney and Littman (2003) found another effective way of deciding whether a word can be considered as positively or negatively charged. Given a set of words that they knew to be positively or negatively charged (using tagged words from Hatzivassiloglou's and McKeown's (1997) experiments and from the General Inquirer Lexicon), they tested how often each word would appear in the context of a set of positive paradigm words (*good, nice, excellent, positive, fortunate, correct, superior*) and a set of negative paradigm words (*bad, nasty, poor, negative, unfortunate, wrong, inferior*). Using a form of point-wise mutual information (Church and Hanks, 1989) and page statistics on word appearance on Altavista and word co-occurrence (within a window of ten words using the Altavista NEAR operator[3]) they classified as positively charged words the words that appeared most significantly with the set of positive paradigm words; and as negatively charged those appearing significantly more often with the negative paradigm words. Using this method, they achieved an accuracy of 98.2% with the 334 most frequently found adjectives in the Hatzivassiloglou and McKeown test set.

1.3 Our Approach

Both groups, Turney and Littman and Hatzivassiloglou and McKeown, begin with a set of words that they consider to be emotionally charged. In our experiments as described below, we try to find words that are probably negatively or positively charged automatically, in order to extend an existing lexicon of affect words.

We see affect words as occupying a ground between stop words, e.g., *the, in, a, is* and content words, e.g., *electricity, transfer, merger*. The boundary is not clear and distinct, as sometimes affect is carried by choice of different content words, e.g., *insurgent* or *terrorist*. And what qualifies as an affect word is ultimately a subjective decision. This notwithstanding, we propose here a method for evaluating the coverage of an affect lexicon, and we demonstrate a means for extending it.

2. The Current Clairvoyance Affect Lexicon

Beginning in the late 1990s, in connection with our development of text-mining configurations of Clairvoyance technology, we began exploring the "extra-semantic" dimensions of text, including emotion. At that time we developed a lexicon of affect words by hand (Subasic and Huettner, 2000a, 2000b, 2001; Huettner and Subasic, 2000). Entries in this lexicon consist of five fields: (i) a lemmatized word form, (ii) a simplified part of speech [adjective, noun, verb, adverb], (iii) an

---

[3] This operator was unfortunately eliminated from Altavista in the Spring of 2004.

affect class, (iv) a weight for the centrality of that word in that class, and (v) a weight for the intensity of the word in that class. The centrality of a word is a hand-assigned value between 0.0 and 1.0 that is intended to capture the relatedness of the word to the affect class. The intensity value attempts to capture the emotional strength of the word. For example in the sample entries given below, one sees that the adjective *gleeful* has been assigned to two affect classes (*happiness* and *excitement*) and that it has been deemed more related to the class *happiness*, with a centrality of 0.7, than it is to the class *excitement*, where the lexicon creators only gave it a centrality of 0.3.

"gleeful"	adj	happiness	0.7	0.6
"gleeful"	adj	excitement	0.3	0.6

In both entries, the word *gleeful* was deemed to have an intensity of 0.6 (out of a maximum intensity of 1). The combination of intensities and centralities made it possible to develop multidimensional weightings of affect in texts (Subasic and Huettner, 2000a, 2000b, 2001).

The existing lexicon contains 3,772 entries. A word form, such as *gleeful*, can appear in more than one entry. There are 2,258 different word forms (ranging from *abhor, abhorrence, abject, absurd, abuse, abusive, acclaim, accomplish* to *worth, wrong, wrongdoing, yawn, yearn, yearning, yen, yucky*). There are 86 different affect classes[4], such as *happiness* and *excitement* shown above. The numbers of entries for each affect class are given in Table 1.

Positive class	Negative class	Positive class	Negative class
Advantage (46)	Disadvantage (59)	Love (37)	Hate (28)
Amity (26)	Anger (28)	Loyalty (20)	Disloyalty (19)
Attraction (71)	Repulsion (70)	Morality (25)	Immorality (64)
Clarity (18)	Confusion (56)	Nurturance (35)	Harm (108)
Comfort (0)	Irritation (56)	Openness (47)	Slyness (82)
Cooperation (21)	Conflict (141)	Peace (21)	Violence (139)
Courage (44)	Fear (71)	Persuasion (26)	Force (102)
Creation (42)	Destruction (75)	Pleasure (33)	Pain (69)
Desire (39)	Avoidance (72)	Praise (36)	Slander (59)
Energy (27)	Fatigue (42)	Predictability (37)	Surprise (56)
Excitement (77)	Boredom (30)	Promise (22)	Warning (24)
Facilitation (13)	Prevention (36)	Public-spiritedness (1)	Crime (77)
Happiness (23)	Sadness (40)	Reasonableness (27)	Absurdity (19)
Health (13)	Sickness (14)	Responsibility (21)	Irresponsibility (33)
Honesty (21)	Deception (83)	Sanity (16)	Insanity (42)
Humility (24)	Pride (46)	Security (25)	Insecurity (24)
Humor (23)	Horror (50)	Selflessness (25)	Greed (55)
Innocence (20)	Guilt (40)	Sensitivity (16)	Insensitivity (32)
Intelligence (49)	Stupidity (32)	Strength (42)	Weakness (57)
Justice (70)	Injustice (41)	Success (43)	Failure (54)
Lively (0)	Death (31)	Superiority (108)	Inferiority (67)
		Surfeit (45)	Lack (75)

Table 1. List of paired (positive-negative) affect classes in the existing Clairvoyance lexicon, with number of headwords present for each class.

---

[4] The Humanity Quest Web site lists more than 500 different human values, similar to our affect classes. See http://web.archive.org/web/20031118174947/http://humanityquest.com/.

In any practical text-analysis application the question always arises whether the lexical resources are sufficient. In our case, we are interested in knowing whether our affect lexicon is complete. To answer this question, we decided to mine the Web using lexical patterns that we thought might be productive indicators of affect words. These patterns are described in the next section.

3. Emotive Patterns

Insults are highly charged with emotional content. Typical insults might be: "he is such a jerk/idiot/know-it-all!" The same pattern "he is such a ..." can also introduce a complimentary characterization: "he is such a prince/magnificent artist/all-around player!" After exploring a few such patterns by typing them into a Web browser and seeing what was brought back, we decided to test the patterns generated by the following procedure systematically:

> Create a pattern by constructing a two word phrase composed of one of these 21 words:
> {*appear, appears, appeared, appearing, feel, feels, feeling, felt, are, be, is, was, were, look, looked, looks, looking, seem, seems, seemed, seeming*}
> followed by one of the 5 words:
> {*almost, extremely, so, too, very*}

For each of these 105 patterns, e.g., "looking extremely...", we sent off a search request and extracted up to 4,000 text snippets containing the pattern from the results pages on www.alltheweb.com[5]. From each context snippet, we extracted the word appearing directly after the pattern. For example, for the pattern "looking extremely," we extracted "dubious" from the following snippet:

> The Christian Science Monitor: Hands-on art gets a grip on athletes inner self
> Famed baseball star Sammy Sosa is standing in a conference room in a downtown hotel here, **looking extremely dubious** about placing his hand in a pan of hot wax. Sculptor Raelee Frazier (in photos at right with Sosa) guides his right ...

The most common words appearing after this particular pattern "looking extremely" were the following:

    77 good
    52 pleased
    47 uncomfortable
    41 bored
    40 happy
    38 promising
    35 tired
    27 pissed
    27 pale

For example, "looking extremely promising" appeared in 38 of the 4000 snippets.

When we produce similar statistics for all the words appearing after any of the 105 patterns, we get the following list:

---

[5] 4,000 was the maximum number of page results that one could obtain from the AllTheWeb browser in 2004. Google and AltaVista limited their responses to 1,000 pages.

8957 good
2906 important
2506 happy
2455 small
2024 bad
1976 easy
1951 far
1745 difficult
1697 hard
1563 pleased

There were 15,111 different, inflected words found at least once immediately following the 105 patterns on the results pages returned by AllTheWeb. Although these patterns seem to give many affect words, e.g., *good, bad*, not all words, even at the top of the list, are affect words. In the next sections, we describe how we can judge whether a pattern is productive for finding affect words.

3.1 Two Gold Standards for Identifying Affect Words

In order to measure the productivity of these patterns, one of the authors examined each of the 4,746 words that appeared more than twice (out of the 15,111 words found at least once) after the patterns and decided subjectively, without referring to the existing affect lexicon, whether the word should be considered an emotion-bearing, affect word (2,988 words) or not (1,758 words). Some of the most frequently appearing words that were marked as an affect word by this author were: *good, important, happy, bad, easy, difficult, hard, pleased, nice, proud, comfortable, tired, helpful, impossible, busy*. Some of the most frequently appearing words that the author did not consider to be affect words were: *small, far, similar, different, high, long, large, close, simple, big, identical, exactly, low, late, real*. We call this adjudicated list the Manual Gold Standard (MGS) in our evaluations.

A second gold standard was produced by listing all the words found in the General Inquirer Lexicon that possessed one of the following affect-related labels: *Pos, Neg, Pstv, Ngtv, Negate, Hostile, Strng, Power, Weak, Subm, Pleasure, Pain, Arousal, EMOT, Feel, Virtue, Vice, IAV, SV, IPadj, IndAdj, EVAL*. (See http://www.wjh.harvard.edu/~inquirer/homecat.htm for explanation of these categories.) Of the 9,051 different headwords found in the General Inquirer Lexicon, 5,574 possessed at least one of these labels, and 3,477 others did not. We will call this set the General Inquirer Gold Standard (GIGS).

Given these two gold standards of affect/non-affect words, we judged both the productivity of the emotive patterns, as well as the coverage of our existing affect lexicon.

3.2 Evaluating the Productivity of Emotive Patterns

Each emotive pattern, e.g., "appears almost...", was evaluated by referring to the gold standard lists of affect/non-affect words described in the previous section. We tabulated the number of words produced by the pattern and found in the gold standard (in the column labeled *found*), the number of these words that the gold standard had listed as an affect word (= *good*) or non-affect word (= *bad*). If a candidate word found by the pattern was not in the gold standard, we did not count it. We discuss these cases below.

Table 2 shows the results for each set of emotive patterns against the Manual Gold Standard. Not all 105 patterns are shown here; each line corresponds to all the variants of a word given in the first column. For example, all the results for "seem almost", "seems almost", "seemed almost" and "seeming almost" are collated in the first line. In that line, we find that these patterns picked up 1,254 of the 4,746 words found in the Manual Gold Standard of affect/non-affect words, with 957 of these 1,254 words (precision 76%) corresponding to affect words. The patterns involving "extremely" had the best precision. and the patterns consisting of versions of "be so" had the best recall of words from the Manual Gold Standard, picking out 1,465 of the 2,988 affect words found there, but with a precision of only 71%.

Emotive pattern		found	good	bad	precision
seem	almost	1254	957	297	0.76
seem	extremely	1170	973	197	0.83
seem	so	1372	1095	277	0.80
seem	too	1220	1006	214	0.82
seem	very	1216	977	239	0.80
feel	almost	1092	785	307	0.72
feel	extremely	1082	860	222	0.79
feel	so	1086	830	256	0.76
feel	too	1120	844	276	0.75
feel	very	1160	905	255	0.78
appear	almost	1063	647	416	0.61
appear	extremely	*618*	*518*	**100**	**0.84**
appear	so	1170	857	313	0.73
appear	too	1178	897	281	0.76
appear	very	1344	1041	303	0.77
look	almost	996	667	329	0.67
look	extremely	1305	1014	291	0.78
look	so	1055	798	257	0.76
look	too	1106	755	351	0.68
look	very	1066	801	265	0.75
be	almost	1320	680	*640*	*0.52*
be	extremely	1541	1157	384	0.75
be	so	**2053**	**1465**	588	0.71
be	too	1393	1019	374	0.73

Table 2. Productivity and precision of emotive patterns against the Manual Gold Standard. The data in each row are summed over all variants of the word form in the first column, e.g., "appear too" covers results from "appears too", "appearing too", etc. The third column shows how many words in the gold standard were found after the patterns. The fourth and fifth columns show how many of these discovered words were marked as Affect or Non-Affect, respectively, in the gold standard. The last column shows the precision of the pattern for finding Affect words. The best numbers are shown in bold and the worst are shown in italics.

Table 3 shows the results for sets of emotive patterns against the General Inquirer Gold Standard. The patterns involving "extremely" once again had the best precision, with the patterns with "so" a close second. As before, the patterns consisting of versions of "be so" had the best recall of words from the gold standard, picking out 1,026 of the 5,574 General Inquirer lexicon words possessing an affect label, with a precision of 83%.

These results demonstrate that it is possible to identify lexical patterns for finding emotion-bearing, affect words with a high precision. The patterns that we used establish contexts for (and, hence, find) adjectives and participles. Other patterns must be used to find verbs and nouns, e.g., maybe a pattern such as *never dare to X* to select verbs.

Emotive pattern		found	good	bad	precision
seem	almost	743	584	159	0.79
seem	extremely	760	656	104	0.86
seem	so	902	766	136	0.85
seem	too	797	664	133	0.83
seem	very	828	693	135	0.84
feel	almost	564	439	125	0.78
feel	extremely	*547*	478	**69**	**0.87**
feel	so	600	512	88	0.85
feel	too	588	477	111	0.81
feel	very	657	547	110	0.83
appear	almost	630	447	183	0.71
appear	extremely	448	380	68	0.85
appear	so	811	685	126	0.84
appear	too	745	606	139	0.81
appear	very	911	766	145	0.84
look	almost	581	*426*	155	0.73
look	extremely	771	634	137	0.82
look	so	691	592	99	0.86
look	too	698	550	148	0.79
look	very	679	564	115	0.83
be	almost	843	576	*267*	*0.68*
be	extremely	1055	865	190	0.82
be	so	**1240**	**1026**	214	0.83
be	too	920	726	194	0.79
be	very	1163	924	239	0.79

Table 3. Productivity and precision of emotive patterns against the General Inquirer Gold Standard. The data in each row are summed over all variants of the word form in the first column, e.g., "appear too" covers results from "appears too", "appearing too", etc. The third column shows how many words in the gold standard were found after the patterns. The fourth and fifth columns show how many of these found words were marked as Affect or Non-Affect, respectively, in the gold standard. The last column shows the precision of the pattern for finding Affect words. The best numbers are shown in bold and the worst are shown in italics.

3.3 Evaluating the Coverage of Existing Affect Lexicons

The second part of our evaluation concerns verifying how many of the affect words identified as such in the hand-tagged gold standard are actually found in the existing affect lexicon developed in previous work (Subasic and Huettner, 2000a, 200b, 2001). There are 2,988 affect words marked in our Manual Gold Standard. Of these words, only 655 were found in our existing lexicon, which therefore has a coverage of 22%. Some of the words from the emotive patterns tested that were not in our lexicon are: *difficult, pleased, nice, comfortable, impossible, busy, young, old, strongly, hot, uncomfortable, expensive, interested, strange, interesting, lucky, sorry, normal, cold, familiar, grateful, professional, new, natural, complex, pretty, welcome, light, relaxed, rare, fast, likely, special, limited, early, lonely, serious, tight, vulnerable, certainly, upset, sweet, blessed, positive, human, unfashionable, unflattering, ungrounded, unhelpful, unhip, unimaginably, uninhibited, unintelligent, uninvolved, unladylike, unmanageable, unmatched, unnerving, unnoticeable, unpalatable, unpolished, unproductive, unqualified, unquestionable, unread, unresponsive, unrestricted, unruly, unsatisfying, unsexy, unspecific, unsuitable, unwatchable, unwelcoming, upfront, uppity, venomous, victimized, vindicated, virile, visceral, wan, watchful, weighty, weirded, wellcome, well-kept, well-qualified, well-read, well-researched.*

The intersection between the General Inquirer and our existing Clairvoyance affect lexicon contains only 1,292 of the 5,574 affect tagged words. Some of these missing words are *abandon, abandonment, abate, abdicate, abide, able, abnormal, abolish, abominable, abound, abrasive, abrupt, abscond, absence, absent, absent-minded, absentee, absolute, absolve, absorbent, absorption, absurdity, abundance, abundant, abyss, accede, accelerate, acceleration, accentuate, accept, acceptable, acceptance, accessible, accession, accident, acclamation, accolade, accommodate, accommodation, accompaniment,...*

The intersection between the Manual Gold Standard and the General Inquirer Gold Standard has 1,295 words. Here are some words not marked with affect labels listed above in the General Inquirer: *young, impressed, slow, complicated, relaxed, obvious, likely, concerned, early, tight, embarrassed, dry, knowledgeable, exclusively, totally, sexy, inclined, instantly, informative, distant, overwhelmed, quickly, quick, nonexistent, carefully, effortless, crowded, isolated, surreal, exhausted, personal, finished, stressed, detailed, easily, sleepy, diverse, loose, restrictive, annoyed,...* Some of these words can be derived from words appearing in the General Inquirer, e.g., *relaxed* from *relax, annoyed* from *annoy,* and other words are not marked with affect labels but with other labels (e.g., *young* is marked as a time interval) since the purpose of the General Inquirer Lexicon is not limited to analyzing affect, but to serve as a resource for more general text analysis.

From this analysis it can be concluded that the definitive affect lexicon has not yet been created and that there is room for improvement in existing affect lexicons.

4. Scoring the Intensity of Candidate Affect Words

In the previous section, it was stated that the 105 emotive patterns had uncovered 4,746 words that appeared in the patterns three or more times from the snippets retrieved. These words were classified by hand as affect or non-affect bearing words to form our Manual Gold Standard. Rather than classifying these terms by hand, as we did to create the gold standard, one might use the automatic ranking technique for calculating the polarity of an unknown word described by Turney and Littman (2003). We replicated this technique of calculating point-wise mutual information with positive-negative paradigm words described in this article and applied it to the words extracted by our emotive patterns.

Our application of this technique proceeded as follows. Each candidate affect word was used to create a series of 14 requests to AltaVista. Each request placed the word with one of the paradigm words using the NEAR operator. For example, given the word *comfortable*, a series of AltaVista requests was created as shown in Table 4, in which we also show the number of pages that AltaVista found containing the pair of words near each (within ten words, according to AltaVista).

Negative Paradigm Queries	Page Counts
comfortable NEAR bad	13127
comfortable NEAR nasty	1008
comfortable NEAR poor	6943
comfortable NEAR negative	3836
comfortable NEAR unfortunate	535
comfortable NEAR wrong	8449
comfortable NEAR inferior	437
Positive Paradigm Queries	Page Counts
comfortable NEAR good	184024
comfortable NEAR nice	57757
comfortable NEAR excellent	95119
comfortable NEAR positive	13259
comfortable NEAR fortunate	1276
comfortable NEAR correct	7952
comfortable NEAR superior	39182

Table 4. Example of some of the raw data used in the Turney and Littman (2003) method. For a given word, here "comfortable," one sends requests to a Web search engine to find how many times the word co-occurs with negative connotation words or with positive connotation words. Here we show the page counts from Altavista.

Nwords	Pages	Pwords	Pages
bad	24576337	good	54596054
nasty	3712598	nice	17084308
poor	10813343	excellent	15955669
negative	7430078	positive	11797788
unfortunate	1174016	fortunate	1357375
wrong	13037886	correct	14187506
inferior	1565672	superior	9377519

Table 5. To calculate point-wise mutual information, one also needs the page counts of the negative and positive paradigm words, such as given here by Altavista in early 2004.

$$\text{SO - PMI}(word) = \log_2 \left(\frac{\prod_{pword \ pwords} \text{hits}(word \text{ NEAR } pword) \cdot \prod_{nword \ Nwords} \text{hits}(nword)}{\prod_{pword \ pwords} \text{hits}(pword) \cdot \prod_{nword \ Nwords} hits(word \text{ NEAR } pword)} \right)$$

Figure 1. The point-wise mutual information formula from Turney and Littman (2003). "Pwords" is the set of positive paradigm words (here, as in that article, we used the set {good, nice, excellent, positive, fortunate, correct, superior}) and "Nwords" is the set of negative paradigm words ({bad, nasty, poor, negative, unfortunate, wrong, inferior}).

Using the point-wise mutual information formula from Turney and Littman (2003), shown in Figure 1, and the Altavista page statistics for the positive paradigm Pwords and the negative paradigm Nwords, shown in Tables 4 and 5, one finds a point-wise mutual information score for *comfortable* of 10.6553. This shows the word is more strongly associated with the positive paradigm words than the negative paradigm words, and thus is probably more positively charged. When the same calculations are applied to all the 4,746 words discovered by the affect patterns of Section 3, eliminating the 156 words that appears fewer than 100 times with all the positive and negative paradigm words (e.g., *sticklike, identical, featurerich*[6], *easytouse, shuai, goodthe,...*), we find the highest and lowest ranking words to be as given in Table 6.

SO-PMI Score	
37.5	knowlegeable
33.6	tailormade
32.9	eyecatching
29.0	huggable
26.2	surefooted
24.6	timesaving
22.9	personable
21.9	welldone
21.0	handdrawn
20.8	commonsensical
20.0	homelike
20.0	hightech
...	...
-15.1	unaccomplished
-15.6	inelegant
-15.9	spindly
-15.9	childishly
-16.2	simpleminded
-16.2	blasphemous
-17.1	underdressed
-17.5	uncreative
-18.1	disapproving
-18.5	meanspirited
-18.6	unwatchable
-22.7	discombobulated

Table 6. Point-wise mutual information scores for some words discovered by the affect patterns.

While the words with very high or very low scores seem to be affect-laden words, as Turney and Littman (2003) have found, the words around 0.0 are less clear-cut. For example, between SO-PMI scores of 0.5 and -0.5 we find word like: *jaunty, julia, jumping, kick, km, know, knowing, labor, ladies, laid, late, learned, lend, liberal, life, lit, lithe, localized, loveable, luscious, magic, main, manmade, materially, military, mindboggling, miss, missed, misty,* some of which we would classify as affect words. This SO-PMI could thus be used to rank words for inclusion in an affect dictionary, with words at extreme points (involving a threshold) included automatically and others treated manually.

---

[6] One step in our text processing removed hyphens from words, so a term like *feature-rich* was treated as the string *featurerich*, which leads to its low counts. *Feature-rich* (with the hyphen) appears often on the web, but was not tested in the experiments described here.

4.1 Automatically Placing Words along other Semantic Axes

Another point to consider in the case of an affect lexicon including not just positive and negative orientation but affect classes as seen in the Clairvoyance affect lexicon (see Section 2) is how to decide in which class the new words should be included. We have been experimenting with extending Turney's and Littman's (2003) technique, as they suggested, to different semantic scales. For each of the 86 affect classes (cf. Table 1) defined in our lexicon, we manually selected 4 to 6 paradigm words. For example, here are the paradigm words we chose for some of these classes:

- **praise** – *acclaim, praise, congratulations, homage, approval*
- **slander** – *bad-mouth, calumniate, calumny, defamation, slander*
- **comfort** – *comfort, comfortable, solace, comforting*
- **irritation** – *aggravate, aggravation, irritation, irritate, bothersome*
- **pleasure** – *pleasure, enjoy, delight, joy, pleasing*
- **pain** – *agony, hurt, pain, nuisance, painful, hurting*
- **excitement** – *agitate, agitation, exciting, excitement, stimulating*
- **boredom** – *boredom, boring, wearisome, tedious, tiresome*
- **humility** – *humble, humility, abject, modest, modesty*
- **pride** – *arrogance, arrogant, proud, prideful, pride*
- **confusion** – *confuse, confusion, unclear, confused, jumbled*

Having chosen such sets for each of the 86 affect classes, we ran queries placing the words that we wish to classify in a semantic class with the NEAR operator and each of these paradigm words as described in Section 3 with positive and negative paradigm words. Since we are not comparing polar endpoints, we used the following formula to produce a score:

$$\text{Score}(word, Class) = \log_2 \left(\frac{\prod_{cword \in Class} \text{hits}(word \text{ NEAR } cword)}{\prod_{cword \in Class} \log_2(\text{hits}(cword))} \right)$$

where *cword* is one of the paradigmatic words chosen for an affect class *Class*, and *hits* is the number of pages found by Altavista. The extra logarithm in the denominator was added only to scale the resulting score, since the counts of the *cword*s were many orders of magnitude larger than the counts of the paired words. Given a candidate affect word, this score is calculated for each of the 86 classes.

As an example of the application of this score, the word *discombobulated* scores highest with paradigm words for semantic classes: **confusion** (score: 0.634), **surprise** (-4.05), **pleasure** (-6.89),… Table 7 gives some other words and the highest scoring classes.

It would seem that this extension of Turney and Littman's (2003) technique to other semantic classes, which relies on finding co-occurrences with paradigms to choose semantic classes, similar to Turney's (2001) work on the finding of the closest synonyms, might allow us to automate the assignment of affect class centrality.

aversion	Hate (15.98), Pain (15.02), ...
award	Success (33.21), Praise (33.12), ...
awful	Pain(28.88), Horror (26.24), ...
back-biting	Deception(4.77), Slander (4.46), ...
back-stabbing	Conflict (4.16), Disloyalty (3.79), ...
banditry	Security (5.48), Violence (3.49), ...
barbaric	Violence (13.89), Horror (12.87), ...
barbarity	Horror (9.20), Surprise (5.66), ...

Table 7. Highest scoring semantic classes for some words discovered by the affect patterns, using an extension of the Turney & Littman (2003) technique to other semantic axes.

Once a class is assigned, intensity might be represented by re-using the SO-PMI formula, but with the paradigm words of the positive and negative class members. For example, for the table above, we see that *awful* is central to *Pain*. In table 1, we see that the *Pain* class is associated with the *Pleasure* class. Using the *Pleasure* paradigm words (*pleasure, enjoy, delight, joy, pleasing*) as the P*words* and the *Pain* paradigm words (*agony, hurt, pain, nuisance, painful, hurting*) as the N*words* gives us an SO-PMI $_{Pleasure-Pain}$ score for *awful* of -1.25, showing that *awful* has a moderate intensity along the negative axis *Pain*.

5. Future Work

In this chapter, we described our use of a few emotive patterns for discovering adjectives. One direction of our future work is to expand the set of emotive patterns used for extracting affect words. We have begun to mine these patterns automatically from the Web using affect words as seeds, gathering a large number of web pages containing both an existing affect word and its affect class name. From such pages, we have begun extracting patterns, e.g., *to their, the most, full of,* appearing before known affect words. These discovered affect patterns may yield new sets of candidate words.

Another direction for future work is confirming that the promising techniques proposed by Turney and Littman (2003) for finding negative–positive polarity can be used for automatically assigning class centrality and intensity, as the results from the previous section promise.

Another avenue to explore concerns alternative methods for placing words along a class axis. Horn (1969) proposed using the pattern *X even Y*, e.g., *silly even ridiculous*, to distinguish which element of *X* and *Y* is more intense along a scaled dimension, such as one of our affect dimensions of Table 1. Such patterns may be usefully explored on the Web as another way to align words along an axis, as suggested by Hatzivassiloglou and McKeown (1993). A quick check on Google in early 2004 shows that the contiguous phrase *silly even ridiculous* can be found on 13 pages, while *ridiculous even silly* is only found once[7]. It might be useful to try this, or other such patterns, to verify an internal ranking along a dimension.

---

[7] Using *silly even...* as a search patterns brings up other adjectives such as *useful* and *offensive* which might not be regarded as belonging to the same affect dimension, so one stills requires a mechanism to find words in the same dimension in order to exploit this *X even Y* pattern.

6. Conclusions

We have explored a method for identifying rich sources for discovering new emotion-laden affect words via emotive lexical patterns. Using the patterns to mine the Web, we retrieved large numbers of affect words. These new words can be used to identify missing items in existing lexicons. We have shown that Turney and Littman's (2003) paradigm word co-occurrence scoring can be used to identify a certain number of the missing items as likely affect words. We have also shown that a similar technique of word co-occurrence with paradigm words might identify the likely centrality of new words among 43 pairs of positively and negatively oriented affect classes. Finally, we have preliminary results that suggest that extending Turney and Littman's approach to these semantic axes may provide an automatic way to find the intensity of new words.

7. Bibliography

Brave, S. and Nass, C. (2002) Emotion in human-computer interaction. In Jacko, J. and Sears, A. (Eds.) *The Human-Computer Interaction Handbook: Fundamentals, Evolving Technologies and Emerging Applications*. Lawrence Erlbaum Associates, Inc., Mahwah, NJ.

Berlin, B. and Kay, P. (1969) *Basic color terms: their universality and evolution*. University of California Press, Berkeley.

Church, K. W. and Hanks, P. (1989) Word association norms, mutual information and lexicography. In *Proceedings of the 27th Annual Conference of the Association of Computational Linguistics*. 76–82.

Deese, J. (1964) The Associative Structure of some Common English Adjectives. *Journal of Verbal Learning and Verbal Behavior 3(5)*. 347–357.

Hatzivassiloglou, V. and McKeown, K. R. (1993) Towards the automatic identification of adjectival scales: Clustering adjectives according to meaning. In *Proceedings of 31st Annual Meeting of the Association for Computational Linguistics*. 172–182.

Hatzivassiloglou, V. and McKeown, K. R. (1997) Predicting the semantic orientation of adjectives. In *Proceedings 35th Annual Meeting of the Association for Computational Linguistics*. 174–181.

Hindle, D. (1990) Noun classification from predicate argument structures. In *Proceedings of the 28th Annual Meeting of the Association for Computational Linguistics*. 268–275.

Horn, L. (1969) A Presuppositional Analysis of Only and Even. In *Papers from the 5th Regional Meeting of the Chicago Linguistics Society*. 98–107.

Huettner, A. and Subasic, P. (2000) Fuzzy Typing for Document Management. In *ACL 2000 Software Demonstration*.

Lasswell, H. D. and Namenwirth, J. Z. (1969) *The Lasswell Value Dictionary*. Yale University Press, New Haven.

Lehrer, A. (1974) *Semantic Fields and Lexical Structure*. North Holland, London.

Levinson, S. C. (1983) *Pragmatics*. Cambridge University Press, Cambridge, UK.

Stone, P. J., Dunphy, D. C., Smith, M. S., and Ogilvie, D. M. (1966) *The General Inquirer: A Computer Approach to Content Analysis*. MIT Press, Cambridge, MA.

Subasic, P. and Huettner, A. (2000a) Affect Analysis of Text Using Fuzzy Semantic Typing. In *Proceedings of FUZZ-IEEE 2000*.

Subasic, P. and Huettner, A. (2000b) Calculus of Fuzzy Semantic Typing for Qualitative Analysis of Text. In *Proceedings of ACM KDD 2000 Workshop on Text Mining*.

Subasic, P. and Huettner, A. (2001) Affect Analysis of Text Using Fuzzy Semantic Typing. *IEEE Transactions on Fuzzy Systems, Special Issue*.

Teufel, S. and Moens, M. (2002) Summarizing Scientific Articles – Experiments with Relevance and Rhetorical Status. *Computational Linguistics, 28 (4)*.

Turney, P. D. (2001) Mining the Web for Synonyms: PMI-IR versus LSA on TOEFL. In *Proceedings of the Twelfth European Conference on Machine Learning (ECML2001)*. 491–502.

Turney, P. D. and Littman, M. L. (2003) Measuring praise and criticism: Inference of semantic orientation from association. *ACM Transactions on Information Systems (TOIS), 21(4)*, 315–346.

Wiebe, J. (2000) Learning subjective adjectives from corpora. In *Proceedings of AAAI 2000*. 735–740.

Chapter 10

A Computational Semantic Lexicon of French Verbs of Emotion

Yvette Yannick Mathieu
Laboratoire de linguistique formelle – CNRS
Université Paris 7
CP.7031, 2 place Jussieu
75251 Paris cedex 05 – France
Email: ymathieu@linguist.jussieu.fr

Abstract

A computational semantic lexicon of French verbs of feeling, emotion, and psychological states is presented here, as well as *FEELING*, a software program using this lexicon to provide an interpretation and to generate paraphrases. Semantic representations are described by means of a set of feature structures. Sixty newspaper "letters to the Editor" were taken as a domain for the evaluation of this work.

Keywords: semantic lexicon, computational lexicon, emotion, feeling, psychological verbs, semantic classes.

1. Introduction

A computational semantic lexicon of verbs of feeling, emotion and psychological states is presented here, as well as *FEELING,* a software program using this lexicon to provide an interpretation and to generate paraphrases. A prototype-based organization of this lexicon with inheritance mechanism, feeling intensity and antonymy graphs, and a linguistic knowledge database is proposed.

2. Semantic Lexicon Description

A corpus of 950 French words for emotions and psychological states was studied. Of them, 600 are verbs, like *aimer* (to love), *effrayer* (to frighten), and *irriter* (to irritate), whereas 350 are nouns, like *amour* (love) and *colère* (anger). A semantic classification in which verbs and nouns are split into semantic classes according to their meaning is proposed. The hypothesis is that language reflects the way one conceptualizes the world, and that words with close meanings have similar formal behaviors. This classification is similar to the works on feelings of Johnson-Laird and Oatley (1989) and Wierzbicka (1996).

2.1 Verbs and Semantic Classes

French verbs for feelings and psychological states occur in two kinds of structures, as illustrated in sentences (1) and (2), respectively.

(1)   *Paul irrite Marie*
       Paul irritates Marie

(2)   *Marie hait Paul*
       Marie hates Paul

These structures differ by the syntactic position of the person (*Marie*), called the "experiencer", who has the feeling or the emotion. In (1), the experiencer is the complement, and the subject (*Paul*) is the cause of her feeling (irritation). In (2), the experiencer is the subject and the complement *Paul* is the object of her feeling (hate). About 500 verbs belong to the first category and 100 belong to the second. Since the linguistic behaviors of these verbs are very different, two separate analyses were made. Verbs of the first category (e.g., irriter) were designated psychological verbs and divided into 33 semantic classes (cf. Table 1), with each class including verbs with the same meaning.

18 classes of **NEGATIVE** (or unpleasant) **FEELING**					
/aigrir/ to embitter	/attrister/ to sadden	/décevoir/ to disappoint	/déconcerter/ to disconcert	/dégoûter/ to disgust	/démoraliser/ to demoralize
/déranger/ to disturb	/effarer/ to alarm	/effrayer/ to frighten	/endurcir/ to harden	/irriter/ to irritate	/froisser/ to hurt
/inhiber/ to inhibit	/lasser/ to tire	/meurtrir/ to bruise	/obséder/ to obsess	/révolter/ to revolt	/tracasser/ to worry

13 classes of **POSITIVE** (or pleasant) **FEELING**					
/calmer/ to calm down	/désarmer/ to disarm	/distraire/ to entertain	/émoustiller/ to titillate	/émouvoir/ to move	/épater/ to impress
/fasciner/ to fascinate	/flatter/ to flatter	/intéresser/ to interest	/passionner/ to inspire passion	/rassurer/ to reassure	/satisfaire/ to satisfy
/vivifier/ to invigorate					

2 classes of **NEUTRAL FEELING**		
/indifférer/ to be indifferent to	/étonner/ to astonish	

Table 1. Semantic classes of French psychological verbs.

Two French dictionaries (Le Grand Robert de la Langue Française 2001, Le Trésor de la Langue Française 1971-1994), the Lexicon-Grammar of French Verbs studied by Gross (1975), and a large electronic corpus, Frantext, (2004) which contains 1250 texts from novels and stories, were used to build this classification. A large panel of native speakers verified this classification.

From a prototypical point of view, one verb of a class represents and can replace all the verbs in a class, and it also names the class. This name is written between slashes. For instance, the class /irriter/ contains verbs which mean "to cause annoyance", such as to aggravate, to irritate, or to exasperate.

The 33 classes of verbs fall into one of three categories of verbs:

a) Negative verbs which indicate the experience or causation of a rather unpleasant feeling, such as irritation, fear, or disappointment. They are divided into eighteen classes, for example, /irriter/, /effrayer/ (= "to cause fear": to affright, to frighten, to scare), or /attrister/ (= "to cause a feeling of sadness": to grieve, to sadden).

b) Positive verbs which mean the experience or the causation of a rather pleasant feeling, such as interest or fascination. They are divided into thirteen classes, for example, /intéresser/ (= "to cause interest": to interest) or /fasciner/ (= "to cause an irresistible attraction or interest": to fascinate).

c) Neutral verbs which mean the experience or the causation of a feeling that is neither pleasant nor unpleasant, like astonishment or indifference. They belong to two classes: /étonner/ (= "to cause a feeling of surprise": to astonish, to surprise) and /indifférer/ (to be indifferent to).

A difficulty is that the polarity of the verbs belonging to /étonner/class depends on the context. For example, in the sentence *La hauteur de la tour Eiffel surprend les touristes* (The Eiffel Tower's height surprises the tourists), the surprise felt by the tourist is neutral, whereas the meaning of *Le cadeau d'anniversaire de Paul surprend Marie* (Paul's birthday gift surprises Marie) is rather pleasant if usually Paul forgets Marie's birthday, and the meaning of *La cruauté de Paul surprend Marie* (Paul's cruelty surprises Marie) is rather unpleasant. Clearly, the classification of /étonner/ as a neutral class does not resolve this problem, which is why the current research is directed towards taking context into account.

2.2 Relationships between Semantic Classes

Semantic classes are linked by three types of relationships: meaning, intensity, and antonymy, which are represented with simple graphs.

Intensity and meaning graphs are connected graphs, shown partially in Figure 1. The figure is divided into three parts: the "unpleasant" classes, with a negative polarity, to the left, the classes with a positive polarity stand to the right, and the neutral classes are in the middle (the /indifférer/ class is not represented in Figure 1). The intensity graph is oriented according to intensity of experienced feeling.

There is a "no feeling state" represented by a white circle noted NFS. Labeled arcs join this state to semantic classes. These arcs can be labeled by more specific features like "admiration", or by intensity degree represented by the symbol ▶ .

For example, the arc labeled "intérêt" (interest) joins the no feeling state to the **/intéresser/** class (to interest, to attract, to tempt, to entice, etc.). An interest increase on **/intéresser/** class verbs is described by **/passionner/** (to inspire passion) class verbs (to devour, to excite, to overexcite, to electrify, to fire, to carry away, to enthuse, etc.).

A stronger emotion of passion is reflected by **/fasciner/** class verbs (to fascinate, to intoxicate, to hypnotize, to mesmerize, etc.).

A graph contains antonymy links between classes. A subset is given in Figure 2, where the antonymy between classes is represented with an arc and the symbol ↔. As an example, the **/irriter/** class is antonymous with the **/calmer/** (to calm) class, meaning that each verb in the first class is antonymous with at least one verb in the second class (to mellow, to calm down, to relax, etc.) and vice versa.

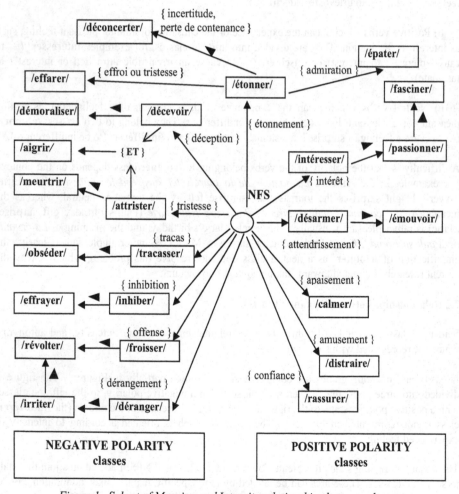

Figure 1. Subset of Meaning and Intensity relationships between classes.

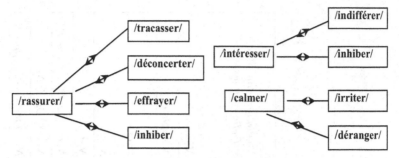

Figure 2. Subset of Antonymy relationships between semantic classes.

2.3 Linguistic Properties of Verbs

The linguistic properties of verbs and classes were examined. Among them, 15 are binary, while others are more complex such as arguments selection or arguments structure. Described here is a subset of these two types of properties (for a full description see Mathieu (2000)).

2.3.1 Simple Properties

A subset of these properties for the /**irriter**/ class is shown in Table 2. The first row represents the whole class (e.g. /**irriter**/), then each following row is a verb (*agacer, courroucer*, etc.), and each column is a property. A plus sign indicates that a verb accepts the property or is accepted in a given sentence form.

A brief description of these properties follows:

- [*Nominalization*]. For each verb (noted *V*), a nominalization (or deverbal, noted *V-n*) is associated, if it exists, as in *irriter/irritation*. This noun denotes either the feeling or emotion felt by the experiencer (*irritation*), or a noun qualifying the subject: in *Luc charme/séduit Marie* (Luc charms Marie), the charm is Luc's charm.

- [*N_0 agentive*]. All the psychological verbs accept a non agentive subject. Some accept an agentive one also. The subject is noted N_0. A plus sign for this property indicates that a sentence like *Luc effraye Marie* (Luc frightens Marie) has two possible meanings: that Luc frightens Marie because he wants (the subject is agentive), or he frightens her unintentionally, by his behavior or his appearance, or something else (the subject is non agentive).

- [*Metaphor*]. Some verbs have a psychological meaning only, like *aimer*, while others, such as *irriter*, have two meanings: one that is "basic" (3), and one that is psychological by metaphor (4):

(3) *Le soleil irrite Marie (sa peau)*
     The sun irritates Marie (her skin)

(4) *Paul irrite Marie* (par son comportement)
     Paul irritates Marie (by his behavior)

		Nominalization (V-n) = feeling felt by N₁	N₀ agentive	Metaphor	Intensifier	N₁ V	N₁ se V	N₁ est Vpp (de ce) que P	N₁ est Vpp de N₀	N₁ est un N (N = Vppadj)
	/irriter/								+	
	agacer	agacement	+	-	neutral	-	+	-	+	-
	courroucer	courroux	+	-	*high*	-	-	+	+	-
	crisper	crispation	+	+	neutral	-	+	+	+	+
	énerver	énervement	+	+	neutral	-	+	+	+	+
	enquiquiner		+	-	neutral	-	-	-	+	-
	enrager	rage	+	-	*high*	+	-	-	+	-
	exaspérer	exaspération	+	-	*high*	-	+	+	+	-
	excéder		+	-	*high*	-	-	-	+	-
	fâcher		+	-	neutral	-	+	+	+	-
	hérisser		-	+	*high*	-	-	+	+	-
	horripiler		-	-	*high*	-	+	-	+	-
IRRITATION	impatienter	impatience	-	-	*high*	-	-	+	+	-
	irriter	irritation	+	+	neutral	-	+	+	+	-
	offusquer		-	-	neutral	-	+	-	+	-
	stresser	stress	+	-	neutral	+	-	-	+	-
	ulcérer		-	+	*high*	-	-	-	+	-

Table 2. Simple properties.

- [***Intensifier***]. Intensity relationships link verbs inside each class, with an order relation. Thus, *exaspérer* (to exasperate) and *irriter* are in the same /**irriter**/ class, but *exaspérer* is stronger than *irriter*. These internal intensity relationships between verbs are described by the property *Intensifier* with the value "neutral" for *irriter*, and the value "high" for *exaspérer*.

The next properties indicates that a verb V can occur in a construction with the complement (= the experiencer N_1) in subject position.

- [*N_1 V*]. The construction is intransitive, as in *Paul enrage* (lit. Paul enrages) or *Paul déprime* (lit. Paul depresses).

- [*N_1 se V*]. The verb becomes a reflexive, as in *Paul s'énerve* or *Paul s'irrite* (lit. Paul irritates himself). Reflexive verbs are common in French: about one third of psychological verbs are reflexive.

- [*N_1 est Vpp de ce que P*], [*N_1 est Vpp de N_0*]. The verb past participle is noted *Vpp*, and *P* represents a sentence. The passive form with the preposition *par* (by) as in *Paul est exaspéré par* *l'attitude de Marie* (Paul is exasperated by Marie's behavior), is possible for all the verbs. This property is implicit. For some verbs, the preposition *de* (of) can also appear in passive constructions, like *Paul est exaspéré de l'attitude de Marie, Paul est exaspéré (de ce) que Marie ait cette attitude* (lit. Paul is exasperated of Marie's behavior, lit. Paul is exasperated of that Marie has this behaviour). The sequence *de ce* is within parentheses because it can be omitted.

- **[N_1 est un N (N=Vppadj)]**. The noun *N* is a conversion of the verb's adjectival past participle *Vppadj*, like *Paul est un énervé* (lit. Paul is an irritated). Adjectival past participles are past participles which have the properties of qualifying adjectives (See also, Kerleroux 1996, Mathieu 2000).

2.3.2 Complex Properties

Whereas simple properties are attribute-value pairs, others are more complex such as argument selection and argument structure.

The form of the subject of the French psychological verbs is free; it can be a sentence, an abstract or concrete noun phrase, or an infinitive.

The complement (= the experiencer) is always a person, like Marie in the sentence (1) *Paul irrite Marie*, or some metonymical expressions referring to a person. The form of these expressions is preferentially "Det N de Nhum" (Determinant Noun of Human-noun). There are three main categories of noun (N), according to how distant the metonymy is from the person (Nhum); it can be (*i*) a body part (or "soul part") like *coeur* (heart) ou *esprit* (mind), (*ii*) a feeling or quality name (anger, vanity, etc.), or (*iii*) a noun such as hopes, convictions, etc.

Some verbs select nouns of the first category only, like *briser* (to break) in *Marie a brisé le coeur de Luc* (Marie broke Luc's heart), some verbs select nouns of the second category also, like *apaiser* or *calmer* in *La chanson a apaisé/calmé la colère de Marie* (The song calmed down Marie's anger), or *blesser* in *Les moqueries de Paul ont blessé l'orgueil de Marie* (Paul's taunts wounded Marie's pride), and other verbs accept nouns of the third category, such as *satisfaire* (to satisfy) in *Les paroles de Marie ont satisfait les espoirs de Luc* (Marie's words satisfied Luc's hopes). Moreover, 110 verbs like *irriter* or *déconcerter* (to disconcert) accept non-human complements, although with difficulty.

The subject and object are linked semantically, as shown by sentences (5) and (6), where a question mark indicates a sentence accepted with difficulty.

(5) a   *La jalousie/ passion ronge le cœur de Marie*
         Jealousy/passion gnaws at Marie's heart

   b   *? La jalousie/ passion ronge l'esprit de Marie*
         ? Jealousy/passion gnaws at Marie's mind

(6) a   *? La peur du chômage ronge le cœur de Marie*
         ? Unemployment fear gnaws at Marie's heart

   b   *La peur du chômage ronge l'esprit de Marie*
         Unemployment fear gnaws at Marie's mind

Even if it is not easy to determine the semantic link between subject and object, one can say that nouns of feeling in the subject position are associated preferentially to the metonymy *le coeur* (the heart) rather than *l'esprit* (the mind), and that to the complement *l'esprit* an abstract subject like a thought is preferentially associated.

3. *FEELING* System

The *FEELING* system is a software program that uses the semantic lexicon to provide an interpretation and to generate paraphrases. It contains four main components: (1) a communication interface, (2) a semantic knowledge database, (3) an inheritance mechanism, and (4) a knowledge treatment module. The following describes how the knowledge is formalized in the database, which knowledge this database contains, and which mechanisms apply to this knowledge (inheritance and inference engine).

3.1 Knowledge Representation

The semantic database contains the knowledge of the classes and verbs, represented in prototype-based format (Rosch, 1975; Kleiber, 1990), and the graphs describing the relationships between classes and a set of rules.

3.1.1 Prototype and Inheritance Mechanism

Studies in cognitive psychology have shown that, for human beings, the real world objects are structured into categories (Rosch, 1975). However, all items from the same category are not equally representative: a prototype is chosen as the medium item, considered the better representative of the category. A set of features shared by most category items characterizes this prototype.

Each class is represented by its prototype, and each verb is a prototype specialisation. An inheritance mechanism allows sharing knowledge between a class and its verbs.

A root prototype contains the knowledge shared by all verb classes, like [the object is human] or the passive construction [N_1 est Vpp par N_0]. An analogy is drawn between semantic classes and prototypes. Each verb is derived from and inherits properties and rules from one prototype. An example is given in Figure 3.

The /**irriter**/ prototype (or semantic class), which has the [subject is agentive] and [Intensifier neutral] properties, inherits the [object is human] property from the root prototype. Each /**irriter**/ class verb, like *exaspérer, énerver,* etc. inherits these two properties. The inheritance is not monotonic: the verb *exaspérer* has the value "high" for the Intensifier, and this value hides the inherited neutral value (written in bold in Figure 3).

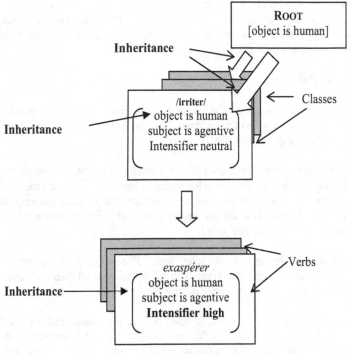

Figure 3. Inheritance.

3.1.2 Inference Engine and Pathfinding Algorithms

An inference engine processes a set of production rules describing conditions to generate well formed paraphrases. These rules are written in declarative format [**Si** (if) condition(s) **Alors** (then) conclusion(s)], without linkage. Simple pathfinding algorithms are associated with the different graphs.

Inheritance mechanisms, inference engines, and pathfinding algorithms are used to exploit the knowledge database.

3.2 Knowledge Database

The knowledge is described by attribute-value pairs and lists, ordered or not ordered, depending on the data type.

3.2.1 Knowledge Associated with Each Class

Each class is characterized by (1) its semantic polarity: negative (unpleasant feeling), neutral (feeling neither unpleasant nor pleasant), or positive (pleasant feeling), (2) the feeling expressed, (3) its antonymous classes, (4) which verbs its contains, (5) the semantic category of the complement (the experiencer metonymy) when a metonymy is possible (is it a complete metonymy, like heart or soul, or a sentiment or a quality ?), (6) a set of simple linguistic properties, with, for each, the value of the representative verb of the class (the prototype), and (7) a list of paraphrasing rules. Each verb is characterized by a set of linguistic properties whose values are different from class values.

3.2.2 Graphs and Rules

The knowledge database also contains the meaning, intensity and antonymy graphs, and a set of 40 paraphrasing rules. Two types of paraphrasing are considered: synonymous words substitution and syntactic restructuring (Mel'čuk, 1992).

Paraphrasing with synonymic substitution does not modify the syntactic structure. In the initial sentence, the verb is exchanged for a verb belonging to the same semantic class. The intensity of the feeling is preserved, either with verbs that have the same value for the property [Intensifier], or with verbs with a different value for this property and with the adjunction of a modifier like *beaucoup* (much), *très* (very), or *peu* (little).

For example, if the verb has an intensity level "high," like *exaspérer*, its synonyms are *excéder, horripiler, hérisser, ulcérer,* etc., or verbs with an intensity level "neutral" and the modifier *beaucoup* like *énerver beaucoup, agacer beaucoup,* etc.

Three types of paraphrasing with syntactic restructuring were used: reflexive sentences (*Paul s'exaspère*) (lit. Paul exasperates himself), nominalization, with complement deletion (*Paul éprouve de l'exaspération*, lit. Paul feels exasperation) or without (*Paul éprouve de l'exaspération devant l'attitude de Marie*, lit. Paul is feeling exasperation at Marie's attitude), and passivization.

There are three types of passivization:

    - with complement deletion as in *Paul est exaspéré* (lit. Paul is exasperated),

    - with complement introduced by p*ar* (by) as in *Paul est exaspéré **par** l'attitude de Marie* (Paul is exasperated by Marie's behavior),

    - and with complement introduced by *de* (of) like *Paul est exaspéré **de** l'attitude de Marie* (lit. Paul is exasperated of Marie's behavior).

The semantics of the verb and its arguments constrain the possibility of paraphrases. Thus, when the subject of the active form is a human name, as *Paul* in *Paul déçoit Luc* (Paul disappoints Luc) or *Paul énerve Luc* (Paul irritates Luc), the passive sentence with "de" is possible only for some verbs. One can say *Luc est déçu de Paul* (lit. Luc is disappointed of Paul) but not **Luc est énervé de Paul*[1] (*Luc is irritated of Paul). An example of such a rule is **Rule *Passiv1*** given in Figure 4.

---

[1] "*" before a sentence means the sentence is ungrammatical.

---

1. **Si**   la phrase à analyser est de la forme $N_0 \, V \, N_1$
        If   the sentence to be analyzed has the form $N_0 \, V \, N_1$

2. **Et si** N_0 est une *infinitive*
        and if N_0 is an *infinitive*

3. **Et si** V est accepté dans la construction N_1 *est Vpp par le fait de N_0*
        and if   V is accepted in the construction N_1 *est Vpp par le fait de N_0*

4. **Et si** V est accepté dans la construction N_1 *est Vpp de N_0*

       Alors   la paraphrase N_1 *est Vpp par le fait de N_0* est valide
       Then   the paraphrase N_1 *est Vpp par le fait de N_0* is valid

       Et   la paraphrase N_1 *est Vpp de N_0* est valide

Figure 4. Rule Passiv1.

Conditions 3 and 4 are redundant and are mentioned here for the reader; **Passiv1** is activated only if the verb V analyzed verifies these 2 conditions.

If **Passiv1** is applied to the sentence *Voir Luc partir exapère Marie* (lit. To see Luc leaving is exasperating Marie), the subject N_0 is an infinitive (= *Voir Luc partir*), the object N_1 is *Marie,* and the verb V is *exaspérer* which is accepted in the two constructions (cf. Table 2). Given these conditions, the paraphrases are:

Marie est exaspérée par le fait de voir Luc partir (= N_1 *est Vpp par le fait de N_0*)
lit. Marie is exasperated by the fact of to see Luc leaving

Marie est exaspérée de voir Luc partir (= N_1 *est Vpp de N_0*)
lit. Marie is exasperated of to see Luc leaving

3.3 *FEELING* Analysis

In order to process a sentence, each token has to be described with its grammatical category (noun, verb) and function (subject, object). For example, **Luc exaspère Marie** is analyzed as:

{ Subject : Luc, *human proper noun ;*
Verb exaspérer ;
Object : Marie, *human proper noun}.*

We rely on Bourigault (2002) and Fabre and Bourigault (2001) to get such syntactic information. The results of the *FEELING* analysis are shown in Figure 5. Given this sentence, *FEELING* provides an interpretation that describes what kind of feeling is expressed (I), then it provides synonymous and antonymous sentences (II and III), it generates several well formed paraphrases (IV), and finally, *FEELING* provides sentences expressing increased and/or decreased feeling (V). Comments (in italics) are added below each category of answer, explaining which knowledge is used by *FEELING*.

I. INTERPRÉTATION (Meaning)
Le sentiment est éprouvé par *Marie*
(The feeling is experienced by *Marie*)

La cause est *Luc*
(The cause is *Luc*)

Le sentiment éprouvé est *plutôt désagréable (négatif)*
(The experienced feeling is **rather unpleasant (negative)**)

Le sentiment éprouvé est *l'exaspération*
(The experienced feeling is **exasperation**)

Comments:
*Exaspérer is a verb of the /**irriter**/ class, a negative class of unpleasant feeling.*
The value of exaspérer for the property [Nominalization] is exaspération which is the feeling experienced by the experiencer.

II. PHRASES SYNONYMES : (Synonymous sentences)
a) *Luc énerve beaucoup Marie*
b) *Luc (courrouce / enrage / excède / hérisse / horripile / ulcère) Marie*

III. PHRASES ANTONYMES (Antonymous sentences)
    Luc apaise Marie
    Luc calme marie

Comments:
*IIa) = verbs of the same semantic class as /**irriter**/ with a neutral intensity and the modifier "beaucoup" to keep the same level of intensity*
*IIb) verbs of the same semantic class as /**irriter**/ with the same intensity level (high)*
III) verbs of antonymous classes

IV. PARAPHRASES
    Marie éprouve de l'exaspération envers Luc
    Marie éprouve beaucoup d'énervement envers Luc
    Marie est (exaspérée / très énervée)
    Marie est (exaspérée / très énervée) par Luc
    Marie éprouve de l'exaspération
    Marie éprouve beaucoup d'énervement
    Marie s'exaspère

Comments:
Application of paraphrasing rules.

V. VARIATION DE L'INTENSITÉ du sentiment exprimé (Feeling intensity variation)

Diminution continue de l'intensité du verbe *exaspérer* (<<) :
(Continuous decreasing intensity of *exaspérer* verb)

a) *Luc (agace / crispe /énerve / fâche / irrite) Marie*

                b) << Luc (dérange / désoblige / emmerde) Marie

c) << *Luc (ennuie / enquiquine /gêne / importune / incommode / indispose) Marie*

Augmentation continue de l'intensité du verbe *exaspérer* (>>) :
(Continuous increasing intensity of *exaspérer* verb)

d) >> *Luc (braque / choque / écœure / scandalise) Marie*
e) >> *Luc (indigne / rebelle / révolte) Marie*

Comments:
Pathfinding of the intensity graph, then inside each class, taking into account the intensity of feeling expressed by the verbs (low, neutral or high).

The order relation between these 3 classes is reviewed below:

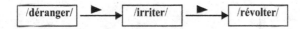

Va) /irriter/ class verbs with neutral intensity (Intensifier property value = neutral)
Vb) /déranger/ class verbs with high intensity (Intensifier property value = high)
Vc) /déranger/ class verbs with neutral intensity (Intensifier property value = neutral)
*   (there is no verb with a low intensity in the class)*
Vd) /révolter/ class verbs with neutral intensity (Intensifier property value = neutral)
Ve) /révolter/ class verbs with high intensity (Intensifier property value = high)

Figure 5. FEELING results.

3.4 FEELING Extension

A *FEELING* system extension, *FEELING-G*, uses the same knowledge database and mechanisms, but produces an oriented-feeling representation, which can be used to process textual data.

Given a sentence, *FEELING-G*, provides a semantic representation of the feelings or psychological states expressed. This representation is a set of complex feature structures: a matrix of attributes with exactly one value assigned to each. Attributes have atomic values but also more complex values, like a complex feature structure. There are three categories of features:

- ***Sentiment*** features describe the meaning, the intensity, and the linguistics properties of the emotion or psychological state,

- *Experiencer* features identify the person (feature **ident**) whose feeling or state is being expressed, and which sentiment he or she feels. The description of this feeling is unified with the *Sentiment* features. This unification mechanism is represented by **#1** in Figure 6.

- *Causeobject* are features showing the cause or the object of feeling or psychological state.

Given the sentence already analyzed *Luc exaspère Marie, FEELING-G* provides a semantic representation shown partially in Figure 6.

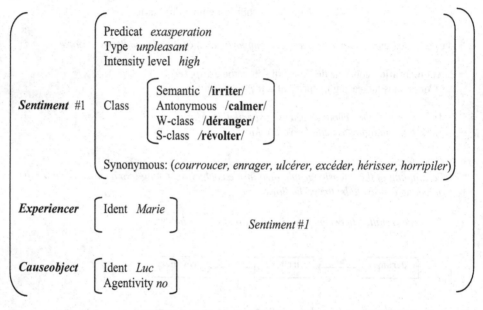

Figure 6. Semantic representation.

4. Evaluation

An evaluation of this work was conducted in two ways. First, a comparison between usual dictionaries and the *FEELING* lexicon was made. A large part of the lexicon, more than 10 percent, contains words which are not described by usual dictionaries as psychological nouns or verbs, like *bétonner* (to concrete) which means *endurcir* (to harden), whereas these words have been found in texts with a psychological meaning.

Secondly, newspaper "letters to the Editor" were analyzed by both *FEELING* and human readers. Three human evaluators classified 60 letters. Those evaluators were instructed to classify sentences as reflecting a "pleasant", an "unpleasant," or a "neutral" feeling, and to give an intensity level of this feeling, on a scale from 1 to 3, with 1 being weak feeling, 2 being medium, and 3 being strong. With the hypothesis that human evaluators do not make mistakes, a comparison between their answers and *FEELING* analysis was made. Without taking Intensity level into account, *FEELING* classified correctly 49 letters and made 11 errors. In taking Intensity level into account, *FEELING* classified correctly 39 letters and made 21 errors.

	Without taking Intensity level into account	Taking Intensity level into account
T: Number of Letters (= correct answers of human evaluators)	60	60
C: Correct answers of *FEELING:*	49	39
Incorrect answers of *FEELING*	11	21
Precision *C/T*	0.81	0.65

Table 3. Comparison between FEELING analysis and Human Evaluations.

Let T be the number of letters (the number of correct answers) and C the number of *FEELING* correct answers. The precision is defined as *Precision=C/T*. The results are given in Table 3.

All letters submitted to *FEELING* contain at least one psychological verb, allowing an interpretation for each letter. If a letter contains several verbs, *FEELING* analyzes only the first one. This is the origin of several errors, when the feeling of the first verb is modified by others which follow it in the letter. Another source of error is the meaning of /**étonner**/ class verbs, whose polarity varies depending on the context. To *FEELING* these verbs are always neutral, whereas human readers are able to interpret the context.

5. Related Work

This approach differs from Wordnet (Fellbaum, 1998) on two points. First, the organization principles are different. For instance, there are no heritage or intensity relationships in Wordnet. Second, Wordnet is a large database resource with no associated knowledge.

The only similar work on French is Mel'čuk's dictionary (1992) in which each word description consists of its linguistics properties and lexical rules. The perspective is rather different in that the focus is on a very detailed description in a semantic field with associated software, whereas Mel'čuk's study is about general language. Furthermore, no system uses the dictionary knowledge.

6. Conclusion

Thus far, *FEELING* analyses only apply to single sentences, as in a text being analyzed as a set of independent sentences. Ongoing work is directed towards extending these analyses to short texts in order to build semantic representations shared by several sentences.

7. Bibliography

Bourigault, D. (2002) Upery : Un Outil d'Analyse Distributionnelle Etendue pour la Construction d'Ontologies à Partir de Corpus. In *Actes de la 9ème Conférence Annuelle Sur le Traitement Automatique des Langues (TALN 2002).* 75-84. Nancy.

Fabre, C. and Bourigault, D. (2001) Linguistic Clues for Corpus-Based Acquisition of Lexical Dependencies. In *Proceedings of the Corpus Linguistics 2001 Conference, UCREL Technical Papers (vol 13),* 176-184. Lancaster University.

Fellbaum, C. (Ed). (1998) *Wordnet: An Electronic Lexical Database.* MIT Press, Cambridge.

Frantext. (2004) Base Textuelle Informatisée. CNRS – Atilf. http://atilf.atilf.fr/frantext.htm.
Gross, M. (1975) *Méthodes en Syntaxe*. Hermann, Paris.

Johnson-Laird, P.N., and Oatley, K. (1989) The Language of Emotions: An Analysis of a Semantic Field. *Cognition and Emotion, 3,* 81-123.

Kerleroux, F. (1996) *La Coupure Invisible*. Presses Universitaires du Septentrion, Paris.

Kleiber, G. (1990) *La Sémantique du Prototype*. Puf, Collection Linguistique Nouvelle. Paris.
Le Grand Robert de la Langue Française 6 volumes. (2001) Le Robert, Paris.

Le Trésor de la Langue Française, 16 volumes. (1971-1994) CNRS Edition, Paris.

Mathieu, Y. Y. (2000) *Les Verbes de Sentiment*. CNRS Edition, Paris.

Mathieu, Y. Y. (1999) Les Prédicats de Sentiment. *Langages, 136*, 41-52.

Mel'čuk, I. (1992) DEC. Dictionnaire Explicatif et Combinatoire du Français Contemporain. Recherches Lexico-Sémantiques III. Les Presses de l'Université de Montréal, Montréal.

Rosch, E. (1975) Cognitive Representations of Semantic Categories. *Journal of Experimental Psychology 104/3*.

Wierzbicka, A. (1996) *Semantics, Primes and Universals*. Oxford University Press, Oxford.

Chapter 11

Extracting Opinion Propositions and Opinion Holders using Syntactic and Lexical Cues

Steven Bethard[†], Hong Yu[*], Ashley Thornton[†], Vasileios Hatzivassiloglou[‡*] and Dan Jurafsky[∞]

†Center for Spoken Language Research, University of Colorado, Boulder, CO 80309
‡Center for Computational Learning Systems, Columbia University, New York, NY 10027
*Department of Computer Science, Columbia University, New York, NY 10027
∞Department of Linguistics, Stanford university, Stanford CA 94305
Email: {steven.bethard, ashley.thornton}@colorado.edu
Email: {hongyu, vh}@cs.columbia.edu
Email: jurafsky@stanford.edu

Abstract

A new task is identified in the ongoing analysis of opinions: finding propositional opinions, sentential complement clauses of verbs such as "believe" or "claim" that express opinions, and the holders of these opinions. An extension of semantic parsing techniques is proposed that, coupled with additional lexical and syntactic features, can extract these propositional opinions and their opinion holders. A small corpus of 5,139 sentences is annotated with propositional opinion information, and is used for training and evaluation. While our results are still quite preliminary (precisions of 43-51% and recalls of 58-68%), we feel that our focus on opinion clauses, and in general the use of rich syntactic features, helps point to an important new direction in opinion detection.

Keywords: opinions, propositions, semantic parsing, opinion-holders, attribution.

1. Introduction

Separating subjective from objective information is a challenging task that impacts several natural language processing applications. Published news articles often contain factual information along with opinions, either as the outcome of analysis or quoted directly from primary sources. Text materials from many other sources (e.g., the web) also mix facts and opinions. Automatically determining which part of these documents is fact and which is opinion would help in selecting the appropriate type of information given an application and in organizing and presenting that information. For example, an information extraction system would likely prioritize factual parts of a document for analysis, while an advanced question answering or summarization system would need to present opinions separately from facts, organized by source and perspective.

This need for identifying opinions has motivated a number of automated methods for detecting opinions or other subjective text passages (Wiebe, Bruce, and O'Hara, 1999; Hatzivassiloglou and Wiebe, 2000; Wiebe, 2000; Wiebe et al., 2002; Riloff, Wiebe, and Wilson, 2003; Yu and Hatzivassiloglou, 2003) and assigning them to subcategories such as positive and negative opinions (Pang, Lee, and Vaithyanathan, 2002; Turney, 2002; Yu and Hatzivassiloglou, 2003). A variety of machine learning techniques have been employed for this purpose, generally based on lexical cues associated with opinions. However, a common element of current approaches is their focus on either an entire document (Pang, Lee, and Vaithyanathan, 2002; Turney, 2002) or on full sentences (Wiebe, Bruce, and O'Hara, 1999; Hatzivassiloglou and Wiebe, 2000; Wiebe, 2000; Wiebe et al., 2002; Yu and Hatzivassiloglou, 2003). This chapter examines an alternative approach that seeks to determine opinion status for smaller pieces of text, not by reapplying existing techniques to the clause level but by adopting a more analytic interpretation. In this approach, distinct components of opinion sentences are annotated with specific roles relative to the opinion, such as the opinion-holder, the topic of this opinion, and the actual subjective part of the opinion sentence, as opposed to additional factual material; often a sentence that contains subjective clauses expresses an opinion only in the main part or one of the clauses.

In this chapter, an opinion is defined as a sentence, or part of a sentence, that would answer the question "How does X feel about Y?" The opinion needs to be directly stated; this does not include inferences that one could make about how a speaker feels based on word choice. Opinions do not include statements verifiable by scientific data nor predictions about the future.

As an example, consider applying this definition of an opinion to the following two sentences:

(1) I believe in the system.
(2) I believe [you have to use the system to change it].

Both (1) and (2) would be considered opinions under the definition—the first answers the question "How does the author feel about the system?", and the second answers the question "How does the author feel about changing the system?" However, in (1), the scope of the opinion is the whole sentence, while in (2) the opinion of the author is contained within the proposition argument of the verb "believe".

In fact, an opinion localized in the propositional argument of certain verbs as in sentence (2) above is a common case of component opinions. In this chapter, such opinions are called propositional opinions. A propositional opinion is an opinion that appears as a semantic proposition, generally functioning as the sentential complement of a predicate. For example, in sentences (3)–(5) below, the underlined portions are propositional opinions, appearing as the complements of the predicates believe, realize, and reply:

(3) I *believe* [you have to use the system to change it].
(4) Still, Vista officials *realize* [they're relatively fortunate].
(5) ["I'd be destroying myself"] *replies* Mr. Korotich.

Not all propositions are opinions. Propositions also appear as complements of verbs like forget, know, guess, imagine, and learn, and many of these complements are not opinions, as the examples below show:

(6) I don't *know* [anything unusual happening here].

(7) I *understand* [that there are studies by Norwegians that show declining UV-B at the surface].

The goal of this chapter is to automatically extract these propositional opinions. An interest in this task derives from interest in automatic question answering, and in particular in answering questions about opinions. Answering an opinion question (like "How does X feel about Y?" or "What do people think about Z?") requires finding which clauses express the exact opinion of the subject. Propositional opinions are an extremely common way to express such third-party opinions. In addition to its key role in opinion question answering, solving the problem of extracting propositional opinions would be an excellent first step toward breaking down opinions into their various components. Finally, this chapter considers propositional opinions because the task was a natural extension from one already addressed: extraction of propositions and other semantic/thematic roles from text. Semantically annotated databases like FrameNet (Baker, Fillmore, and Lowe, 1998) and PropBank (Kingsbury, Palmer, and Marcus, 2002) already mark semantic constituents of sentences like AGENT, THEME, and PROPOSITION, data which could be expected to help in extracting propositional opinions and opinion-holders.

The technique presented here for extracting propositional opinions augments an algorithm developed in earlier work on semantic parsing (Gildea and Jurafsky, 2002; Pradhan et al., 2003) with new lexical features representing opinion words. In the semantic parsing work, sentences were labeled for thematic roles (AGENT, THEME, and PROPOSITION among others) by training statistical classifiers on FrameNet and PropBank. In the techniques of this chapter, the actual semantic parsing software described in (Pradhan et al., 2003) is used, modifying its role labels so that it performs a binary classification (OPINION-PROPOSITION versus NULL). Words that are associated with opinions are used as additional features for this model; these words are automatically learned by bootstrapping from smaller sets of known such words. A classifier is examined that directly assigns opinion status to propositions using these features as well as a two-tiered approach that classifies propositions recognized by the semantic parser. Finally, results are presented from a three-way classification where sentence constituents are labeled as either OPINION-PROPOSITION, OPINION-HOLDER, or NULL.

To be able to train different classification models, 5,139 sentences were annotated, marking opinion propositions and opinion-holders in them. This data and its annotation is discussed, and then the opinion word sets used and the methodology by which they were constructed is presented. This chapter's approaches to the detection of propositions are described in detail, followed by the results obtained. A brief discussion of these results and their likely impact on continued efforts on extracting and labeling opinion components concludes the chapter.

2. Data

This chapter addresses the problem of extracting propositional opinions as a supervised statistical classification task, based on hand-labeled training and test sets. In order to label data with propositional opinions, a set of labeling instructions was first established, and then several resources were drawn upon to build a small corpus of propositional-opinion data.

2.1 Labels

In each of the hand-labeling tasks, sentences from a corpus were labeled with one of three labels:
- NON-OPINION

- OPINION-PROPOSITION
- OPINION-SENTENCE

In each of these labels, OPINION indicates an opinion as in the definition above. Thus, the label NON-OPINION means any sentence that could not be used to answer a question of the form "How does X feel about Y?" The remaining two labels, OPINION-PROPOSITION and OPINION-SENTENCE both indicate opinions under the definition, but OPINION-PROPOSITION indicates that the opinion is contained in a propositional verb argument, and OPINION-SENTENCE indicates the opinion is outside of such an argument.

For example, the sentence

(8) I *surmise* [PROPOSITION this is because they are unaware of the shape of humans].
would be labeled NON-OPINION because this sentence does not explain how the speaker feels about the topic; it only makes a prediction about it. By contrast, the sentence
(9) [PROPOSITION It makes the system more flexible] *argues* a Japanese businessman.
would be labeled OPINION-PROPOSITION because the propositional argument in this sentence explains how the businessman feels about "it". Finally, an OPINION-SENTENCE contains an opinion, but that opinion does not fit within the proposition. For example:
(10) It might be *imagined* by those who are not themselves Anglican [PROPOSITION that the habit of going to confession is limited only to markedly High churches] but this is not necessarily the case.

Here, the opinion expressed by the author is not "that the habit of going to confession is limited only to markedly High churches", but that the imaginings of non-Anglicans are not necessarily the case. Thus the opinion is not contained within the proposition argument and so the sentence is labeled OPINION-SENTENCE.

It is worth noting that the labels OPINION-PROPOSITION and OPINION-SENTENCE can occasionally occur in the same sentence. For example:

(11) You may sincerely *believe* yourself [PROPOSITION capable of running a nightclub] and as far as the public relations and administration side goes that's probably true.

Here there are two opinions: the listener's, that they are capable of running a nightclub, and the speaker's, that the listener is probably right. The first of these is contained in the proposition, and the second is not.

2.2 FrameNet

FrameNet (Baker, Fillmore, and Lowe, 1998) is a corpus of over 100,000 sentences which has been selected form the British National Corpus and hand-annotated for predicates and their arguments. In the FrameNet corpus, predicates are grouped into semantic frames around a target verb which have a set of semantic roles. For example the Cognition frame includes verbs like think, believe, and know, and roles like COGNIZER and CONTENT. Each of these roles was mapped onto more abstract thematic roles like AGENT and PROPOSITION via hand-written rules as described in (Gildea and Jurafsky, 2002), and later modified by our collaborator Valerie Krugler.

A subset of the FrameNet sentences was selected for hand annotation with opinion labels. As this chapter is concerned primarily with identifying propositional opinions, only the sentences in

FrameNet containing a verbal argument labeled PROPOSITION were taken. Each of these sentences was then individually annotated with one or more of the labels above. This produced a dataset of 3,041 sentences, 1,910 labeled as NON-OPINION, 631 labeled OPINION-PROPOSITION, and 573 labeled OPINION-SENTENCE.

2.3 PropBank

PropBank (Kingsbury, Palmer, and Marcus, 2002) is a million word corpus consisting of the Wall Street Journal portion of the Penn TreeBank that was then annotated for predicates and their arguments. Like FrameNet, PropBank gives semantic/thematic labels to the arguments of each predicate. For an earlier project on semantic parsing, the PropBank labels (ARG0, ARG1, . . .) were again mapped into the abstract thematic roles (AGENT, PROPOSITION, etc.) by Valerie Krugler and Karen Kipper.

Again only a subset of PropBank was selected for hand annotation with opinion labels. Using the FrameNet data set, some verb-specific information was extracted. For each verb, the frequency with which that verb occurred with an OPINION (PROPOSITION or SENTENCE) label was measured. These statistics gave an idea of how highly a given verb's use correlates with opinion-type sentences.

A number of verbs that seemed to correlate highly with OPINION sentences were then selected, in order to focus further annotation on sentences more likely to contain opinions. Specifically, the selected verbs were:

accuse	*comment*	*express*	*pledge*	*reply*	*suggest*
argue	*confirm*	*forget*	*realize*	*scream*	*think*
believe	*criticize*	*frame*	*reckon*	*show*	*understand*
castigate	*demonstrate*	*know*	*reflect*	*signal*	*volunteer*
chastise	*doubt*	*persuade*			

For each of these verbs, all of the PropBank sentences containing these verbs as targets were labeled, labeling in the same manner as for the FrameNet sentences. This produced a dataset of 2,098 sentences, 1,203 labeled NON-OPINION, 618 labeled OPINION-PROPOSITION, and 390 labeled OPINION-SENTENCE.

2.4 Opinion-Holders

In addition to labeling propositional opinions, this chapter also reports initial experiments in labeling the holder of the opinions. Because the focus is on propositional opinions, this chapter is mainly interested in extracting opinion-holders of each OPINION-PROPOSITION. Example (12) below shows a correctly labeled example:

(12) [OPINION-HOLDER You] can *argue* [OPINION-PROPOSITION these wars are corrective].

To create training and test sets, each OPINION-PROPOSITION labeled in the FrameNet and PropBank corpora was taken, and for each one an OPINION-HOLDER was hand-labeled. For efficiency, a semi-automated labeling process was used, relying on the fact that these PropBank and FrameNet sentences had already been labeled for semantic roles like AGENT. The vast majority of OPINION-HOLDERs of propositional opinions had been observed to be the AGENTs of those sentences (as was the case, for example, in (12) above). Thus each AGENT of an OPINION-PROPOSITION was automatically labeled as an OPINION-HOLDER, and then hand-checked to correct mistakes. For example, (13) shows a sentence in which the AGENT was not in fact the OPINION-HOLDER, and which had to be hand-corrected to mark "these people" as the OPINION-HOLDER.

(13) Why should [AGENT I] *believe* [OPINION-HOLDER these people] [OPINION-PROPOSITION that one small grey lump which they showed me on a screen is a threat to my life]?

In all, only 10% of the OPINION-HOLDERs in PropBank and FrameNet combined turned out not to be AGENTs and had to be corrected.

Not all opinion-holders were explicitly mentioned in the sentences. In 72 sentences (6%) the opinion-holder was the "speaker", while in 42 (4%) the opinion-holder was unlexicalized. For the purposes of scoring the automatic OPINION-HOLDER labeler, these sentences were counted as if there were no OPINION-HOLDER at all.

3. Opinion-Oriented Words

Previous work indicated that words that associate with opinions are strong clues for determining phrase and sentence-level subjectivity (Wiebe et al., 2002; Riloff, Wiebe, and Wilson, 2003; Yu and Hatzivassiloglou, 2003). This chapter therefore hypothesizes that including such opinion words as additional features may enhance the performance of methods for identifying propositional opinions.

Earlier approaches for obtaining opinion words included manual annotation, as well automatic extension of sets of opinion words by relying on frequency counts and expression patterns. This chapter uses as a starting set a collection of opinion words identified by Janyce Wiebe, Ellen Riloff, and colleagues using the approaches described above. The collection includes 1,286 strong opinion words and 1,687 weak opinion words. Examples of strong opinion words include *accuse*, *disapproval*, and *inclination*, while weak opinion words include *abandoned*, *belief*, and *commitment*.

Experiments were performed with using either the strong opinion words in that collection or both the strong and weak opinion words together. Additional methods were explored to obtain additional, larger sets of opinion words and assign an opinion score to each word.

The first method relies on differences in the relative frequency of a word in documents that are likely to contain opinions versus documents that contain mostly facts. For this task, the TREC 8, 9, and 11 text collections, which consist of more than 1.7 million newswire articles, were used. This corpus includes a large number of Wall Street Journal (WSJ) articles, some of which contain additional headings such as editorial, letter to editor, business, and news. 2,877, 1,695, 2,009 and 3,714 articles were extracted in each of these categories, and the ratio of relative frequencies for each word in the editorial plus letter to editor versus the news plus business articles (taken to be representative, respectively, of opinion-heavy and fact-heavy documents) was calculated.

The second approach used co-occurrence information, starting from a seed list of 1,336 manually annotated semantically oriented adjectives (Hatzivassiloglou and McKeown, 1997), which were considered to be opinion words (Wiebe, 2000). A modified log-likelihood ratio for all words in the TREC corpus was calculated depending on how often each word co-occurred in the corpus in the same sentence with the seed words. Using this procedure, opinion words were obtained from all open classes (adjectives, adverbs, verbs, and nouns).

Knowledge in WordNet (Miller et al., 1990) was also used to substantially filter the number of words labeled as opinion words by the above methods. A supervised Naïve Bayes classifier was built that utilized as features the hypernyms of each word. For training, a randomly selected set of nouns from the TREC corpus was manually annotated with FACT or OPINION labels, and 500 FACT nouns and 500 OPINION nouns were selected. A model was trained using the hypernyms of these nouns as features, so as to produce a classifier that predicts a FACT or OPINION label for any given noun.

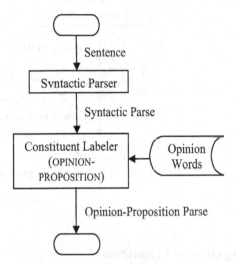

Figure 1: One-tiered architecture

The performance of each of these techniques was evaluated. WordNet part-of-speech information was used to divide the 1,286 strong opinion words into 374 adjectives, 119 adverbs, 951 nouns, and 703 verbs, which were then used as the gold standards. Different methods proved best for different syntactic classes of opinion words. The first method was appropriate for verbs while the second method worked better for adverbs and nouns. The WordNet filtering technique was applied to the results of the second method for nouns. There was a trade-off for adjectives—the first method resulted in higher recall while the second method resulted in higher precision. The first method was adopted for adjectives after comparing the average of precision and recall obtained by the two methods in an earlier run, using a subset of the 1,286 strong opinion words manually tagged as adjectives. This first set of adjectives was used only for choosing one of the two methods for extending the set, and the first method was subsequently applied to the full set of 374 adjectives identified with WordNet part-of-speech information, as described above. In that manner, a total of 19,107/14,713, 305/302, 3,188/22,279 and 2,329/1,663 subjective/objective adjectives, adverbs, nouns and verbs were obtained, respectively. The evaluation demonstrated a precision/recall of 58%/47% for adjectives, 79%/37% for adverbs, 90%/38% for nouns, and 78%/18% for verbs.

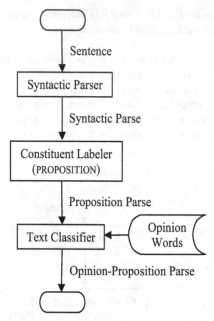

Figure 2: Two-tiered architecture

4. Identifying Opinion Propositions

Having identified a large number of opinion-oriented words, two approaches to the opinion identification task were considered. The first, pictured in Figure 1, directly modifies the semantic parser, restricting the target labels to those relevant to opinion propositions and incorporating the opinion words as additional features, but otherwise uses the same machinery to directly assign labels to sentence constituents. The second approach, pictured in Figure 2, performs the task in two steps: it first uses a version of the semantic parser to obtain generic semantic constituents (such as PROPOSITION) and then classifies propositions as opinions or not.

4.1 One-Tiered Architecture

The one-tiered architecture is a constituent-by-constituent classification scheme. That is, for each constituent in the syntactic parse tree of the sentence, that constituent is classified as either OPINION-PROPOSITION or NULL.

As an example, consider the sentence "The young Sheikh kept grumbling that the TV was wrong", which has the parse tree in Figure 3. In this situation, each node in the tree, e.g. S1, S, NP, DT, JJ, NNP, VP, etc., is assigned one of the two labels. For this sentence, the correct classification would be to label the SBAR node as OPINION-PROPOSITION, and the remaining nodes as NULL.

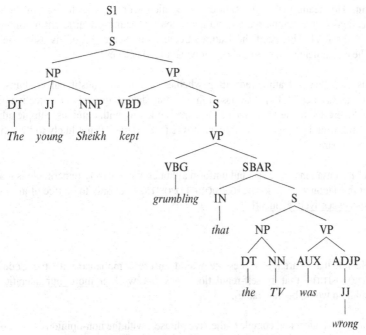

Figure 3: A syntactic parse tree. The SBAR constituent is a propositional opinion.

To perform this classification, the Support Vector Machine (SVM) (Joachims, 1998) paradigm proposed in (Pradhan et al., 2003) for semantic parsing was used, in fact making use of the actual semantic parsing code itself. In that paradigm, semantic roles like AGENT, THEME, PROPOSITION, and LOCATION are labeled by training SVM classifiers. Instead of labeling 20 semantic roles, the task was changed to label only one: OPINION-PROPOSITION. The classification task was thus a binary one: OPINION-PROPOSITION versus NULL.

For the semantic parsing task, Pradhan et al. used eight features as input to the SVM classifier— the verb, the cluster of the verb, the subcategorization type of the verb, the syntactic phrase type of the potential argument, the head word of the potential argument, the position (before/after) of the potential argument relative to the verb, the syntactic path in a parse tree between the verb and the potential argument, and the voice (active/passive) of the sentence. A detailed description of each of these features is available in (Gildea and Jurafsky, 2002).

The initial experiments used exactly this feature set. In follow-on experiments, several additional features, derived mainly from the opinion-oriented words described in the previous section, were considered.

Counts: This feature counts for each constituent the number of words that occur in a list of opinion-oriented words. Several alternatives for that list were considered: the strong opinion words identified by Wiebe and colleagues (referred to as "external strong"), both the strong and weak opinion words from that work (referred to as "external strong+weak"), and various subsets of the automatically constructed list of opinion words from this chapter, obtained by requiring different minimums on each word's opinion score for inclusion in the list.

Score Sum: This feature takes the sum of the opinion scores for each word in the constituent. Several versions of the feature were again generated by requiring a different minimum score for inclusion in the total. That is, if the feature "Score Sum [Score $\geq$ 2.0]" is used, the sum of all words in the constituent with scores above or equal to 2.0 is taken.

ADJP: This is a binary feature indicating whether or not the constituent contains a complex adjective phrase as a child. Explorations of the training data suggested that adjective phrases with forms like "interested in the idea" seemed to correlate highly with opinions. Simple adjectives, on the other hand, would provide many false positives (e.g., "large" is not likely to be an indicator of opinions). Compare

(14) The accusations were flat and uniform although what is truly remarkable is that the youth of the nation were *believed* [OPINION-PROPOSITION not only to be free of all discipline but also <u>excessively affluent</u>].

and

(15) He felt that shareholder pressure would ensure compliance with the Code but *added* [PROPOSITION that if self-regulation does not work a <u>more bureaucratic</u> legislative solution would be inevitable].

which include the underlined complex adjective phrases, with the non-opinion

(16) He *added* [PROPOSITION that there might be a sufficient pool of volunteers to act as a new breed of civil justices].

Using different subsets of these features, several SVM models were trained for labeling propositional opinion constituents. For training and testing data, all the sentences labeled NON-OPINION and all the sentences labeled OPINION-PROPOSITION were taken from both the FrameNet and PropBank datasets. The constituents for propositional arguments in the OPINION-PROPOSITION sentences were labeled as propositional opinions, while all other constituents were labeled NULL.

Some normalization was required to join the two datasets before training the models. First, both FrameNet and PropBank data were stripped of all punctuation as in (Pradhan et al., 2003). In addition, propositional arguments in PropBank were slightly altered if they used the complementizer "that". FrameNet labelers were instructed to include "that" in propositional arguments when it occurred as a complementizer, while PropBank labelers were instructed the opposite—"that" was not to be included in the argument. Note that the inclusion of "that" in the argument changes which constituent should receive the propositional-opinion label. Consider the parse tree in Figure 3. The propositional-opinion, as labeled, is shown in the FrameNet style—"that" is included in the proposition—and so the node to receive the label is the SBAR. Under the PropBank labeling style, "that" would not have been included in the proposition, and so the node to receive the label would have been the lower S node. Because the methods of this chapter learn constituent-by-constituent, it is important to normalize for this sort of labeling so that the data for similar propositional opinion constituents can be shared.

After normalization, both the PropBank and FrameNet data were divided into three randomly selected sets of sentences—70% for training data, 15% for development data, and 15% for testing data. The combined training, development and testing sets were formed by joining the corresponding sets in FrameNet and PropBank. This produced datasets whose sentences were distributed proportionally between FrameNet and PropBank. The distributions of propositional opinion and null constituent labels in each of these datasets are shown in Table 1.

Dataset	OPINION-PROPOSITION	NULL
Training	912	90,729
Development	178	19,247
Testing	183	19,031

Table 1: Distribution of constituents as opinion propositions or null.

In addition to identifying propositional-opinions, the task of identifying the holders of these opinions was also considered. As mentioned above, all OPINION-PROPOSITION sentences were labeled with opinion-holders as well. Using the same datasets as above, new models were trained with one additional label: OPINION-HOLDER. The distributions of constituent labels for this three-way classification task are shown in Table 2.

Dataset	OPINION-PROPOSITION	OPINION-HOLDER	NULL
Training	912	769	89,960
Development	178	149	19,098
Testing	183	162	18,869

Table 2: Distribution of constituents as opinion propositions, opinion holders or null.

In addition to treating OPINION-HOLDER as a third label in a single classification task, labeling OPINION-HOLDERs was also approached as a separate task, following the OPINION-PROPOSITION classification task. For this purpose, the sentences that had contained OPINION-PROPOSITIONs were used to train an OPINION-HOLDER vs. NULL constituent classifier.

4.2 Two-Tiered Architecture

A two-tiered approach for detecting opinion propositions was also explored. The bottom tier was a version of the semantic parser, trained using the Support Vector Machine paradigm proposed in (Pradhan et al., 2003) to identify the role of PROPOSITION only (other semantic roles were dropped).

Independent classifiers were then built on top of the modified semantic parser to distinguish whether the propositions identified were opinions or not. For this part, a previous machine-learning approach (Yu and Hatzivassiloglou, 2003), initially designed for sentence-level opinion and fact classification, was applied.

Three machine-learning models, all based on Naive Bayes learning, were considered. The first model trains on sentences of which labels are inherited from Wall Street Journal document metadata as described earlier in the section on opinion words; sentences in editorials and letters to the editor are labeled to be opinion sentences, and sentences in news and business articles are labeled to be factual. This avoids the need for obtaining individual sentence annotations for training and evaluation, and relies instead on the expectation that documents classified as opinion on the whole (e.g., editorials) will tend to have mostly opinion sentences, and conversely documents placed in the factual category will tend to have mostly factual sentences. Wiebe et al. (2002) report that this expectation is borne out 75% of the time for opinion documents and 56% of the time for factual documents. Predictions are then made for the entire sentence a new proposition is in, and propagated to the individual proposition. The second model keeps the training at the sentence level with approximate labels as before, but calculates the predictions only on the text of the proposition which is being classified as opinion or not. Finally, the third model trains directly on propositions using the same kind of approximate, inherited labels, and also predicts on propositions.

All three models use the same set of features which include the words, bigrams, and trigrams in the sentence or proposition, part-of-speech information, and the presence of opinion and positive/negative words; see (Yu and Hatzivassiloglou, 2003) for a detailed description of these features. For training the first and second models, 20,000 randomly selected sentences from 2,877 editorials and 3,714 news articles from the WSJ were used. The third model was trained on all 5,147 propositions extracted by the modified semantic parser from these documents. The three models were evaluated on the set of opinion propositions manually annotated from FrameNet and PropBank.

5. Results

This section evaluates the one-tiered and two-tiered architectures using the OPINION-PROPOSITION labeled data. For comparison, a baseline system which labels all SBAR constituents as OPINION-PROPOSITIONS, gives a precision of 18.07%, a recall of 50.27%, and an F-score of 26.59%.

5.1 One-Tiered Architecture

Table 3 shows the results for identifying propositional opinion constituents. The first version of the system used only the features from (Pradhan et al., 2003), and no opinion words, and achieved precision of 50.97% and recall of 43.17%.

All of the other systems used at least one of the features presented in the description of the one-tier approach. The counts of subjective words identified in earlier work (the "external" sets of strong and weak opinion words) were not very good predictors in this task—the systems trained using these features performed nearly identically to the system without them. The counts of the opinion oriented words identified in the section of this chapter on opinion words were better predictors, gaining the system, in most cases, several percent (absolute) in precision and recall. Taking advantage of the scores produced for these words, instead of just their counts, gave similar results.

Interestingly, the complex adjective phrase (ADJP) feature provided as much predictive power as the best of the opinion-word based features. Using this feature in combination with the best opinion-oriented word feature achieved precision of 58.02% and recall of 51.37%, about a 40% (absolute) increase in precision and over the baseline system.

Features	Precision	Recall
No opinion words	50.97%	43.17%
Counts (external, strong)	50.65%	42.62%
Counts (external, strong+weak)	50.00%	43.72%
Counts (Score $\geq$ 2.0)	52.76%	46.99%
Counts (Score $\geq$ 2.5)	54.66%	48.09%
Counts (Score $\geq$ 3.0)	54.27%	48.63%
Score Sum (Score $\geq$ 0.0)	51.97%	43.17%
Score Sum (Score $\geq$ 2.0)	52.12%	46.99%
Score Sum (Score $\geq$ 2.5)	55.35%	48.09%
Score Sum (Score $\geq$ 3.0)	54.84%	46.45%
ADJP	56.05%	48.09%
ADJP, Score Sum (Score $\geq$ 2.5)	58.02%	51.37%

Table 3: One-tiered approach results for opinion propositions.

5.1.1 Combined Opinion-Proposition, Opinion-Holder Task

Table 4 shows the results for the more difficult, three-way classification into OPINION-PROPOSITION, OPINION-HOLDER, and NULL. Note that the system with no opinion features here performs slightly better than the same system in the two-way classification task, while the best system here performs slightly worse than the best two-way system. Still, the results here are remarkably similar to those achieved in the easier, two-way classification task which indicates that the system described here is able to achieve the same performance for propositional opinions and opinion-holders as it did for propositional opinions alone.

Features	Precision	Recall
No opinion words	53.43%	42.90%
Counts (external, strong)	51.81%	41.45%
Counts (external, strong+weak)	51.04%	42.61%
Counts (Score $\geq$ 2.0)	54.09%	44.06%
Counts (Score $\geq$ 2.5)	53.90%	44.06%
Counts (Score $\geq$ 3.0)	54.93%	45.22%
Score Sum (Score $\geq$ 0.0)	52.46%	43.19%
Score Sum (Score $\geq$ 2.0)	54.36%	45.22%
Score Sum (Score $\geq$ 2.5)	54.74%	45.22%
Score Sum (Score $\geq$ 3.0)	54.48%	44.06%
ADJP	55.71%	45.22%
ADJP, Score Sum (Score $\geq$ 2.5)	56.75%	47.54%

Table 4: One-tiered approach results for opinion propositions and opinion holders.

5.1.2 Separate Opinion-Proposition, Opinion-Holder Tasks

In the final constituent-labeling experiment, a separate classifier was trained to classify OPINION-HOLDERS after OPINION-PROPOSITIONS had already been classified. In this case, none of the opinion word features were considered because OPINION-HOLDER constituents were expected mainly to contain names or pronouns, not opinion words. For this reason, only one such OPINION-HOLDER classifier was trained. This classifier was able to identify OPINION-HOLDERS in OPINION-

PROPOSITION sentences with 90.85% precision and 89.10% recall. This suggests that once a sentence has been identified as containing an OPINION-PROPOSITION, identifying the OPINION-HOLDER is a much simpler task.

5.2 Two-Tiered Architecture

The first step in the two-tier approach was to train a version of the semantic parser using only propositions and target verbs as labels. Performance in that task was 62% recall and 82% precision, corresponding to an increase of 10% (absolute) in precision over the more general version of the parser with more semantic roles (Pradhan et al., 2003).

Table 5 lists the results obtained by the Naive Bayes classifiers trained over weak, inherited labels from the document level. The highest precision (up to 68%) was generally obtained when the opinion/semantic-oriented words were incorporated as features. This configuration however usually attained lower recall than just using the words as features, while the bigrams and trigrams offered a slight benefit in most cases. Part-of-speech information did not help either recall or precision. In general, significantly higher precision values were obtained with the two-tier approach as compared to the one-tier approach (68% versus 58%), but at the cost of substantially lower recall (43% versus 51%).

| Train on | Predict on | Measure | Features | | | | |
			Words	Bigrams	Trigrams	POS	Orientation
Sentence	Sentence	Recall	33.38%	29.69%	30.09%	30.05%	43.72%
		Precision	67.84%	63.13%	62.50%	65.55%	67.97%
Sentence	Proposition	Recall	37.48%	37.32%	37.79%	36.03%	28.81%
		Precision	53.95%	59.00%	59.83%	55.00%	68.41%
Proposition	Proposition	Recall	42.77%	38.07%	37.84%	35.01%	25.75%
		Precision	59.56%	61.63%	60.43%	58.77%	61.66%

Table 5: Two-tiered approach results for opinion propositions.

Comparing the three training/prediction models examined, one notes that Model 1 (training and predicting on entire sentences) generally performed better than Models 2 (training on sentences, predicting on propositions) and 3 (training and predicting on propositions). Models 2 and 3 had similar performance. One possible explanation for this difference is that Model 1 used longer text pieces and thus suffered less from sparse data issues.

Overall, the best model in the two-tier category obtained 43% recall and 68% precision, a 25% increase in precision and an 18% increase in recall over the baseline system. Still, these results were lower than earlier results that evaluated against manually annotated sentences from the WSJ corpus (Yu and Hatzivassiloglou, 2003). This performance difference is probably due in part to the difference between the WSJ text, which was used for training, and the BNC corpora, from which some of the evaluation propositions were drawn.

6. Error Analysis

In an attempt to find directions for future work, we investigated the errors of our best system, the one tier architecture with results described at the end of Table 3. Overall we found a number of areas where we miss opinion propositions and opinion holders. One key problem was that our current system was based on sentences with punctuation stripped out; it turns out that quotation marks are an important cue to opinion-propositions. We therefore did not detect the opinion-propositions in the following two examples:

(17) [OPINION-PROPOSITION "That must be a comfort,"] *rejoined* [OPINION-HOLDER Ella] as she shut the kitchen door behind her.

(18) [OPINION-PROPOSITION "Liar!"] *snarled* [OPINION-HOLDER her mother]

A related problem was when the opinion was split into two parts, before and after the target; we missed the following split proposition:

(19) [OPINION-PROPOSITION-1 The police] [OPINION-HOLDER he] *concluded* [OPINION-PROPOSITION-2 must possess an unswerving commitment to communication and consultation within which police and the community are equal partners]

We also often missed opinions when the proposition was expression with a noun phrase rather than a full sentential complement, such as the following

(20) [OPINION-HOLDER Mr Chalmers the SNP 's prospective candidate for Glasgow in the European elections] *expressed* [OPINION-PROPOSITION the growing desire within party ranks for an end to the public attacks on the leadership].

Finally, our system is very sensitive to the target opinion verb. Performance on the verb *believe*, for example (P/R=.72/.78) was much higher than average verbs like *argue* (.61/.58), while completely missed detection of opinion clauses (P/R=0/0) for certain verbs (*snarl, know, chuckle* and *trumpet*), suggesting obvious directions for improving our system. In addition, our system was quite sensitive to genre; we performed about twice as well on PropBank data as on FrameNet data.

We also examined errors in the opinion holder detection described in section 5.1.1. The major source of errors seemed to be false positives; detecting far too many opinion holders. In many cases we seemed to incorrectly label 2 or even 3 phrases as the opinion holder, caused by the fact that our current architecture makes the opinion-holder decision about each phrase independently, a problem we plan to address. Another such case was when the true opinion holder is the author. We believe these deserve much more attention in the future; the following is such an example:

(21) It does not relieve the need for our market-opening efforts for both goods and services but it does *suggest* [OPINION-PROPOSITION that it is our exports of services and not just borrowing that is financing our imports of goods].

7. Discussion

Two new tasks in opinion detection were introduced: detecting propositional opinions and detecting the holders of these opinions. While these problems are far from solved, the initial experiments of this chapter are encouraging. Even these initial experiments have led to some interesting conclusions. First, the one-tiered and two-tiered approaches offered complementary results, with the one-tiered approach achieving recall and precision of 51%/58% and the two-tiered approach achieving lower recall at a higher precision (43%/68%). Thus, both approaches seem to merit further exploration. Second, classification was significantly improved by using lists of opinion words which were automatically derived with a variety of statistical methods, and these extended lists proved more useful than smaller, more accurate manually constructed lists. This is a testament to the robustness of those word lists. In general, syntactic structures based on from the semantic-role-detection literature proved useful. A new syntactic feature, the presence of complex adjective phrases, also improved the performance of opinion proposition detection. Finally, the results on opinion-holder detection show that the approach based on identifying and labeling semantic constituents is promising, and that opinion-holders can be identified with accuracy similar to that of opinion propositions.

8. Acknowledgments

This work was partially supported by a DHS fellowship to the first author, and by ARDA under AQUAINT project MDA908-02-C-0008. Any opinions, findings, or recommendations are those of the authors and do not necessarily reflect the views of the sponsors. Many thanks to Valerie Krugler and Karen Kipper for mapping roles in the PropBank and FrameNet databases, to Lauren Asia Hall-Lew for help in the error analysis, and to Janyce Wiebe and Ellen Riloff for making available to us their lists of opinion oriented words. We are also grateful to Ed Hovy, Jim Martin, Kathy McKeown, Rebecca Passonneau, Sameer Pradhan, Wayne Ward, and Janyce Wiebe for many helpful discussions and comments.

9. Bibliography

Baker, C., Fillmore, C., and Lowe, J. (1998) The Berkeley FrameNet project. In *Proceedings of the Joint Conference on Computational Linguistics and the 36th Annual Meeting of the ACL (COLING-ACL98)*. Montreal, Canada: Association for Computational Linguistics.

Gildea, D. and Jurafsky, D. (2002) Automatic labeling of semantic roles. *Computational Linguistics* 28(3):245–288.

Hatzivassiloglou, V. and McKeown, K. R. (1997) Predicting the semantic orientation of adjectives. In *Proceedings of the 35th Annual Meeting of the ACL and the 8th Conference of the European Chapter of the ACL*, 174–181. Madrid, Spain: Association for Computational Linguistics.

Hatzivassiloglou, V. and Wiebe, J. (2000) Effects of adjective orientation and gradability on sentence subjectivity. In *Proceedings of the Conference on Computational Linguistics (COLING-2000)*.

Joachims, T. (1998) Text categorization with Support Vector Machines: Learning with many relevant features. In *Proceeding of the European Conference on Machine Learning*.

Kingsbury, P., Palmer, M., and Marcus, M. (2002) Adding semantic annotation to the Penn TreeBank. In *Proceedings of the Human Language Technology Conference*.

Miller, G., Beckwith, R., Fellbaum, C., Gross, D., and Miller, K. (1990) Introduction to WordNet: An on-line lexical database. *International Journal of Lexicography* 3(4):235–312.

Pang, B., Lee, L., and Vaithyanathan, S. (2002) Thumps up? Sentiment classification using machine learning techniques. In *Proceedings of the 2002 Conference on Empirical Methods in Natural Language Processing (EMNLP-02)*.

Pradhan, S., Hacioglu, K., Ward, W., Martin, J., and Jurafsky, D. (2003) Semantic role parsing: Adding semantic structure to unstructured text. In *Proceedings of the International Conference on Data Mining (ICDM-2003)*.

Riloff, E., Wiebe, J., and Wilson, T. (2003) Learning subjective nouns using extraction pattern bootstrapping. In *Proceedings of the Seventh Conference on Natural Language Learning (CoNLL-03)*.

Turney, P. (2002) Thumps up or thumbs down? Semantic orientation applied to unsupervised classification of reviews. In *Proceedings of the 40th Annual Meeting of the Association for Computational Linguistics*.

Wiebe, J., Bruce, R., and O'Hara, T. (1999) Development and use of a gold standard data set for subjectivity classifications. In *Proceedings of the 37th Annual Meeting of the Association for Computational Linguistics (ACL-99)*, 246–253.

Wiebe, J. (2000) Learning subjective adjectives from corpora. In *Proceedings of the 17th National Conference on Artificial Intelligence (AAAI-2000)*.

Wiebe, J., Wilson, T., Bruce, R., Bell, M., and Martin, M. (2002) Learning subjective language. Technical Report TR-02-100, Department of Computer Science, University of Pittsburgh, Pittsburgh, Pennsylvania.

Yu, H., and Hatzivassiloglou, V. (2003) Towards answering opinion questions: Separating facts from opinions and identifying the polarity of opinion sentences. In *Proceedings of the Conference on Empirical Methods in Natural Language Processing (EMNLP-03)*.

Chapter 12

Approaches for Automatically Tagging Affect: Steps Toward an Effective and Efficient Tool

Nathanael Chambers
The Institute for Human and Machine Cognition
40 South Alcaniz Street
FL 32502, U.S.A.
Email: nchambers@ihmc.us

Joel Tetreault and James Allen
University of Rochester
Department of Computer Science
NY 14627, U.S.A.
Email: tetreaul@cs.rochester.edu and james@cs.rochester.edu

Abstract

The tagging of discourse is important not only for natural language processing research, but for many applications in the social sciences as well. This chapter describes an evaluation of a range of different tagging techniques to automatically determine the attitude of speakers in transcribed psychiatric dialogues. It presents results in a marriage-counseling domain that classifies the attitude and emotional commitment of the participants to a particular topic of discussion. It also gives results from the Switchboard Corpus to facilitate comparison for future work. Finally, it describes a new Java tool that learns attitude classifications using our techniques and provides a flexible, easy to use platform for tagging of texts.

Keywords: affect, automatic tagging, cats, stochastic affect, affect tool, psychological models.

1. Introduction

Detecting affect in written or spoken language has several potential benefits. First and most obvious, human-computer interaction can benefit by tailoring the computer's responses (or lack of) according to the affect detected in the human. A more natural and effective interaction will ensue. Conversely, if computers can detect affect, then they can also help humans understand the concept of affect itself. For example, by observing the changes in emotion and attitude in people conversing, psychologists can determine correct treatments for patients. Computers can aid this sort of study by allowing more data to be collected and analysed, leading to more reliable treatments and theories.

In this study, the data from psychologists at the University of Rochester is used to test their hypothesis that poor interactions between married couples in a time of stress, such as a major illness, can actually exacerbate the illness. The premise is that emotion and communication are important to mental and physical health and that there is a direct correlation between how well a couple copes with a serious illness and how well they interact to deal with it. Good interactions can lead to quicker recovery while poor interactions, such as disengagement during conversations, can at times exacerbate the illness. They tested this hypothesis by observing the engagement levels of conversation between married couples presented with a "what-if?" scenario of one of the participants having a major illness (Alzheimer's Disease). The participants are then asked to discuss how they would deal with the sickness. The transcriptions of the conversations were tagged with affect related codes to look for correlations between communication and marital satisfaction.

Hodson, Shields, and Rousseau (2003) have shown that this tagging operation is very useful in analyzing patients' interactions and providing assistance to them. However, tagging by hand can be extremely time consuming and tends to be unreliable, so automated tools that can quickly learn tagging schemes from small amounts of data would be very useful. This chapter describes the evaluation of several different tagging approaches with respect to their tagging accuracy, ranging from simple n-gram approaches with statistical models that are easy to learn and apply, to more complex information retrieval techniques that require significant computation to produce the models. The goal is to identify the most promising techniques to use in an automatic tagging tool. This tool will then be used to develop tagging models for new domains and to use these models to automatically tag new data in the domains.

The approaches in this chapter were evaluated on two corpora. The Rochester Marriage-Counseling Corpus (Shields, 1997) was used because it provides a rich dialogue between married couples, providing informal utterances that are tagged for the attitude each spouse has toward a particular topic. The conversations are frank, sometimes intense dialogues between people who have known each other for years. It is a unique domain that provides excellent data for analyzing attitude and affect in dialogue. The results were compared with the Switchboard Corpus (Godfrey, Holliman, and McDaniel, 1992) for the two-fold purpose of comparing our results to previous work and future approaches in determining dialogue attitude. The two corpora are ideal because they are meticulously hand-tagged and are relatively informal dialogues in which the attitude and affect of the participants is not repressed by a simulated experiment.

2. Background

Work in textual Affective Computing has spawned a myriad of approaches to identify the emotions expressed by a sentence or discourse. The earliest approaches involve searching a text for predetermined keywords and other cue phrases that convey strong emotion, thus tagging the sentence depending on which keywords (if any) it contains. While this method has the advantage of speed, it fails in sentences with negation and is limited by the list of keywords.

Boucouvalas and Ze (2002) found that a tagged dictionary can identify the basis of emotion in phrases and then use grammatical features to determine which of the words in the sentence carry some emotional weight. Its main advantage is that it has a scaled model of emotion, but has the drawback of having to create a tagged dictionary that encompasses the target domain.

Statistical methods have the advantage of being free from the pretagged list constraints but are dependent on having a large enough tagged corpus for training and, in some instances, do not fare well with tagging at the sentence level. Goertzel's Webmind (2000) project uses latent semantic analysis for affect classification in its domain. Wu (2002) uses transformation-based learning for tagging affect in chat-conversation analysis. The method works by automatically generating rules for tagging and then refining the rules by comparing them with a tagged corpus (ground truth) and iterating until no more improvements in the rules can be made.

One successful technique is used by Liu (2003); he created an affect tagger for email that uses a corpus of common-sense rules. The premise is that to successfully identify affect, one must take into account everyday knowledge (which for them was manually encoded) that would not be captured in statistical approaches.

Our approach differs from past approaches in two ways. First, it describes different statistical methods based on computing n-grams and individually tags sentences as opposed to tagging whole documents or paragraphs. The approaches are based on techniques that have been successful in another domain, discourse act tagging. Second, these approaches are incorporated into a tagging tool that a user interacts with to better tag a transcribed session.

3. Rochester Marriage-Counseling Corpus

The initial studies used a corpus of 45 annotated transcripts of conversations between married couples. These transcripts were provided by researchers from the Center for Future Health at the University of Rochester. At the start of each conversation, the moderator gave a husband and wife the task of discussing how they would cope if one of them developed Alzheimer's disease. Each transcript is broken into *thought units*, one or more sentences that represent how the speaker feels toward the topic. Each thought unit takes into account positive and negative words, comments on health, family, jobs, emotion, travel, sensitivity, detail, and many more. There are roughly two dozen tags, but the five major ones are given here:

- **GEN** verbal content towards illness is vague or generic. Discussion tends to be about outcomes. It can also can indicate that the speaker does not take ownership of emotions. (i.e. "It would be hard," "I think that it would be important.")
- **DTL** speaker's verbal content is distinct with regards to illness, emotions, dealing with death, etc. Speaker tends to describe the process rather than the outcome. (i.e. "It would be hard for me to see you so helpless," "I would take care of you.")
- **SAT** statements about the task; couple discusses what the task is and how to go about it. (i.e. "I thought I would be the caregiver.")
- **TNG** tangents; statements that are not related to the task. Thought unit contains no emotional content related to the central issues of the task. (i.e. talking about a friend with a disease.)
- **ACK** acknowledgments of the other speaker's comments. (i.e. "yeah" and "right")

The corpus contains a total of 14,390 unigrams and bigrams, of which 9,450 occur only once. There are 4,040 total thought units. The distribution of tags is as follows: GEN: 1964 (41.51%), ACK: 1075 (22.72%), DTL: 529 (11.18%), SAT: 337 (7.12%), TNG: 135 (2.85%).

4. Approaches to Tagging

We investigated two classes of approaches to automatic tagging. The first is based solely on building n-gram statistical models from training data. The second is a vector-based approach that builds sentence vectors from the n-grams in the training data.

4.1 N-gram Based Approaches

An n-gram approach tags a thought unit based on previously seen n-grams in the training data. The approach is motivated by the assumption that there are key phrases in each thought unit that identify which tag (emotion, attitude, etc.) should be used. Depending on the size of the n-grams being collected, a significant amount of word ordering can also be captured. However, n-gram models often lose many long range dependencies that extend beyond the n length of the n-gram.

The following approaches all use n-grams ranging from unigrams to 5-grams. Any n-gram that appears only once in the training corpus is considered sparse and is ignored. In addition, all unigrams, bigrams, and trigrams that appear only twice are thrown out. Due to the greater information content of the high n-grams, those that appeared twice are deemed helpful and are not ignored. The start of the thought unit was also considered a word (i.e. <s> *well* is a bigram in a sentence that begins with the word *well*).

4.1.1 Naive Approach

The Naive Approach to tagging the thought units is the most basic approach; it simply selects the *best* n-gram that appears.

$$P(tag_i \mid utt) = \max_{j,k} P(tag_i \mid ngram_{jk})$$

Where tag_i ranges over the set of available tags (GEN, DTL, SAT, TNG, ACK) and $ngram_{jk}$ is the *jth* n-gram of length k (k-gram) in the current thought unit *utt* of the test set. The example below illustrates how the naive approach would tag a sentence, showing the n-gram with the highest probability of each n-gram length.

Ex: I don't want to be chained to a wall

N-Gram Size (tag)	Top N-gram	Probability
1: (GEN)	don't	0.665
2: (GEN)	to a	0.692
3: (GEN)	<s> I don't	0.524
4: (DTL)	don't want to be	0.833
5: (DTL)	I don't want to be	1.00

The highest n-gram is *I don't want to be* with 1.00 probability, indicating that this phrase always appeared with the DTL tag in the training set. Therefore, the unit is tagged DTL.

4.1.2 Weighted Approach

The Weighted Approach builds upon the Naive by assuming that higher n-grams provide more reliable information and that the sum of all n-gram probabilities will give a broader estimation. Each n-gram that appears in the given thought unit is multiplied by a weight assigned to the length of the n-gram. In more detail, the probability of a thought unit being tagged is:

$$P(tag_i \mid utt) = \sum_{k=0}^{m} ((\max_j P(tag_i \mid ngram_{jk})) * weight_k)$$

Where m is the length of the longest n-gram ($m=5$ in this study) and again, $ngram_{jk}$ is the jth n-gram of length k. $weight_k$ is the weight of an n-gram of length k. We will refer to the weights 0.4, 0.4, 0.5, 0.8, 0.8 (i.e. unigrams and bigrams are weighted 0.4, trigrams are 0.5, etc.) whenever the Weighted Approach is used. Many different weights can be assigned, each between 0 and 1 to try and obtain better results. However, the improvement is both minimal and approximately the same no matter which weights are chosen (as long as the longer n-grams are weighted more than unigrams and bigrams).

As above, the same example sentence is given here to illustrate this approach. The top GEN and DTL n-grams are shown.

Ex:I don't want to be chained to a wall		
N-Gram Size (tag)	Top N-gram	Probability
1: (GEN)	don't	0.665
1: (DTL)	want	0.452
2: (GEN)	to a	0.692
2: (DTL)	want to	0.443
3: (GEN)	<s> I don't	0.524
3: (DTL)	I don't want	0.592
4: (GEN)	I don't want to	0.27
4: (DTL)	don't want to be	0.833
5: (GEN)	<s> I don't want to	0.25
5: (DTL)	I don't want to be	1.00

GEN sum (w/weights) 1.255
DTL sum (w/weights) 2.086

Ignoring the other possible tags in this example, it is easy to see that DTL gains ground in the higher probabilities, 0.833 for the 4-gram and 1.00 for the 5-gram. DTL's final sum of the n-gram weighted probabilities is clearly higher and the sentence is correctly tagged DTL.

The added weights do not differ much from the Naive Approach in this example, but one of the many cases where it does differ can be seen in the utterance, "*and really decide if there were places we wanted.*" The Naive Approach pulls out the unigram *really* as the highest single probability and tags it GEN. However, the Weighted Approach sums the max of each n-gram for the tags and DTL wins because *decide if there* has a higher probability than GEN's top trigram. Trigrams are weighted higher than the lower n-grams where GEN is considered more likely, so the Weighted Approach chooses DTL while the naive approach would incorrectly choose GEN.

4.1.3 Lengths Approach

The Lengths Approach also builds upon the Naive Approach by adding the lengths of each thought unit as a type of weight (much like the Weighted Approach) to compute the maximum n-gram probabilities. During training with the training set, the number of words are counted in each tag's thought units. By calculating the average utterance length for each tag and its corresponding standard deviation, the length weight for each new thought unit in the test corpus can be obtained.

$$lenWeight_{ts} = \frac{e^{(-(n_s - n_t)^2)/(2*dev_t^2)}}{\sqrt{2\pi} * dev_t}$$

Where n_s is the number of words in utterance s, n_t is the average word length for the tag t, and dev_t is the length standard deviation for tag t. The length weights from our example sentence of nine words are as follows:

GEN	DTL	ACK	SAT	TNG
0.0396	0.0228	0.0004	0.0613	0.0354

The above table shows that the weights are relatively equal except for the ACK and SAT tags. Acknowledgment phrases tend to be very short and concise, one or two words long, so this low weight for a sentence of nine words is consistent with the motivation for this approach. Once these tag weights are computed, we choose our tag by the following:

$$P(tag_i \mid utt) = (\max_{j,k} P(tag_i \mid ngram_{jk})) * lenWeight_{im}$$

Where m is the word length of utt. Below shows how this method influences our example utterance. Again, only the top n-gram for each is shown.

Ex: I don't want to be chained to a wall		
1: (GEN) don't	.665 * .0396 =	.026
2: (GEN) to a	.692 * .0396 =	.027
3: (GEN) <s> I don't	.592 * .0396 =	.021
4: (DTL) don't want to be	.833 * .0228 =	.019
5: (DTL) I don't want to be	1.00 * .0228 =	.023

The highest weighted n-gram is now the bigram, *to a*, with 0.027 final probability. The length weight effectively changes the Naive Approach's result to GEN. The majority of cases where the Lengths Approach differs the most can be found in ACK thought units. For example, the utterance *I don't either* should be tagged ACK, but none of the three words are strong indicators of the ACK tag and the training set does not contain this trigram. However, the length weight of ACK is 0.174 while the nearest tag, GEN, is 0.029. The Naive Approach normally considers this sentence three times more likely to be GEN than ACK. However, the length weight takes the short length of this utterance and correctly weights the ACK probability higher than GEN.

4.1.4 Weights with Lengths Approach

After finding only minor improvements over both the Weighted and Lengths approaches, we combined the two together. The example above is continued here by recalling the results of the Weighted Approach followed by the addition of the lengths weight:

GEN	sum (w/weights)	1.255
DTL	sum (w/weights)	2.086
GEN	weight/length	1.255 * 0.0396 = 0.0497
DTL	weight/length	2.086 * 0.0228 = 0.0476

Adding the length weight to this example reverses the Weighted Approach's DTL tag to a GEN tag. This occurs because DTL utterances typically are very long, while GEN utterances are very often under 10 words long (as is our example).

4.1.5 Analytical Approach

Many of the ACK utterances were found to be mis-tagged as GEN by the above approaches. Most of these were grounding utterances that repeated some of what was said in the previous utterance. For example, the second utterance below is mis-tagged:

B - so then you check that your tire is not flat

A - check the tire

This is a typical example of grounding where speaker A repeats a portion of B's last utterance in order to indicate understanding. Instead of adding another weight to our already growing list on the Naive Approach, a new model can be created that takes repeated words and the length of the two utterances into account (the repeated phrase is usually shorter than the original).

$$P(w_1 | T) * P(w_2 | T) * \mathsf{L} \ * P(w_n | T) *$$
$$P(R_{w_1} | O_{w_1}, L, L_p, T) * \mathsf{L} \ * P(R_{w_n} | O_{w_n}, L, L_p, T) *$$
$$P(L | T) * P(T)$$

Where w_i is a unigram in the utterance and $0 \le i < n$ where n is the length of the utterance, O_{wi} is a unigram occurring in the previous utterance, R_{wi} is the repeated unigram (i.e. the unigram appeared in this utterance as well), L is the length of the current utterance, and L_p is the length of the previous utterance. The third line of the equation is the length weight brought over from the Lengths Approach. Due to the obvious sparseness of the data for such an ambitious statistic, we put each unigram in one of four buckets according to its number of occurrences in the training data (5, 30, 100, infinity). The sentence lengths are thrown into only two buckets (2, 100000). Since most acknowledgements are two or less words in length, this statistic should help find the majority of them while the repeated unigrams will find the rest.

This method produced worse results than the Naive Approach. Other bucket sizes were experimented with, but none significantly altered the result. This may be a direct result from the frequency of tags GEN and ACK. These two tags make up 64% of the 5 tags that occur in the corpus and the probability $P(L|T)$ heavily favors one of the two tags (ACK dominates short sentences and GEN dominates the rest). Unfortunately, it seems to pull down the overall results when it is a factor in any calculation.

4.2 Information Retrieval-Based Approaches

Two vector-based methods for automatically tagging the utterances in the marriage corpus are discussed in this section. The first method is based on the Chu-Carroll and Carpenter routing system (1999). The second method dispenses with matrix construction of exemplar vectors and compares test sentences against a database of sentences.

4.2.1 Chu-Carroll and Carpenter

Chu-Carroll and Carpenter's domain is a financial call center with 23 possible caller destinations. The algorithm to route callers to the appropriate destination is summarized here. First, the caller's voice request is sent to a parser and a routing module. If the module generates only one destination, then the call is routed to that department. If more than one destination is generated, the system tries to generate a disambiguation query. If such a query cannot be generated, then the call defaults to a human operator (calls are also sent to human operators if the routing module does not generate a destination). When the clarifying query is generated, the algorithm is repeated with the caller's disambiguating response to the query.

The routing module is the most important part of the system. It consists of a database of a large collection of documents (previous calls) where each document is a vector in n-dimensional space. A query is a sentence transformed into a single vector and compared to each document (or destination) in the database. The document most similar to the query vector is the final destination.

Creation of the database of documents consists of the following training process; each word of the input is filtered morphologically, stop-words are removed, and all unigrams, bigrams and trigrams are extracted. The database or term-document matrix is an $M \times N$ matrix where M is the number of salient terms and N is the number of destinations. $A_{t,d}$ is the number of times term t occurs in calls to destination d. This matrix is then normalized for n-grams:

$$B_{t,d} = \frac{A_{t,d}}{\sqrt{\sum_{1 \leq e \leq n} A_{t,e}^2}}$$

A second normalizing metric, inverse document frequency (IDF), is also employed to lower the weight of a term that occurs in many documents since it is not a good indicator of any destination:

$$IDF(t) = \log_2 \frac{n}{d(t)}$$

where n is the number of documents in the corpus and $d(t)$ is the number of documents containing term t. Each entry in the matrix thus becomes:

$$C_{t,d} = IDF(t) \times B_{t,d}$$

Query matching consists of transforming the input call to a vector in the same manner as above. A cosine distance metric is then used to compare this vector against the n destinations in the matrix.

4.2.2 Method 1: Routing-Based Method

A modified version of Chu-Carroll and Carpenter's algorithm was also analyzed; it is described here. Stop-word filtering is not done, so some common stop words such as "hmmm" or "uh" are included in the list of n-grams. A 2-gram model is used, so the term extraction phase generates all unigrams and bigrams. The same weighting principles and IDF metrics are employed for the matrix construction phase. The modification to the algorithm is the introduction of the entropy (amount of disorder) of each term. If a term is found in several documents then it exhibits low entropy, or a low amount of disorder. On the other hand, terms such as *yeah* or *right*, which appear in several tags, are bad exemplars and should be pruned from the database given their entropy. The following formula for determining the entropy of a term was used:

$$entropy(t) = -\sum_{1 \le e \le n} \frac{A_{t,e}}{\sum_{1 \le f \le n} A_{t,f}} \times \frac{\log A_{t,e}}{\sum_{1 \le f \le n} A_{t,f}}$$

A pruning threshold must be determined in order to use entropy to eliminate unhelpful terms. In the marriage-counseling corpus, the maximum entropy for any term was 2.9. The testing algorithm was repeated starting with this cutoff value and decrementing by 0.1 for each new test. Figure 1 shows how this method would assign the DTL tag to the sentence, *I don't want to be chained to a wall*. After the matrix of canonical vectors is created, the test sentence (in vector form) is compared to each of the vectors. The one that is closest to our example thought unit is DTL, if only by a small margin over GEN. Hence it is selected, correctly, as the tag. It should be noted that figure 1 is purely conceptual. In reality, the cosine test is done over an n-dimensional space (as opposed to 2) where n in this test is 38,636.

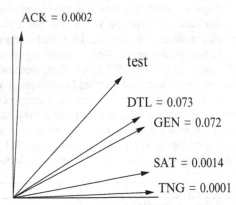

ACK = 0.0002

test

DTL = 0.073

GEN = 0.072

SAT = 0.0014

TNG = 0.0001

Figure 1. IR Method 1 Results of Test Sentence (not to scale)

Length	GEN	ACK	TNG	DTL	SAT
1-2	218	991	10	13	42
3-4	389	140	26	29	68
5-6	400	49	31	68	55
7-8	312	20	15	72	63
Over	1107	19	54	426	126

Figure 2. Distribution of the lengths of thought units for each tag.

In addition, we created two more vectors to raise the tagging accuracy: sentence length and repetition. The intuition behind the former is that tags tend to be correlated with sentences of a certain length. For example, ACK utterances are usually one or two words in length because most of them are phrases such as "yeah" or "yeah ok." On the other hand, tags that tend to communicate more, such as DTL, would have longer sentences. The distribution can be seen in figure 2. Additional vectors are added to the matrix for each sentence length and the frequencies above are encoded in these vectors using the normalization schemes. During the test phase, the length of the test sentence is included in its vector representation.

The intuition behind the repetition metric is that ACK's can be better modeled by taking into account repeated words from the previous thought unit. If key words are repeated then it is likely that the second speaker used those words to signal a backchannel. Repetition, or percent overlap, is calculated by dividing the number of n-grams in the intersection of the current and previous utterance by the number of current utterance n-grams. A "bin" system is used as was done in the sentence length metric, making new tags of 0% repetition, 1- 25%, 26-50%, 51-75%, 76-100% and 100% overlap. All unigrams are thrown out under the assumption that they won't add any useful information since higher order n-grams are better predictors. Keeping them results in a 1% drop in performance.

4.2.3 Method 2: Direct Comparison of Sentence Vectors

The Direct Comparison method directly compares a test vector to a database. Unlike the Chu-Carroll and Carpenter algorithm, there is no construction of n-grams and normalizing of data.

Each thought unit is converted to a vector in which the index of the vector is a term. The cosine test is again used to determine similarity, but here it is used somewhat differently. Every other vector in the database is compared with our test vector. The ten highest cosine scores (highest similarities) are kept and used to calculate the best tag. First, each of the ten thought units' tags are normalized to 100%, so if a thought unit had multiple tags and tag counts of ((GEN 2) (DTL 1)), the result would be (GEN 66.67%) and (DTL 33.33%). Next, these percents are normalized by multiplying by the respective cosine score and dividing by the sum of all ten cosine scores. This makes vectors that are very close to the test vector more significant (weighting). Finally, each tag is summed across the ten thought units and the one with the highest sum is returned as the most likely tag. Using the same test example, the top five sentences selected using this method are shown in figure 3. Weighting the tags appropriately, the scores are: DTL = 0.3741, SAT = 0.2169, GEN = 0.2045, TNG = 0.2044, ACK = 0. Thus, DTL is correctly selected.

Cosine Score	Tag	Sentence
0.6396	SAT	Are we supposed to get them?
0.6030	GEN	That sounds good
0.6030	TNG	That's due to my throat
0.5583	DTL	But if I said to you I don't want to be Ruth and I don't want to get anywhere close to being Ruth, that I would expect that you would respect my wishes
0.5449	DTL	If it were me, I'd want to be a guinea pig to try things

Figure 3. IR Method 2 results of test sentences

5. Evaluations

The different methods discussed in this paper were evaluated based on a six-fold cross validation of their percent accuracy. In regards to the Marriage-Counseling Corpus, the corpus is divided into six equal portions and cross validation was used (train on five, test on the remaining one) to extract the final tagging accuracy percentage for each approach. All six combinations of the validation were tested and the average of the six is used as the final percentage.

5.1 N-Gram Based Approaches

The five n-gram approaches performed relatively the same on the marriage corpus. The results are given in figure 4. The Weighted Approach performed the best, scoring almost one percent above the Naive Approach and more so above the others. The Naive, which simply takes the n-gram with the highest probability, performed better than the other added metrics.

5.1.1 IR Method 1

Several instantiations of the modified Chu-Carroll and Carpenter algorithm were evaluated by toggling these pruning methods:

- **Prune-1:** terms that occur only once are pruned
- **Entropy:** the above entropy method is used
- **IDF:** terms are pruned using IDF

To determine which values were best, all six combinations of the three pruning methods were tested. The X's in figure 5 denote which pruning method was used.

The results in figure 5 show that only using the entropy model (with or without terms that occur only once) offers roughly a 4% advantage over the IDF method. The top two combinations of models (using entropy with/without Prune-1) were then run on the entire corpus with the model eliminating values that occur only once. This resulted in an average of 66.16% over the 6 cross-validation sets, while the model not using Prune-1 averaged 65.69%.

Using the best instantiation (Prune-1 and Entropy) from the first six tests, new n-grams for sentence length were made: sentences less than 2, of length 3 or 4, of length 5 or 6, and so forth so the final new n-gram was sentences 10 words or longer. Only a marginal increase in performance was found at 66.76%.

Naïve	Weighted	Lengths	Weight w/Length	Analytical
66.80%	67.43%	64.35%	66.02%	66.60%

Figure 4. Percent correct comparison of the five n-gram approaches for the UR Marriage Corpus.

Prune-1	Entropy	IDF	Accuracy
X	X		66.16%
	X		65.69%
			65.17%
X	X	X	61.56%
	X	X	61.40%
X		X	61.37%

Figure 5. IR Method 1 results

5.1.2 IR Method 2

The result (using cross-validation as in Method 1 and the best instantiation: Prune-1 and Entropy, but no IDF) is an overall average of 63.16%, slightly lower than Method 1. See figure 6.

Prune-1	Entropy	IDF	Accuracy
	X	N/A	63.10%
X	X	N/A	65.25%

Figure 6. IR Method 2 results

Metric	Accuracy
Sentence Length	66.76%
Repetition: No Unigrams	66.39%
Repetition: All N-grams	65.59%

Figure 7. IR Extension Metrics

6. Discussion

Of the two vector approaches, the Routing-Based Method achieved the best result with almost a 1% improvement over the Direct Method. Both approaches did best when Prune-1 and Entropy were factored in. Pruning terms that appeared only once helped in most cases (except for IDF, adding Prune-1 lowered the score); this intuitively makes sense. Words with only one occurrence do not convey accurate information and tend to bring the accuracy down. The entropy factor also improved performance, adding 1.5% to IDF and almost 2% to the combination of Prune-1 and IDF. When Prune-1 and entropy were combined, they resulted in the highest Routing-Based and Direct Method results. However, with a score of 66.16%, the Routing-Based Prune-1 and Entropy scored almost 1% over the Direct's 65.25%.

The N-Gram Approaches proved to be much more versatile than was initially thought. The Naive Approach does surprisingly well, scoring a half percentage higher than the best Routing-Based method, 66.80%. Several additions to the Naive were tried to improve performance, but nothing significantly improved the results. Giving the n-grams different weights produced the most accurate results with a 6-fold cross validation score of 67.43%. Putting the lengths of the thought units into consideration actually hurt the results in the marriage corpus. The Analytical Approach looks the most promising since it seems to capture the length of utterances and repeated words more precisely than the Naive Approach; however, the Analytical performs relatively the same as the Naive, scoring just 0.2% lower.

The Weighted Approach performed the best on the marriage corpus out of all the methods discussed in this chapter. This result goes against intuition and shows us that a simple n-gram comparison between the training set and the testing set performs as well and even better than the more complicated vector based approaches. Further, adding different weights to the Naive often hurts and very rarely improves the performance. Choosing the most indicative n-gram for the correct tag produces the most accurate results.

6.1 Switchboard Corpus Evaluation

6.1.1 Switchboard Data Set

To further determine the effectiveness of a tagging system, it is necessary to compare it to other methods on a common corpus. The Stolcke et al. modified Switchboard Corpus of spontaneous human-to-human telephone speech (Godfrey, Holliman, and McDaniel, 1992) from the Linguistic Data Consortium was chosen for this purpose. Unlike the Marriage-Counseling data set, the Switchboard set is composed of conversations of random topics as opposed to planned task-oriented ones. In addition, the data set has a much richer tagging set, being composed of 42 Dialog Acts (DA's) that are the Switchboard's version of thought unit tags. The five most prominent tags, which comprise 78% of the corpus, are (and their percentage of the corpus): Statement (36%), Backchannel/Acknowledgement (19%), Opinion (13%), Abandoned/Uninterruptible (6%), Agreement/Accept (5%). The tagged corpus consists of 205,000 utterances and 1.4 million words making it significantly larger than any other similarly tagged corpora.

6.1.2 Evaluation Method and Results

After splitting the Switchboard Corpus into six subsets as was done with the Marriage Corpus, a six fold cross-validation test was run. All the results are averages over the six combinations of training on five subsets and testing on one.

Figure 8 shows the results of the vector-based approaches on the Switchboard Corpus. The base model uses the original Chu-Carroll and Carpenter formalism of pruning entries that occur once and using IDF. The second method adds the entropy metric. The following approaches incorporate sentence length and word repetition as n-grams in the vector. As in the Marriage-Counseling corpus, these improve accuracy slightly. The Direct Approach performs significantly better than it did in the other corpus, mostly due to the fact there is more data to compare with.

Figure 9 shows the results of the five n-gram approaches described in section 4.1. The performance is similar to that on the Marriage Corpus (figure 4), but the Analytical Approach experiences a drop of 7.8%. This can be attributed to an even denser clustering of tags in the Switchboard corpus, where the three most frequent tags appear 71% of the time in the corpus. The length probability in the Analytical Approach favors them greatly (so it is often used instead of the correct tag). It can be seen, however, that the Weighted with Lengths Approach out-performs the other approaches. It correctly tags 1.6% more than the closest approach, breaking 70%.

Base Model	Entropy & IDF	Repeated Words	Length	Repeated & Length	Direct Approach
58.42%	57.26%	60.93%	60.92%	60.93%	63.53%

Figure 8. Percent Correct in the Information Retrieval Approaches for the Switchboard Corpus

Naïve	Weighted	Lengths	Weight w/Length	Analytical
68.41%	68.77%	69.01%	70.08%	61.40%

Figure 9. Percent Correct comparison of the five n-gram approaches for the Switchboard Corpus

7. CATS Tool

The culmination of this research has led to the development of a first version of an easy to use tool that is based off of the Naive Approach. Written in Java for multi-platform portability, this automated tagging system (CATS) employs the Lengths Approach, but uses only unigrams and bigrams. One of the main concerns during development of CATS was the hardware limitation that exists for a helpful tool. The methods discussed in this chapter require intensive computing resources and would be too slow to be of use to a human user. However, it was found that the Naive Approach performs as well as the vector-based approaches yet requires much less computing power. In addition, using just unigrams and bigrams performs almost as well as including the higher order n-grams. This is most likely the result of sparse data, but sparse data is usually the norm for untagged corpora. As a result, CATS employs a unigram-bigram Naive Approach with length weights. Computing time is acceptable and the results are comparable.

The program's main goal is ease of use for the researcher. As can be seen in figure 10, the main tagging attributes (case #, speaker, tag, text) are contained in separate windows to keep a clean workspace. Features such as auto-completion, tag flexibility, model customization, and others make the program both a text editor and an automated tagger. One can build a naive method model off of data by loading any text file with thought units and tags into the CATS program. A simple click of the button builds the model. To tag new text based off of this model, a new file of thought units (without tags obviously) can be loaded and automatically tagged with another click of the mouse.

CATS splits the new thought units into unigrams and bigrams and draws its tags using the naive length weighted approach discussed in this paper. A certainty percentage, the tagger's assessment of its tag choices, is given with each tag as well. The percent is based off of the second highest tag choice for the thought unit (high / (high + 2nd high) x 100). Low certainty measurements are colored red to bring the researcher's attention to a potentially incorrect tag.

Currently, there is no program that can train on data with a click of the mouse and instantly build a statistical model based on the given tags. Tagging new data is completed in seconds with CATS, saving the researcher weeks or even months of work. We have worked closely with the Center for Future Health and have received good feedback on the interface and ease of use of the tool. Preliminary results have even been seen of 80 to 90% accuracy (based on smaller tag sets than the one discussed in this paper) with this tool when there is enough data to train on.

The fields of anthropology, linguistics, and psychology frequently employ several undergraduates and graduates to tag speech dialogues for information content. The process is extremely tedious and can take months. However, a tool like CATS has the potential to cut the process down to a few seconds. Once an initial dataset of adequate size is tagged, CATS trains itself on the data and is able to accurately and quickly tag new data. We feel that the tool is a good first step at automating the time intensive task of tagging text for the research community.

7.1 Future Tools

CATS fails in many aspects to fulfill the need of a fully functional tagging tool, both in its graphical interface and in its results. Although the results haven't been found scientifically, there are reports that making a list of *high importance* words and using them to tag utterances is more effective than the automated approaches. If a given utterance contains a word in this list, it is tagged as the list specifies. These lists must be created by hand.

The n-gram models discussed above should take into account high importance words, but these anecdotes show that users are often distrustful of black box tools and require other options to manipulate the models themselves. Also, n-gram models only represent relations between adjacent words, losing the correspondence between words on opposite sides of an utterance or paragraph. It may be that the high importance list captures more of these relations than n-gram and vector based approaches are able. Also, when data is too sparse to train on, automatic tools need fallback methods such as word lists to be effective. More work is needed to build larger and more general models that are robust enough to be used in an automated tagging tool.

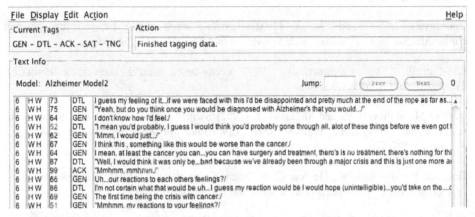

Figure 10. CATS tags data and gives a certainty measure to its left. Low certainty tags can be glanced over by the researcher to assure correctness.

8. Related Work

Stolcke (2000) developed a dialogue model that is "based on treating the discourse structure of a conversation of a hidden Markov model and the individual dialogue acts are modeled via a dialogue act n-gram." Whereas word n-grams form the basis of analysis for both metrics discussed in this paper, word n-grams are part of a set of methods used to implement the statistical dialogue grammar. Decision trees and neural nets are also used. In addition, while our methods only look at written text, Stolcke et al. have models that integrate prosody and speech.

Their model fared about the same as the Lengths and Weights metric, tagging 71% correctly. In comparison, their study of human annotators had human annotation scoring 84% and a baseline of 35%.

9. Conclusion

This chapter has described several vector and n-gram based approaches to automatically tagging text. It describes a new domain involving married couples in which its approaches perform reasonably well, but without much variation from each other. The computationally expensive vector based approaches for recognizing the emotional content of a speaker is outperformed by much more simple n-gram approaches. It has also described a platform independent tagging tool that can be employed by researchers to learn tagging patterns and automatically tag large corpora of dialogues or written text. Finally, the approaches in this chapter have shown to perform similarly on the Switchboard Corpus and have provided scores for others to compare future work on automatic tagging.

10. Acknowledgments

We would like to thank Dr. Cleveland Shields for insight and the evaluation dialogues. This work was supported in part by ONR grant 5-23236 and the National Institute on Deafness and Other Communication Disorders grant T32 DC00035-10.

11. Bibliography

Boucouvalas, A. C. and Zhe, X. (2002) Text-to-emotion engine for real time internet communication. In *Proc. International Symposium on CSNDSP 2002*. 164-168.

Chu-Carroll, J. and Carpenter, B. (1999) Vector-based natural language call routing. *Computational Linguistics*. 361-388.

Godfrey, J., Holliman, E., and McDaniel, J. (1992) Switchboard: Telephone speech corpus for research and development. In *Proc. IEEE Conference on Acoustics, Speech and Signal Processing*. 517-520.

Goertzel, B., Silverman, K., Hartley, C., S. Bugaj, S., and Ross, M. (2000) The baby webmind project. In *Proc. Artificial Intelligence and the Simulation of Behaviour*.

Hodson, J. H., Shields, C. G., and Rousseau, S. L. (2003) Disengaging communication in later-life couples coping with brest cancer. *Family Systems and Health*. 145-163. Campbell, Maryland.

Liu, H., Lieberman, H., and Selker, T. (2003) A model of textual affect sensing using real-world knowledge. In Proc. Seventh International Conference on Intelligent User Interfaces. 125-132.

Shields, C. (1997) Annotation scheme. *For Center for Future Health, University of Rochester*. Rochester, New York.

Stolcke, A., Ries, K., Coccaro, N., Shriberg, E., Bates, R., Jurafsky, D., Taylor, P., and Martin, R. (2000) Dialogue act modeling for automatic tagging and recognition of conversational speech. *Computational Linguistics*. 339-373.

Wu, T., Khan, F. M., Fisher, T. A., Shuler, L. A., and Pottenger, W. M. (2002) Posting act tagging using transformation-based learning. In *Proc. Workshop on Foundations of Data Mining and Discovery, IEEE International Conference on Data Mining*.

Chapter 13

Argumentative Zoning for Improved Citation Indexing

Simone Teufel
University of Cambridge
Computer Laboratory,
JJ Thomson Avenue
Cambridge CB1 3PY, UK
Email: Simone.Teufel@cam.ac.uk

Abstract

We address the problem of automatically classifying academic citations in scientific articles according to author affect. There are many ways how a citation might fit into the overall argumentation of the article: as part of the solution, as rival approach or as flawed approach that justifies the current research. Our motivation for this work is to improve citation indexing. The method we use for this task is machine learning from indicators of affect (such as *"we follow X in assuming that...",* or *"in contrast to Y, our system solves this problem")* and of presentation of ownership of ideas (such as *"We present a new method for...",* or *"They claim that...").* Some of these features are borrowed from Argumentative Zoning (Teufel and Moens, 2002), a technique for determining the rhetorical status of each sentence in a scientific article. These features include the type of subject of the sentence, the citation type, the semantic class of main verb, and a list of indicator phrases. Evaluation will be both intrinsic and extrinsic, involving the measurement of human agreement on the task and a comparison of human and automatic evaluation, as well as a comparison of task-performance with our system versus task performance with a standard citation indexer (CiteSeer, Lawrence et al., 1999).

Keywords: citation analysis, sentiment, machine learning, automatic summarisation.

1. Citation Indexing and Citation Maps

Automatic indexing, as exemplified by the highly successful tool CiteSeer (Lawrence et al., 1999; Giles et al., 1998), has become the method of choice for literature searches; as a result, CiteSeer receives more than 8000 hits a day. CiteSeer automatically citation-indexes all scientific articles reached by a web-crawler, making them available to searchers via authors or keywords in the title.

However, keywords are not everything in literature searches. Shum (1998) states that researchers, particularly experienced researchers, are often interested in relations between articles. They need to know if a certain article criticises another and what the criticism is, or if the current work is based on that prior work. This type of information is hard to come by with current search technology. Neither the author's abstract, nor raw citation counts help users in assessing the relation between articles. And even though CiteSeer shows a text snippet around the physical location for searchers to peruse, there is no guarantee that the text snippet provides enough information for the searcher to infer the relation.

Being able to interpret the rhetorical status of a citation at a glance would add considerable value to citation indexes, as shown in Figure 1. Here differences and similarities are shown between the example paper from which the search starts (Pereira et al., 1993) and the papers it cites, as well as the papers that cite it - within the universe of our smallish corpus of scientific papers. The citation relation is depicted by arrows. We distinguish *contrastive* links (arrows shown in grey) - links to rival papers and papers the current paper contrasts itself to -- and *continuative* links (shown in black) - links to papers that are taken as starting point of the current research, or as part of the methodology of the current paper. In the citation map, the most important textual sentence about each citation can be displayed; these sentences are extracted from the original text. For instance, the map tells us which aspect of Hindle (1990) the Pereira et al. paper criticises, and in which way Pereira et al.'s work was used by Dagan et al. (1994).

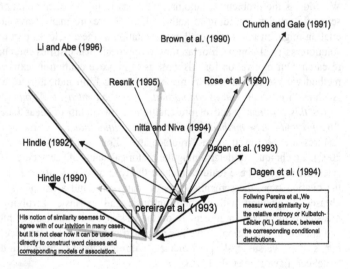

Figure 1. A Rhetorical Citation Map.

In a larger context (i.e., with thousands of citations automatically citation-indexed), we would be able to trace the citation relations of our example paper across time; Figure 2 shows part of such information (with sentence numbers indicating where in the text these sentences were taken from).

Simple citation parsing and displaying of sentences containing citations is not enough to achieve this type of output. CiteSeer makes the simplifying assumption that the most important information about a citation is always local to the physical citation, but this assumption does not hold. In the annotated corpus from Teufel and Moens (2002), where sentences are marked up according to rhetorical context, we found that 69% of the 600 evaluative **Contrast** sentences and 21% of the 246 **Basis** sentences do not contain the corresponding citation; the citation is found in preceding sentences instead. Therefore, CiteSeer will miss to display the evaluative statement in many cases. Nanba and Okumura (1999) present an automatic citation indexer which, like ours, automatically classifies contexts (in their case, into "positive" and "negative" contexts). However, they display a large context of around 3 sentences per citation, assuming that the important sentence expressing author affect is in this area. In our approach, we aim to find the single sentence containing the evaluative statement that connects two papers, even if that sentence is textually removed from the citation. We rely on corpus-based discourse analysis to find this sentence. Therefore, our approach is in a position to produce maximally short and informative descriptions.

Pereira et al. (1993) →(basis) Dagan et. al (1993)	**155** The data for this test was built from the training corpus for the previous one in the following way, based on a suggestion by Dagan et al. (1993)	
Pereira et al. (1993) →(contrast) Resnik (1992)	**11** While it may be worthwhile to base such a model on pre-existing sense classes (Resnik, 1992), in the work described here we look at how to derive the classes directly from distributional data.	
Resnik (1995) →(contrast) Pereira et al. (1993)	**0** Word groupings useful for language processing tasks are increasingly available [...] (e.g., Bensch and Savitch (1992), [...], Pereira et al. (1993), Schuetze (1993)	**1** However, for many tasks, one is interested in relationships among word senses, not words.

Figure 2. Some of Pereira et al. (1993)'s Citation Relations in Our Corpus.

The task of building citation maps can be formulated as a statistical classification problem. For each evaluative statement identified by Argumentative Zoning, we determine a set of potential candidate citation identifiers nearby, and use machine learning to associate the correct candidate identifier with the evaluative statement. The output of the classifier is a citation and a corresponding evaluative statement (a sentence), which can be displayed in the citation map.

2. Argumentative Zoning and Author Affect

Scientific writing is supposed to be objective and affect-free, but it is not. In fact, scientific texts are often so full of subjective statements, fixed phrases and hedges that even rather shallow techniques can exploit this fact to improve text understanding.

One example of such a technique is Argumentative Zoning (AZ; Teufel and Moens, 2002), a shallow method of discourse analysis which automatically determines the rhetorical status of each sentence in a text as one of the seven rhetorical roles defined in Figure 3 (examples come from our corpus, with CMP_LG identifiers (Computation and Language Archive, 1994).

The categories **Contrast** and **Basis** are directly relevant to the citation classification work described here. These two types of sentences are also the ones which are particularly concerned with affect, as they correspond roughly to positive and negative descriptions of other researchers' work. Of course, "positive" and "negative" affect are oversimplifications of much finer classification schemes developed in the field of Content Citation Analysis. This work has concentrated on manual annotation of citation function (cf. Weinstock's (1971) overview).

While we feel that our two categories are a workable approximation of these schemes for automation purposes, we remain interested in the fuller annotation schemes for the longer-term future.

AZ is based on machine learning with the Naive Bayes classifier, as in the Kupiec et al., (1995) approach to statistical sentence extraction. 15 features are used (cf. the overview in Figure 4), some of which are borrowed from the sentence extraction literature (such as location of a sentence in the article, or the sum of the relative term frequencies of the content words contained in it), and some of which are new and linguistically more interesting (such as the attribution-type of the subject; feature 14).

Aim	Specific research goal of the current paper	We describe and experimentally evaluate a method for automatically clustering words according to their distribution in particular syntactic contexts (9408011).
Textual	Statements about section structure	This section presents a morphographemic model which handles error detection in non-linear strings (9504024).
Own	(Neutral) description of own work presented in current paper	Our model associates phrases with relation graphs (9408014).
Background	Generally accepted scientific background	Semitic is known amongst computational linguists for its highly inflexional morphology (9504024).
Contrast	Comparisons with, criticism of or contrast to other work	However, Solomonoff does not give a concrete search algorithm and only makes suggestions as to its nature (9504034).
Basis	Statements of agreement with other work or continuation of other work	We use the framework for the allocation and transfer of control of Whittaker and Stenton (1988) (9504007).
Other	(Neutral) description of other researchers' work	The semidirectional Lambek calculus (henceforth SDL) is a variant of J. Lambek's original calculus of syntactic types (Lambek, 1958) (9605016).

Figure 3. Argumentative Zoning: Categories and Examples.

For instance, in order to find out if a sentence is part of the Background section or the Own section, knowing that the subject of the sentence is "our system" might bias one towards the Own section. Feature determination is shallow in that it requires only POS-tagging. The material used to train the system were 80 papers collected from the Computation and Language archive (around 12,000 sentences) which were manually annotated, with good inter- and intra-annotator agreement (Teufel, Carletta and Moens, 1999).

The original application of AZ was summarisation: Extractive summaries can be formed by choosing particularly important labels (e.g., Aim, Contrast and Basis) and by selecting those sentences which have the highest probabilistic score for that given label. The experiment in (Teufel, 2001), where the task used to evaluate the quality of abstracts was to list related articles and their relationship to the current paper, indicates that AZ information could be very useful in the short run to improve citation indexes. Subjects given AZ-extracts were able to perform this task almost as well as a control group given the full papers.

1. Absolute Location	Position of sentence absolutely in document; 10 segments A-J
2. Section Structure	Relative and absolute position of sentence within section (e.g., first sentence in section; anywhere in last third of section); 7 values
3. Paragraph Structure	Relative position of sentence within a paragraph; Initial, medial or final.
4. Headline Type	16 classes (e.g., Introduction, Results)
5. Sentence Length	Is the sentence longer than a threshold (currently 12 words)? Binary.
6. Title Word Overlap	Does the sentence contain words also occurring in the title or the internal headlines? Binary.
7. TF*IDF Word Overlap	Docs the sentence contain "significant terms" as determined by the TF*IDF measure? Binary.
8. Voice of Main Verb	Voice of first finite verb in sentence; Active or Passive or NoVerb
9. Tense of Main Verb	Tense of first finite verbgroup in sentence; 9 simple or complex tenses or NoVerb
10. Modality of Main Verb	Is the first finite verb a modal auxiliary? Binary.
11. Citations	Does the sentence contain a citation or the name of an author? If it contains a citation, is it a self citation? Where does the citation or author name occur? Type= Cit.(other), Cit.(self), Author Name, or None X Location=Beginning, Middle, End
12. History	Most probable rhetorical category of previous sentence; 7 Categories (cf. Figure 3) or "BEGIN"
13. Formulaic Patterns	Type of formulaic pattern occurring in sentence (e.g., "in this paper"); 18 Types or 9 Agent types or None
14. Type of Subject (Agent)	Semantic type of agent/subject; 9 Agent types or None
15. Type of Main Verb (Action)	Semantic type of action/verb, with our without negation; 27 Action types or None

Figure 4. Features Used for Argumentative Zoning.

3. Meta-discourse

One set of features particularly interesting for citation classification are the so-called meta-discourse features. As meta-discourse we understand here, in the sense of Myers (1992), the set of expressions that talk *about* the act of presenting research in a paper, rather than the research itself.

Swales (1990) found that the argumentation of the paper is rather prototypical; it might start by convincing us that the research done in the paper is hard or difficult, and that there is a gap in the current literature. This gap, for instance, is often indicated by a phrase such as "*to our knowledge, no method for ...*" or "*As far as we aware*". The Formulaic feature (Feature 13) collects 1762 such phrases and their variations.

The Agent feature (feature 14) models the succession of grammatical subjects in meta-discourse, which often signal who the ideas in a given paragraph are attributed to. For instance, in a paragraph describing related work, we expect to find references to other people in subject position more often than in the section detailing the authors' own methods, whereas in the background section, we often find general subjects such as "*researchers in computational linguistics*" or "*the computer science literature*". There is also a strong segmental aspect to the phenomenon of attribution of authorship: in sentences without meta-discourse, one assumes that the same sets of players (the authors, their rivals, or general researchers in the area) are still active. These assumptions are modelled in the Agent feature, which maps every sentence to 10 different classes of agents.

From a viewpoint of lexical semantics, it is interesting to look at the main verbs involved in meta-discourse. This is expressed in the Action feature. For instance, there is a set of verbs that is often used when the overall scientific goal of a paper is defined. These are the verbs of presentation, such as "*propose, present, report*" and "*suggest*"; in the corpus we found other verbs in this function, but with a lower frequency, namely "*describe, discuss, give, introduce, put forward, show, sketch, state*" and "*talk about*". There are specialised verb clusters which co-occur with **Basis** sentences, e.g., the verb semantics of continuation of ideas (cf. first row of Figure 5) or of change (second row).

On the other hand, the semantics of verbs in **Contrast** sentences is often concerned with failing of other researchers' ideas (cf. third row in Figure 5) or of contrast to these researchers' ideas (fourth row).

Currently the verb clusters we use are manually collected; the Action feature maps them onto 20 features (in theory, there are twice as many as negation of the sentence is also taken into account and combined with these 20 groups – in practice only 27 of these Action Types occur in our corpus as negation is rare). In future work, we are interested in how to automate the process of verb cluster determination.

Verbs of Continuation	*adopt, agree with, base, be based on, be derived from, be originated in, be inspired by, borrow, build on, follow, originate from, originate in, side with*
Verbs of Change	*adapt, adjust, augment, combine, change, decrease, elaborate on, expand, extend, derive, incorporate, increase, manipulate, modify, optimize, refine, render, replace, revise, substitute, tailor, upgrade*
Verbs of Failure	*abound, aggravate, arise, be cursed, be incapable of, be forced to, be limited to, be problematic, be restricted to, be troubled, be unable to, contradict, damage, degrade, degenerate, fail, fall prey, fall short, force oneself, force, hinder, impair, impede, inhibit, lack, misclassify, misjudge, mistake, misuse, neglect, obscure, overestimate, overfit, overgeneralize, overgenerate, overlook, pose, plague, preclude, prevent, resort to, restrain, run into problems, settle for, spoil, suffer from, threaten, thwart, underestimate, undergenerate, violate, waste, worsen*
Verbs of Contrast	*be different from, be distinct from, conflict, contrast, clash, differ from, distinguish oneself, differentiate, disagree, disagreeing, dissent, oppose*

Figure 5. Some Verb Classes (Continuation, Change, Failure and Contrast).

4. Human Annotation of Author Affect

In order to machine learn author affect, we have created a corpus of human annotated citation, starting from the annotations in Teufel and Moens (2002), where every sentence was associated with one of the seven categories. In that work, we used three annotators, written guidelines of 17 pages, and a formal training procedure of 7 hours. As a measure of agreement, we use Kappa (Siegel and Castellan, 1986).

We measured intra- and inter-annotator agreement. Intra-annotator agreement, i.e., the similarity of the annotation of *one* annotator after a time period long enough for the annotator to have forgotten the original annotation, is important as it justifies the well-definedness of the semantic labels of an annotation scheme. We concluded that our scheme was reasonably stable (K=.82, .81, .76) and reproducible (K=.71). The distribution of categories was very skewed: 67% **Own**, 16% **Other**, 6% **Background**, 5% **Contrast**, and 2% each for **Basis, Aim** and **Textual**. Further analyses showed that **Aim** and **Textual** are categories the annotators were particularly good at determining, whereas **Basis** and **Contrast** were relatively more difficult.

For the new project, a different type of annotation was necessary: for each evaluative statement (**Contrast** and **Basis**), our annotators had to identify one or more (or zero) citations in the text. These citations could be either in the current sentence, or in sentences before or after the evaluative statement.

In Citation-indexing, more than one target classification must be determined:

- More than one citation can be associated with an evaluative statement
- The citation concerned can be in the text before or after the evaluative statement

- The distance of the sentence expressing the evaluative statement from the citation must also be determined.

We have written a new set of guidelines, and currently have 1000 annotated sentence/citation pairs. We have not yet measured human agreement on the task.

Figure 6 shows two example contexts from our sample paper with their citation annotation. In the first example, the evaluation of the citation *Hindle (1990)* is contrastive, and the evaluative statement is found 4 sentences after the sentence containing the citation. In the second example, the citation *Rose et al. (1990)* is evaluated as a continuation; the evaluative statement can be found in the same sentence as the physical citation.

During the annotation, we noticed typical patterns of citation and evaluation, which is illustrated in Figure 7. The little square box signifies the citation itself; light grey background **Contrast** evaluation, medium grey a neutral description of other work (**Other**), the black zone signifies **Basis,** and white signifies **Own**. a) and b) show normal cases there other work is cited, and either **Contrast** or **Basis** evaluation is expressed a few sentences later. In case c), the approach is identified (by citation) and criticised in the first sentence, and only later is the approach described. This pattern is rarer than the corresponding pattern a). Pattern d) shows an approach which is cited but receives no evaluation. While citing without stating why one cites is against good writing advice, this pattern nevertheless occurred frequently in our corpus. Pattern e) is quite frequent for **Basis** sentences: as they are often used to describe which other work forms part of the own methodology, **Basis** sentences often occur embedded in **Own** sentences. In these cases, the citation and the evaluation are typically present in the same sentence.

---

5 Hindle (1990) (Contrastive, +4) proposed dealing with the sparseness problem by estimating the likelihood of unseen events from that of "similar" events that have been seen.
6 For instance, one may estimate the likelihood of that direct object for similar verbs.
7 This requires a reasonable definition of verb similarity and a similarity estimation method.
8 In Hindle's proposal, words are similar if we have strong statistical evidence that
they tend to participate in the same events.
9 His notion of similarity seems to agree with our intuitions in many cases, but it is not clear how it can be used directly to construct word classes and corresponding models of association.

113 The analogy with statistical mechanics suggests a deterministic annealing procedure for clustering **(Rose et. al, 1990). (Continuation, 0)**

Figure 6. Citation Annotation Examples.

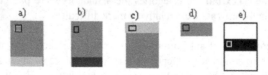

*Figure 7. Patterns of Citing and Author Stance Statements. Light grey stands for a **Contrast** zone, medium grey for a neutral **Other** zone, white for a **Own** zone, and black for a **Basis** zone. The little squares represent the references.*

5. Features for Author Affect

The 15 features used for Argumentative Zoning were presented in Figure 4 above, and the meta-discourse features were explained above. We will reuse some of the features used for Argumentative Zoning for the new citation classification task. In particular, the most successful features for Argumentative Zoning were (in descending order of usefulness): Absolute Sentence Location, Agent, Citations, Headlines, History, Formulaic, and Action. The other features only minimally improved results.

One of the AZ features, the history feature, models local context: it takes the category of the previous sentence as a feature, as there are often patterns of categories following each other. During testing, the category of the previous sentence is only probabilistically known, which is why beam search is performed. We expect this feature to be equally important for citation relation learning.

Other methods from co-reference resolution will be newly implemented for this project. The task of finding associations is loosely related to anaphora resolution. The differences between anaphora links and citation associations is that the latter appear less frequently in text, but seem to build links which are stronger, less ambiguous, and more global than anaphoric links. Constraining factors such as agreement information and WordNet relations, which prove very useful for anaphora resolution, are probably of less use for this task. We plan to borrow features from work such as Ge et al.'s (1998): type of candidate identification, type of alternative candidates, type of citation (self citation or foreign citation), location in the document of the evaluative statement, direction of identification (forward in text, or backward) and saliency factors such as (estimated) grammatical function of identification phrase, verb and verb tense.

In addition to these features, we will also exploit regularities such as the ones described in Figure 7 (patterns of citations and author stance).

6. Evaluation

Intrinsic evaluation of Argumentative Zoning was performed by measuring similarity of system annotation with human annotation, expressed in Kappa (Siegel and Castellan, 1988) and Macro-F (Lewis, 1991) (with respect to precision and recall of each of the seven categories). Our system showed an annotation accuracy of F=.50 (K=.45), beating a text classification baseline of F=.30 (K=.30), but remaining well under human performance (F=.69; K=.71). Extrinsic evaluation (Teufel, 2001) showed that for a question-answering task which concentrated on relations between articles, AZ-enhanced sentence extracts were significantly more useful than any other short document representation (including authors' abstracts and traditional sentence extracts).

For the new project, two types of evaluation are planned. Again, the intrinsic evaluation will compare system annotation with human annotation. The extrinsic evaluation will evaluate the usefulness of citation maps in comparison with alternative document surrogates, using specific questions created for our development corpus. We will create 20 pairs of document + question pairs about related work in the CL domain. For instance, the question for an article which uses manual rules for genre identification might be "*Name another article with a different method for genre identification*", or "*Does this article use the same classification as Karlgren (1994)?*" We will ask experts to verify the correctness of our answers. We can then measure the accuracy and time required to answer these questions using citation maps, as opposed to using CiteSeer or a standard search engine such as Google.

7. Conclusion

The automatic detection of subjectivity and point-of-view is traditionally associated with genres such as novels and newspaper texts (e.g., Wiebe, 1994), and tasks such as sentiment classification have used reviews of financial services or movies as their texts (Pang et al., 2002). We believe that scientific text also contains subjective content, and that this content can be determined and exploited for tasks such as summarisation and better citation indexing. Here, we have described a new task for citation-indexing that uses positive or negative spin on citations to guide users during their literature searches. This is an early project report; at this stage, we have created the training material and are currently adapting the features from Argumentative Zoning to this task.

8. Bibliography

Computation and Language Archive (1994). http://xxx.lanl.gov/cmp-lg

Ge, N. Hale, J., and Charniak, E. (1998). A statistical approach to anaphora resolution. In *Proceedings of the Sixth Workshop on Very Large Corpora*.

Giles, C, Bollacker, K., and Lawrence, S. (1998). Citeseer: An automatic citation indexing system. In *Proceedings of the Third ACM Conference on Digital Libraries*.

Kupiec, J. ,Pedersen, J., and Chen, F. (1995). A trainable document summarizer. In *Proceedings of the 18th Annual International Conference on Research and Development in Information Retrieval (SIGIR-95)*.

Lawrence, S., Giles, C., and Bollacker, K. (1999). Digital libraries and autonomous citation indexing. *IEEE Computer 32(6)*.

Lewis, D. (1991). Evaluating text categorisation. In *Speech and Natural Language: Proceedings of the ARPA Workshop of Human Language Technology*.

Myers, G. (1992). In this paper we report...- speech acts and scientific facts. *Journal of Pragmatics* 17(4).

Nanba and Okumura (1999). Towards multi-paper summarization using reference information. In *Proceedings of IJCAI-99*.

Pang, B., Lee, L., and Vaithyanathan, S. (2002). Thumbs up? Sentiment classification using machine learning techniques. In *Proceedings of the Conference on Empirical Methods in Natural Language Processing (EMNLP)*.

Shum, S. (1998). Evolving the web for scientific knowledge: First steps towards an "HCI knowledge web". *Interfaces, British HCI Group Magazine* 39.

Siegel, S. and Castellan, N. (1988). *Nonparametric Statistics for the Behavioral Sciences*. Berkeley, CA: McGraw-Hill, 2nd edition.

Swales, J. (1990). *Genre Analysis: English in Academic and Research Settings*. Chapter 7: Research articles in English. Cambridge, UK: Cambridge University Press.

Teufel, S. and Moens, M. (2002). Summarising scientific articles – experiments with relevance and rhetorical status. *Computational Linguistics* 28(4).

Teufel, S., Carletta, J., and Moens, M. (1999). An annotation scheme for discourse-level argumentation in research articles. In *Proceedings of the Ninth Meeting of the European Chapter of the Association for Computational Linguistics (EACL-99)*.

Teufel, S. (2001). Task-based evaluation of summary quality: Describing relationships between scientific papers. In *Proceedings of NAACL-01 Workshop "Automatic Text Summarization"*.

Weinstock, M. (1971). Citation Indexes. In *Encyclopaedia of Library and Information Science*, volume 5, New York, NY: Dekker.

Wiebe, J. (1994). Tracking point of view in narrative. *Computational Linguistics* 20(2).

Chapter 14

Politeness and Bias in Dialogue Summarization: Two Exploratory Studies

Norton Trevisan Roman
State University of Campinas
Instituto de Computação,Universidade Estadual de Campinas
Avenida Albert Einstein 1251
Cx. Postal 6176
CEP 13084-971,Campinas, SP, Brazil
Email: norton@ic.unicamp.br

Paul Piwek
University of Brighton
ITRI, University of Brighton, UK.
Email: Paul.Piwek@itri.brighton.ac.uk

Ariadne Maria Brito Rizzoni Carvalho
State University of Campinas
Computing Institute, State University of Campinas, Brazil.
Email: ariadne@ic.unicamp.br

Abstract

In this chapter, two empirical pilot studies on the role of politeness in dialogue summarization are described. In these studies, a collection of four dialogues was used. Each dialogue was automatically generated by the NECA system and the politeness of the dialogue participants was systematically manipulated. Subjects were divided into groups who had to summarize the dialogues from a particular dialogue participant's point of view or the point of view of an impartial observer. In the first study, there were no other constraints. In the second study, the summarizers were restricted to summaries whose length did not exceed 10% of the number of words in the dialogue that was being summarized.

Amongst other things, it was found that the politeness of the interaction is included more often in summaries of dialogues that deviate from what would be considered normal or unmarked. A comparison of the results of the two studies suggests that the extent to which politeness is reported is not affected by how long a summary is allowed to be. It was also found that the point of view of the summarizer influences which information is included in the summary and how it is presented. This finding did not seem to be affected by the constraint in our second study on the summary length.

Keywords: automatic dialogue summarization, automatic summarization, natural language processing, politeness, bias.

1. Introduction

To build an automatic summarization system capable of producing more "human like" dialogue summaries, one must first understand *how* humans summarize dialogues, *i.e.*, *what* they consider important to report in the summary and *how* they report it. The focus of this paper is on one aspect about which little is known. It concerns the nature of the interaction and, in particular, the politeness of the interlocutors. The question that is addressed is whether politeness is important enough to be mentioned in the summary and, if so, how it is mentioned.

So far, work on both language interpretation and generation has concentrated mainly on interpretation to and generation from truth-conditional representations of content, with some early exceptions such as (Hovy, 1988). The underlying assumption has been that the content of a natural language utterance is captured by the conditions under which it is true. When considering dialogue, the limitations of a strictly truth-conditional approach are apparent. Many types of dialogue acts do not yield to a purely truth-conditional analysis (greetings, acknowledgments, closings, etc.) and the way a dialogue proceeds is often affected by the emotional states of the interlocutors (Craggs and Wood, 2003; Fischer, 1999; Schmitz and Quantz, 1996; Reithinger et al., 2000).

Recent research on the influence of emotions on interpretation and generation includes work on recognizing the user's emotional state, e.g., anger (Huber et al., 2000), so that a computer dialogue system can adapt its own behaviour to prevent such feeling; the use of humour to facilitate interaction with users (Nijholt, 2003); and strategies to establish a social and personal relationship with the user by means of "small talk" (Bickmore and Cassell, 2000; Bickmore, 2002). An overview of the literature on affect/emotion in natural language generation can be found in (Piwek, 2003). Although there is a body of work on politeness in dialogue generation and interpretation (e.g., Ardissono et al., 1999; and Walker et al., 1997), as far as we know, there is not yet any systematic work on the role of politeness in dialogue summarization and, more specifically, on how politeness is reported in dialogue summaries.

Work on automated summarization (e.g., Mani, 2001; Mani and Maybury, 1999; Marcu, 2000) and more specifically dialogue summarization (e.g., Alexandersson and Poller, 2000; Kipp et al., 1999; Reithinger et al., 2000) has concentrated on summarizing informational content, at the expense of reports on the quality of interaction, such as the politeness of the interlocutors. Approaches so far to politeness in generation and interpretation mainly follow the ideas of Brown and Levinson (1987) about face threatening. These ideas were criticized, amongst others, by Eelen (2001), who pointed out that Brown and Levinson do not provide a balanced account of both polite and impolite behavior; they are mainly concerned with polite behaviour. Watts (2003) argues that impoliteness is an important feature of interaction. In particular, he has argued that people are more likely to comment on impolite than polite behaviour.

In this chapter, two pilot studies are presented. In both studies, the following hypothesis, based on Watts' (2003) aforementioned supposition concerning impolite behaviour, is tested:

Hypothesis 1: If a dialogue contains very impolite behaviour by the dialogue participants, this behaviour tends to be reported in the dialogue summary.

This hypothesis was confirmed by the studies, *i.e.*, subjects actually reported politeness for the very impolite dialogues. This is an important result, to the extent that it shows *when* an automatic summarizer should report politeness.

The second tested hypothesis concerns *how* people report politeness. In particular, the way the point of view of a summarizer can bias reports of politeness is investigated. This hypothesis was formulated along the lines of Walton's definition of biased arguments. According to Walton (1999, p.86) "... a biased argument is a one-sided argument, consisting of pure pro-argumentation for one side of an issue in a dialogue, while failing to genuinely interact with the other side on a balanced way. A balanced argument, in contrast, considers all the relevant arguments on both sides and exhibits the characteristics of flexible commitment, empathy, open-mindedness, critical doubt, and evidence sensitivity." The second hypothesis is:

Hypothesis 2: Reporting of politeness in a dialogue summary is biased as a result of the point of view of the summarizer.

Again, the studies confirmed this second hypothesis, *i.e.*, the findings suggest that people bias their summaries according to their point of view.

In the studies, the subjects were instructed to summarize a carefully selected set of automatically generated dialogues. The resulting collection of human-authored summaries constituted the data. The two studies that were carried out differed in only one respect. Whereas in the first study the summarizers were not provided with any instructions concerning the length of their summaries, in the second study, summarizers were given a maximum summary size. The purpose of having two studies was to test the third hypothesis:

Hypothesis 3: Severely restricting the summary length has no influence on Hypotheses 1 and 2.

This third hypothesis, as it will be shown in the sections ahead, was confirmed. No changes in the results pertaining to hypotheses 1 and 2 were found when subjects faced a maximum summary size of 10% of the number of words of the corresponding dialogue.

The eventual aim is to use the insights gained from these studies in the construction of an automatic dialogue summarizer, which will be folded into the NECA system (Krenn et al., 2002). NECA (*Net Environment for Embodied Emotional Conversational Agents*) is a conversational agent platform in which the user can create characters by specifying their roles, personalities and interests. Based on these settings, the system automatically generates dialogues between the characters. The result of the generation process is a script that can be performed by two or more embodied agents (Piwek et al., 2002; Piwek and van Deemter, 2003). Potential applications are for the purpose of, for instance, entertainment, infotainment and education. The system has been developed for two domains: *eShowRoom* (infotainment), which concerns car sales, and *Socialite* (entertainment), which concerns characters who are inhabitants of a student district in Vienna.

The dialogues for the current studies were taken from the eShowRoom domain (first version of October 2002) where an agent is the vendor while the other is the customer. NECA's scripted dialogues were used as a test corpus because the NECA system allowed us to systematically change, amongst other characteristics, the agents' politeness.

2. First Study: Politeness and Bias in Unconstrained Dialogue Summarization

2.1 Method

The subjects in this study were students and former students from the State University of Campinas, Brazil. Figure 1 shows the educational level and field of study of the subjects. From the total amount of subjects, 18 were men and 12 women. Subjects were given the dialogues, hardcopies or by e-mail, and asked to summarize those dialogues and return the summaries to the researchers, either by e-mail or on paper, typed or handwritten.

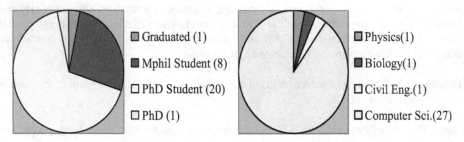

Figure 1. Educational level and field of study of subjects.

The study was carried out during July and August 2003 at the State University of Campinas, Brazil. It was conducted as follows. First, four dialogues were generated using the NECA *eShowroom* system. Each dialogue involved a customer and a vendor: a character named Ritchie tries to sell a car to another character named Tina. The dialogues can be found in Appendix I. For the purpose of this study, the politeness of both interlocutors in the dialogues was varied. This was possible because NECA allows us to control some dialogue parameters. These include (a) the interlocutors' interests, which influence the length of the dialogue (if the customer is interested in many features of the car, the dialogue will be longer), (b) their agreeableness, which also influences the dialogue length, for it determines how easily the customer is persuaded to buy the car, or how easily the vendor will give up the sale, and (c) their politeness, which determines how polite the interlocutors will be (currently the system allows only two politeness degrees: polite and impolite).

Transcripts of the automatically generated dialogues were presented to the subjects in the following order:

- Dialogue D_1 showed an interaction in which both vendor and customer were polite and do not use language that is likely to cause offence. The dialogue began with the vendor attending to the customer, and ended with the customer buying the car;
- D_2 showed an interaction in which the vendor is polite and the customer is impolite. The interaction began with the customer not finding the vendor in the showroom (i.e., the vendor was apparently absent for a moment) and ended with the customer not buying the car;
- D_3 showed an interaction in which the vendor is impolite and the customer is polite. Again, the dialogue began with the vendor being apparently absent for a moment, and ended with the customer not buying the car;

- D$_4$ showed a very short interaction in which both vendor and customer were polite again. Like the first dialogue, it began with the vendor introducing himself to the customer, and ended with the customer buying the car.

The subjects were told to summarize the dialogues as if they had been present during the dialogue and were telling a friend what happened. Subjects were divided into three groups. Firstly, ten subjects were told to summarize the dialogue from the point of view of the customer, i.e., they were asked to pretend that they had been the customer. Secondly, another ten subjects were told to summarize the dialogues as if they were the vendor. Finally, a third group of ten subjects were told to summarize the dialogues as if they had overheard the dialogue without directly participating in it. The subjects were given no other constraint. It was up to the subjects to decide how long the summary should be, as well as whether they should quote parts of the dialogue or rephrase them. Although the dialogues were in English, the summarizers were instructed to summarize them either in Portuguese or English, depending on their preference.

The produced summaries were manually annotated by one of the researchers, sentence by sentence, for whether or not the sentences reported (positive or negative) behaviour. The summaries as a whole were classified based on whether they contained a sentence reporting the interlocutors' behaviour. Thus, a summary was classified as *behav* if it contained at least one sentence concerning the behaviour, such as "I asked a very disgusting vendor..." (negative), "I was extremely attentive..." (positive), "I was in a bad mood..." (negative), and "Ritch, showing lack of respect and politeness..." (negative); and *no behav* otherwise.

For the annotation of bias, Walton's (1999) definition was used. Following Walton, a biased summary was defined as *a summary in which the summarizer strongly defends his/her position in the dialogue, by arguing in favor of it and not genuinely taking the other side in a balanced way.*

To implement the notion of bias based on Walton's work, the reporting of positive/negative behaviour by the vendor or customer was manually annotated on a sentence-by-sentence basis. Examples of sentences that were classified as negative reports were "I lost my patience and rudely said...", "Besides being ill-treated today...", "disgusting vendor", "she was angry and impatient", "what a 'nice' person I received today" (sarcastic), "a loser came...", "annoying customer", "(Ritchie) is an awful vendor", "I was impatient, the vendor came along with small talk...", and "I was not in the mood...she asked silly questions". Similarly, examples of sentences that were classified as positive reports were "I was extremely attentive", "I gently apologized", "Ritchie served her politely", "therefore I preferred to be polite...", "she didn't loose her calm" and "Ritchie showed... with patience".

In order to classify the annotated summaries, two mutually exclusive, but not exhaustive, categories were defined:

Definition 1 (Exclusively Negative Report -- *ENR* -- of an agent A) A summary is classified as an *ENR(A)* if and only if:
1. It has at least one sentence where agent A's behaviour is reported negatively and this behaviour is not blamed on another agent B; and
2. It has no positive report about the agent at all.

Definition 2 (Exclusively Positive Report -- *EPR* -- of an agent A) A summary is classified as an *EPR(A)* if and only if:
1. It has at least one sentence reporting the agent A's behaviour positively; and

2. It has no negative report about the agent at all.

Within this framework, a summary can either be classified as *ENR(V)*, when it exclusively reports the vendor's behaviour as negative, or *ENR(C)*, when it exclusively reports the customer's behaviour as negative. Similarly, they can also either be classified as *EPR(V)*, when they exclusively positively report the vendor's behaviour, or *EPR(C)*, when the positively reported agent is the customer. Summaries that do not fit the above categories are left out of consideration, for the moment.

The summary classification mentioned above can now be used to implement this chapter's definition of a biased summary, based on the collective behaviour of the subjects. If one finds that the number of summaries classified as *ENR(V)* and *ENR(C)* varies significantly according to the point of view given the same dialogue, this suggests that subjects did not report the interaction in a balanced way and were biased. The same idea applies to *EPR* summaries.

2.2 Results and Analysis

Figure 2 summarizes the study's results for behaviour reporting[1]. In this figure, the bars differentiate among (a) the users who only reported some party's behaviour (*behav (only)*), ignoring technical information, (b) the users who reported the behaviour, along with technical information (*behav*), and those who did not report any behaviour at all (*no behav*), i.e., those who only included the exchanged technical information in the summary. For each dialogue, behaviour reporting is displayed for each of the three points of view adopted by subjects, i.e., the customer's (**C**), the vendor's (**V**) and an observer's (**O**) point of view.

This Figure shows that although for D_1 and D_4 there was a small percentage of subjects who included the behaviour of some party in the summary (respectively, 7% for D_1 and 17% for D_4), this percentage is remarkably higher for D_2 and D_3 (respectively, 67% for D_2 and 93% for D_3). This percentage consists of the sum of the subjects who have taken the behaviour into account and those who have only taken the behaviour into account.

---

[1] There are some minor differences between the data in this table and those given in previous technical reports on this research (see Roman *et. al.* (2004a), (2004b) and (2004c)). These differences are due to the correction in this chapter of a typo and a counting mistake. Note that although there are some minor differences between the numbers, the main conclusions have not been affected and are the same for this chapter and the technical reports that predate it.

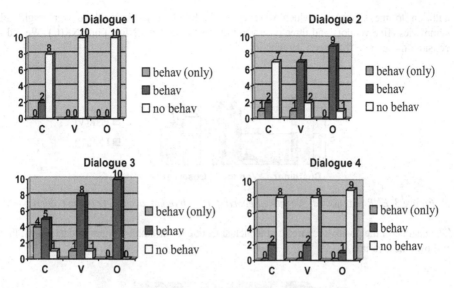

Figure 2. Behaviour reporting data for the first study.

The differences might be explained by the fact that D_2 and D_3 show unusual situations for car sales dialogues. In the first dialogue the customer and in the second the vendor manifested rude behavior. D_1 and D_4, on the other hand, are more usual, or "neutral", dialogues. If one groups D_1 and D_4, and D_2 and D_3 together, one finds approximately 12% of the subjects mentioning the behaviour in D_1 and D_4, and 80% mentioning it in D_2 and D_3. A 2×2 χ^2 analysis reveals that this is a significant difference, χ^2 (1, N=120) = 56.43, at the significance level of p = 0.001. This suggests that whether subjects report some party's behaviour/politeness in a summary depends on the interaction's politeness degree.

Another point that is worth mentioning is the higher number of subjects who reported the behaviour in D_4, when compared to D_1 (from 2 subjects in D_1 to 5 in D_4). This might be because D_2 and D_3 present such an unusual interaction that the subjects notice that in the last dialogue the interaction is again "normal". The difference between D_1 and D_4 in this respect is, however, not statistically significant.

Furthermore, if the total number of summaries mentioning politeness/behaviour and those that do not are counted, and related to the point of view they were summarized under, one has 16 summaries reporting the behaviour (and 24 not reporting it at all) for the customer's viewpoint, 19 reporting (and 21 not reporting) for the vendor's, and 20 reporting (and 20 not reporting) for the observer's. This presents no statistically significant relation between whether politeness/behaviour is reported and the point of view.

Figure 3 shows the bias annotation results. In this figure, the bars differentiate amongst the negatively reported behaviour, for each viewpoint. Applying a χ^2 analysis to the data in Figure 3 results in χ^2 (2, N=40) = 20.39. This indicates that whether subjects report the vendor's or the customer's behaviour exclusively negatively, depends on their point of view at the significance level of p = 0.001. These data lead to the conclusion that there exists a bias: subjects are apparently trying to advocate their side by reporting mostly the counterpart's behaviour. In addition to the summaries which were either ENR(V) or ENR(C), there were eight other summaries (five vendors and three observers) that were neither ENR(V) or ENR(C). We did not consider these more "balanced" summaries.

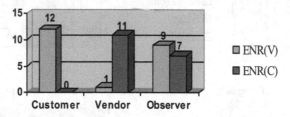

Figure 3. ENR (Exclusively Negative Report) for each agent, according to the point of view.

The results for the positive reports are inconclusive, due to the small number of data points. Figure 4 shows these results.

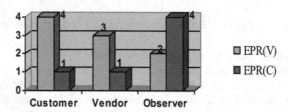

Figure 4. EPR (Exclusively Positive Report) for each agent, according to the point of view.

3. Second Study: Politeness and Bias in Constrained Dialogue Summarization

3.1 Method

This study was also carried out over a period of two months - November and December 2003 - at the State University of Campinas, Brazil. In order to compare results, the same set of dialogues as in the first study was used. The same procedure as for the first study was followed (see Section 2.1 for details). Subjects were asked to produce a summary for each dialogue according to the same point of view they assumed in the first study; the only difference being that the summary length was restricted to 10% of the number of words in the dialogue. For annotation of the summaries, the procedure as described in Section 2.1 was followed.

3.2 Results and Analysis

Figure 5 summarizes the results of the study. In this figure, like in Figure 2, the bars differentiate among the subjects who have only taken some party's behaviour into account (*behav (only)*), the subjects who have taken the behaviour into account as well as technical information (*behav*), and those who have not taken it into account at all (*no behav*).

For this study, the percentage of subjects who included some party's behaviour in the summary, for D_1 and D_4, is 3%. This percentage is 47% and 90% for D_2 and D_3, respectively. Again there is a greater number of subjects who report behaviours when the dialogue is unusual with respect to the politeness that is displayed. Interestingly, the upper bound on the summary length may have caused summarizers who reported some behaviour to leave out technical information.

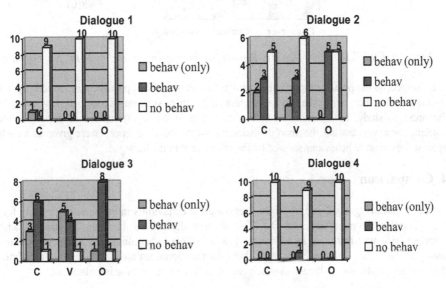

Figure 5. Behaviour data for the second study.

If one groups D_1 and D_4, and D_2 and D_3, one has approximately 3% of the subjects mentioning some behaviour in D_1 and D_4, and 68% mentioning it in D_2 and D_3. A 2×2 χ^2 analysis revealed that this was a significant difference, χ^2 (1, N=120) = 55.13, at the significance level of p = 0.001. Thus, this provides evidence that there may be a relationship between the politeness of the dialogue and subjects reporting dialogue behaviour in the summary, even with the restriction on the summary length.

Notice that the number of subjects who included behaviour in the summaries for D_1 and D_4 is exactly the same, i.e., apparently, the fact that D_4 was presented after two unusual dialogues did not affect the subjects in this second study, where there was a constraint on summary length.

Counting again the total number of summaries mentioning some behaviour and those not mentioning it at all, and relating them to the assumed viewpoint, one has 15 summaries mentioning it and 25 not mentioning it, for the customer's point of view; 14 and 26, respectively, for the vendor's; and 14 and 26 for the observer's. This presents no statistically significant relation between whether summaries report behaviour and the point of view.

Figure 6 summarizes the bias annotation results for this second study. In this figure, like in Figure 3, the bars differentiate amongst the reported behaviour. If one applies a 3×2 χ^2 analysis to the data in Figure 6, one has χ^2 (2, N=39) = 7.91, which is significant at the p = 0.02 level. This result suggests that if subjects report some behaviour, they bias their reports according to their point of view. For this classification, two summaries (one for the vendor's viewpoint and another for the observer's) fit neither in ENR(V) nor in ENR(C).

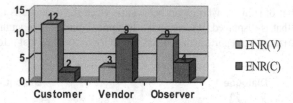

Figure 6. ENR (Exclusively Negative Report) for each agent, according to the point of view.

With respect to the positive reports, the customer's behaviour was positively reported only in one summary (customer), while the vendor was reported in three summaries (one per viewpoint). As in the previous study, no conclusion can be drawn due to the small amount of data. It is worth noticing, however, that for the impolite dialogues, all the positive reports were given as a contrast against the negative behaviour showed by the other party in the dialogue.

4. Comparison

In both studies (Figures 2 and 5) subjects reported the behaviours in the summary mainly for the more impolite dialogues (D_2 and D_3). This did not depend on the summary size. When the summary size was restricted to a value as low as 10% of the number of words present in the dialogue, subjects still included remarks about the emotional state of the interlocutors, related to their politeness, for the dialogues in which one of the interlocutors was impolite/rude.

If, however, one counts the summaries in which subjects reported some behaviour (*behav* and *behave(only)*) and those in which they do not (*no behav*), and groups them according to the study they belong to, then one has no statistically significant evidence ($p = 0.20$) that the overall number of summaries reporting some behaviour depends on the study, i.e., it does not depend on whether subjects are restricted to a 10% summary size or not. Figure 7 summarizes the results.

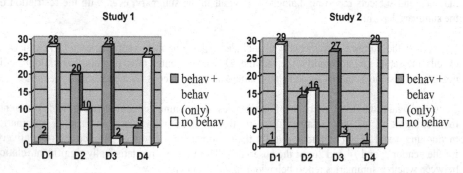

Figure 7. Summaries reporting some behaviour for both studies.

A last point about this part of the studies is that the difference between the number of summaries including behaviour in D_1 and D_4 for the first study is not reproduced in the second study. If the fact that D_4 was presented after two unusual dialogues affected the summaries in the first study, it might be that the restriction on the summary size in the second study suppressed this effect.

Concerning bias, both studies provide evidence that the way people describe the behaviour of some party, and more specifically, which party they describe negatively, depends on the point of view under which they are summarizing, *i.e.*, it is biased. Not only that, but a closer look at Figure 3 and Figure 6 shows that the negatively reported party tends to be the counterpart in the dialogue, as opposed to the summarizer's point of view (vendors negatively reporting customers and *vice versa*). This fact is in accordance with Walton (1999), in the sense that these summaries consist of "pure advocacy for one side of an issue in a dialogue, without genuinely considering the other side in a balanced way".

Comparing data from figures 3 and 6, one has 22 summaries classified as *ENR(V)* and 18 as *ENR(C)*, for the first study, and 24 *ENR(V)* and 15 *ENR(C)*, for the second study. A χ^2 analysis of these data leads to no statistically significant results, meaning that most probably the negative report of behaviours does not depend on the study, i.e., on whether the summary has a fixed length of 10% or no constrain at all.

With respect to the positive reporting of behaviours, the amount of data collected is not enough to lead to any conclusion. Interestingly, the number of positive remarks is 15 in the first study and four in the second study. This could suggest that, as subjects face severe constraints on the summary size, they drop the positive remarks, keeping only the reports on the negative behaviors.

5. Conclusion and Outlook

In this chapter, two exploratory studies were described. These studies were designed to gather information about how people summarize dialogues. More specifically, the studies were intended to shed light on how people deal with politeness/behaviour in dialogues and how their point of view influences their summaries. The eventual goal is to use the results to inform the construction of an automatic dialogue summarization system. The envisaged system should be capable of considering dialogue politeness (through its participants' behaviour) and point of view when summarizing. The underlying rationale is that by basing our work on experiments into the behavior of human summarizers, our system will eventually produce automatically generated summaries that are perceived to be "natural". In practical terms, we intend to evaluate this by finding out to what extent system produced summaries are indistinguishable from summaries produced by humans.

In both studies, the percentage of summaries reporting some behaviour was higher when the dialogues were more impolite. This result was independent of the point of view and summary size. The order in which the dialogues were presented appeared to have little influence on whether people included behaviour information in the summary. No statistically significant differences were found with respect to the reporting of behaviour for the neutral dialogue before the two impolite dialogues, and the neutral dialogue after them.

Regarding the question how people report behaviour, when they do so, it was observed that the point of view adopted by the summarizer influences reporting of behaviours. In particular, whose behaviour is negatively reported (vendor or customer), depends on the point of view of the summarizer rather than the actual dialogue behaviour. This is an indication that people bias their summaries. In our studies, this result did not depend on whether the summary was restricted to 10% of the dialogue size or not.

There is tentative evidence that positive reporting is less subject to bias. The number of data points on this was, however, too limited to apply any statistics. Further studies into positive reporting and bias are required to come to a firm conclusion. Interestingly, the number of subjects positively reporting some of the behaviours is lower in the second than in the first study: it decreases with the shortening of the allowed summary size, indicating that there could be a relationship between them.

The currently used dialogues are automatically generated. In further studies it would be interesting to test the obtained results from these preliminary studies with more complex dialogues, like those produced by human writers for TV, theatre, etc. Currently, the results presented here are being used to build an algorithm for automatic dialogue summarization that takes politeness, behaviours and point of view into account. The algorithm will be tested through an implementation that is embedded in the NECA platform and which takes as input a NECA scripted dialogue. The system will generate the summary according to a point of view defined by the user, and include the politeness of the interaction, if requested by the user.

6. Acknowledgements

This research was sponsored by CNPq - Conselho Nacional de Desenvolvimento Científico e Tecnológico - and CAPES - Coordenação de Aperfeiçoamento de Pessoal de Nível Superior. Part of it was also supported by the EC Project NECA IST-2000-28580.

7. Bibliography

Alexandersson, J. and Poller, P. (2000) Multilingual Summary Generation in a Speech-to-Speech Translation System for Multilingual Dialogues. In *Proc. International Natural Language Generation Conference (INLG-2000)*. Mitzpe Ramon, Israel.

Ardissono, L., Boella, G. and Lesmo, L. (1999) Politeness and Speech Acts. In *Proc. Workshop on Attitude, Personality and Emotions in User-Adapted Interaction*. 41-55. Banff, Canada.

Bickmore, T. and Cassell, J. (2000) How About this Weather? Social Dialogue with Embodied Conversational Agents. In *Proc. AAAI Fall Symposium on Socially Intelligent Agents*. North Falmouth, USA.

Bickmore, T. (2002) Social Dialogue is Serious Business. In *Proc. CHI 2002 Workshop on Socially Adept Technologies*. Minneapolis, USA.

Brown, P. and Levinson, S. (1987) *Politeness: Some Universals in Language Usage*. Cambridge University Press.

Craggs, R. and Wood, M. (2003) Annotating Emotion in Dialogue. In *Proc. 4th SIGdial Workshop on Discourse and Dialogue*. Sapporo, Japan.

Eelen, G. (2001) *A Critique of Politeness Theories*. St. Gerome, Manchester.

Fisher, K. (1999) Annotating Emotional Language Data. *Technical Report 236*. Verbmobil Project.

Hovy, E. (1988) *Generating Natural Language Under Pragmatic Constraints*. Lawrence Erlbaum, New Jersey.

Huber, R., Batliner, A. Buckow, J., Nöth, E., Warnke, V. and Niemann, H. (2000) Recognition of Emotion in a Realistic Dialogue Scenario. In *Proc. International Conference on Spoken Language Processing*. Beijing, China.

Kipp, M., Alexandersson, J. and Reithinger, N. (1999) Understanding Spontaneous Negotiation Dialogue. In *Proc. International Joint Conferences on Artificial Intelligence (IJCAI-1999)*. Stockholm, Sweden.

Krenn, B., Pirker, H., Grice, M., Baumann, S., Piwek, P., van Deemter, K., Schroeder, M., Klesen, M. and Gstrein, E. (2002) Generation of Multimodal Dialogue for Net Environments. In Busemann, S. (Ed.) *KONVENS 2002, Deutsches Forschungszentrum fuer Kuenstliche Intelligenz (DFKI)*. 91-98. Saarbruecken, Germany.

Mani, I. and Maybury, M. (1999) *Advances in Automatic Text Summarization*. MIT Press, Cambridge, MA.

Mani, I. (2001) *Automatic Summarization*. John Benjamins, Amsterdam.

Marcu, D. (2000) *The Theory and Practice of Discourse Parsing and Summarization*. MIT Press.

Nijholt, A. (2003) Humor and Embodied Conversational Agents. *CTIT Technical Report Series 03-03*. University of Twente.

Piwek, P., Krenn, B., Schröder, M., Grice, M., Baumann, S. and Pirker, H. (2002) RRL: A Rich Representation Language for the Description of Agent Behaviour in NECA, In *Proc. Workshop "Embodied Conversational Agents – Let's Specify and Evaluate Them!"*. Bologna, Italy.

Piwek, P. (2003) An Annotated Bibliography of Affective Natural Language Generation. *Technical Report ITRI-02-02*. ITRI – University of Brighton.

Piwek, P. and van Deemter, K. (2003) Dialogue as Discourse: Controlling Global Properties of Scripted Dialogue. In *Proc. AAAI Spring Symposium on Natural Language Generation in Spoken and Written Dialogue*. Menlo Park, CA.

Reithinger, N., Kipp, M., Engel, R. and Alexandersson, J. (2000) Summarizing Multilingual Spoken Negotiation Dialogues. In *Proc. 38th Meeting of the Association for Computational Linguistics (ACL-2000)*. Hong Kong, China.

Roman, N., Piwek, P. and Carvalho, A. (2004a) Politeness and Summarization: an Exploratory Study. In *Proc. AAAI Spring Symposium Exploring Affect and Attitude in Text: Theories and Applications (AAAI-EAAT-2004)*. Palo Alto, USA.

Roman, N., Piwek, P. and Carvalho, A. (2004b) Be Polite or Be Summarized. *Technical Report ITRI-04-05*. ITRI – University of Brighton.

Roman, N., Piwek, P. and Carvalho, A. (2004c) Politeness and Summarization: to Bias or not to Bias. *Technical Report ITRI-04-06*. ITRI – University of Brighton.

Schmitz, B. and Quantz, J. (1996) Dialogue Acts in Automatic Dialogue Interpreting. *Technical Report 173*, Verbmobil Project.

Walker, M., Cahn, J. and Whittaker, S. (1997) Improvising Linguistic Style: Social and Affective Bases for Agent Personality. In *Proc. Conference on Autonomous Agents (AGENTS-97)*. Marina del Rey, USA.

Walton, D. (1999) *One-Sided Arguments: A Dialectical Analysis of Bias*. State University of New York Press.

Watts, R. (2003) *Politeness*. Cambridge University Press.

8. Appendix I

The four dialogues used in the experiment, in the same order they were presented to the subjects.

Dialogue 1	Dialogue 3
Size: 99 words. Summary size: 10 words.	Size: 124 words. Summary size: 12 words.

Dialogue 1

R: Hello! I am Ritchie.
T: Can you tell me something about this car?
R: It is very safe.
R: It has anti-lock brakes.
R: It has airbags.
T: How much does it consume?
R: It consumes 8 litres per 60 miles.
T: Interesting.
T: What kind of luggage compartment does this car have?
R: It has a spacious luggage compartment.
T: Excellent!
T: What kind of interior does this car have?
R: It has a spacious interior.
T: Excellent! (Tina)
T: How much does this car cost?
R: It costs 25 thousand Euros.
T: Well, well.
T: All in all this is a perfect car. It is a deal!
R: Really? I am sure you wont regret it.

Dialogue 2
Size: 182 words. Summary size: 18 words.

T: Anybody here? I haven't got all day.
R: I am sorry to have kept you waiting. I will be with you in a moment.
R: How can I help you?
T: I want you to tell me about this car.
R: It is very friendly for the environment.
R: It is made of recyclable materials.
R: It has a catalytic converter.
T: How much does it consume?
R: It consumes 8 litres per 60 miles.
T: It is not exactly very friendly for the environment.
R: Just consider this.
R: This car is very prestigious.
R: It has leather seats.
R: It has broad tires.
R: It drives 100 and 10 miles per hour.
R: It has 80 horse power.
T: What kind of luggage compartment does it have?
R: It has a spacious luggage compartment.
T: Well, well.
T: What kind of interior does this car have?
R: It has a spacious interior.
T: Well, well.
T: How much does this car cost?
R: It costs 25 thousand Euros.
T: It is not exactly very cheap.
R: Just consider this.
R: This car is very safe.
R: It has anti-lock brakes.
R: It has airbags.
T: Enough is enough! You keep your car!
R: Well, sorry that I cannot help you.

Dialogue 3

T: Anybody in today?
R: Yeah yeah, keep your calm.
T: Can you tell me something about this car?
R: It is very safe.
R: It has anti-lock brakes.
R: It has airbags.
T: Does it have power windows?
R: What do you think? Of course not!
T: This car is not exactly very prestigious.
R: Just consider this.
R: This car has leather seats.
R: It has broad tires.
R: It drives 100 and 10 miles per hour.
R: It has 80 horse power.
T: What kind of luggage compartment does it have?
R: It has a spacious luggage compartment.
T: Well, well.
T: What kind of interior does this car have?
R: For god's sake, how should I know?
T: No problem.
T: Thank you for your help. I have to think a bit more about this.
R: Great! Thanks for wasting my time.

Dialogue 4
Size: 53 words. Summary size: 5 words.

R: Hello! My name is Ritchie.
R: What can I do for you?
T: Could you tell me something about this car?
R: This is a very sporty car.
R: It can drive 100 miles per hour.
T: How much does it consume?
R: It consumes 8 litres per 60 miles.
T: Not bad.
T: Ok! I'll take it.
R: Congratulations! Exquisite taste.

Chapter 15

Generating More-Positive and More-Negative Text

Diana Zaiu Inkpen
University of Ottawa
School of Information Technology and Engineering
University of Ottawa, Ottawa
ON, Canada, K1N 6N5
Email: diana@site.uottawa.ca

Ol'ga Feiguina and Graeme Hirst
University of Toronto
Dept. of Computer Science, University of Toronto, Canada
Email: {olga,gh}@cs.toronto.edu

Abstract

We present experiments on modifying the semantic orientation of the near-synonyms in a text. We analyze a text into an interlingual representation and a set of attitudinal nuances, with particular focus on its near-synonyms. Then we use our text generator to produce a text with the same meaning but changed semantic orientation (more positive or more negative) by replacing, wherever possible, words with near-synonyms that differ in their expressed attitude.

Keywords: near-synonyms, lexical nuances, text generation, attitude, semantic orientation.

1. Near-Synonyms and Attitudinal Nuances

The choice of a word from among a set of near-synonyms that share the same core meaning but vary in their connotations is one of the ways in which a writer controls the nuances of a text. In many cases, the nuances that differentiate near-synonyms relate to expressed attitude and affect. For example, if a writer wants to express a more-favorable view of the appearance of a relatively narrow person, he or she can use the words *slim* or *slender*; if the writer wants to express a less favorable view, the word *skinny* is available.

This level of attitude expression is distinct from that of the opinions expressed in the text as a whole, and may in fact contradict it. In particular, *euphemism* is the expression of a critical or unpleasant message in relatively positive or favorable terms; *dysphemism* is the converse (Allan and

Burridge, 1991). Nonetheless, the term *semantic orientation* has been used to describe attitudes at both levels.

Any natural language understanding or generation system must be sensitive to this kind of nuance in text if it is to do its work well. A machine translation system, especially, must recognize such nuances in the source text and *preserve* them in the target text. If the source is, say, polite, angry, or obsequious, then the translation must be too.

Nonetheless, in this paper we look at *changing* the nuances of a text rather than preserving them. We see this primarily as an exercise in the control of nuances in text, and hence a test of a natural language generation system, rather than as a useful application that is an end in itself. That is, any system that purports to accurately preserve nuances should be equally able to change nuances as desired, and render its input in a variety of ways. A system that can change the nuances of a text could sometimes be helpful — for example, in the customization of texts for users. When generating text that expresses a strong opinion, a negative or positive tone may reflect the speaker's point of view. In this paper, we propose to automatically transform the low-level semantic orientation of a text by choosing near-synonyms accordingly.

In our previous work (Inkpen, 2003; Inkpen and Hirst, 2001) we automatically acquired a lexical knowledge-base of near-synonym differences (LKB of NS) from the explanatory text of a special dictionary of synonym discrimination, *Choose the Right Word* (hereafter CTRW) (Hayakawa 1994). The main types of distinctions (nuances) that we extracted were: stylistic (for example, *inebriated* is more formal than *drunk*), attitudinal (for example, *skinny* is more pejorative than *slim*), and denotational (for example, *blunder* implies *accident* and *ignorance*, while *error* does not). The computational model we use for representing the meaning of near-synonyms was initially proposed by Edmonds and Hirst (2002).

We enriched the initial LKB of NS with additional information extracted from other sources. Knowledge about the collocational behavior of the near-synonyms was acquired from free text (Inkpen and Hirst, 2002). More knowledge about distinctions between near-synonyms was acquired from machine-readable dictionaries: attitudinal distinctions from the *General Inquirer*, and denotational distinctions from word definitions in the *Macquarie Dictionary*. These distinctions were merged with the initial LKB of NS, and inconsistencies were resolved. Our final LKB of NS has 904 clusters containing a total of 5,425 near-synonyms.

The *General Inquirer* (Stone et al., 1966) is particularly important in this facet of our work. It is a computational lexicon compiled from several sources, including the Harvard IV-4 dictionary and the Lasswell value dictionary. It contains 11,896 word senses, each tagged with markers that classify the word according to an extensible number of categories. There are markers for words of pleasure, pain, virtue, and vice; markers for words indicating overstatement and understatement; markers for places and locations; etc. The definitions of each word are very brief. Some example entries in GI are presented in Table 1.

The *General Inquirer* category of interest to our work is Positiv/Negativ. (The abbreviations Pstv/Ngtv in Table 1 are earlier versions of Positiv/Negativ.) A positive word corresponds to a favorable attitude; a negative one corresponds to a pejorative attitude. There are 1,915 words marked as Positiv (not including words for *yes*, which is a separate category of 20 entries), and 2,291 words marked as Negativ (not including the separate category *no* in the sense of refusal). An attitudinal distinction was asserted in our LKB of NS for each near-synonym in CTRW that was marked Positiv or Negativ in GI.

CORRECT #1	H4Lvd Positiv Pstv Virtue Ovrst POSAFF Modif 21% adj: Accurate, proper
CORRECT #2	H4Lvd Positiv Pstv Strng Work IAV TRNGAIN SUPV 54% verb: To make right, improve; to point out error (0)
CORRECT #3	H4Lvd Positiv Pstv Virtue Ovrst POSAFF Modif 25% adv: "Correctly" – properly, accurately
CORRECT #4	H4Lvd Virtue TRNGAIN Modif 0% adj: "Corrected" – made right

Table 1. General Inquirer entries for the word "correct".

In this paper, we focus on the attitudinal distinctions stored into our LKB of NS, acquired from CTRW and GI. For our near-synonyms, we extracted 1,519 attitudinal distinctions from GI, and 384 from CTRW. The information acquired from the two sources was merged and conflicts were resolved through a voting scheme. After merging, we were left with 1,709 attitudinal distinctions in our LKB of NS. The rest of the near-synonyms are considered neutral by default.

2. Related Work

There is much recent work on the classification of text (at the document level or at the sentence level) as objective or subjective (Riloff and Wiebe, 2003), and the classification of subjective text as positive or negative (Turney, 2002; Pang, Lee and Vaithyanathan, 2002; Yu and Hatzivassiloglou, 2003). Work on generation using pragmatic nuances, including the attitude of the speaker and of the hearer was presented by Hovy (1990). Elhadad (1997) presented work on unification-based constraints for lexical choice in generation. Similarly, our generator uses collocations to constrain the lexical choice, but it also includes the possibility of expressing lexical nuances.

Our work in this paper has a different focus, on the analysis of subjective text, extracting its lexical nuances (including attitude), and generating a text with the same meaning but a new semantic orientation. This is, in effect, translating from English to English via an interlingual representation, changing the semantic orientation before the generation phase.

3. Estimating the Relative Semantic Orientation of Text

We extracted paragraphs from the British National Corpus (BNC) that contain at least three of our set of near-synonyms. We chose to use paragraphs because we believe that the change in orientation will be more noticeable than at the sentence level and more localized than at the document level (because we cannot be sure that the semantic orientation does not change from paragraph to paragraph in the BNC).

We did not classify the complete texts according to their semantic orientation. We only estimated, semi-automatically, the orientation of each selected paragraph from the semantic orientation of its words. We labelled as many words (except stopwords) as we could as positive, negative, or neutral as follows. First, we checked whether the word is a near-synonym in our LKB of NS. If so, we consulted the LKB regarding the attitude of the near-synonym. We did sense disambiguation as described in the next section. We consulted the GI for the attitude of all the other words. The sense disambiguation mechanism for this part is also described in the following section. A majority vote gave us an estimate of the attitude of the paragraph: Favorable,

Pejorative, or Neutral. We declared a paragraph to be Neutral (not subjective) if fewer than three pejorative or favorable words were discovered.

There are several problems with this approach, related to the fact that we look at individual words and ignore longer expressions. First, neighboring words can change the attitude of a word (e.g., not good is negative while good is positive). Second, words may have different attitudes when they are used as part of an expression or collocation (e.g., out to lunch is negative while the individual words are neutral or positive) (Baron and Hirst, 2004). Lastly, the author may be employing irony or sarcasm, which is not detected by our method. Another limitation is that if the information in the LKB of NS for a word was acquired from CTRW, the near-synonyms are classified as favorable, pejorative, or neutral only in comparison to other near-synonyms in their cluster; that is, the classification is relative. For example, mistake is Favorable in the LKB of NS because it's better than blunder, but the word mistake itself is not very positive. Despite these problems, because we look at the words in a paragraph and take a majority vote, we can determine the probable correct semantic orientation of the paragraph.

We also experimented with paragraphs from Epinions (*www.epinions.com*), a Web site where users review and rate books, movies, music, and various products and services. The reviews are typically several paragraphs long, and are accompanied by a rating on a scale of one to five stars. If a user rates an item with four or five stars, we can assume that the text of the associated review is positive. If the rating is one or two stars, we can assume that the text is negative.

4. Word Sense Disambiguation

When looking up the attitude of a word in our LKB or in GI, we needed to first disambiguate it, because the nuances of a word may depend on the sense in which it is being used. Since the BNC text is POS-tagged, we could rule out senses with a different part of speech. After that, when looking up words in the GI, we just took the most frequent sense. In our LKB of NS, different senses of a near-synonym can belong to different clusters of near-synonyms. We also had situations when a word in the paragraph, considered a potential near-synonym, was used in a sense that was not in the LKB of NS. For example, the word blue is in the LKB in the sense of sad, but not in the sense of a color. So, we had to consider every cluster and decide whether it is the right sense. We attempted to do this by checking whether the intersection of the paragraph and the text of the CTRW entry for this cluster (both considered as bags of words, with stopwords removed) was empty or not, but this did not work well. So we completed the near-synonym sense disambiguation in a semi-automatic manner, by hand-correcting the wrong decisions. In later work, we hope to improve the sense disambiguation module by using semantic relatedness instead of a simple intersection. Disambiguation of near-synonym senses is also used in the analysis module that will be presented in the next section.

5. Analysis

Figure 1 presents the global architecture of our system. Each sentence of the paragraph was parsed with Charniak's parser (Charniak, 2000), and we applied an input construction tool, which produces a shallow interlingual representation (IL) from each parse tree. This will be described in the next section. We then substituted a meta-concept — a disjunction of the near-synonyms of the initial near-synonym — for each near-synonym in the interlingual representation.

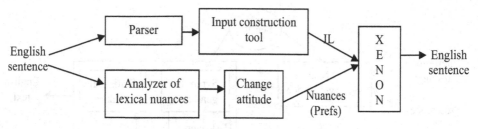

Figure 1. The architecture of the system.

6. Generation

After analysis of the input, the resulting interlingual representation and the set of lexical nuances are input to the generator module, which is named Xenon (see Figure 1). The set of lexical nuances becomes preferences to be satisfied by Xenon. But before the lexical nuances are passed to Xenon, those relating to attitude may be modified as desired by the user.

Xenon (Inkpen and Hirst, 2003) is our natural language generation system, capable of distinguishing between near-synonyms in generation. Xenon integrates a new near-synonym choice module and a near-synonym collocation module with the HALogen sentence realization system (Langkilde and Knight, 1998; Langkilde-Geary, 2002). HALogen is a broad-coverage general-purpose natural language sentence generation system that combines symbolic rules with a language model derived from large text corpora. For a given input, it generates all the possible English sentences into a compact forest representation and then ranks the sentences according to its language model, in order to choose the most likely sentence as output. Xenon extends this, using the LKB of NS and a set of desired nuances to possibly override the choice that HALogen would otherwise make.

The IL input to Xenon, like the input to HALogen, is expressed in an interlingua developed at the Information Sciences Institute, University of Southern California (ISI). This language contains a specified set of 40 roles, and the fillers of the roles can be words, concepts from Sensus (Knight and Luk, 1994), or complex representations (Langkilde-Geary, 2002). Xenon extends this representation language by adding meta-concepts that correspond to the core denotation of the clusters of near-synonyms (disjunctions of all the near-synonyms in a cluster).

Figure 2 presents the architecture of Xenon. The input is a semantic representation and a set of preferences to be satisfied. The final output is a set of sentences and their scores. An example of input and output is shown in Figure 3. The first sentence (the highest-ranked) is considered to be the solution. In this example, *fib* was chosen from the cluster *lie, falsehood, fib, prevarication, rationalization, untruth* to represent the meta-concept generic_lie_n.

The near-synonym choice module chooses the near-synonym from each cluster that best matches the input preferences. The preferences, as well as the distinctions between near-synonyms stored in the LKB of NS, are of three types. Stylistic preferences express a certain formality, force, or concreteness level and have the form: (*strength stylistic-feature*), for example (low formality).

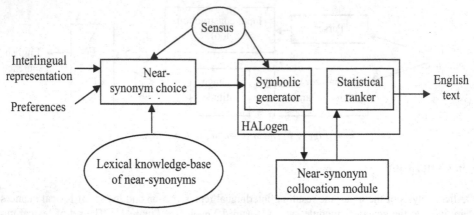

Figure 2. The architecture of Xenon.

Denotational preferences connote a particular concept or configuration of concepts and have the form: (*indirectness peripheral-concept*), where *indirectness* takes one of the values suggest, imply, denote. An example is: (imply (C / assessment :MOD (OR ignorant uninformed))). The peripheral concepts are expressed in the ISI interlingua. Attitudinal preferences, which are the ones that are of special interest here, express a favorable, neutral, or pejorative attitude and have the form: (*stance entity*), where *stance* takes one of the values favor, neutral, disfavor. An example is: (disfavor :agent).

The near-synonym collocations module ensures that the text generated does not contain unacceptable collocations. Near-synonyms that would violate collocational constraints are assigned lower weights, so that they will not be chosen by later processes. Possible collocations are detected in the forest representation that is output by HALogen's symbolic generator, the weights are decreased as needed, and the modified forest representation is input to HALogen's statistical ranker to finish the generation. The near-synonym collocations module is important in generating text with different semantic orientations, because by simply replacing a negative near-synonym with a positive one we might violate collocational constraints.

7. Experiments

We ran Xenon on the IL representations that resulted from the analysis, as described above, of each of the paragraphs that we selected from the BNC and from Epinions. Figure 4 shows an example of paragraph from Epinions, part of a negative review with an accompanying rating of two stars.

In the first two experiments, the set of preferences contained only one element, an attitudinal preference. We generated paragraphs with positive orientation, using the preference (favor :agent). The paragraph generated for our example paragraph is presented in Figure 5. We did not consider the semantic orientation of the initial paragraph; we simply generated positive or negative text. If the original paragraph was negative, the generated text is expected to be more positive; if the original paragraph was already positive, the generated text should be the same or slightly more positive. Similarly, we generated negative paragraphs with the input preference (disfavor :agent).

Input:	Output:	
	The boy told fibs.	− 40.8177
(A9 / tell	Boy told fibs.	− 42.3818
:agent (V9 / boy)		
:object (O9 / generic_lie_n))	Boys told fibs.	− 42.7857
	A boy told fibs.	− 43.0738
Input preferences:	Some boys told fibs.	− 46.4388
((DISFAVOR :AGENT)		
(LOW FORMALITY)	Any boy told fibs.	− 50.0306
(DENOTE (C1 / TRIVIAL)))	An boy told fibs.	− 50.15
	Were told fibs by the boy.	− 55.3801

Figure 3. Example of input and output of Xenon.

The paragraph generated for our example is presented in Figure 6. In our example, the initial paragraph was relatively negative (two stars), but we expect it to become even more negative (corresponding to a one-star rating). Note that in order to focus on the lexical-choice issues, rather than choice of syntactic structures and the limitations of HALogen and Xenon, Figures 5 and 6 do not show the actual output, but rather the crucial lexical choices substituted back into the original paragraph. The actual output is very close to the text we showed, with a few small grammar errors made by the generator.

We also experimented with a set of preferences that preserves the original nuances of near-synonyms in the text, and adds (favor :agent) or (disfavor :agent). The attitudinal preference is given a higher importance than the rest of the preferences in order to increase the change in semantic orientation as much as possible. In these experiments, we expected a near-synonym in the paragraph to change only if there was another near-synonym in the same cluster with the desired orientation and with lexical nuances that are not incompatible with the initial nuances. The resulting positive paragraph is very similar to the one presented in Figure 5, with small differences; but the word *aroma* was replaced by the word *smell*, which was also used in the original paragraph. This is what we expected to obtain by preserving lexical nuances; the word *aroma* is more positive, but it introduces the nuance of a very pleasant smell, which is not the case in this text. The negative paragraph is very similar to that presented in Figure 6, with the difference that more words were chosen as in the original paragraph: *stink* was replaced by *smell*, *propose* by *offer*, and *good* by *able*.

Sometimes, when we expect a specific word to be chosen because of its semantic orientation, another word might be chosen instead by HALogen's statistical ranker, as it tends to favor frequent words. Also, notice that the choice of near-synonyms can be sometimes infelicitous. For example, the choice of *good to* instead of *able to* in Figure 6 makes the sentence sound odd. The word *good* was included in the near-synonym cluster of *able* by the lexicographers who wrote CTRW, but it was intended as a modifier (e.g., *a good teacher*). We would have expected HALogen's trigram language module to prefer *able to*, since it favours good collocations with function words. Xenon's collocations module favours good collocations between near-synonyms and content words, but the coverage of our collocational knowledge-base is limited.

During my trip to Aruba a few years back, my boyfriend and I rented a car and drove around the island. While looking for the natural bridge we found a tourist spot called the "Tunnel of Love". Essentially, it's a big cave that you pay to walk through. We thought it would be nice to experience some of the natural beauty Aruba had to **offer**. I had just hurt my ankle in a jet-skiing incident and asked if I would be **able** to walk through with a gimpy leg. The women at the entrance told me I should have no **trouble**. The cave starts out as a pretty large enclosed space, with some external light and quite **easy** to manoeuvre. As you progress inward and downward, the space gets narrower, darker and more difficult to walk through. At approximately halfway through I literally had to hunch over to pass through. That's when the funny **smell**, strange noises and incredible heat kicked in and my light switched off! So here we are in the pitch-blackness of a hot and **humid cave**. When our light flickered on for a few moments, the rays of illumination happened to pass over our fellow cave dwellers — a colony of bats. I later learned that the funny **smell** is bat waste! This is where I almost had a coronary and picked up the pace forward. When we finally reached the end I found out that instead of walking out, you climb out! With only one good leg and the other to use only as a support, I had a lot of **trouble** getting out. Luckily the **smell** of bat urine, got me moving. As a reasonable healthy bodied person I was slightly inconvenienced but **elderly** and sickly people who visit the Tunnel of Love may have some serious issues with this tourist spot.

Figure 4. An example of original paragraph.

During my trip to Aruba a few years back, my boyfriend and I rented a car and drove around the island. While looking for the natural bridge we found a tourist spot called the "Tunnel of Love". Essentially, it's a big cave that you pay to walk through. We thought it would be nice to experience some of the natural beauty Aruba had to **offer**. I had just hurt my ankle in a jet-skiing incident and asked if I would be **able** to walk through with a gimpy leg. The women at the entrance told me I should have no **exertion**. The cave starts out as a pretty large enclosed space, with some external light and quite **easy** to manoeuvre. As you progress inward and downward, the space gets narrower, darker and more difficult to walk through. At approximately halfway through I literally had to hunch over to pass through. That's when the funny **aroma**, strange noises and incredible heat kicked in and my light switched off! So here we are in the pitch-blackness of a hot and **humid tunnel**. When our light flickered on for a few moments, the rays of illumination happened to pass over our fellow cave dwellers — a colony of bats. I later learned that the funny **aroma** is bat waste! This is where I almost had a coronary and picked up the pace forward. When we finally reached the end I found out that instead of walking out, you climb out! With only one good leg and the other to use only as a support, I had a lot of **exertion** getting out. Luckily the **odor** of bat urine, got me moving. As a reasonable healthy bodied person I was slightly inconvenienced but **elderly** and sickly people who visit the Tunnel of Love may have some **serious** issues with this tourist spot.

Figure 5. Generated positive text.

During my trip to Aruba a few years back, my boyfriend and I rented a car and drove around the island. While looking for the natural bridge we found a tourist spot called the "Tunnel of Love". Essentially, it's a big cave that you pay to walk through. We thought it would be nice to experience some of the natural beauty Aruba had to **propose**. I had just hurt my ankle in a jet-skiing incident and asked if I would be **good** to walk through with a gimpy leg. The women at the entrance told me I should have no **trouble**. The cave starts out as a pretty large enclosed space, with some external light and quite **simplistic** to manoeuvre. As you progress inward and downward, the space gets narrower, darker and more difficult to walk through. At approximately halfway through I literally had to hunch over to pass through. That's when the funny **stink**, strange noises and incredible heat kicked in and my light switched off! So here we are in the pitch-blackness of a hot and **oppressive tunnel**. When our light flickered on for a few moments, the rays of illumination happened to pass over our fellow cave dwellers — a colony of bats. I later learned that the funny **stink** is bat waste! This is where I almost had a coronary and picked up the pace forward. When we finally reached the end I found out that instead of walking out, you climb out! With only one good leg and the other to use only as a support, I had a lot of **trouble** getting out. Luckily the **stink** of bat urine, got me moving. As a reasonable healthy bodied person I was slightly inconvenienced but **old** and sickly people who visit the Tunnel of Love may have some **grave** issues with this tourist spot.

Figure 6. Generated negative text.

N.	Paragraph Pair	J_1	J_2	J_3	J_4	J_5	J_6
1	$P1$ and $P1$-positive	=	<	>			
2	P_2 and P_2-positive	<	<	=			
3	$P3$ and P_3-positive	=	>	=			
4	$P1$ and $P1$-negative				=	>	=
5	P_2 and P_2-negative				<	=	<
6	$P3$ and $P3$ -negative				<	>	<

Table 2. Evaluation of the generated texts by judges J1 to J6.

8. Evaluation

Our evaluation is at a preliminary stage. We conducted an evaluation that involved human judges comparing paragraphs in terms of attitude. We selected three paragraphs from the BNC, and generated the positive and negative versions of each of them. Hence, we had six pairs of paragraphs for which we wanted the judges to decide, for two paragraphs P_1 and $P2$ whether:

- $P1$ is more positive (less negative) than P_2 ($P1$ < P_2); or
- $P1$ is more negative (less positive) than $P2$ ($P1$ < P_2); or
- $P1$ and $P2$ are equally positive/negative ($P1$ = P_2).

We had six judges in total. Each pair of original paragraph and generated paragraph was presented to three judges. No judge saw the original paragraph more than once. The order of pairs and paragraphs in pairs was randomized. The results are presented in Table 2, where Pi < Pj means Pi was judged to be more negative (or less positive) than Pj. In an ideal case, if the generated texts had the intended semantic orientation, the expected judgments would be '<' for the upper half of the table (the rows numbered 1, 2, and 3) because the original paragraph should be less positive than the positive-generated one, and '>' for the lower part (the rows numbered 4, 5, and 6), because the original paragraph should be more positive than the negative-generated one. For the positive texts, the judgments were closer to the expectations than for the negative texts, for which there were too many cases when the judgment was opposite to the expected one. The '=' answers are sometimes consistent with our expectations. This depends on how negative or positive the initial text was. For example, if a text is positive to start with, the more-positive version that we generated might be only slightly more positive, in which case both '>' and '=' should be expected judgments. We have yet to include this factor in our results.

The task proved to be difficult for the judges, who were native speakers of English but had no knowledge of computational linguistics. The instructions were short, relying on the judges' intuition of what a positive or negative text is. The results of the preliminary evaluation are not very conclusive; the scale of the experiment was too small. We plan to redo it with more paragraphs from Epinions, which have the advantage that we know their initial semantic orientation. We also plan to choose paragraphs with a higher number of near-synonyms that have positive and negative alternatives in their clusters, and to use more paragraphs and more, better-instructed judges in order to conduct a more conclusive evaluation.

9. Conclusion

In our experiments we changed individual words in order to change the semantic orientation of a text. We made the changes in the semantic representation of the sentences. We could modify the semantic representations so that the sentences would express the same meaning but with a different emphasis, focus, or point of view. This could make the text more suitable for achieving specific communication goals, such as changing the listener's convictions relative to a subject. Another extension, more straightforward to implement, is to include special treatment of contextual valence shifters (Polanyi and Zaenen, 2004): for example, replacing a word with a more positive synonym does not achieve the desired effect if the word is modified by negation.

The work reported here is a pilot for research that is presently in progress, and we have yet only a small amount of data and analysis. We need to experiment with more texts and with changes a higher number of words in each text. In future work, we need to increase the coverage of our LKB of NS, which at the moment is large, but not large enough. We need to know what the near-synonyms of all the content words in a paragraph are. It would be useful to know the near-synonyms at least of all the words from GI for which the semantic orientation is known. We could acquire these near-synonyms from corpora. Steps in this direction were taken by Glickman and Dagan (2003) and Lin et al. (2003). We also need to acquire attitudinal nuances for the newly-added near-synonyms.

Once the coverage of our LKB of NS is increased, we plan to use other texts, such as movie reviews for which the semantic orientation is known, to generate the same texts with changed orientation. We can also use texts whose semantic orientation is determined by one of the existing classifiers mentioned in the related work section.

10. Acknowledgements

We thank Irene Langkilde-Geary for making HALogen and the input construction tool available. Our work is financially supported by the Natural Sciences and Engineering Research Council of Canada, the University of Toronto, and the University of Ottawa.

11. Bibliography

Allan, K. and Burridge, K. (1991) *Euphemism and Dysphemism*. Oxford University Press.

Baron, F. and Hirst, G. (2004) *Collocations as cues to semantic orientation*. Unpublished manuscript.

Charniak, E. (2000) A maximum-entropy-inspired parser. In *Proceedings of the 1st Conference of the North American Chapter of the Association for Computational Linguistics and the 6th Conference on Applied Natural Language Processing (NAACL-ANLP 2000)*, 132–139. Seattle.

Edmonds, P. and Hirst, G. (2002) Near-synonymy and lexical choice. *Computational Linguistics 28 (2)*:105–145.

Elhadad, M., McKeown, K., and Robin, J. (1997) Floating constraints in lexical choice. *Computational Linguistics 22 (4)*:1–44.

Glickman, O. and Dagan, I. (2003) Identifying lexical paraphrases from a single corpus: A case study for verbs. In *Proceedings of the International Conference RANLP-2003 (Recent Advances in Natural Language Processing)*, 166–173. Borovets, Bulgaria.

Hayakawa, S.I. (1994) *Choose the Right Word.* Second Edition, revised by Eugene Ehrlich. HarperCollins Publishers.

Hovy, E. (1990) Pragmatics and language generation. *Artificial Intelligence 43*:153–197.

Inkpen, D.Z. and Hirst, G. (2001) Building a lexical knowledge-base of near-synonym differences. In *Proceedings of the Workshop on WordNet and Other Lexical Resources, Second Meeting of the North American Chapter of the Association for Computational Linguistics (NAACL 2001)*, 47–52. Pittsburgh.

Inkpen, D.Z. and Hirst, G. (2002) Acquiring collocations for lexical choice between near-synonyms. In *Proceedings of the Workshop on Unsupervised Lexical Acquisition, 40th Annual Meeting of the Association for Computational Linguistics (ACL 2002)*, 67–76. Philadelphia.

Inkpen, D.Z. and Hirst, G. (2003) Near-synonym choice in natural language generation. In *Proceedings of the International Conference RANLP-2003 (Recent Advances in Natural Language Processing)*, 204–211. Borovets, Bulgaria.

Inkpen, D. (2003) *Building a Lexical Knowledge-Base of Near-Synonym Differences.* Ph.D. Dissertation, University of Toronto.

Knight, K. and Luk, S. (1994) Building a large knowledge base for machine translation. In *Proceedings of the 12th National Conference on Artificial Intelligence (AAAI-94)*, 773–778. Seattle.

Langkilde, I. and Knight, K. (1998) Generation that exploits corpus-based statistical knowledge. In *Proceedings of the 36th Annual Meeting of the Association for Computational Linguistics joint with 17th International Conference on Computational Linguistics (ACL-COLING '98)*, 704–712. Montreal.

Langkilde-Geary, I. (2002) *A Foundation for a General-Purpose Natural Language Generation: Sentence Realization Using Probabilistic Models of Language.* Ph.D. Dissertation, University of Southern California.

Lin, D., Zhao, S., Qin, L., and Zhou, M. (2003) Identifying synonyms among distributionally similar words. In *Proceedings of the Eighteenth Joint International Conference on Artificial Intelligence (IJCAI-03)*, 1492–1493. Acapulco.

Pang, B., Lee, L., and Vaithyanathan, S. (2002) Thumbs up? Sentiment classification using machine learning techniques. In *Proceedings of the 2002 Conference on Empirical Methods in Natural Language Processing (EMNLP-02)*, 79–86. Philadelphia.

Polanyi, L. and Zaenen, A. (2004) *Contextual valence shifters.* In this volume.

Riloff, E. and Wiebe, J. (2003) Learning extraction patterns for subjective expressions. In *Proceedings of the 2003 Conference on Empirical Methods in Natural Language Processing (EMNLP-03)*, 105–112. Sapporo.

Stone, P.J., Dunphy, D.C., Smith, M.S., Ogilvie, D.M., and associates. (1966) *The General Inquirer: A Computer Approach to Content Analysis*. The MIT Press.

Turney, P. (2002) Thumbs up or thumbs down? Semantic orientation applied to unsupervised classification of reviews. In *Proceedings of the 40th Annual Meeting of the Association for Computational Linguistics (ACL 2002)*, 417–424. Philadelphia.

Yu, H. and Hatzivassiloglou, V. (2003) Towards answering opinion questions: Separating facts from opinions and identifying the polarity of opinion sentences. In *Proceedings of the 2003 Conference on Empirical Methods in Natural Language Processing (EMNLP-03)*, 129–136. Sapporo.

Chapter 16

Identifying Interpersonal Distance using Systemic Features

Casey Whitelaw and Jon Patrick
University of Sydney
Language Technology Research Group
School of Information Technologies
University of Sydney
NSW 2006 Australia
Email: {casey, jonpat}@it.usyd.edu.au

Maria Herke-Couchman
Macquarie University
Centre for Language in Social Life
Division of Linguistics and Psychology
Macquarie University
NSW 2109 Australia
Email: maria.couchman@ling.mq.edu.au

Abstract

This chapter uses Systemic Functional Linguistic (SFL) theory as a basis for extracting semantic features of documents. We focus on the pronominal and determination system and the role it plays in constructing interpersonal distance. By using a hierarchical system model that represents the author's language choices, it is possible to construct a richer and more informative feature representation with superior computational efficiency than the usual bag-of-words approach. Experiments within the context of financial scam classification show that these systemic features can create clear separation between registers with different interpersonal distance. This approach is generalizable to other aspects of attitude and affect that have been modelled within the systemic functional linguistic theory.

Keywords: interpersonal distance, document classification, machine learning, feature representation, systemic functional linguistics, register.

1. Introduction

This paper explores the categorization of text based on meaning. Rather than classify on the content matter of a document, we aim to capture elements of the manner in which the document is written. In particular, we use a computational model of a part of Systemic Functional Linguistic theory to identify the interpersonal distance of a text.

Previous work has looked at extracting other semantic properties of documents. This has included the subjectivity or objectivity of whole texts (Kessler et al., 1997) or individual sentences (Wiebe, 1990; Riloff et al., 2003), and classifying reviews as positive or negative (Turney, 2002). Here, we investigate the interpersonal distance of an entire document, which partially describes the type of relationship established between author and reader.

Much of the prior research has focused on semantic categories of adjectives (Turney, 2002) and nouns (Riloff et al., 2003). This paper focuses on the closed class of pronominals and determiners. These are terms that have often been placed in stop lists, due to their frequent usage and apparent lack of relevance to classification tasks. While the use of these individual words may provide some semantic information, it is through placing them in a system of language choice that patterns of usage may be correlated with interpersonal distance.

Interpersonal distance is, briefly, the relationship established between the author / speaker and reader / listener in a text. It sets the environment in which the information is presented, and can affect the way this information is processed. This research was undertaken as part of a study into the language used in financial scams on the internet. One common characteristic of some types of scams was their 'friendly' and 'casual' manner, and it was hoped to exploit these traits within a traditional document classification task.

Systemic Functional Linguistics (SFL) provides the necessary framework to approach notions such as interpersonal distance. SFL uses multistratal analysis that encompasses both the ideational and non-ideational phenomena of a text. Attitude, affect, judgement, and subjectivity are all addressed within SF theory.

It is important to understand the fundamental bases of SFL, and its approach to describing language in general, and specifically its characterization of interpersonal distance. Section 2 includes a brief introduction to SFL theory, and explains why it is appropriate for use in this field. For SFL to be applied in practise, a suitable computational model is required. Section 3 describes such a computational representation that covers some elements of SFL, and how this can be used within a standard document classification and machine learning environment. This approach is evaluated in Section 4 through an initial series of experiments in classifying financial scams. The results confirm the usefulness of this approach and show that SFL is well-suited to identifying document-level characteristics of language use, especially the aspects of non-denotational meaning that have traditionally confounded keyword-based classification systems.

2. Systemic Functional Linguistics

Systemic Functional Linguistics (SFL) is a framework for describing and modelling language in functional rather than formal terms. The theory is *functional* in that language is interpreted as a resource for making meaning, and descriptions are based on extensive analyses of naturally occurring written and spoken text (Halliday, 1994). The theory is also *systemic* in that it models language as systems of choices (Matthiessen, 1995).

System networks have been used in SFL for more than 40 years as a way of representing the paradigmatic organization of choices within the language system (Matthiessen, 2000: 65). Initially formalized and applied by Halliday in his work on intonation (Halliday, 1963), network diagrams have been used extensively in all areas of theoretical, descriptive and applied SFL research. Systems are organized in terms of increasing *delicacy*, enabling language choice to be viewed from the most general to the most specific. The system network has served as a useful resource in computational linguistics for more than thirty years (Matthiessen 2000:66); Section 3 proposes one approach for its use in document classification.

Systemic Functional theory is a linguistic theory that describes a text in terms of the multiple meanings that it makes. While these meanings are realized by words or orthographic strings, both grammatical and lexical, a text in the first instance is viewed as a semantic unit (Halliday and Hasan, 1985). In a study such as this that seeks to categorize texts according to the meanings that they make in a systematic way, rather than just the set of words that it uses most frequently, SF theory presents itself as an extremely useful model. The proposed methods for computing aspects of SFL operate on raw text. The present research is not dependent on external semantic resources or parsers, and the text representation used is constructed only according to the specific SF meaning system under focus.

SF theory describes the use of language in context. It conceptualizes language as a multi-dimensional semiotic space showing the organization of language both globally as a meaning making system and locally as sub-systems of language use. Here we will focus on the three global dimensions that are implicated in the semantic phenomenon of interpersonal distance - the hierarchy of stratification, the spectrum of metafunction and the cline of instantiation.

2.1 The Hierarchy of Stratification

One key global dimension of SFL is the hierarchy of stratification. Language itself is modelled as an ordered series of levels or strata encompassing semantics, lexicogrammar and graphology / phonology, as shown in Figure 1. This in turn is modelled as being embedded stratally within context. Interpersonal distance, the phenomenon being investigated here, is located as a pattern of meaning within the semantic stratum. This pattern of meaning is realized as patterns of wording in the lexicogrammar, and it is at this level that it is exposed to current NLP techniques. The aim, then, is to recreate the semantic characterization of interpersonal distance through modelling its visible effects in the lexicogrammar of a text.

The outermost stratum shown in Figure 1 is that of context, and is frequently overlooked in NLP tasks. The social situation in which a text takes place influences and is influenced by all aspects of language choice; this is partially captured by the notion of register, as discussed below.

2.2 The Spectrum of Metafunction

The metafunctions refer to the three separate strands of meaning that contribute to the overall meaning in the text (Halliday, 1994). These three metafunctions are deployed simultaneously and are the textual, the interpersonal and the ideational:

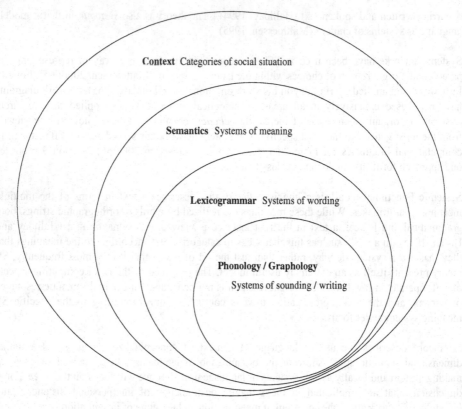

Figure 1. Modelling language stratally (Hasan, 1996)

- The textual metafunction provides 'the resources for presenting information as text in context' (Matthiessen, 1995).
- The interpersonal metafunction provides the resources for enacting social roles and relations as meaning.
- The ideational metafunction provides the resources for construing our experience of the world.

Interpersonal distance is located within the interpersonal metafunction and relates to the tenor of the relationship between the writer and reader within the context. Metafunction is orthogonal to the strata shown in Figure 1; the interpersonal metafunction is evidenced in context, semantics, lexicogrammar, and orthography.

2.3 Characterizing Registers

A register is a group of texts whose language selections vary from the general language system in similar ways. A register can be characterized by properties of its field, tenor, and mode. Registers are skewings "of probabilities relative to the general systemic probabilities" (Matthiessen, 1993). Register is the instantiation of particular situation types within the system. This characterization of registers as probabilistic is key to SFL and to this study: a register is relatively, not rigidly. This provides a formal basis for the feature representation choices made in Section 3.

Register is a realization of diversification in the context of situation (Matthiessen, 1993:234) and, in turn, register is realized by variation in meanings and wordings. While a register groups documents on the basis of the meanings they make, these meanings are realized in the semantics and lexicogrammar of the texts, and so may be analysed on these terms. In particular, registerial differences should be exposed through the patterns of language choice within a system.

A register can be described in terms of the language selections it makes within all the various language sub-systems. While the meaning of a particular text is constructed by all the selections across all the sub-systems simultaneously, examination of just a single system will still give insight into a specific type of meaning being made within the text. If this system contains characteristic variation between registers, it may be a strong enough basis for classification without further unpacking.

2.4 Attitude, Affect, and SFL

The systemic functional approach to language is well suited to the broader study of attitude and affect in text. Traditional areas of interest such as semantic orientation, opinion, polarity, and modality are developed, from one perspective, within the framework of Appraisal theory (Martin, 2004). Appraisal, encompassing systems such as Judgement and Appreciation, is itself only one element of the interpersonal metafunction. The study of attitude and affect must be a study of all aspects of the interpersonal; and it is through the application of these systems, both individually and as interacting elements, that a deeper understanding will be reached.

As computational techniques for identifying systemic features improve, these models of attitude and affect provide a reasoned and functional basis for classification at all levels of a text. The current level of sophistication is showing results in analysing modality (Argamon and Dodick, 2004) and appraisal (Taboada and Grieve, 2004), as well as this work on interpersonal distance.

2.5 Interpersonal Distance

Interpersonal distance is a measure of the distance being constructed by the text in the relationship between the speaker or writer and the addressee (Eggins et al., 1993). Typically, spoken discourse that unfolds in a context of maximum oral and visual contact is representative of minimal interpersonal distance whereas written discourse with no visual, oral or aural contact represents maximal interpersonal distance.

Interpersonal distance can be determined by analysing various systemic language choices made within a text. Examples of such an analysis might include measuring the degree and frequency of participant nominalization deployed within a text as well as the frequency and type of interactant reference (Couchman, 2001).

An example of a text with very close interpersonal distance would be one that includes direct speech, such as the following (Biggs, 1990):

> *Kupe went to Muturangi's village and spoke of the bad behaviour of the animal*
> *with regard to his people's bait, saying, 'I have come to tell **you** to kill **your***

> *octopus', Muturangi replied, 'I won't agree to my pet being killed. Its home is in*
> *the sea.' 'Well', said Kupe, 'if you won't take care of your pet, I will kill it.'*
> *Kupe went back home and said to his people, 'Prepare my canoe as well.'*
> *Maataa-hoorua was made ready and Kupe set off to go.*

In the above text, degree and frequency of nominalization is low and selections from the Interactant system, shown in bold face, are high.

A written history text is a good example of a text that constructs maximum interpersonal distance, partly by making no selections from within the Interactant system (Biggs, 1997):

> *The discovery of Hawaii from the Marquesas was a remarkable achievement,*
> *but at twenty degrees north latitude Hawaii is still within the zone of the trade*
> *winds that blow steadily and predictably for half of each year. New Zealand lies*
> *far to the South of the trade winds, in the stormy waters and unpredictable*
> *weather of the Tasman Sea. The Southern hemisphere, moreover, has no Pole*
> *Star to provide a constant compass point.*

Work on Nigerian emails has indicated that close interpersonal distance might be characteristic of that particular register (Herke-Couchman, 2003). As mentioned above, interpersonal distance can be analysed through various systemic language choices. One key system, and that focused upon here, is the closed set of pronominals and determiners.

2.6 The Pronominal & Determination System

The Pronominal and Determination system (DETERMINATION) is a language system that includes within it the interpersonal resource for modelling the relationship between the interactants in the dialogue. The system is a closed grammatical system that includes realizations of both interactant (speaker, speaker-plus and addressee) and non-interactant reference items. A portion of the full DETERMINATION system is shown in Figure 2.

It is expected that very close interpersonal distance in a text would be characterized by frequent selections from the interactant system. For example, a text seeking to establish patterns of familiarity between author and reader would show foregrounded patterns of speaker (*I, me, my, mine*) and addressee (*you, your, yours*) usage. Contrastively, a text that is constructing a more formal and distant tenor will typically make little use of the interactant system but may instead show strong patterns of usage of more generalized alternative meaning systems.

The full list of terms included in this system are as follows: *my, mine, i, me, our, ours, we, us, your, yours, you, her, hers, she, his, he, him, its, it, their, theirs, they, them, one's, one, whose, who, whom, this, these, that, those, the, which, what, no, not any, no one, noone, nobody, nothing, each, each one, every, everyone, everybody, both, all.*

3. Representing System Networks

For systemic information to be extracted from a document, there must be a suitable computationally-feasible language model. While SFL is a comprehensive and multidimensional linguistic theory, and is not obviously computationally tractable, we can develop a more restricted model that allows us to work with specific systems such as DETERMINATION.

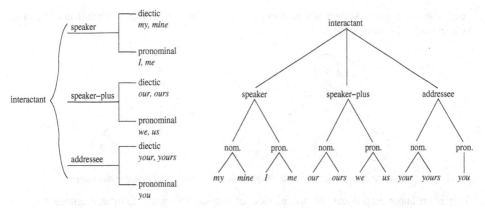

Figure 2. The interactant subsystem modelled systemically and as a tree

3.1 SFL in Computational Linguistics

Most of the computational work using systemic functional grammar has focused upon generation. The multi-stratal approach of SFG has been shown to be very effective at generating individual sentences (Mann and Matthiessen, 1985) and rhetorically linked texts using Rhetorical Structure Theory (Mann and Thompson, 1988). Functional parsing has proved more problematic in part due to the need for manual creation of broad-coverage grammars (O'Donnell, 1994).

Much less work has been done in performing automated functional analysis. Many view parsing as the fundamental basis of any text analysis, but this is not necessarily the case; machine learning techniques have been used to classify sentences by function (O'Donnell, 2002), and to automatically induce the functional properties of nominal groups (Munro, 2003). By putting to one side the complexities of full parsing, relevant aspects of SFG have been used successfully in practise.

By modelling the SFL system of DETERMINATION, the aim is to produce a model of the relevant elements of a text's meaning, and in doing so be able to efficiently classify documents based on the interpersonal distance they create. The representation used must be sufficient to capture the range of expression displayed in the system, but be amenable to use with current machine learning techniques.

The richness and reach of SF theory has meant that the linguistic analysis has typically been associated with manual qualitative text analysis. However, it is important to remember that the development of the theory has been firmly based on quantitative observations about language (Matthiessen, 2003).

3.2 System as Hierarchy

As is shown in Figure 2, this system can intuitively be modelled as a tree. Each internal node represents a subsystem or category: a pattern of possible language choice. Each leaf gives a realization of its parent system as a word or phrase. A system may contain both lexical realizations (leaves) and subsystems (nodes).

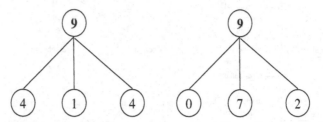

Figure 3. Aggregating counts smoothes differences at greater delicacy

This is an impoverished but still useful view of a system network. Language choice does not always result in a specific word or phrase; an in-depth manual analysis of a text would show that grammatical and lexical units of various sizes contribute to the overall meaning. Further, interaction between systems can result in networks that are not strictly hierarchical, and richer representations will be required to model these processes effectively. A more general computational model for extracting systemic features is proposed by Whitelaw and Argamon (2004) as an extension of this purely hierarchical approach. The current representation is sufficient to capture language choice for a system such as DETERMINATION, which is a closed class and fully lexically realized.

The usage of a system in a document can be represented by a system instance. Each occurrence of each lexical realization in the document is counted, and these counts are accumulated upwards through the network. The count at an internal node is the sum of the counts of its sub-categories. This process is no more costly than constructing a feature vector in traditional text classification methods.

3.3 Leveraging Systemic Structure

In a standard 'bag-of-words' approach, the contribution of a word to a document is given by its relative frequency; how rarely or often that word is used. This implicitly uses a language model in which all words are independent of each other. Crucially, this does not and cannot take into account the *choice* between words, since there is no representation of this choice. Placing words within a system network provides a basis for richer and more informative feature representation. There are two main advantages to be gained from systemic information:

Firstly, it allows for categorical features that are based on semantically-related groups of words, at all levels in the network. By collecting aggregate counts, individual variations within a category are ignored. Figure 3 shows the raw counts of the same system in two documents; at the lower level, closer to lexis, the distributions of counts are highly dissimilar. At the higher level, these differences have been smoothed, and the documents look the same.

For a given register, it may be the case that important and characteristic language choice occurs at a very fine level, distinguishing between usages of individual words. This word-level information is kept intact, as in a bag-of-words approach. In another register, it may be the usage of a category, such as interactant, that is characteristic. The usage of any words within the category may appear random while maintaining consistent category usage. These higher-level features are not available in a traditional bag-of-words approach, hence these patterns may be lost as noise.

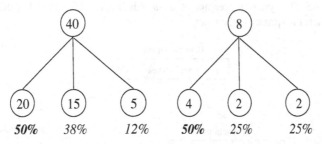

Figure 4. Proportional features are a local and size-independent measure

The second and more important difference to traditional feature representation is the representation of language *choice*. SF theory treats language use as a series of selections within systems; at any point in the system network, or tree as it has been modelled here, the selection is restrained to the immediate sub-systems. The choice is not between one word and any other, or even one system and any other, but a series of semantically-driven choices within the system. A bag-of-words model can model only choice between one word and any other; a choice between arbitrary words such as 'dog' and 'elegant'. Comparative features such as these can only be used within an appropriate theory-driven structure, which is provided here through the use of SFL and system networks. Figure 4 shows the potential for comparative features to reveal similarities not immediately apparent in a text.

3.4 Representing Systemic Features

Figure 5 shows a portion of the DETERMINATION system for two documents of different sizes, belonging to the same register. Four possible feature representations are given: from left to right, each node shows the total count, term frequency, system percentage, and system contribution. Each feature representation captures a different aspect of system usage in a document and register.

Raw counts (first column). The summed feature count, shown in the leftmost column, presents these two documents as highly dissimilar. Note also that this is only the top portion of the system, and that multiple levels exist below those shown. Raw term counts are usually not used directly as features, as they are heavily influenced by document length.

Term frequency (second column) is the standard basis for bag-of-words representations; it gives the proportion of the document accounted for by this term. Term frequency is commonly used since it normalizes for document length; most topic-based document classification assumes that the document length is not important (Sebastiani, 2002). In creating features for each sub-system, this representation can still take advantage of the aggregation and smoothing provided by the system, but does not take further advantage of the known structure.

System percentage (third column) gives the proportion of total system usage made up by this sub-system. In Document A, *addressee* occurs three times from a total of fifteen occurrences of *determination* in the document, giving it a system percentage of 20%. Within a document, system percentage is directly proportional to term frequency, but is independent to system *density*. If another 800 words were added to Document A, but no more uses of DETERMINATION, the term frequency for a feature would halve while the system percentage remained constant. This makes it a suitable representation where distinctions are made not on how often a feature occurs, but the manner of its use. The system percentage of *speaker* is higher in Document A than Document B, despite higher term frequency in the latter.

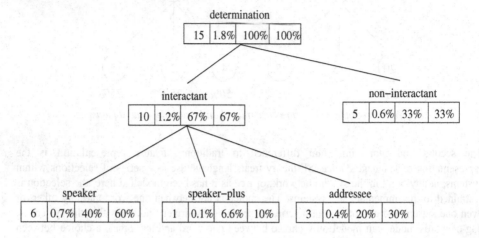

Document A: 800 words

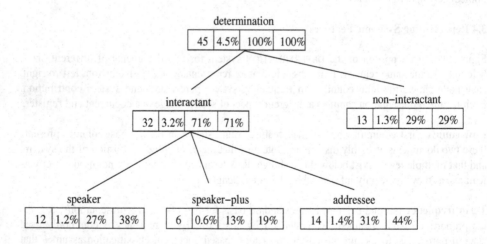

Document B: 1000 words

count	term frequency	system %	system contribution

Figure 5. Different feature representations portray a text differently

System contribution (fourth column) shows the ratio of sub-system to super-system occurrence. Again in Document A, *speaker* occurs six times and its super-system, *interactant*, occurs ten times, giving a system contribution of 60%. This is a strictly local measure of usage, and captures most directly the systemic notion of choice: once the decision to use a given super-system has been made, how often was this sub-system chosen as the realization? This is a relative feature, and as such is independent of document length, total system usage, and usage of other portions of the system (see Figure 4). Despite the differences in lower-level choices, and in the raw counts of system usage, the system contribution of *interactant* in Documents A and B are very similar.

System contribution is not proportional or strongly correlated to term frequency, and the two measures provide useful and complementary information. Term frequency reports the percentage of a document that is made up of a given term. Within a system instance, term frequency can be used to report the term frequency not just of terms but of systems as well. Unlike term frequency, system contribution does not capture how often a system is used, but rather its usage in relation to the other possible choices. In the same way as a register may be characterized by choice, it may also be characterized by frequent usage of a particular system. The three complementary representations given here may each be useful in discerning characteristic system usage in general, and interpersonal distance in particular.

In implementing these representations, it is worth noting that not all system contribution features are necessary. Systems with a single child will always give 100%, and do not add information since there is no choice. In a system with a binary choice, either one of the features may be discarded since they have unit sum. Both system percentage and system contribution are meaningless at the root level, and system percentage and system contribution are identical at first level below the root. This feature reduction can be performed deterministically before any further feature selection.

By mapping only the relevant portions of a document's meaning, systemic features also have the potential to increase computational efficiency by reducing the number of attributes used in machine learning systems, in comparison to broader bag-of-words methods.

4. Identifying Registers

As discussed in Section 2, a register is constrained in the types of meanings it is likely to construct. A register may be characterized as establishing a certain interpersonal distance. If the choice within the determination system reflects this semantic position, it should be possible to classify documents on this basis.

Not all registers are distinguishable by interpersonal distance. This is but one of many of the semantic properties that characterize documents, such as formality, modality, and evaluation. Note also that the identification of a register is not the same as identifying the *topic* of a document; instances of the 'newspaper article' register may have very different content that is all presented in the same fashion.

4.1 Corpora

We chose corpora that were clearly separated into different registers. From prior manual analysis, it was expected that these registers would have different characteristic interpersonal distance.

Previous work has examined the use of the determination system in so-called 'Nigerian emails'. These are fraudulent emails in which the author attempts to establish an illegal business relationship (money transfer) with the recipient. One of the most salient characteristics of this register is the way in which the author, despite having no prior relationship with the reader, works to set up a sense of familiarity and trust. These semantic strategies suggest closer interpersonal distance than would usually be expected in the setting up of a legitimate business relationship, particularly since the texts are written rather than spoken. This corpus contained 67 manually collected Nigerian emails.

The Nigerian emails were contrasted with a collection of newspaper articles taken from the standard Reuters text classification corpus. Since many of the newswire texts are very short, only texts with more than one thousand words were kept, resulting in 683 documents. As a result of the context in which they unfold, it was expected that the Reuters newswire texts would make different language choices in order to realize the different meanings they construct. More specifically, it is expected that this register constructs a greater and more formal interpersonal distance between author and reader.

The third register was taken from the British National Corpus and consists of 195 documents marked as belonging to the 'spoken / leisure' category. These are mostly transcriptions of interviews and radio shows covering a wide range of topics. As stated above, the interpersonal distance constructed in spoken text is almost always much closer than that constructed in written texts. Including this corpus allowed us to explore whether the perceived close interpersonal distance in the Nigerian email corpus would be confused with the close interpersonal distance that is typical of spoken texts.

These corpora differ greatly in both field and tenor, and can be separated easily using standard bag-of-words techniques. In using these corpora, we aim not to show improved performance, but to show that the determination system provides sufficient evidence to separate documents on the basis of interpersonal distance. For this to be possible, the words and categories in this system must be used in a regular and learnable fashion, which reflects the semantic positioning of the text. The systemic organization proposed by SFL is only one possible structure; if this is a sensible semantic description of language use, as SFL asserts it to be, the resulting systemic features should be useful in classification.

4.2 Features Used

The behaviour of a system within a document can be represented as a system instance. As discussed in Section 3, a system instance stores hierarchical information at every level from the full system to individual lexical realizations. System usage may differ at any or all of these levels: some registers may make very specific lexical choices, while others may be differentiable by more general trends. In its entirety, the determination system consists of 109 nodes including 48 lexical realizations. From these, various subsets were used to test the performance and robustness of the system.

- **all**: All 109 system and lexis nodes
- **lexis**: The 48 lexical realizations in the system.
- **system**: All 61 non-lexical features.
- **top10**: Top 10 features on the basis of information gain
- **top5**: Top 5 features on the basis of information gain

	#attributes	NB	J48	SVM
all	109	**99.4%**	97.9%	**99.6%**
lexis	48	98.6%	**98.6%**	**99.6%**
system	61	98.6%	98.1%	99.5%
top10	10	98.9%	97.7%	98.6%
top5	5	96.2%	98.1%	98.2%

Table 1. Classification accuracy using system contribution

	#attributes	NB	J48	SVM
all	109	92.8%	98.2%	98.3%
lexis	48	93.8%	98.1%	**98.4%**
system	61	93,9%	98.4%	98.3%
top10	10	96.1%	**98.6%**	97.9%
top5	5	**97.3%**	98.1%	97.8%
baseline	109	98.4%	97.5%	100%

Table 2. Classification accuracy using term frequency

Each set of features was computed once using term frequency and again using system contribution. Classification was performed using three different machine learners, all commonly used in text classification tasks: a Naive Bayes probabilistic classifier (NB), a decision tree (J48), and a support vector machine (SVM). All implementations are part of the publicly available WEKA machine learning package (Witten and Eibe, 1999).

4.3 Results

Results from using system contribution and term frequency are shown in Tables 1 and 2 respectively. All of the feature sets and classifiers produced clear separation of the classes, using only features from the determination system. The best result of 99.6% came from the use of an SVM using the system contribution data of either all features or lexical features. It is clear from these results that these corpora are separable using features related to interpersonal distance.

Better results were achieved using system contribution than term frequency. By measuring the system choice, rather than system usage, this feature representation highlights the salient aspects of language use. This contrastive description is made possible by placing words in a system network.

In all tests, the Nigerian and Reuters corpora were clearly separated. These registers have markedly different and strongly characteristic interpersonal distance. The spoken corpus exhibited a small amount of confusion with the Nigerian texts, showing evidence that their language is more like spoken than written text.

Feature selection exhibits different effects on the two types of features used. Best performance for system contribution features came from using all features, or only lexical features. Best performance for term frequency features, however, came from using fewer features. Since there is a high degree of correlation between term frequencies within a system network, this can skew results when using classifiers that assume independent features, as Naive Bayes does.

system	term	bag-of-words
addressee / pronominal	addressee / nominal	*your*
addressee / nominal	*your*	*my*
speaker / pronominal	*my*	*you*
speaker / nominal	interactant	*me*
I	addressee	*said*
interactant	speaker / nominal	*I*
Non-interactant	addressee / pronominal	*er*
your	*you*	*that's*
me	*I*	*erm*
my	speaker / pronominal	*us*

Table 3. Top ten features show pronominals and speech markers

Table 3 shows the top 10 features as ranked using the information gain metric (Quinlan, 1993). For systemic features, almost all are located within the *interactant* subsystem. This is further confirmation that the discerning features are not random discrepancies between classes, but are evidence of the underlying semantic intent. Also shown are the most significant features in the bag-of-words approach. Despite being informed by all the words in the documents, the most significant were still those located in the determination system, together with transcribed discourse markers such as 'er' and 'erm', which were of use in separating the spoken texts of the BNC documents.

5. Conclusion

SFL is fundamentally a theory of meaning. As such, language choices can be identified as both formal lexical or grammatical selections as well as in terms of systemic meaning selections. The relationship between these two complementary perspectives is one of abstraction or generalization; a meaning system is more abstract than the grammar or lexis that realizes it (Martin and Rose, 2003). This realization ensures that a meaning phenomenon such as interpersonal distance is characterizable in terms of both systemic choice and lexicogrammatical structure.

In this paper, we have shown that one aspect of the interpersonal distance of a document can be characterized by the use of the determination system. We have further shown that registers that construct variable interpersonal meaning can be separated solely using the features from the Pronominal and Determination system. This can be achieved by modelling SFL at the lexical level without specific external resources.

Interpersonal distance is but one property of the tenor of a document. Similarly, the determination system is but one small part of SFL theory. As our ability to computationally model and extract system networks increases, these systems and their interactions will provide more features by which the semantic properties of a document may be discerned.

6. Bibliography

Argamon, S. and Dodick, J. *Conjunction and Modal Assessment in Genre Classification: A Corpus-Based Study of Historical and Experimental Science Writing*. In this volume, Shanahan J. G., Qu Y., Wiebe J. (Eds.) *Computing Attitude and Affect in Text*. Springer, Berlin.

Biggs, B. (1990) *In the Beginning, The Oxford Illustrated History of New Zealand.* Oxford University Press, Oxford.

Biggs, B. (1997) *He Whirwhiringa Selected Readings in Maori.* Auckland University Press, Auckland.

Couchman, M. (2001) *Transposing culture: A tri-stratal exploration of the meaning making of two cultures.* Honours thesis, Macquarie University.

Eggins, S., Wignell, P. and Martin, J. R. (1993) *Register analysis: theory and practice.* In *The discourse of history: distancing the recoverable past,* 75-109, Pinter, London.

Halliday, M. A. K. and Hasan, R. (1985) *Language, Context and Text: a social semiotic perspective.* Geelong, Victoria: Deakin University Press.

Halliday, M. A. K. (1994) *Introduction to Functional Grammar.* Edward Arnold, second edition.

Halliday, M. A. K. (1995) Computing Meaning: some reflections on past experience and present prospects. Paper presented to PACLING95, Brisbane, April, 1995.

Hasan, R. (1996) *Ways of saying, ways of meaning: selected papers of Ruqaiya Hasan.* Cassell, London.

Herke-Couchman, M. A. (2003) *Arresting the scams: Using systemic functional theory to solve a hi-tech social problem.* In Australian SFL Association Conference 2003.

Iedema, R., Feez, S. and White, P. (1995) *Media literacy.* Sydney, Metropolitan East Disadvantaged Schools Program.

Kessler, B., Nunberg, G., and Shutze, H. (1997) *Automatic detection of text genre.* In Philip R. Cohen and Wolfgang Wahlster (Eds), *Proceedings of the Thirty-Fifth Annual Meeting of the ACL and Eigth Conference of the EACL,* 32-38, Somerset, New Jersey.

Mann, W. C. and Matthiessen, C. M. I. M. (1985). *Nigel: A systemic grammar for text generation.* In Benson, R. and Greaves, J. (Eds), *Systemic Perspectives on Discourse: Selected Papers from the 9th International Systemic Workshop.* Ablex.

Mann, W. C. and Thompson, S. A. (1988) *Rhetorical structure theory: Toward a functional theory of text organisation.* Text, 8 (3), 243-281.

Martin, J. R. and Rose, D. (2003). *Working with Discourse: Meaning Beyond the Clause.* Continuum, London and New York.

Martin, J. R. (2004) *Mourning: how we get aligned.* In Discourse & Society 15.2/3 (Special Issue on 'Discourse around 9/11'). 321-344.

Matthiessen, C. M. I. M (1993) *Register analysis: theory and practice.* In *Register in the round: diversity in a unified theory of register.* 221-292. Pinter, London.

Matthiessen, C. M. I. M (1995) *Lexico-grammatical cartography: English systems.* International Language Sciences Publishers.

Matthiessen, C. M. I. M. (2003). *Frequency Profiles of some basic grammatical systems: an interim report.* Macquarie University.

Munro, R. (2003) *Towards a computational inference and application of a functional grammar,* Honours thesis, University of Sydney, 2003.

O'Donnell, M. (1994) *Sentence analysis and generation: a systemic perspective.* PhD thesis, University of Sydney.

O'Donnell, M. (2002) *Automating the coding of semantic patterns: applying machine learning to corpus linguistics.* In *Proceedings of the 29th International Systemic Functional Workshop.* University of Liverpool.

Quinlan, J. R. (1993) *C4.5: Programs for Machine Learning.* Morgan Kaufmann.

Riloff, E., Wiebe, J. and Wilson, T. (2003), *Learning subjective nouns using extraction pattern bootstrapping.* In *Proceedings of CoNLL-2003,* 25-32. Edmonton, Canada.

Sebastiani, F. (2002) *Machine learning in automated text categorization.* ACM Computing Surveys, 34 (1), 1-47.

Sebastiani, F. (2004). Text Categorization. In Alessandro Zanasi (Ed.), *Text Mining and its Applications,* WIT Press, Southampton, UK.

Taboada, M. and Grieve, J. *Analysing Appraisal Automatically.* In Shanahan J. G., Qu Y., Wiebe J. (Eds.) *Computing Attitude and Affect in Text.* Springer, Berlin.

Turney, P. (2002) *Thumbs up or thumbs down? Semantic orientation applied to unsupervised classification of reviews.* In *Proceedings 40th Annual Meeting of the ACL (ACL'02),* 417-424

Wiebe, J. (1990) *Recognizing Subjective Sentences: A Computational Investigation of Narrative Text.* PhD thesis, State University of New York at Buffalo.

Witten, I.H. and Eibe, F. (1999) *Data Mining: Practical Machine Learning Tools and Techniques with Java Implementations.* Morgan Kaufmann.

Whitelaw, C. and Argamon, S. (2004) *Systemic Functional Features for Stylistic Text Categorization.* In *Proceedings of the AAAI 2004 Fall Symposium on Style and Meaning in Language, Art, Music, and Design.* AAAI Press.

Wu, C. (2000) *Modelling Linguistic Resources: A Systemic Functional Approach.* Unpublished PhD thesis, Macquarie University, Sydney.

Chapter 17

Corpus-Based Study of Scientific Methodology: Comparing the Historical and Experimental Sciences

Shlomo Argamon
Illinois Institute of Technology
Department of Computer Science
10 W 31st Street
Chicago, IL 60616, U.S.A.
Email: argamon@iit.edu

Jeff Dodick
The Hebrew University of Jerusalem
Science Teaching Center
Givat Ram Campus
Jerusalem 91904, ISRAEL
Email: jdodick@vms.huji.ac.il

Abstract

This chapter studies the use of textual features based on systemic functional linguistics, for genre-based text categorization. We describe feature sets that represent different types of conjunctions and modal assessment, which together can partially indicate how different genres structure text and may prefer certain classes of attitudes towards propositions in the text. This enables analysis of large-scale rhetorical differences between genres by examining which features are important for classification. The specific domain we studied comprises scientific articles in historical and experimental sciences (paleontology and physical chemistry, respectively). We applied the SMO learning algorithm, which with our feature set achieved over 83% accuracy for classifying articles according to field, though no field-specific terms were used as features. The most highly-weighted features for each were consistent with hypothesized methodological differences between historical and experimental sciences, thus lending empirical evidence to the recent philosophical claim of multiple scientific methods.

Keywords: Text classification, systemic functional linguistics, computational stylistics, philosophy of science, science education.

1. Introduction

Research in automatically using features of a text to determine its stylistic character has a long history, going back to Mosteller and Wallace's landmark study on authorship attribution of the *Federalist Papers* (Mosteller and Wallace 1964). The kind of features typically used in such studies has not changed much over the years: frequencies of different function words (Mosteller and Wallace 1964), frequencies of different kinds of syntactic constituents (Baayen et al. 1996; Stamatatos et al. 2001), and various measures of sentence complexity (Yule 1938; Losee 1996). The implicit understanding is that such lexical, syntactic, or complexity-based features serve as useful proxies for the 'behind-the-scenes' pragmatic or contextual factors that determine stylistic variation, because such factors are realized in specific texts via word choice and syntactic structure. However, for the most part, computational stylistics research has not explicitly examined the semantics or pragmatics of such features. In particular, although it is clear that different textual genres use different rhetorical modes and different generic document structures (Martin 1992), the relation of low-level stylistic features to aspects of rhetorical structure remains obscure. Our highest-level goal is to elucidate this relationship by exploring genre-based text categorization problems where particular rhetorical or cognitive communicative needs can be identified. In the future, this approach may be enhanced by incorporating rhetorical 'parsing' of the text (see the recent work of Marcu (2000)).

In this chapter we outline an approach to defining linguistically-motivated features for genre classification based on systemic functional principles, and present an initial implementation of the approach. The specific domain we study here is that of scientific discourse, with the aim of gaining a better understanding of the nature and methods of science. We apply our system to a corpus-based study of genre variation between articles in a historical science (in this case paleontology) and an experimental science (in this case physical chemistry), where we expect to find significant rhetorical differences. Our results show how computational stylistic techniques can give a consistent picture of differences in methodological reasoning between scientists in the two fields. This line of research also has the potential to contribute to the philosophy of science, by enabling empirical investigation of hypothesized methodological differences among fields. (See for example the work of Cleland (2001; 2002) where she strongly argues for such methodological differences.) Also, since properly understanding different forms of scientific reasoning is critical for science education (Dodick and Orion 2003), we hope to contribute eventually to the development of better pedagogical practices.

2. Background

2.1 Genre, Register, and Systemic Choice

The linguistic framework we assume is that of systemic functional linguistics (Halliday 1994). Systemic functional linguistics (SFL) construes language as a set of interlocking choices for expressing meanings: "either this, that, or the other", with more general choices constraining the possible specific choices. For example: "A message is either about doing, thinking, or being; if about doing, it is either standalone action or action on something; if action on something it is either creating something or affecting something pre-existent," and so on. A *system*, then, is a set of options for meanings to be expressed, with *entry conditions*, i.e., when that choice is possible – for example, if a message is not about doing, then there is no possible choice between expressing standalone action or action on something. Each option has also a *realization specification*, which gives constraints (lexical, featural, or structural) on statements that express the given option. Options often serve as entry conditions for more detailed systems, which we will term here *subsystems*.

By structuring language as a complex of choices between mutually exclusive options, the systemic approach is particularly appropriate to examining variation in language use. Thus a systemic grammar specification allows us to ask:

> In places where a meaning of type A is to be expressed in a text (e.g., "connection between two clauses"), what sorts of more specific meanings (e.g., "extension by new information" or "elaboration by qualification") are most likely to be expressed in different contexts?

While much of the meaning potential of language is determined by the sort of ideas being expressed, the specific form of an utterance is underdetermined by its purely representational meaning. Other layers of meaning in terms of interpersonal relations, attitude towards propositions, and intratextual logical or rhetorical connections (cohesion) are also present, as well as subtle choices of focus. As an example of a cohesive system in English, when *expanding* the meaning of one clause by conjoining another clause, one may choose between three possibilities: *elaboration* (deepening by restatement, comment, or exemplification: "He left, which was good", commenting on the event), *extension* (adding new information: "He left, and I felt better", adding on a related event), and *enhancement* (qualification by reference to circumstance, cause, manner, or result: "He left, so I rejoiced", creating a short causal chain). Note that all three examples have similar representational meanings, though more subtle distinctions are drawn. A general preference for one or another option is thus largely a question of *style* or of *attitude*, in which individual and social/contextual factors come to bear. Such preferences can be measured by evaluating the relative probabilities of different options by tagging their realizations in a corpus of texts (Halliday 1991). By comparing how these probabilities vary between situations with different characteristics, we may determine how those characteristics affect linguistic behavior.

By examining differences between systemic preferences across scientific genres, we are performing a quantitative analysis of register. *Register* denotes functional distinctions in language use related to the context of language use (Eggins and Martin 1997), and may be considered to comprise: *mode*, the communication channel of the discourse (interaction between producer and audience); *tenor*, the effect of the social relation between the producer and the audience; and *field*, the domain of discourse. We study here the field distinction between historical and experimental science, with mode and tenor held relatively constant, by using articles written by working scientists drawn from peer-reviewed journals. Our hypothesis, borne out by our results below, is that the difference in the types of reasoning needed by historical and experimental sciences leads to correlated differences in rhetorical preferences (perhaps best understood as 'functional tenor' (Gregory 1967)), which are realized by how the writer expresses attitudes towards assertions in the text (via modal assessment), as well as by what strategies they use for cohesion.

Previous work in this vein has investigated the relationship between choice probabilities and contextual factors. For example, Plum and Cowling (1987) demonstrate a relation between speaker social class and choice of verb tense (past/present) in face-to-face interviews. Similarly, Hasan has shown, in mother-child interactions, that the sex of the child and the family's social class together have a strong influence on several kinds of semantic choice in speech (Hasan 1988). The methodology that has been applied in these works has two stages: first hand-coding a corpus for systemic-functional and contextual variables and second comparing how systemic choice probabilities vary with contextual factors, using correlation statistics or multivariate analysis techniques (such as principal components analysis). This chapter presents a first attempt at extending this idea to larger corpora using automated text analysis and machine learning.

2.2 Scientific Language

Our domain of interest in this study is scientific discourse, which we approach by examining peer-reviewed journal articles. Our goal in analyzing scientific communication is to study the nature and methods of science. Paradigmatic of this general approach is research on how scientists communicate with each other while doing science. It is clear that group communication between the various scientists working in a laboratory is often crucial to scientific success (Dunbar 1995). The particular uses of language by scientists serve to create a sort of "collaborative space", whose background worldview makes possible communication about complex observations and hypotheses (Goodwin 1994). Analysis of specific linguistic features can help elucidate important features of the way discourse contributes to problem solving, as in the study by Ochs et al. (1994) of physicist's metaphoric talk of travel in a variety of graphical spaces.

2.3 Historical and Experimental Science

Increasingly, philosophers of science recognize that the classical model of a single "Scientific Method" based on experimentation does a disservice to sciences such as geology and paleontology, which are no less scientific by virtue of being historically, rather than experimentally, oriented. Rather, differences in method may stem directly from the types of phenomena under study. Experimental science (such as experimental physics) attempts to formulate general predictive laws, and so relies heavily on repeatable series of manipulative experiments to refine hypotheses about such laws (Latour and Woolgar 1986). Historical science, on the other hand, deals with *contingent* phenomena, involving study of specific individuals and events from the past, in an attempt to find unifying explanations for effects caused by those events (Diamond, 1999; Mayr 1976). Based on these differences, reasoning in historical sciences is understood as a form of *explanatory* reasoning, as opposed to the reasoning from causes to effects more characteristic of experimental science (Gould 1986; Diamond 1999). Indeed, as far back as the 19th century philosopher William Whewell (1837, v3, p. 617) noted that in (the historical science of) geology "the effects must themselves teach us the nature and intensity of the causes which have operated".

An important element of historical reasoning is the need to differentially weight the evidence. Since any given trace of a past event is typically ambiguous as to its possible causes, many pieces of evidence must be combined in complex ways in order to form a confirming or disconfirming argument for a hypothesis (termed *synthetic* thinking by Baker (1996)). Such synthetic thinking is, as Cleland (2002) argues, a necessary commitment of historical science (as opposed to experimental science), due to the fundamental asymmetry of causation. A single cause will often have a great many disparate effects, which if taken together would specify the cause with virtual certainty; however, since all the effects cannot actually be known, and moreover since some effects are not historically connected to a specific cause, the evidence must be carefully weighed to decide between competing hypotheses (a methodology sometimes known as "multiple working hypotheses").

This chapter describes our first steps towards the analysis of linguistic and rhetorical features of scientific writing in experimental and historical science, using several types of linguistically-motivated document features together with machine learning methods. Our goal is to show how linguistic features that are indicative of different classes of scientific articles may be usefully correlated with the rhetorical and methodological needs of historical and experimental sciences.

To make this more concrete, note that the posited methodological differences described above generate the following linguistic predictions:

- First, we expect historical science's posited focus on *observation* and *explanation* to result in language containing more delicate shadings of likelihood and frequency of occurrence than that of experimental science, where we expect more direct assessments of necessity and possibility.

- Second, the focus of historical science on *explanation* in order to find *ultimate causes* implies that its argumentation will involve combinations of multiple lines of evidence of differing validity and generality, due to the complexity of the phenomena and the asymmetry of causation (Cleland 2002). This further implies that historical science will use more complex and explicit qualifications of likelihood. On the other hand, since experimental science is posited to rely more on *manipulation* of *variables in nature* and is focused on consistency with *prediction*, we would expect its language to more often qualify assertions as to their predictive value or consistency with predictions.

- Third, the fact that historical scientists study *complex* and *unique* entities by *observation* and *comparison* implies that they might tend to use 'panoramic' language, in which many different independent pieces of information are linked together by geographical or comparative links. Consider a geologist describing a particular site—connections between statements are likely to be geographical ("...and near that is...") or temporal ("when that process completed, then..."). Conversely, since experimental science focuses on finding deep causal descriptions of essentially uniform entities, we expect a more 'unifocal' prose, where links between assertion are based on tight causal, conditional, or temporal connections (e.g., "X causes Y whenever Z").

3. Systemic Indicators as Textual Features

The features used in this study are the relative frequencies of sets of keywords and phrases which indicate that a particular part of the text realizes a certain system in the language. For example, an occurrence of the word "certainly" usually indicates that the author is making a high-probability modal assessment of an assertion. Such a keyword-based approach has obvious practical advantages in the current absence of a reliable general systemic parser. The primary drawback, of course, is the possibility of ambiguity, in that the proper interpretation of such a keyword depends crucially on its context. By using as complete a set of such *systemic indicators* as possible for each system we represent, and then by using only measures of *comparative* frequency between such aggregated features, we hope to reduce the effect of ambiguity. In addition, since we use very large sets of indicators for each system, it is unlikely that such ambiguity would introduce a systematic bias, and so such noise is more likely to just reduce the significance of our results instead of biasing them.

We describe in this section the features we developed (Figure 1) which are based on the options within three main systems, following Matthiessen's (1995) grammar of English, a standard SFL reference. Keyword lists were constructed starting with the lists of typical words and phrases given by Matthiessen, and expanding them to related words and phrases taken from Roget's

Interactive Thesaurus[1] (manually filtered for relevance to the given feature). The keyword lists were constructed entirely independently of the target corpus.

CONJUNCTION: Joining two clauses
  Elaboration: Deepening the content of the context
    Appositive: Restatement or exemplification
      in other words, for example, to wit
    Clarifying: Correcting, summarizing, or refocusing
      to be more precise, in brief, incidentally
    Extension: Adding new related
    Verifying: Adjusting content by new information
      instead, except for, alternatively
  Enhancement: Qualifying the context
    Matter: What are we talking about
      here, as to that, in other respects
    Spatiotemporal: Relating context to space/time
      Simple: Direct spatiotemporal sequencing
        then, now, previously, lastly
      Complex: More complex relations
        soon, that day, meanwhile, immediately
    Manner: How did something occur
      in the same way, similarly, likewise
    Causal/Conditional:
      Causal: Relations of cause and effect
        so, therefore, for this reason
      Conditional: Logical conditional relations
        then, in that case, otherwise

(a) Options and indicators for CONJUNCTION

COMMENT: Status of the message in discourse
  Admissive: Message is assessed as an admission
    frankly, to tell the truth, honestly
  Assertive: Emphasizing the reliability of the message
    really, actually, positively, we confirm that
  Presumptive: Dependence on other assumptions
    evidently, presumably, reportedly, we suspect that
  Desiderative: Desirability of some content
    fortunately, regrettably, it was nice that, hopefully
  Tentative: Assessing the message as tentative
    tentatively, initially, depending on, provisionally
  Validative: Assessing scope of validity
    broadly speaking, in general, strictly speaking
  Evaluative: Judgement of actors behind the content
    wisely, sensibly, foolishly, justifiably, by mistake
  Predictive: Coherence with predictions
    amazingly, fortuitously, as expected

(b) Options and indicators for COMMENT

TYPE: What kind of modality?
  Modalization: How 'typical' is it?
    Probability: How likely is it?
      probably, maybe, perhaps, might, are likely to
    Usuality: How frequent/common is it?
      often, sometimes, rarely, is frequent
  Modulation: Will someone do it?
    Readiness: How ready are they (am I)?
      will, able to, decided to
    Obligation: Must I (they)?
      should, is needed, will permit, must, required to

ORIENTATION: State of mind or attribute of the message?
  Objective: Modality as an attribute of the message
    probably, perhaps, usually, frequent, it is necessary
  Subjective: Modality expressed as a state of mind
    I think, we imagine, we know, it ought, it will allow

VALUE: What degree of the relevant modality scale?
  Median: In the middle of the normal range
    will, likely, we expect, usually, should
  High: More than normal
    must, should, certainly, always, never, we require
  Low: Less than normal
    might, perhaps, seldom, rarely, is unusual, will allow

MANIFESTATION: In the clause, or as a projection?
  Implicit: Modality in the clause as an adjunct or auxiliary
    possibly, maybe, shall, should, definitely, ought to
  Explicit: Modality in a verb with a projected clause
    I think, we require, it is necessary that, it is likely that

(c) Systems, options, and indicators for MODALITY

Figure 1. Systems and indicators used in the study.

---

[1] http://www.thesaurus.com

We use systems and subsystems within: CONJUNCTION, linking clauses together (either within or across sentences); MODALITY, giving judgments regarding probability, usuality, inclination, and the like; and COMMENT, expressing modal assessments of attitude or applicability. MODALITY and COMMENT relate directly to how propositions are assessed in evidential reasoning (e.g., for likelihood, typicality, consistency with predictions, etc.), while CONJUNCTION is a primary system by which texts are constructed out of smaller pieces[2].

3.1 Conjunction

On the discourse level, the system of Conjunction serves to link a clause with its textual context, by denoting how the given clause *expands* on some aspect of its preceding context. Similar systems also operate at the lower levels of noun and verbal groups, 'overloading' the same lexical resources which, however, generally denote similar types of logico-semantic relationships, e.g., "*and*" usually denotes "additive extension".

The three options within CONJUNCTION are *Elaboration, Extension,* and *Enhancement.* Each of these options (subsystems) has its own options which we also use as features. (Note that the system network can be deepened further (Matthiessen 1995, p. 521), but our keyword-based method allows only a relatively coarse analysis.) The hierarchy of CONJUNCTION SYSTEMS WITH THEIR OPTIONS IS given in Figure 1(a), along with examples of the indicator keyphrases we used. Note that the features by which we represent an article are the frequencies of each option's indicator features, each measured relative to its siblings. So, for example, one feature is Elaboration/*Appositive,* whose value is the total number of occurrences of Appositive indicators divided by the total number of occurrences of Elaboration indicators (Appositive + Clarifying). The relative frequencies of Elaboration, Extension, and Enhancement within CONJUNCTION are also used as features.

3.2 Comment

The system of COMMENT is one of modal assessment, comprising a variety of types of "comment" on a message, assessing the writer's attitude towards it, or its validity or evidentiality. Comments are generally realized as adjuncts in a clause (and may appear initially, medially, or finally). Matthiessen (1995), following Halliday (1994), lists eight types of COMMENT, shown in Figure 1(b), along with representative indicators for each subsystem.

3.3 Modality

The features for interpersonal modal assessment that we consider here are based on Halliday's (1994) analysis of the MODALITY system, as formulated by Matthiessen (1995). In this scheme, modal assessment is realized by a simultaneous choice of options within the four systems[3] shown in Figure 1(c). The cross-product of all of these systems and subsystems creates a large number of modality assessment types, each of which is realized through a particular set of indicators. We consider as *simple* features, each option in each system above (for example, Modalization/*Probability* opposed to Modalization/*Usuality*) as well as *complex* features made up

---

[2] Other textual/cohesive systems, such as PROJECTION, TAXIS, THEME, and INFORMATION cannot be easily addressed, if at all, using a keyword-based approach.

[3] Note that we did not consider here the system of POLARITY , since it too cannot be properly addressed without more sophisticated parsing.

of pairwise combinations[4] of simple features. The indicator set of keyphrases for each such combined feature is the intersection of the indicator sets for the two component features. For example, the complex feature Modalization/*Probability*:Value/*Median* will have as indicators all keyphrases that are indicators for both Modalization/*Probability* and Value/*Median*. Frequencies are normalized by the total set of options in both primary systems.

Journal	*# Art.*	*Avg. Words*	*Total Size*
Palaios	116	4584	3.4 Mb
Quaternary Res.	106	3136	2.0 Mb
J. Phys. Chem. A	169	2734	3.2 Mb
J. Phys. Chem. B	69	3301	1.6 Mb

Table 1. Peer reviewed journals included in the corpus.

4. Experimental Study

4.1 The Corpus

The study reported here was performed using a corpus of articles (Table 1) drawn from four peer-reviewed journals in two fields: *Palaios* and *Quaternary Research* in paleontology, and *Journal of Physical Chemistry A* and *Journal of Physical Chemistry B* in physical chemistry. (These particular journals were chosen initially in part for ease of access.) *Palaios* is a general paleontological journal, covering all areas of the field, whereas *Quaternary Research* focuses on work dealing with the quaternary period (approximately 1.6 million years ago to the present). The two physical chemistry journals are published in tandem but have separate editorial boards and cover different subfields of physical chemistry, specifically: studies on molecules (*J. Phys Chem A*) and studies of materials, surfaces, and interfaces (*J. Phys Chem B*). The numbers of articles used from each journal and their average (preprocessed) lengths in words are given in Table 1.

4.2 Methodology

We took the preprocessed articles in our corpus and converted each of them into a vector of feature values (relative frequencies of system options), as described above. Throughout, classification models were constructed using the SMO learning algorithm (Platt 1998) as implemented in the Weka system (Witten and Frank 1999), using a linear kernel, no feature normalization, and the default parameters. (Using other kernels did not appear to improve classification accuracy, so we used the option that enabled us to determine easily the relevant features for the classification.) SMO is a support vector machine (SVM) algorithm; SVMs have been applied successfully to many text categorization problems (Joachims 1998). By using a

---

[4] For simplicity, we did not consider 3- or 4-way combinations here. We may address this in future work.

linear kernel, we can easily evaluate which features contribute most to classification, by examining their weights.

4.3 Experimental Results

We first tested the hypothesis that paleontology articles are distinct from physical chemistry articles (along the field-independent linguistic dimensions we defined). Table 2 presents average classification accuracy using 20-fold cross-validation. In all four cross-disciplinary cases, classification accuracy is 83% and above, while in the two intra-disciplinary cases, accuracy is noticeably lower; Palaios and *Quat. Res.* are minimally distinguished at 74%, while *J. Phys. Chem. A* and *J. Phys. Chem. B* are entirely undistinguishable (note that 68% of the articles are from *J. Phys. Chem. A*, the majority class). This supports our main hypothesis, while pointing towards a more nuanced possible analysis of the difference between the two paleontology journals. Such a difference would be expected, since, unlike *Palaios*, which covers most subdisciplines of paleontology, *Quaternary Research* deals with analysis of just the last 1.6 million years of earth history, including the use of a wider variety of chemical and physics based research tools, and hence we may expect a rhetoric closer to that of physical chemistry. A more detailed analysis is clearly needed.

We now consider if a consistent linguistic picture of the difference between the two classes of scientific articles (paleontology and physical chemistry) emerges from the patterns of feature weights in he learned models. To do this, we ran SMO on all the training data for each of the four pairs of a paleontology with a physical chemistry journal, and ranked the features according to their weight for one or the other journal in the weight vector. Table 3 shows graphically which features were most indicative for each journal in its two trials. We restrict consideration to cases where a feature was strong (i.e., among the 30 weights with largest magnitude) for a single class across all journal pairs (note that there were a total of 101 features). Even with this strong restriction, several striking patterns emerge. Space limits us to discussing the most important.

	Historical		Experimental	
	Palaios	*Quat Res*	*Ph Ch A*	*Ph Ch B*
Palaios	--	*74%*	*91%*	*91%*
Quat Res	*74%*	--	*83%*	*86%*
Ph Ch A	*91%*	*83%*	--	*68%*
Ph Ch B	*91%*	*86%*	*68%*	--

Table 2. Accuracy for linear SMO learning (with feature normalization) for pairs of journals, using 20-fold cross-validation.

First, in the textual system of CONJUNCTION, we see a clear opposition between Extension, indicating paleontology, and Enhancement, indicating physical chemistry. This implies (as predicted) that paleontological text has a higher density of discrete informational items, linked together by extensive conjunctions, whereas in physical chemistry, while there may be fewer information items, each is more likely to have its meaning deepened or qualified by related clauses. This corroborates the understanding that paleontological articles are more likely to be primarily descriptive in nature, as they focus on wide scale systems, thus requiring a higher information density, whereas physical chemists focus their attention deeply on a single phenomenon at a time. At the same time, this linguistic opposition may also reflect differing principles of rhetorical organization: perhaps physical chemists prefer a single coherent 'story line' focused on enhancements of a small number of focal propositions, whereas paleontologists may prefer a multifocal 'landscape' of connected propositions. Future work may include also interviews and surveys of the two types of scientists, regarding these points.

Next, in the system of COMMENT, the one clear opposition that emerges is between preference for Validative comments by paleontologists and for Predictive comments by physical chemists. This linguistic opposition can be directly related to methodological differences between the historical and experimental sciences. The (historical) paleontologist has a rhetorical need to explicitly delineate the scope of validity of different assertions, as part of synthetic thinking process (Baker 1996) about complex and ambiguous webs of past causation (Cleland 2002). This is not a primary concern, however, of the (experimental) physical chemist; his/her main focus is prediction: the predictive strength of a theory and the consistency of evidence with theoretical predictions.

Finally, we consider the (complicated) system of MODALITY. At the coarse level represented by the simple features (in Table 3), we see a primary opposition in Type. The preference of the (experimental) physical chemist for Modulation (assessing what 'ought' or 'is able' to happen) is consistent with a focus on prediction and manipulation of nature. The (historical) paleontologist's preference for Modalization (assessing 'likelihood' or 'usuality') is consistent with the outlook of a "neutral observer" who cannot directly manipulate or replicate outcomes. This is supported also by patterns within the complex features crossing modality **Type** and **Manifestation** (see Table 4). In Manifestation, we might say that Implicit variants are more likely for options that are well-integrated into the expected rhetorical structure, while Explicit realizations are more likely to draw attention to less characteristic types of modal assessment. We find that Modalization is preferably Implicit for paleontology but Explicit for physical chemistry; just the reverse holds true for Modulation. In this way, Modalization is integrated smoothly into the overall environment of paleontological rhetoric, and similarly Modulation is a part of the rhetorical environment of physical chemistry.

Systemic Features				Historical				Experimental			
				Palaios		QR		PCA		PCB	
				PC A	PC B	PC A	PC B	Pal	QR	Pal	QR
Conjunction	Elaboration										
		Appositive									
		Clarifying									
	Extension										
		Additive									
		Adversative									
		Verifying									
	Enhancement										
		Manner									
		Matter									
		S/T									
			Simple								
			Complex								
		CC									
			Cause								
			Cond.								
Comment	Admissive										
	Assertive										
	Presumptive										
	Desiderative										
	Tentative										
	Validative										
	Evaluative										
	Predictive										
Modality	Type	Modalization									
			Probability								
			Usuality								
		Modulation									
			Obligation								
			Readiness								
	Value	Median									
		High									
		Low									
	Orientation	Objective									
		Subjective									
	Manifest	Implicit									
		Explicit									

Table 3. Significant simple features for each class in classification tests pairing each historical science journal in the study with each experimental journal. Features were sorted according to their weights learned in each two journal classification test (e.g., Palaios vs. Phys. Chem. A in the first column, Palaios vs. Phys. Chem. B in the second, and so forth). Black squares represent features whose weights are in the top 15 for the main class of the column, and grey squares those with weights in the second 15.

		Value Med	High	Low	Orientation Obj	Subj	Manifestation Impl	Expl
Type	Modal	Q/B P/B Q/A P/A	B/Q P/B A/Q P/A	Q/B P/B Q/A P/A	Q/B P/B Q/A P/A	Q/B B/P Q/A A/P	Q/B P/B Q/A P/A	B/Q B/P A/Q A/P
	Prob	Q/B P/B A/Q A/P	Q/B B/P A/Q P/A	B/Q B/P A/Q A/P	Q/B P/B A/Q A/P	B/Q B/P A/Q A/P	Q/B P/B Q/A P/A	B/Q B/P A/Q A/P
	Usual	Q/B P/B Q/A P/A	Q/B P/B A/Q P/A	B/Q B/P Q/A P/A	Q/B P/B Q/A P/A	B/Q B/P A/Q A/P	B/Q B/P A/Q A/P	Q/B P/B Q/A P/A
	Modul	B/Q B/P A/Q A/P	Q/B P/B Q/A P/A	B/P A/Q A/P	B/Q B/P A/Q A/P	B/Q B/P A/Q A/P	B/Q B/P A/Q A/P	Q/B P/B Q/A P/A
	Oblig	B/Q B/P A/Q A/P	Q/B P/B Q/A P/A	Q/B P/B Q/A P/A	B/Q B/P A/Q A/P	Q/B P/B Q/A P/A	Q/B P/B Q/A P/A	Q/B P/B Q/A P/A
	Readi	Q/B P/B A/Q A/P	Q/B P/B Q/A P/A	B/Q B/P A/Q A/P	B/Q B/P A/Q A/P	B/Q B/P A/Q A/P	B/Q B/P A/Q A/P	—
Value	Median				Q/B P/B Q/A P/A	B/Q B/P A/Q A/P	Q/B B/P Q/A P/A	B/Q P/B A/Q P/A
	High				B/Q B/P A/Q P/A	Q/B P/B A/Q A/P	B/Q P/B A/Q A/P	B/Q B/P Q/A A/P
	Low				B/Q P/B A/Q P/A	Q/B B/P Q/A A/P	B/Q B/P Q/A P/A	Q/B P/B A/Q A/P
Orient	Objective	Q/B P/B Q/A P/A	B/Q B/P A/Q P/A	B/Q P/B A/Q P/A			Q/B B/P Q/A P/A	B/Q P/B A/Q P/A
	Subjective	B/Q B/P A/Q A/P	Q/B P/B A/Q A/P	Q/B B/P Q/A A/P			B/Q B/P A/Q A/P	Q/B B/P A/Q A/P
Manif	Implicit	Q/B B/P Q/A P/A	B/Q P/B A/Q A/P	B/Q B/P Q/A P/A	Q/B B/P Q/A P/A	B/Q B/P A/Q A/P		
	Explicit	B/Q P/B A/Q P/A	B/Q B/P Q/AA/P	Q/B P/B A/Q A/P	B/Q P/B A/Q P/A	Q/B B/P A/Q A/P		

Table 4. Combined features from Modality. Each cell in the table represents a feature corresponding to a modal indicator realizing options from two Modality systems simultaneously. For example, the top-left cell gives results for the aggregate of indicators realizing Type/Modalization and also Value/Median. In each cell are listed the models in which the corresponding feature is associated: A=J. Phys. Chem A, B=J. Phys. Chem. B, P=Palaios, Q=Quaternary Res. The lower portion of each notation shows the "opposing" class for a given model, i.e., P/A represents the model that classifies an article as being from Palaios as opposed to J. Phys. Chem. A, and so forth. The heavily outlined cells are those whose preferring classes are consistent, i.e, either all historical (P, Q) or all experimental (A, B).

5. Example Texts

We now consider two short illustrative passages from articles in our corpus. These have been marked up (by hand) for the three main oppositions we identified above—we have marked realizations of each of the six features: EXTENSION, *enhancement*, validative comment, *predictive comment*, modalization, and *modulation*.

Paleontology

Biologists agree that global warming is **likely** to produce changes in the diversity and distribution of species, BUT the magnitude, timing and nature of such responses remains unclear. Animals **may** be affected directly by altered temperature and/or moisture regimes, for example, OR indirectly through associated vegetation changes. For herbivores in particular, direct effects are **likely** to be compounded by vegetation changes, especially in the case of animals with specialized habitat affinities or relatively small home ranges. Climatic change **may** ALSO occur too rapidly for animals to adapt, OR they **may** be unable to adapt because of physiological or phylogenetic constraints. Under such circumstances, species **may** become locally extinct. Estimating the potential range of adaptive response to climatic and vegetative shifts is **clearly** crucial to an understanding of the effects of global warming on terrestrial ecosystems, YET *it requires* a more thorough understanding of life history and ecosystem function than is **often** available.
(Smith and Betancourt 2003)

Physical Chemistry

In this experiment, the oxidation scan was run *first and then followed* by the reduction scan in the reverse direction. Above E=0.4V, the Cu(II) spin density reaches an average plateau value *indicating that* no spin coupling occurs between the neighboring copper centers. HOWEVER, in addition to this plateau, obtained in the oxidation scan, three local maxima in spin density are clearly observed at 0.48, 0.78, and 1.1 V, which very well correlate with the redox waves observed in the CV of poly[1,3,cu+]. Interestingly, in the reduction scan, the polymer film gives rise to only two spin density maxima at potential values close to those of the redox waves *corresponding to* the reduction of copper AND to the first redox wave of the polymer reduction. *Surprisingly*, the matrix spin density is very low AND reaches only ca. 5% of the copper(II) spin density, *whereas* both oxidizable components of poly[1,3,Cu+] show comparable electroactivity. In the simplest interpretation, such behavior **can be** regarded as a clear manifestation of the recombination of initially formed radical cations to spinless dications. *This is not unexpected*, *since* bipolarons are the dominant charge-storage configurations in essentially all thienylene-based conducting polymers. The onset of the spin appearance **can be** correlated with the onset of the first oxidation wave of the polymer oxidation. HOWEVER, contrary to the case of copper spin response, the spin response of the polymer is smooth and monotonic AND does not follow the current peaks recorded in the CV experiment. This underlines the efficiency of the polaron recombination process.
(Divisia-Blohorn et al. 2003)

Briefly, in the first passage above, from *Quaternary Research*, we see in a short space how frequent use of extension allows the construction of a complex of interrelated propositions, with no one focal point (though all are related to the basic theme of "global warming" and "climatic change"). We also see a clear preference for modalization, involving multiple levels of probabilistic assessment (e.g., "may", "likely", "clearly"), placing most propositions explicitly on a scale of variable likelihood. The use of validative comments ("under such circumstances") also serves to circumscribe the validity of the assertions in the passage.

In the passage from *J. Phys. Chem. B*, on the other hand, we see the use of enhancement (primarily temporal and causal) in creating a narrative story-line which serves to organize presentation both of the experimental procedure but also of the interpretation of results. Extension is used mostly to construct small local structures which fit as a whole into the larger narrative line. Predictive comments are used ("surprisingly", "not unexpected") to emphasize certain results and also to place them into the larger context. Note also that the ambiguous modal assessment "can be" is used here to realize modulation (i.e., "it can be regarded..." = "we are able to regard it as...").

6. Conclusions

This chapter has demonstrated how the use of machine learning techniques combined with a set of linguistically-motivated features can be used to provide empirical evidence for rhetorical differences between writing in different scientific fields. Further, by analyzing the models' output by the learning procedure, we can see what features realize the differences in register that are correlated with different fields. This method thus provides indirect empirical evidence for methodological variation between the sciences, insofar as rhetorical preferences can be identified which can be linked with particular modes of methodological reasoning. This study thus lends empirical support to those philosophers of science who argue against a monolithic "scientific method".

The current study is only the beginning, of course. To make more general and stable conclusions, a much larger corpus of articles, from a wider variety of journals, will be needed. We are currently working on collecting and processing such a corpus. More fundamentally, there are serious limitations to using keyword/phrase counts as indicators for systemic options. Overcoming this limitation will require the construction of an accurate shallow systemic parser, which can enable a more general and more precise way to analyze the systemic functional options realized in a text. The rhetorical parsing methods developed by Marcu (2000) are an important step in this direction. Also, automatic methods for discovering rhetorically important features, similar to the subjectivity collocations of Wiebe et al. (2001) may be helpful.

It should also be noted that the current study treats each article as an indivisible whole. However, as noted by Lewin et al. (2001) in their analysis of social science texts, the rhetorical organization of an article varies in different sections of the text—future work will include studying how systemic preferences vary also across different sections of individual texts, by incorporating techniques such as those developed by Teufel and Moens (1998).

7. Acknowledgements

Thanks to Jonathan Fine for feedback on an early version of the manuscript, as well as to the editors and anonymous reviewers for their very helpful comments.

8. References

Argamon, S., Koppel, M., Fine, J., and Shimoni, A. R. (2003a) Gender, Genre, and Writing Style in Formal Written Texts. *Text*, **23**(3).

Argamon, S., Šarić, M., and Stein, S. S. (2003b) Style mining of electronic messages for multiple authorship discrimination: First Results. In *Proceedings of ACM Conference on Knowledge Discovery and Data Mining 2003*.

Baayen, H., van Halteren, H., and Tweedie, F. (1996) Outside the cave of shadows: Using syntactic annotation to enhance authorship attribution, *Literary and Linguistic Computing*, **11**.

Baker, V.R. (1996) The pragmatic routes of American Quaternary geology and geomorphology. *Geomorphology* **16**, pp. 197-215.

Cleland, C.E. (2002) Methodological and epistemic differences between historical science and experimental science. *Philosophy of Science*.

Diamond, J. (1999) *Guns, Germs, & Steel*, New York: W. W. Norton and Company.

Divisia-Blohorn, B., Genoud, F., Borel, C., Bidan, G., Kern, J-M., and Sauvage, J-P. (2003) Conjugated Polymetallorotaxanes: In-Situ ESR and Conductivity Investigations of Metal-Backbone Interactions, *J. Phys. Chem. B*, **107**, pp. 5126-5132.

Dodick, J. T. and Orion, N. (2003) Geology as an Historical Science: Its Perception within Science and the Education System. *Science and Education*, **12**(2).

Dunbar, K. (1995) How scientists really reason: Scientific reasoning in real-world laboratories. In Sternberg, R.J. and Davidson, J. (Eds.). *Mechanisms of Insight*. Cambridge MA: MIT Press, pp. 365-395.

Eggins, S. and Martin, J. R. (1997) Genres and registers of discourse. In van Dijk, T. A. (Ed.) *Discourse as structure and process. A multidisciplinary introduction*. Discourse studies 1. London: Sage, pp. 230–256.

Goodwin, C. (1994) Professional Vision. *American Anthropologist*, **96**(3), pp. 606-633.

Gould, S. J. (1986) Evolution and the Triumph of Homology, or, Why History Matters, *American Scientist*, Jan.-Feb. 1986:60-69.

Gregory, M. (1967) Aspects of varieties differentiation, *Journal of Linguistics* **3**:177-198.

Halliday, M.A.K. (1991) Corpus linguistics and probabilistic grammar. In Karin Aijmer & Bengt Altenberg (Ed.) *English Corpus Linguistics: Studies in honour of Jan Svartvik*. (London: Longman), pp. 30-44.

Halliday, M.A.K. (1994). *An Introduction to Functional Grammar*. Edward Arnold, London.

Hasan, R. (1988) Language in the process of socialisation: Home and school. In Oldenburg, J., v Leeuwen, Th., and Gerot, L. (ed.), *Language and socialisation: Home and school;* Proceedings from the Working Conference on Language in Education, 17-21 November, 1986. North Ryde, N.S.W., Macquarie University.

Holmes, D. I. and Forsyth, R. S. (1995). The federalist revisited: New directions in authorship attribution. *Literary and Linguistic Computing*, 10(2):111-126

Joachims, T. (1998) Text categorization with Support Vector Machines: Learning with many relevant features. In Machine Learning: ECML-98, Tenth European Conference on Machine Learning, pp. 137-142.

Koppel, M., Argamon, S., and Shimoni, A. R. (2003) Automatically categorizing written texts by author gender. *Literary and Linguistic Computing* 17(4).

Latour, B. and Woolgar, S. (1986) *Laboratory Life: The Construction of Scientific Facts*, Princeton: Princeton University Press.

Lewin, B.A., Fine, J. and Young, L. (2001) Expository Discourse: A Genre-Based Approach to Social Science Research Texts, Continuum Press.

Losee, R. M. (1996) Text Windows and Phrases Differing by Discipline, Location in Document, and Syntactic Structure. *Information Processing & Management*, 32(6):747-767.

Marcu, D. (2000) The Rhetorical Parsing of Unrestricted Texts: A Surface-Based Approach. *Computational Linguistics*, 26(3):395-448.

Martin, J. R. (1992) *English Text: System and Structure*. Amsterdam: Benjamins.

Matthews, R. A. J. and Merriam, T. V. N. (1997) Distinguishing literary styles using neural networks. In Fiesler, E. and Beale, R. (Eds) *Handbook of Neural Computation*, chapter 8. Oxford University Press.

Matthiessen, C. (1995) *Lexicogrammatical Cartography: English Systems.* International Language Sciences Publishers: Tokyo, Taipei & Dallas.

Mayr, E. (1976). *Evolution and the Diversity of Life.* Cambridge: Harvard University Press.

Mosteller, F. and Wallace, D. L. (1964) *Inference and Disputed Authorship: The Federalist Papers,* Reading, Mass.: Addison Wesley.

Ochs, E., Jacoby, S., and Gonzales, P. (1994) Interpretive journeys: How physicists talk and travel through graphic space, *Configurations* 1:151-171.

Platt, J. (1998) *Sequential Minimal Optimization: A Fast Algorithm for Training Support Vector Machines,* Microsoft Research Technical Report MSR-TR-98-14.

Plum, G. A. and Cowling, A. (1987) Social constraints on grammatical variables: Tense choice in English. In Steele, R. and Threadgold, T. (Eds.), *Language topics. Essays in honour of Michael Halliday.* Amsterdam: Benjamins.

Sebastiani, F. (2002) Machine learning in automated text categorization, *ACM Computing Surveys*, 34(1):1-47.

Smith, F. A. and Betancourt, J. L. (2003) The effect of Holocene temperature fluctuations on the evolution and ecology of Neotoma (woodrats) in Idaho and northwestern Utah, *Quaternary Research* **59**:160 -171.

Stamatatos, E., Fakotakis, N., and Kokkinakis, G. (2001) Computer-based authorship attribution without lexical measures, *Computers and the Humanities* **35**.

Teufel, S. and Moens, M. (1998) Sentence extraction and rhetorical classification for flexible abstracts. In *Proc. AAAI Spring Symposium on Intelligent Text Summarization*.

Wiebe, J., Wilson, T., and Bell, M. (2001) Identifying Collocations for Recognizing Opinions. In *Proc. ACL/EACL '01 Workshop on Collocation, Toulouse, France, July 200*.

Whewell, W. (1837) *History of the Inductive Sciences*, John W. Parker, London.

Witten, I.H. and Frank E. (1999)   *Weka 3: Machine Learning Software in Java;* http://www.cs.waikato.ac.nz/~ml/weka.

Yule, G.U. (1938) On sentence length as a statistical characteristic of style in prose with application to two cases of disputed authorship, *Biometrika*, **30**:363-390.

Chapter 18

Argumentative Zoning Applied to Critiquing Novices' Scientific Abstracts

Valéria D. Feltrim[1], Simone Teufel[2], Maria das Graças V. Nunes[1] and Sandra M. Aluísio[1]
[1]University of São Paulo
NILC,ICMC, Universidade de São Paulo,
Av. do Trabalhador São-Carlense, 400
13560-970, São Carlos, SP, Brasil.
Email: {vfeltrim, gracan, sandra}@icmc.usp.br

[2]University of Cambridge
Computer Laboratory, University of Cambridge,
JJ Thomson Avenue, Cambridge CB3 0FD, U.K.
Email: Simone.Teufel@cam.ac.uk

Abstract

We present a system that applies Argumentative Zoning (AZ) (Teufel and Moens, 2002), a method of determining argumentative structure in texts, to the task of advising novice graduate writers on their writing. For this task, it is important to automatically determine the rhetorical/argumentative status of a given sentence in the text. On the basis of this information, users can be advised that a different sentence order might be more advantageous or that certain argumentative moves are missing. In implementing such a system, we had to port AZ from English to Portuguese, as our system is designed to help the writing of Brazilian PhD theses in Computer Science. In this chapter, we report on the overall system, named SciPo, the porting exercise, including a human annotation experiment to verify the reproducibility of our annotation scheme, and the intrinsic and extrinsic evaluation of the AZ module of the system.

Keywords: academic writing, Argumentative Zoning, machine learning.

1. Introduction

It is widely acknowledged that academic writing is a complex task, since it involves the complexities of the writing process as well as those specific to the academic genre (Sharples and Pemberton, 1992). It can be even harder for novice writers, who are usually not well acquainted, if at all, with the requirements of the academic genre. Even when the basic guidelines on scientific writing are explicit and known, it can be very difficult to apply them to a real text. To improve the quality of academic texts produced by novice and/or non-native writers, a number of writing tools have been described in the literature (Sharples et al, 1994; Broady and Shurville, 2000; Narita, 2000; Aluísio et al., 2001).

The project SciPo (short for Scientific Portuguese) aims at analysing the rhetoric structure of Portuguese academic texts — in terms of schematic structure, rhetorical strategies and lexical patterns — to derive models for supporting the creation and evaluation of computational writing tools and its outcomes. This project is currently being developed at *Núcleo Interinstitucional de Lingüística Computacional* (NILC)[1], University of São Paulo. To make it feasible, the analysis has focused on specific sections of theses in Computer Science, namely the abstract and the introduction, which are the most studied in the literature (Swales, 1990; Weissberg and Buker, 1990; Liddy, 1991; Santos, 1996). In conjunction with conclusions, these particular sections have also been pointed out as the most difficult ones to be written in a questionnaire applied to graduated students of Computer Science from University of São Paulo. The reasons for working on this kind of text and domain were threefold: firstly, in the Brazilian University system, theses have to be written in Portuguese, unlike research articles, which are preferably written in English; secondly, there exists a high degree of standardization in Computer Science texts, as in other scientific research areas; and thirdly, SciPo's developers are familiar with the Computer Science domain, as it is being developed in a Computer Science department.

As the approach being followed is corpus-based, an analysis of a specific corpus was carried out by human annotators, based mainly on Swales's (1990) and Weissberg and Buker's (1990) models. The used annotation scheme has the following rhetorical categories: Background, Gap, Purpose, Methodology, Results, Conclusion and Outline. Examples of sentences for each category are presented in Figure 1. For convenience, the examples are presented in English although our corpus is in Portuguese and were collected from Anthony and Lashkia (2003) (except the example sentence for Outline). The results of this analysis have been used as basis for a computational model using (good and bad) examples and rules. Moreover, this analysis helped us to understand the problems novice writers face when writing in a new genre. We have identified some writing problems that are specific to the academic genre, such as misuse of lexical patterns and verbal tenses, inefficient organization and inappropriate emphasis on some specific components. On the basis of these results, we believe that especially novice writers may benefit from a writing support tool that provides critiques about text structure, a repository of good and bad examples of structure, writing strategies and lexical patterns. In the next section we introduce the SciPo system, focusing on its architecture and linguistics resources.

2. The SciPo System

Inspired by the Amadeus system (Aluísio et al., 2001), SciPo is a system whose ultimate goal is to support novice writers in producing academic writing in Portuguese, specially abstracts and

---

[1] http://www.nilc.icmc.usp.br/nilc/index.html

introductions of Computer Science theses. Its current main functionalities can be summarized as: (a) browsing and searching on a base of authentic thesis abstracts manually annotated according to our structure model (Feltrim et al., 2003) for all occurrences of a specific rhetorical strategy and/or structural component; (b) browsing and searching on a base of authentic thesis introductions manually annotated according to an adaptation of Aluísio and Oliveira Jr.'s (1996) model, in the same way of the abstracts base; (c) support to build a structure for the writer to use as a starting point for his/her text; (d) application of critiquing rules to the created structure; and (e) recovery of authentic cases that are similar to the writer's structure. Also, the existing lexical patterns from the case base are highlighted allowing the writer to easily add such patterns to a previously built structure. Examples of lexical patterns are underlined in Figure 1.

---

1 **Background**
"The research article (RA) or paper is one of the most important genres that both scientists and engineers will write."
2 **Gap**
"When faced with the tasks of reading and writing a complex technical paper, many nonnative scientists and engineers (...) lack an adequate knowledge of commonly used structural patterns at the discourse level."
3 **Purpose**
"In this paper, we propose a novel computer software tool that can assist these people in the understanding and construction of technical papers (...)."
4 **Methodology**
"The software uses a supervised learning approach, in which the system first "learns" the characteristic features of text structure in a particular discipline using a small number of training examples."
5 **Results**
"We can see that the system performs consistently across the different data sets, with an average accuracy of 68%."
6 **Conclusion**
"The system is tested using research article abstracts and is shown to be fast, accurate, and useful aid in the reading and writing process."
7 **Outline**
"In the next section we present the contextualization of this work and details about the used methodology."

Figure 1. Example sentences for each category with lexical patterns underlined.

SciPo contains four knowledge bases, namely the Abstracts Case Base, Introductions Case Base, Rules and Similarity Measures, and Critiquing Rules. As explained before, the Case Bases were built through manual annotation, based on predefined rhetorical schemes. The Abstract Case Base has 52 instances of schematic structures of authentic abstracts, describing the rhetorical components, strategies and lexical patterns of each case. The Introduction Case Base has 48 instances and represents the same kind of information described for abstracts. The Rules and Measures of Similarity are based on similarity rules among lists (pattern matching) and on nearest neighbours matching measure (Kriegsman and Barletta, 1993). These rules are used in the case recovery process, when a search is performed according to the writer's request of a specific schematic structure. The Critiquing Rules are based on prescriptive guidelines for good writing in the literature and on structural problems observed in the annotated corpus, as an attempt to anticipate and correct problematic structural patterns the writer might construct. The rules cover two distinct types of problems: content deviations (absence of components) and order deviations (occurrence order of components and strategies inside the overall structure). Thus, we have four classes of rules: content critiques, order critiques, content suggestions and order suggestions. We use critiques for serious problems such as, detecting absence of the purpose component, or for generating suggestions for structures that do not have serious problems but can be enriched by adding new components and/or reorganizing existing ones.

An example of an abstract with poor structure is [P M B G P], where the main purpose (first P) is followed by the Methodology (M) used to accomplish that purpose. Next, the most natural move would be to present results; however, the writer used a background component, followed by a gap (B G), providing more detail of the previously stated purpose and the introduction of yet other purposes. The presence of background and gap in the middle of the abstract, separating the main purpose from its subsequent detail, confuses the reader, who may lose track of the main purpose of the related research. Also, the sequence [M B] disrupts the cohesion of the text and may cause the reader to feel that "something is missing".

Using the resources mentioned above, the writer can build his/her own structure by choosing components/strategies from a predefined list, get feedback from the system until an acceptable structure has been built, recover authentic similar examples and use example lexical patterns (as found in the corpus) in his/her own writing. These can be very helpful for the writer to organize the structure of his/her text before the actual writing, but once the text has been constructed, the system cannot say anything about its structure. To overcome this drawback, we decided to provide a critiquing tool capable of giving feedback on the organization of the text after its writing, instead of just aiding its composition. For a tool to supply the writer with such information, it has to be able to elicit the schematic structure of texts automatically. Such analysis has been proved to be feasible by means of a text classifier (Teufel and Moens, 2002; Burstein et al., 2003; Anthony and Lashkia, 2003). With information about the rhetorical status of each textual part, SciPo could apply the critiquing rules previously mentioned to actual texts, instead of building structures. Figure 2 presents a simplified version of the SciPo's architecture, including the aforementioned critiquing tool.

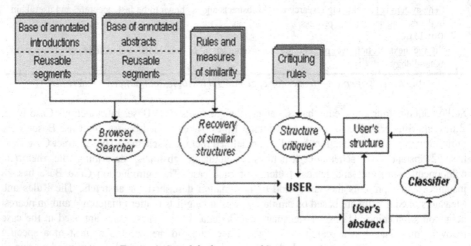

Figure 2. Simplified version of SciPo's architecture.

After analyzing previous work reporting on this kind of classification task (Teufel and Moens, 2002; Burstein et al., 2003; Anthony and Lashkia, 2003), we have found that Teufel and Moens's approach, named Argumentative Zoning, might suit our purpose better, considering the category scheme we wanted to use and the cost of adapting the feature extraction process to work on

Portuguese texts. To evaluate this assumption, we have run an experiment using a feature extraction pipeline similar to AZ's and the Weka implementation of a Naïve Bayes classifier (Witten and Frank, 2000). As we have got encouraging results, we decided to implement our own classifier, named AZPort (as it is based on AZ), so we could take the context into account during classification. Details on both experiments are presented in the next section. We also present information about the manual annotation of the abstracts used as training material.

3. Argumentative Zoning for Portuguese Texts

Argumentative zoning is the task of breaking a text containing a scientific argument into linear zones (i.e. contiguous sentences) of the same argumentative status, or zones of the same intellectual attribution (Teufel and Moens, 2000). The zone segmentation is done automatically by a statistical classifier, based on textual features that can be readily read off the text. The parameters of the statistical model, a simple Naive Bayesian classifier, are learned from human-annotated texts. For Portuguese abstracts, we followed a similar approach, adapting the textual features and the set of target categories to fit our purposes. We assumed the seven categories presented in Figure 1 as the target ones.

The first step was to select the set of features to be applied in the experiment. Considering that we want to classify abstracts sentences, we decided to use seven features, derived from the original AZ feature set, namely:

- Sentence length (*Length*);
- Sentence location (*Location*);
- Presence of citations (*Citation*);
- Presence of formulaic expressions (*Formulaic*);
- Verb tense (*Tense*);
- Voice (*Voice*);
- Presence of modal verb (*Modal*).

The *Length* feature classifies a sentence as short, medium or long length, based on two thresholds (20 and 40 words) that were estimated using the average sentence length found in our corpus.

The *Location* feature identifies the position occupied by a sentence within the abstract. We use four values for this feature: first, medium, 2ndlast and last. We believe that these values characterize common locations for some specific categories of our scheme. In fact, experiments using other values showed these to be the best ones.

The *Citation* feature flags the presence of citations in a sentence. As we are not working with full texts, it is not possible to parse the reference list in order to identify self-citations. Nevertheless, as we are dealing with a theses corpus, that usually may not contain self-citations, we believe that such distinction would not affect the classification task.

The *Formulaic* feature identifies the presence of a formulaic expression in a sentence and the category (within our category scheme) to which an expression belongs. In order to recognize these expressions, we built a set of 377 regular expressions. The sources for the construction of the regular expressions set came from corpus observations, and the literature (translated into Portuguese).

Due to the relatively abundant inflectional morphology of Portuguese, much of the porting effort went into adapting verb-syntactic features. The *Tense*, *Voice* and *Modal* features report syntactic properties of the first finite verb phrase in indicative or imperative mood. Only if no indicative or imperative verb form is found, a subjunctive form is considered. This decision was made to avoid focusing on a verb of a subordinate clause. *Tense* may assume 14 values, namely 'noverb' for verbless sentences, 'Imp' for imperatives, or some identifier in the format 'SimpleTense-(not)perfect-(not)continuous', where 'SimpleTense' refers to the tense of the finite component in the verb phrase, and '(not)perfect/(not)continuous' flags the presence of perfect/continuous auxiliary "*ter* | *haver* / *estar*". As verb inflection in Portuguese has a wide range of simple tenses – many of which are rather rare in general and even absent in our corpus – we collapsed some of them. As a result, 'SimpleTense' may assume one single value 'Past'/'Future', to the detriment of the three/two morphological past/future tenses. In addition, 'SimpleTense' neutralizes mood distinction. The *Voice* feature may assume 'noverb', 'Passive' or 'Active'. Passive voice is understood here in a broader sense, collapsing some Portuguese verb forms and constructs that are usually used to omit an agent, namely (i) regular passive voice (analogous to English, by means of auxiliary "*ser*" plus past participle), (ii) synthetic passive voice (by means of passivizating particle "*se*") and (iii) a special form of indeterminate subject (also by means of particle "*se*"). The *Modal* feature may assume 'noverb' or flag the presence of a modal auxiliary.

The next step was to determine the corpus that would be used as training material, as AZ uses supervised learning. We decided to use a corpus of 52 abstracts in Portuguese (366 sentences) from Computer Science theses collected in a previous study (Feltrim et al., 2003). In order to verify the reproducibility of our annotation scheme (Figure 1) and whether the annotated corpus could be used as valid training material, we performed an annotation experiment.

Based on our annotation scheme and using specific annotation guidelines similar to the original AZ guidelines, we trained three human annotators, one of them being the first author. They were already knowledgeable of the corpus domain and familiar with scientific writing, so the training focused on defining each category and interpreting the stated guidelines. Our corpus presents a high number of sentences with "overlapping rhetorical roles", which often leads to doubt about the correct category to be assigned. Therefore, the full understanding of the guidelines is very important since they state strategies to deal with conflicts between categories. We used 6 abstracts in the training phase, which was performed in three rounds, each round consisting of explanation, annotation, and discussion. We found that the training phase was crucial to calibrate the annotators' knowledge about the annotation task. After training, the annotators were asked to annotate 46 abstracts sentence by sentence, assigning exactly one category per sentence. We used the *Kappa* coefficient K (Siegel and Castellan, 1988) to measure reproducibility among k annotators on N items. In our experiment, items are sentences. The use of the *Kappa* measure is appropriated in this kind of task since it discards random agreement. The formula for the computation of Kappa is:

$$K = \frac{P(A) - P(E)}{1 - P(E)}$$

where *P(A)* is pairwise agreement (the proportion of times judges agree) and *P(E)* is random agreement, (the proportion of times that we would expect judges to agree by chance). *Kappa* varies between -1 and 1. It is -1 for maximal disagreement, 0 for if agreement is only as would be expected by chance annotation following the same distribution as the observed distribution, and 1 for perfect agreement.

The results show that our scheme is reproducible (K=0.69, N=320, k=3). Considering the subjectivity of this task, these results are acceptable. In a similar experiment, (Teufel et al., 1999) measured the reproducibility of their scheme as slightly higher (K=0.71, N=4261, k=3). One reason why our agreement rate is lower than theirs might be that our scheme refines their Own category into more specific categories Methodology, Results and Conclusion, increasing the complexity of the task. Collapsing these three categories increases our agreement significantly (K=0.82, N=320, k=3). When comparing our results to (Teufel et al., 1999), it is important to bear in mind that our corpus is much smaller. Based on these results, we concluded that trained humans can distinguish our set of categories and thus the data resulting from this experiment are reliable enough to be used as training material for an automatic classifier.

3.1 Experiment Using Weka

For the extraction of features values, the abstracts were automatically pre-processed, starting with the segmentation into sentences using XML tags and tokenization. Citations in running text were also marked with an XML tag and the sentences were POS-tagged according to a simplification of the NILC tagset (Aires et al., 2000). The target categories are the seven categories in the annotation experiment described above. As baselines, we considered a random choice of categories weighted by their distribution in the corpus (Baseline 1) and classification as the most frequent category (Baseline 2). The categories distribution in our corpus is presented in Figure 3.

Category	%
Background	21
Gap	10
Purpose	18
Methodology	12
Result	32
Conclusion	5
Outline	2

Figure 3. Distribution of components in the abstract corpus.

We used the Naive Bayesian classifier from the Weka system (Witten and Frank, 2000) for our experiments and the performance was measured by comparing the system's prediction with one human annotation. We assumed the annotation performed by one of the subjects in the previous annotation experiment as our "gold standard" and used it as training material. The agreement between the system and the human annotator was K=0.58, when compiled with a 13-fold cross-validation, and K=0.56 when using 66% of the data for training and the remainder for testing. This is encouragingly high amount of agreement (compared to Teufel and Moens' figure of K=0.45). Such a good result might be in part due to the fact that we are dealing with abstracts instead of longer texts (full papers). This result is also better than the baselines (Baseline 1: K=0 and Baseline 2: K=0.26).

Further analysis of our results shows that, apart from category Outline, the classifier performs well on the others categories, cf. the confusion matrix in Figure 4. This result is not surprising, since we are dealing with a corpus of abstracts, which is low in outline sentences (total of 6 sentences in the whole corpus). Many machine learning algorithms, including the Naïve Bayes classifier, perform badly on infrequent categories due to the lack of sufficient training material. Regarding the other categories, the best performance of the classifier is for Purpose (*F-measure*=0.82), followed by Gap (*F-measure*=0.70). We calculated *F-measure* as:

$$\frac{2*P*R}{P+R}$$

where P is *precision* and R is *recall*. We attribute the high performance on these categories to the presence of strong discourse markers on these kinds of sentences (modelled by feature *Formulaic*).

We were also interested in measuring the impact of taking the context of the sentence into account in our classification task. It is known that some argumentative zones tend to follow other particular zones. This property is even more apparent in self-contained texts such as abstracts (Feltrim et al., 2003). In our corpus, some particular sequences of argumentative zones are very frequent. For example, the pattern Background followed by Gap, with repetition or not, and then followed by Purpose, i.e. ((BG) | (GB)+)P, occurs in 30.7% of the corpus. So, we decided to use a context feature *History* that holds the category of the sentence classified previously, as was used in the original AZ.

		Weka Naive Bayesian Classifier							
		B	G	P	M	R	C	O	Total
	B	48	7	0	2	19	0	1	77
	G	7	24	0	0	5	0	0	36
	P	3	0	52	0	9	1	0	65
Human	M	1	0	0	27	17	0	0	45
	R	6	1	9	4	93	3	1	117
	C	0	0	0	0	14	6	0	20
	O	0	0	0	0	5	1	0	6
	Total	65	32	61	33	162	11	2	366

Figure 4. Confusion matrix: Weka Naive Bayesian classifier vs. human.

During training, the value of *History* can be calculated by simple corpus observation. For unseen texts, however, it has to be estimated as a second pass process during testing, using the posterior probabilities of all categories (values) obtained for the previous sentence. As Weka does not give access to the posteriors, and as this would facilitate the integration of the classifier into the SciPo system, we implemented our own Naïve Bayes classifier, named AZPort. For the estimation of the feature *History*, we performed a beam search with width three among the candidate categories for the previous sentence to reach the most likely classification, following Teufel and Moens (2002). In the next section, we present the classification results of AZPort.

3.2 Experiment Using AZPort

AZPort is a Naïve Bayesian classifier that renders each input sentence a set of possible rhetorical status with their respective estimated probabilities. Similarly to the AZ classifier, it estimates the probability P that a sentence S has category C given the values of its feature vector V. The category with the highest probability is chosen as the output for the sentence. The implemented classifier is presented in Figure 5.

Again, the results of classification were compiled by applying 13-fold cross-validation to our 52 abstracts (training sets of 48 texts and testing sets of 4 texts). We considered the same baselines of the previous experiment. Comparing our classifier, trained with the full feature pool (the seven features described above plus *History*), to one human annotator, the agreement reaches $K=0.65$ (system accuracy of 74%). This is a better result than the previous one ($K=0.58$) and also much better than Baseline 1 (K=0 and accuracy of 20%) and Baseline 2 (K=0.26 and accuracy of 32%). It shows that taking the context into account is a helpful heuristic, as it improved our result significantly, by 12%.

$$P(C \mid F_0, ..., F_{n-1}) \approx P(C) \frac{\prod_{j=0}^{n-1} P(F_j \mid C)}{\prod_{j=0}^{n-1} P(F_j)}$$

$P(C \mid F_0, ..., F_{n-1})$: Probability that a sentence has target category C, given its feature values $F_0, ..., F_{n-1}$;

$P(C)$:   (Overall) probability of category C;

$P(F_j \mid C)$:   Probability of feature-value pair F_j, given that the sentence is of target category C;

$P(F_j)$:   Probability of feature value F_j;

Figure 5. Naïve Bayesian classifier (Teufel and Moens, 2002).

Looking at the contribution of single features, the power of the feature *History* can be confirmed. In Figure 6, the second column gives the predictiveness of the feature on its own, in terms of *Kappa* between the classifier (actually, the 13 classifiers obtained in cross-validation) and one human annotator (gold standard). As can be observed, *Formulaic* is still the strongest feature, followed by *History*. Apart from these two, all other features are outperformed by both baselines. Syntactic features -- *Tense*, *Voice* and *Modal* -- and *Citation* are the weakest. We believe that the *Citation* feature would perform better in other kind of text than abstracts (e.g. introductions). The third column in Figure 6 gives *Kappa* coefficients for experiments using all features except the one given in the first column. As shown, apart from syntactic features, all features contribute some predictiveness in combination with others.

Feature	Alone	Left out
Length	-0.106	0.620
Location	-0.047	0.624
Citation	-0.272	0.630
Formulaic	0.557	0.345
Tense	-0.166	0.642
Voice	-0.018	0.644
Modality	-0.287	0.650
History	0.251	0.540
Baseline 1 (Random by distribution): K=0		
Baseline 2 (most frequent category): K=0.26		

Figure 6. Potential of individual features in 13-fold cross-validation.

		AZPort						
		B	G	P	M	R	C	O	Total
	B	57	10	2	1	7	0	0	77
	G	11	23	0	0	2	0	0	36
	P	6	1	49	0	8	1	0	65
Human	M	5	0	0	26	14	0	0	45
	R	2	2	0	9	101	3	0	117
	C	0	0	0	0	9	10	1	20
	O	0	0	0	0	5	1	0	6
	Total	81	36	51	36	146	15	1	366

*Figure 7. Confusion matrix: **AZPort** automatic annotation in 13-fold cross-validation vs. human.*

The analysis of the confusion matrix presented in Figure 7 shows that AZPort and Weka Naive Bayes has a similar behaviour. However, AZPort is more accurate. Its best performance is for Purpose sentences (*F-measure*=0.84), followed by Result sentences (*F-measure*=0.77). The worst performance is for Outline (*F-measure*=0). As pointed out earlier, the classifier performed badly on this category due to the lack of sufficient training material. Figure 8 presents *precision, recall* and *F-measure* for each category.

The results for the AZPort classifier are reasonably in agreement with our previous experimental results for human classification. We also observed that the confusion categories of the automatic classification are similar to the confusion categories of our human annotators. As can be observed in Figure 7, the classifier has problems in distinguishing the categories Methodology, Result and Conclusion and so do our human annotators. As mentioned previously, collapsing these three categories in one raises the human agreement considerably, which suggests distinction problems amongst these categories even for humans.

Category	Precision	Recall	F-Measure
Background	0.70	0.74	0.72
Gap	0.64	0.64	0.64
Purpose	0.96	0.75	0.84
Methodology	0.72	0.58	0.64
Result	0.69	0.86	0.77
Conclusion	0.67	0.50	0.57
Outline	0	0	0

Figure 8. Precision, Recall and F-Measure per category.

We concluded that the performance of AZPort, although lower than human, is promising and acceptable to be used as part of SciPo's critiquing tool. In the next section, we describe briefly the critiquing tool and how it works on unseen abstracts. We also report on an evaluation experiment.

4. Evaluation of SciPo's Critiquing Tool

One of the main ideas underlying SciPo's critiquing tool is that a good abstract must provide factual and specific information about a work. Thus, our aim is to help academic writers to produce more "informative" abstracts, in which the reader is likely to learn quickly what is most characteristic of and novel about the work at hand.

As previously mentioned, the critiquing tool is composed of two agents: a classifier, which detects the schematic structure elements of an abstract; and a critiquing component that analyzes the detected structure. We use AZPort for the classification task and the critiquing rules described in Section 2 for the critiquing component. Figure 9 presents the critiques and suggestions generated by the critiquing tool when analysing an abstract with the structure [B G P].

In order to evaluate how well real users would interact with the critiquing tool and to which extent it would improve their writing, we made an experiment with four students who had just finished their Master's dissertation in Computer Science at the University of São Paulo. We were also interested in observing the impact of the mistakes made by the classifier on the overall result of the critiquing tool.

Critiques and Suggestions

Critique: Essential components are missing!

– Add Methodology

It is important to inform the reader about the methodology used in your work

– Add Result

It is important to inform the reader about the main findings of your work

Suggestion: You can enrich your abstract!

– You can add some Conclusions

Conclusion sentences is a nice way to finish up an abstract as they make it look more self-contained and add to its cohesion

---

Figure 9. Output of the critiquing tool when analyzing the structure [B G P].

The students were asked to use SciPo to rewrite the abstracts of their dissertations. One of the developers/authors was present, but intervened only when prompted by the student. Before starting the experiment, all students were asked to read a document explaining SciPo's main funcionalities, as we were not interested in assessing system interface, but rather, its effectiveness as a critiquing tool. After the evaluation, all four students filled in a questionnaire, which asked for general impressions about the system.

During the evaluation experiment, the students were asked to input their abstracts into the classifier for structure detection. Before submitting the detected structure to the critiquer, the students could correct the automatic classification, if desired. Two students made corrections, while the other two assumed the classification as totally correct. The four students got suggestions/critiques from the system and changed their abstract to some extent.

Although aware of the accuracy rate of the classifier, the students considered its results very reliable and this affected the way they interacted with the tool. The classifier made mistakes in three of the four abstracts, with different impact on the resulting critiques. The observerd misclassifications were: (a) Gap vs. Background, (b) Purpose vs. Background, (c) Methodology vs. Result and (d) Purpose vs. Conclusion. (a) and (c) occurred simultaneously in a single abstract (Student 1). (b) and (d) occurred in two different abstracts (Students 2 and 3). Student 1 did not correct any of the two mistakes. Students 2 and 3 did correct the classification mistakes on their abstracts. We believe that this difference in behaviour might be caused by the kind of misclassifications made by the system. In (b) and (d), the classifier confounded very dissimilar categories and thus less problematic to be corrected, as the writer is likely to perceive such mistakes. On the other hand, mistakes like (a) and (c) are a major problem, as these categories are hard to distinguish even for trained annotators. Thus, Student 1 was not able to perceive the mistakes and then accepted the automatic results as correct. This caused the system to emit unhelpful critiques and suggestions on Student 1's abstract.

Regarding the questionnaire, the four students reported their experience with SciPo as positive. As commented above, they considered the classifier reliable. They also considered the critiques and suggestions relevant, except for one student that considered the suggestions not relevant. All students evaluated SciPo as a useful tool and reported their intention of using it again on a real situation.

To evaluate if there were improvements in the writing, we used two sets of abstracts: the original ones and the ones rewritten using SciPo. Then we asked an expert judge, experienced at academic writing, to analyse both sets and point out if there were any improvements in the rewritten abstracts regarding structure. The expert was knowledgeable of the abstract model used by the system.

The results of the expert's analysis showed the rewritten abstracts to be more informative in the sense that they contain more factual information than the original ones. However, they cannot be classified as "better quality" abstracts, as other kinds of writing problems still remain. The system focuses only on the rhetorical structure and there are other quality factors involved in the writing task, such as phrasing, grammar usage, register, etc. Nevertheless, the experiment showed that SciPo's critiquing tool offers potentially useful guidance towards more informative and genre-compliant abstracts.

5. Conclusions

We have reported on the porting of Argumentative Zoning from English to Portuguese. The features that were mostly affected by this porting were the syntactic ones: *Tense*, *Modal* and *Voice*, and also the *Formulaic* feature. Regarding the classification task (i.e. to assign one of the seven target categories to each sentence in our abstract corpus), we reported here the results of three experiments: (1) agreement results for human annotation, (2) intrinsic evaluation of automatic annotation and (3) intrinsic evaluation of automatic annotation taking context information into account. Our results are similar to Teufel and Moens's original results for English and they are very encouraging, particularly as the largest part of the porting could be performed in a matter of weeks.

The framework in which we use Argumentative Zoning is that of an automatic critiquing tool that is part of a bigger system for academic writing support in Portuguese, named SciPo. Being able to automatically determine the rhetorical status of a sentence put us in a position to implement a fully automatic critiquer, in addition to the currently implemented guided writing assistance. We reported an initial evaluation of the critiquing tool, which showed that Argumentative Zoning, although with some limitations, is suitable for this kind of application.

6. Acknowledgements

We would like to thank the financial support from the Brazilian funding agencies CAPES and FAPESP. We also want to thank Jorge Marques Pelizzoni and Lucas Antiqueira for their invaluable help implementing AZPort and SciPo.

7. Bibliography

Aires, R. V. X., Aluísio, S. M., Kuhn, D. C. S., Andreeta, M. L. B. and Oliveira Jr., O. N. (2000) Combining Multiple Classifiers to Improve Part of Speech Tagging: A Case Study for Brazilian Portuguese. In *Proceeding of SBIA 2000*. Atibaia, SP, Brazil.

Aluísio, S.M., Barcelos, I., Sampaio, J. and Oliveira Jr., O. (2001) How to learn the many unwritten "Rules of the Game" of the Academic Discourse: A hybrid Approach based on Critiques and Cases. In *Proceedings of the IEEE International Conference on Advanced Learning Technologies*. 257-260. Madison/Wisconsin.

Aluísio, S.M. and Oliveira Jr., O.N. (1996) A Detailed Schematic Structure of Research Papers Introductions: An Application in Support-Writing Tools. *Revista de la Sociedad Espanyola para el Procesamiento del Lenguaje Natural*, 19, 141-147.

Anthony, L. and Lashkia, G.V. (2003) Mover: A Machine Learning Tool to Assist in the Reading and Writing of Technical Papers. *IEEE Transactions on Professional Communication*, 46 (3), 185-193.

Broady, E. and Shurville, S. (2000) Developing Academic Writer: Designing a Writing Environment for Novice Academic Writers. In E. Broady (Ed.) *Second Language Writing in a Computer Environment*. 131-151. CILT, London.

Burstein, J., Marcu, D. and Knight, K. (2003) Finding the WRITE Stuff: Automatic Identification of Discourse Structure in Student Essays. *IEEE Intelligent Systems: Special Issue on Natural Language Processing*, 18 (1), 32-39.

Feltrim, V., Aluísio, S. and Nunes, M.G.V. (2003) Analysis of the rhetorical structure of computer science abstracts in Portuguese. In *Proceedings of the Corpus Linguistics 2003*, Dawn Archer, Paul Rayson, Andrew Wilson and Tony McEnery (eds.), UCREL Technical Papers, Vol. 16, Part 1, Special Issue (2003) 212-218.

Kriegsman, M. and Barletta, R. (1993) Building a Case-based Help Desk Application. *IEEE Expert*, December, 18-26.

Liddy, E.D. (1991) The Discourse-Level Structure of Empirical Abstracts: An Exploratory Study. *Information Processing & Management*, 27 (1), 55-81.

Narita, M. (2000) Corpus-based English Language Assistant to Japanese Software Engineers. In *Proceedings of MT-2000 Machine Translation and Multilingual Applications in the New Millennium*. 24-1 – 24-8.

Santos M. (1996) The textual organisation of research paper abstracts. *Text*, 16 (4), 481-499.

Sharples, M., Goodlet, J. and Clutterbuck, A. (1994) A comparison of algorithms for hypertext notes network linearization. *International Journal of Human-Computer Studies*, 40 (4), 727-752.

Sharples, M. and Pemberton, L. (1992) Representing writing: external representations and the writing process. In P.O. Holt and N. Williams (Eds.) *Computers and Writing: State of the Art*. 319-336. Intellect, Oxford.

Siegel, S. and Castellan, N. (1988) *Nonparametric Statistics for the Behavioral Sciences,* McGraw-Hill.

Swales, J.M. (1990) *Genre Analysis: English in Academic and Research Settings,* Cambridge University Press. Cambridge, UK.

Teufel, S. and Moens, M. (2002) Summarising Scientific Articles – Experiments with Relevance and Rhetorical Status. *Computational Linguistics*, 28 (4), 409-446.

Teufel, S. and Moens, M. (2000) What's yours and what's mine: Determining Intellectual Attribution in Scientific Text. In *Proceedings of the 2000 Joint SIGDAT Conference on Empirical Methods in Natural Language Processing and Very Large Corpora*. Hong Kong.

Teufel, S., Carletta, J. and Moens, M. (1999) An annotation scheme for discourse-level argumentation in research articles. In *Proceedings of the Ninth Meeting of the European Chapter of the Association for Computational Linguistics (EACL-99)*, 110-117.

Weissberg, R. and Buker, S. (1990) *Writing up Research: Experimental Research Report Writing for Students of English*, Prentice Hall.

Witten, I. and Frank, E. (2000) *Data Mining: Practical Machine Learning Tools and Techniques with Java Implementations*, Morgan Kaufmann.

Chapter 19

Using Hedges to Classify Citations in Scientific Articles

Chrysanne Di Marco and Frederick W. Kroon
Dept. Of Computer Science, University of Waterloo,
Waterloo, Ontario, Canada
Email*: cdimarco@uwaterloo.ca*

Robert E. Mercer
Dept. Of Computer Science, The University of Western Ontario,
London, Ontario, Canada
Email*: mercer@csd.uwo.ca*

Abstract

Citations in scientific writing fulfil an important role in creating relationships among mutually relevant articles within a research field. These inter-article relationships reinforce the argumentation structure intrinsic to all scientific writing. Therefore, determining the nature of the exact relationship between a citing and cited paper requires an understanding of the rhetorical relations within the argumentative context in which a citation is placed. To determine these relations automatically, we have suggested that various stylistic and rhetorical cues will be significant. One such cue that we are studying is the use of hedging to modify the affect of a scientific claim. We provide evidence that hedging occurs more frequently in citation contexts than in the text as a whole. With this information we conjecture that hedging is a significant aspect of the rhetorical structure of citation contexts and that the pragmatics of hedges may help in determining the rhetorical purpose of citations. A citation indexing tool for biomedical literature analysis is introduced.

Keywords: automatic citation analysis, hedges, rhetoric of science, science writing.

1. Scientific Writing, the Need for Affect, and Its Role in Citation Analysis

Since the inception of the formal scientific article in the seventeenth century, the process of scientific discovery has been inextricably linked with the actions of writing and publishing the results of research. Rhetoricians of science have gradually moved from a purely descriptive characterization of the science genre to full-fledged field studies detailing the evolution of the scientific article. During the first generation of rhetoricians of science, (e.g., Myers, 1991, Gross, 1996, Fahnestock, 1999), the persuasive nature of the scientific article, how it contributes to making and justifying a knowledge claim, was recognized as the defining property of scientific writing. Style (lexical and syntactic choice), presentation (organization of the text and display of the data), and argumentation structure were noted as the rhetorical means by which authors build a convincing case for their results. Recently, second-generation rhetoricians of science (e.g., Hyland, 1998, Gross et al., 2002) have begun to methodically analyze large corpora of scientific texts with the purpose of cataloguing specific stylistic and rhetorical features that are used to create the pragmatic effects that contribute to the author's knowledge claim. One particular type of pragmatic effect, *hedging*, is especially common in scientific writing and can be realized through a wide variety of linguistic choices.

We believe that pragmatic attitudes such as hedging (Hyland, 1998), politeness (Myers, 1989), and persuasion play an essential role in building the argumentative structure of the scientific article, and in conveying the nuances that help to support the author's knowledge claims. Moreover, we believe that these pragmatic effects work together with both global discourse structure—e.g., the traditional Introduction, Methods, Results, and Discussion (IMRaD) design of scientific discourse—and local text structure, including lexical choice, syntactic arrangement, citation placement and other aspects of scientific presentation, to create the overall rhetorical effect of a research article. In particular, we are studying the pragmatic function of citations in providing a textual means of relating articles in the space of documents which defines a research community. Studies in citation analysis indicate that the author's intent in including a citation at a particular point in the text reflects the pragmatic purpose of the citation, whether, for example, it indicates supporting or contrasting work to the topic under discussion. Our basic hypothesis is that the specific pragmatic function of citations may be determined through the analysis of fine-grained linguistic cues in the surrounding text.

We are presently studying the analysis of hedging cues in scientific writing as a means of classifying the purpose of citations in scientific texts. Hedging analysis seems well-suited as a means of approaching this problem: hedging in scientific writing is both pervasive and often readily detectable by surface textual features, while hedging cues have been well-studied (e.g., Hyland, 1998) in terms of their pragmatic function.

We have started to apply our citation classification methodology in the biomedical field. We believe that the usefulness of automated citation classification in literature indexing can be found in both the larger context of managing entire databases of scientific articles and for specific information-extraction problems such as mining the literature for protein-protein interactions.

2. Hedging in Scientific Writing

Hyland (1998) elaborates on "hedging", the term introduced by Lakoff (1972) to describe "words whose job it is to make things more or less fuzzy.": "[Hedging] has subsequently been applied to the linguistic devices used to qualify a speaker's confidence in the truth of a proposition, the kind of caveats like *I think*, *perhaps*, *might*, and *maybe* which we routinely add to our statements to avoid commitment to categorical assertions. Hedges therefore express tentativeness and possibility in communication, and their appropriate use in scientific discourse is critical (p1)".

The following examples illustrate some of the ways in which hedging may be used to deliberately convey an attitude of uncertainty or qualification. In the first example, the use of the verb *suggested* hints at the author's hesitancy to declare the absolute certainty of the claim:

(1) The functional significance of this modulation is suggested by the reported inhibition of MeSo-induced differentiation in mouse erythroleukemia cells constitutively expressing c-myb.

In the second example, the syntactic structure of the sentence, a fronted adverbial clause, emphasizes the effect of qualification through the rhetorical cue *Although*. The subsequent phrase, *a certain degree*, is a lexical modifier that also serves to limit the scope of the result:

(2) Although many neuroblastoma cell lines show a certain degree of heterogeneity in terms of neurotransmitter expression and differentiative potential, each cell has a prevalent behavior in response to differentiation inducers.

Hedging may be used in different rhetorical contexts within a scientific article to convey persuasive effect and enhance the knowledge claims of the author. For example, hedging may be realized through various linguistic cues in the Introduction, Results section, a controversial Discussion section, or generally throughout the research paper.

Within the Introduction to a scientific article, the use of hedging may serve both to establish the results within a wider research context and highlight the significance of this new work. In the extract below, the authors repeatedly use the key phrase *is/are consistent with* to first establish the reliability of their results, and then turn to more-hesitant cues (*provide circumstantial evidence, may be responsible, Regardless of the validity of this specific proposal*) to support, yet not overreach, their assertions. Nevertheless, the authors still manage to get their claims across through a number of subtle but signficant cues: *not appear to, we reasoned, would.*

(3) Transgenic Arabidopdis seedlings over expressing phytochrome B exhibit enhanced sensitivity to Rc but wild-type responsiveness to FRc (Wagner *et al*, 1991; McCormac *et al*, 1993). This result is consistent with the behaviour of endogenous phytochrome B deduced from the *hy* 3 mutant studies...By contrast, transgenic Arabidopdis over expressing phytochrome A exhibits enhanced sensitivity to FRc (Whitelam *et al*, 1992; McCormac *et al*, 1993). Together these results are consistent with the possibility, although do not prove, that the capacity to mediate the FR-HIR may be an intrinsic property of phytochrome A.

Accumulated biochemical and physiological data also provide circumstantial evidence that phytochrome A may be responsible for the FR-HIR...[the data] are consistent with the possibility that this photolabile phytochrome pool may be responsible for the FR-HIR.

Regardless of the validity of this specific proposal, however, because phytochrome B does not appear to be involved in the FR-HIR, we reasoned that mutants defective in the activity of the phytochrome mediating this response would retain phytochrome B, and, therefore, retain responsiveness to Rc...

The Results section of a scientific paper, whether implicit or set off as a formal structure, tends to be lengthy and subdivided according to topic (Hyland, 1998, p193). The topics present the paper's findings, while associated hedges may be used to enhance the persuasive effects of the authors' interpretations of the findings and the resulting claims.

In the following example, the authors appear to be hedging certainty, putting forth their claim, but tempering the persuasive effect. They have chosen a modal verb, *would*, rather than a strong positive verb, such as *indicates*, so that the effect of the claim is restrained. Then, the following sentence seems to signal the possibility of a strong contrast by the explicit discourse marker,

However, and use of a negative phrase, *cannot be ruled out*. Overall, the rhetorical effect is one of hesitance and tentativeness on the author's part.

(4) The faint 21-kD band observed in the PBM lane (Figure 2) <u>would</u> reflect the transient passage of this protein across the PBM from the plant cell cytoplasm to the bacteroids. <u>However, the opposite is also possible</u>, and it <u>cannot be ruled out</u> that the 21-kD polypeptides seen in the bacteroid lane and in the soluble proteins lane are totally different proteins with the same apparent molecular weight.

Hedging may be used not only in enhancing or mitigating the persuasive effects of an author's specific knowledge claims, but in setting up a strong 'protective' position from which to defend a highly controversial position. Hyland (1998, p196) describes a text in which the writer has proposed a radical explanation for a process that is a core issue in her research area. As he analyzes the text, he points out how the writer goes even further, in making serious challenges to current theories. Not only is the writer concerned about supporting her own scientific claim, Hyland observes, but with protecting her position in her research community: "In making this proposal, the writer implicitly attributes serious inadequacies in current theories in their interpretations of critical data. She therefore runs the very real risk of having the claim rejected by a community of peers who, she perceives, have a great deal invested in the existing view and who are likely to defend it without giving serious consideration to her work" (p. 196).

How then does this writer manage to simultaneously put forth her own claim, challenge established theory, and protect her position in the community? Not surprisingly, the paper is thick with hedges: modal verbs and adverbs, epistemic lexical verbs, indefinite quantifiers, and admissions of limiting conditions, all contriving to "[create] a rhetorical and interpersonal context which seeks to pre-empt the reader's rejection" (Hyland, 1998, p196).

As these examples illustrate, hedging effects are commonly used throughout scientific articles, while the ways in which hedging may be realized are both varied and easy to recognize. These characteristics suggested to us that the detection of hedging effects might be used as the basis for locating linguistic cues in scientific texts that might then help to determine the intended communicative effect of citations placed in the surrounding text.

3. Classifying Citations in Scientific Writing

Scientific citations play a crucial role in maintaining the network of relationships among mutually relevant articles within a research field. Customarily, authors include citations in their papers to indicate works that are foundational in their field, background for their own work, or representative of complementary or contradictory research. But, determining the nature of the exact relationship between a citing and cited paper is often difficult to ascertain. To address this, the aim of formal citation analysis has been to categorize and, ultimately, automatically classify scientific citations.

A *citation* may be formally defined as a portion of a sentence in a citing document which references another document or a set of other documents collectively. For example in sentence (5) below, there are two citations: the first citation is *Although the 3-D structure...progress*, with the set of references (Eger et al., 1994; Kelly, 1994); the second citation is *it was shown...submasses* with the single reference (Coughlan et al., 1986).

(5) Although the 3-D structure analysis by x-ray crystallography is still in progress (Eger *et al.*, 1994; Kelly, 1994), it was shown by electron microscopy that XO consists of three submasses (Coughlan *et al.*, 1986).

The primary purpose of scientific citation indexing is to provide researchers with a means of tracing the historical evolution of their field and staying current with on-going results. Citations link researchers and related articles together, and allow navigation through a space of mutually relevant documents which define a coherent academic discipline. Citation statistics play an important role in academic affairs, including promotion and tenure decisions and research grant awards. Scientific citations are thus a crucial component in the research and administrative life of the academic community. However, with the huge amount of scientific literature available, and the growing number of digital libraries, standard citation indexes are no longer adequate for providing precise and accurate information. What is needed is a means of better judging the relevancy of related papers to a researcher's specific needs so that only those articles most related to the task at hand will be retrieved. In previous work, Garzone and Mercer (Garzone, 1996, Garzone and Mercer, 2000) presented a system for citation classification that relied on characteristic syntactic structure to determine citation category. We are now extending this idea to develop a method for using fine-grained rhetorical cues within citation sentences to provide such a stylistic basis for categorization (Mercer and Di Marco, 2003, Di Marco and Mercer, 2003, Mercer et al., 2004).

3.1 Related Work in Citation Classification

The usefulness of citation categorization for other applications is directly related to the comprehensiveness (breadth and granularity) of the citation classification scheme. Garzone and Mercer (Garzone, 1996, Garzone and Mercer, 2000) proposed a citation classification scheme with 35 categories. This scheme is more comprehensive than the union of all of the previous schemes: it has a finer granularity than the often-used scheme of Garfield (1965) and Weinstock (1971) and the one which previously had the most categories, (Duncan et al., 1981), and it includes the full breadth of the other schemes (Cole, 1975, Finney, 1979, Frost, 1979, Lipetz, 1965, Moravscik and Murugesan, 1975, Peritz, 1983, Small, 1982, and Spiegel-Rösing, 1977). The Garzone and Mercer scheme and its relationship to the previous ones is discussed in detail in Garzone (1996).

We list a few of the citation categories (slashes indicate separate categories):

- Citing work disputes/corrects/questions some aspect of cited work.
- Citing work confirms/illustrates some aspect of cited work.
- Use of materials, equipment, or tools/methods, procedures, and design/theoretical equation/definition/numerical data.

We have a prototype citation classification system that takes journal articles (currently only biochemistry and physics) as input and maps each citation into one of the 35 citation categories. The prototype system relies on a large number of cue words (for example, discourse cues, nouns, and verbs which are closely related to the science and its methodology), some simple syntactic relationships, and knowledge about the IMRaD structure.

In direct contrast to Garzone and Mercer, which we take as our own starting-point, Teufel (1999) questions whether fine-grained discourse cues do exist in citation contexts, and states that "many instances of citation context are linguistically unmarked." (p93). She adds that while "overt cues" may be recognized if they are present, the problems of detecting these cues by automated means are formidable (p125). Teufel thus articulates the dual challenges facing us: to demonstrate that fine-grained discourse cues can play a role in citation analysis, and that such cues may be detected by automated means. While Teufel represents a counterposition to our approach, her work does complement ours in a number of ways. Teufel's research has a different goal to ours – it is aimed at generating summaries of scientific articles – but she does acknowledge the importance of a recognizable discourse structure in scientific articles, the IMRaD structure, and she also relies on local rhetorical structure to help determine where to find specific types of information to construct her 'fixed-form' summaries. However, Teufel voices her concern about the "potentially high level of subjectivity" (p92) inherent in judging the nature of citations, a task made more difficult by the fine granularity of her model of argumentation and the absence, she claims, of reliable means of mapping from citations to the author's reason for including the citation. As a consequence, Teufel confines her classification of citation categories to only two clearly distinguishable types: the cited work either provides a basis for the citing work or contrasts with it.

Nanba and Okumura (1999) and Nanba et al. (2000) also present work in automated citation classification that is complementary to ours: their aim is to automatically generate review articles in a specific subject domain using citation types as the basis for the classification of papers. Like Teufel, they rely on two primary citation categories (works that provide a supporting basis for the citing paper, works that have a contrasting or 'negative' relationship), but also add a third 'others' category to indicate some form of unspecified relationship exists between the citing and cited papers. Collections of 'cue phrases' (including discourse markers, lexical usage, specific phrases), are used to classify citations into the different categories but these cues are heuristically motivated rather than theoretically based. In contrast, the types of cues we are using to detect the purpose of a citation are based in discourse analysis (Mercer and Di Marco, 2003) and the rhetoric of science (Mercer et al., 2004).

We can thus summarize the differences between our approach to citation categorization and that of Teufel and Nanba et al. as follows:

- Our aim is a literature indexing tool using the rhetoric of science.
- We use a fine-grained citation categorization scheme with a greater number and variety of categories.
- We rely on cue phrases derived from formal linguistic theories as the basis for the detection and classification of citations.

4. Determining the Importance of Hedges in Citation Contexts

The surface features through which hedging is realized in scientific texts have been copiously catalogued, in particular by Hyland. Using several corpora, both scientific and general academic, Hyland (1998) carried out a detailed analysis of hedging at several levels of linguistic description, including surface-level cataloguing of hedges and pragmatic analysis of their functions (pp98–99). The results of the study yielded a detailed catalogue of hedging cues including a large number of modal auxiliaries, epistemic lexical verbs (most commonly, *suggest, indicate, predict*), epistemic adjectives, adverbs, and nouns (representing half the major grammatical classes expressing hedging), as well as a variety of non-lexical, discourse-based hedges.

We believe that hedging cues may provide a prime source of fine-grained discourse cues that can be used to determine the intent of citations in the surrounding text. Hedging cues seem ideally suited for this purpose because the various types of hedging in scientific discourse have been extensively studied and catalogued by rhetoricians of science, (Hyland, 1998), in particular, and because the surface cues that give rise to hedging are readily recognizable by linguistic analysis, e.g., modal auxiliaries, specific lexical choice, and the use of discourse markers.

In our initial study (Mercer and Di Marco, 2003), we analyzed the frequency of discourse cues in a set of scholarly scientific articles. We reported strong evidence that these cue phrases are used in the citation sentences and the surrounding text with the same frequency as in the article as a whole. We noted in this study that citations appeared to occur quite often in sentences marked by hedging cues. For example, sentence (1) above contains the hedging verb *suggested*, and a citation about earlier work by other authors. We may assume that the hedge and the citation are linked in some way: hesitancy in the current work may be offset by the support of earlier related research.

In sentence (2) above, the lexical and syntactic cues (*Although, a certain degree*) express qualification of the claim, but now the accompanying use of several citations serves to bolster the authoritative nature of the underlying argument. (Indeed, two of the citations refer to papers published more than five years earlier, and the third reference is 17 years old.)

Frame Sentence	\<p\> To test this idea further, we also analyzed a construct where the third Val residue in the V18 segment was changed to Pro.
Citation Sentence	We have previously shown that the introduction of a Pro residue in corresponding positions in a L23V transmembrane segment leads to a reduction in the MGD value of about 2.5 residues, <u>presumably</u> as a result of a break in the poly-Leu -helix caused by the Pro residue [\<citation/\>14].
Frame Sentence	Indeed, the initial drop in the glycosylation profile for the V18(P3) construct was ~2 residues, Fig. 4B, while the shift in the location of the second drop was only ~1 residue.
Normal Sentence	This is consistent with the <u>possibility</u> that V18 molecules with MGD ~ 15.5 residues indeed have already formed a transmembrane-helix at the time of glycosylation, whereas the remaining ones have not.

Figure 1. A paragraph (starts with \<p\>) containing all sentence types. There are two hedge cues (underlined) in this example, one in the citation frame, and one outside the citation window.

We have followed up on our hypothesis that hedging cues tend to occur in citation contexts with a frequency analysis of hedging cues in citation contexts in a 985 biology journal article subset from the BioMed Central corpus, and obtained statistically significant results indicating that hedging is indeed used more frequently in citation contexts than the whole text (Mercer et al., 2004). Given the presumption that writers make stylistic and rhetorical choices purposefully, we propose this as further evidence that hedging cues are an important aspect of the rhetorical structure of citation contexts and the pragmatic functions of hedges may help to determine the purpose of citations.

Each sentence in the corpus was identified as one or more of the following (see Figure 1):

- A citation sentence, if the sentence contains one or more citations.
- A citation frame sentence, if the sentence contains no citation and is immediately adjacent to a citation sentence that is within the same paragraph.
- A normal sentence, if it is neither a citation nor a citation frame sentence.
- A hedge sentence, if the sentence contains one or more hedging cues.

Several tallies were computed. We kept track of each citation sentence and frame, noting whether each contained a hedging cue. In addition, each citation window, which comprises both the citation sentence and the citation frame, was noted as either containing or lacking a hedging cue. Finally, we tallied the total number of sentences that contain a hedging cue, the total number of sentences that contain a citation, and the total number of sentences that fall into a citation frame.

It was often the case that citation windows overlapped in the text. This is especially evident in the citation-rich background section. When this occurred, care was taken to avoid double-counting hedging cues. When a hedging cue occurred in the intersecting region of two citation windows, the cue was counted as belonging to only one of the two windows. If it was in the citation sentence of one of the two windows, it was counted as belonging to the citation sentence in which it fell. If it fell in the intersection of two citation frames, it was counted as belonging to the citation that had no other hedge within its window. If neither window contained any other hedging cues, it was arbitrarily treated as belonging to the first of the two windows.

Table 1 shows the counts and Table 2 shows the frequencies of citation sentences, frame sentences, and hedge sentences. Any given sentence may belong to only one of the citation/frame categories. Since citation windows may overlap, it is sometimes the case that a citation sentence may also be part of the frame of another window. In this case, the sentence is counted only once, as a citation sentence, and not as a citation-frame sentence. Note that in Table 2, the frequencies do not add to 1, since there are sentences that neither occur in a citation window nor contain hedging cues. Data about these sentences has not been listed in Table 2.

Section	Total Sentences	Citation Sentences	Frames	Hedge Sentences Verb	Non-verb	Total
background	22321	10172	6037	2891	2785	5278
methods	36632	5922	5585	2132	1480	3468
results+disc	87382	16576	16405	13602	12040	23198
conclusions	5145	587	647	1049	760	1635

Table 1. Number of sentences, by sentence type.

Section	Citation Sentences	Frames	Hedge Sentences Verb	Non-verb	Total
background	0.46	0.27	0.13	0.12	0.24
methods	0.16	0.15	0.06	0.04	0.09
results+disc	0.19	0.19	0.16	0.14	0.27
conclusions	0.11	0.13	0.20	0.15	0.32

Table 2. Proportion of total sentences, by sentence type.

Section	Verb Cues Cite	Frame	All	Non-verb Cues Cite	Frame	All	All Cues Cite	Frame	All
background	0.15	0.11	0.13	0.13	0.13	0.12	0.25	0.22	0.24
methods	0.09	0.06	0.06	0.05	0.04	0.04	0.14	0.10	0.09
results+disc	0.22	0.16	0.16	0.15	0.14	0.14	0.32	0.27	0.27
conclusions	0.29	0.22	0.20	0.18	0.19	0.15	0.42	0.36	0.32

Table 3. Proportion of sentences containing hedging cues, by type of sentence and hedging cue category.

Hedge sentences are further subdivided into verb and non-verb categories depending on whether the hedging cue is a verb or a non-verb. Note that a sentence may belong to both of these categories. The reason for this is that the sentence may contain two cues, one from each category. In all cases, a sentence containing more than one hedging cue is counted only once as a hedge sentence (reported in the 'Total' column). This single-counting of sentences containing multiple cues explains why the number of hedge sentences does not total to the number of hedging cues.

Table 3 shows the proportions of the various types of sentences that contain hedging cues, broken down by hedging-cue category. For all but two combinations, citation sentences are more likely to contain hedging cues than would be expected from the overall frequency of hedge sentences at a significance level of 0.01. The two combinations for which there are no significant differences are non-verb hedging cues in the background and conclusion sections. It is interesting to note that there are, however, significantly (at a significance level of 0.01) more non-verb cues than expected in citation frames in the conclusion section.

With the exception of the above combination (non-verb cues in the conclusion section), citation frame sentences seem to contain approximately the same proportion of hedging cues as the overall text. However, this being said, there is little indication that they contain fewer cues than expected. The one major exception to this trend is that citation frame sentences in the background section appear less likely to contain verbal hedging cues than would be expected. It is not clear whether this is due to an actual lack of cues, or is simply an artifact of the fact that since the background section is so citation rich, there are relatively few citation frames counted (since a sentence is never counted as both a citation sentence and a citation frame sentence).

Section	n citation	frame	Verb Cues citation	frame	Non-verb Cues citation	frame	All Cues citation	frame
background	10172	6037	32.66	22.19	0.97	0.93	15.69	5.65
methods	5922	5585	118.75	0.94	13.53	0.03	113.82	1.33
results+disc	16576	16405	451.48	0.58	20.53	2.01	288.36	4.19
conclusions	587	647	24.50	1.17	5.57	9.92	26.86	6.16

Table 4. Chi2(1,n) values for observed versus expected proportion of citation sentences and frames containing hedging cues. Chi2 (crit) is 9.14 after Bonferroni correction.

Section	Windows #	%	Sentences #	%	Frames #	%
background	3361	0.33	2575	0.25	2679	0.26
methods	1089	0.18	801	0.14	545	0.09
results+disc	7257	0.44	5366	0.32	4660	0.28
conclusions	338	0.58	245	0.42	221	0.38

Table 5. Number and proportion of citation windows containing a hedging cue, by section and location of hedging cue.

Section	Windows #	%	Sentences #	%	Frames #	%
background	1967	0.19	1511	0.15	1479	0.15
methods	726	0.12	541	0.09	369	0.06
results+disc	4858	0.29	3572	0.22	2881	0.17
conclusions	227	0.39	168	0.29	139	0.24

Table 6. Number and proportion of citation windows containing a verbal hedging cue, by section and location of hedging cue.

Section	Windows #	Windows %	Sentences #	Sentences %	Frames #	Frames %
background	1862	0.18	1302	0.13	1486	0.15
methods	432	0.07	295	0.05	198	0.03
results+disc	3751	0.23	2484	0.15	2353	0.14
conclusions	186	0.32	107	0.18	111	0.19

Table 7. Number and proportion of citation windows containing a non-verb hedging cue, by section and location of hedging cue.

The chi2(1,n) values for observed versus expected proportion of citation sentences and frame sentences containing hedging cues are summarized in Table 4. The chi2(1,n) values were computed by comparing the actual versus expected frequencies of hedging cues in each sentence type. The expected frequencies are obtained simply from the overall frequency of each sentence type. Thus, if hedging cues were distributed randomly, and 24% of sentences overall had hedging cues, one would expect that approximately 24% of citation sentences would contain cues, assuming there is no relationship between hedging and citations. In order to correct for multiple tests, Bonferroni correction (Miller, 1981) was applied.

Tables 5, 6, and 7 summarize the occurrence of hedging cues in citation windows. Table 8 shows the proportion of hedge sentences that either contain a citation, or fall within a citation frame. Note that this is not the same thing as the proportion of *hedging cues* that fall within a citation sentence or frame. If more than one hedging cue falls within a single sentence, the sentence is counted as a single hedge sentence.

Section	Verb Cues Cite	Verb Cues Frame	Verb Cues None	Non-verb Cues Cite	Non-verb Cues Frame	Non-verb Cues None	All Cues Cite	All Cues Frame	All Cues None
background	0.52	0.23	0.25	0.47	0.28	0.25	0.49	0.26	0.26
methods	0.25	0.16	0.59	0.20	0.15	0.65	0.23	0.16	0.61
results+disc	0.26	0.19	0.55	0.21	0.19	0.60	0.23	0.19	0.58
conclusions	0.16	0.14	0.70	0.14	0.16	0.70	0.15	0.14	0.71

Table 8. Proportion of hedge sentences that contain citations or are part of a citation frame, by section and hedging cue category.

Table 8 suggests (last 3-column column) that the proportion of hedge sentences containing citations or being part of citation frame is at least as great as what would be expected just by the distribution of citation sentences and citation windows. Table 3 indicates that in most cases the proportion of hedge sentences in the citation windows is greater than what would be expected by the distribution of hedge sentences. Taken together, these conditional probabilities support the conjecture that hedging cues and citation contexts correlate strongly. Rather than occurring by chance, writers purposefully use these cues. With this knowledge, the strong correlation would indicate that the hedging cues are being used in synergy with the citation contexts. Hyland has catalogued a variety of pragmatic uses of hedging cues, so it is reasonable to speculate that these uses map over to the rhetorical structure that is found in citation contexts.

5. A Citation Indexing Tool for Biomedical Literature Analysis

We are presently developing a biomedical literature indexing tool to automate the classification of citations using the rhetoric of science through the following tasks:

- Adapting existing computational linguistic tools (e.g., online lexicons, part-of-speech taggers, discourse marker analyzers) for the detection of hedging cues and other cue phrases within citation contexts.
- Building test corpora of citation sentences from biomedical and scientific articles.
- Developing methods and tools for automatically classifying the pragmatic functions of hedging cues and other cue phrases in the citation corpora.

Our goal in studying the effects of hedging in scientific writing is to identify linguistic cues that may be used as a means of determining the pragmatic function of citations. Ultimately, we can expect to be able to associate hedging cues and other pragmatic cues with rhetorical relations as determiners of citation function.

Indexing tools, such as CiteSeer (Bollacker et al., 1999), play an important role in the scientific endeavour by providing researchers with a means of navigating through the network of scholarly scientific papers using the connections provided by citations. Citations relate articles within a research field by linking together works whose methods and results are in some way mutually relevant. Customarily, authors include citations in their papers to indicate works that are foundational in their field, background for their own work, or representative of complementary or contradictory research. Another researcher may then use the presence of citations to locate articles she needs to know about when entering a new field or to read in order to keep track of progress in a field where she is already well-established. But, with the explosion in the amount of scientific literature, a means of providing more information in order to give more intelligent control to the navigation process is warranted. A user normally wants to navigate more purposefully than "Find all articles citing a source article". Rather, the user may wish to know whether other experiments have used similar techniques to those used in the source article, or whether other works have reported conflicting experimental results. In order to navigate a citation index in this more-sophisticated manner, the citation index must contain not only the citation-link information, but also must indicate the function of the citation in the citing article. But, the author's purpose for including a citation is not apparent in the citation per se. Determining the nature of the exact relationship between a citing and cited paper, often requires some level of understanding the text that the citation is embedded in.

The goal of our citation indexing tool project is the design and implementation of an indexing tool for scholarly biomedical literature which uses the text surrounding the citation to provide information about the binary relation between the two papers connected by a citation. In particular, we are interested in how the scientific method structures the way in which ideas, results, theories, etc. are presented in scientific writing and how the style of presentation indicates the purpose of citations, that is, what the relationship is between the cited and citing papers. Our interest in the connections among scientific literature (our focus), ontologies, and databases is that the content and structure of each of these three repositories of scientific knowledge has its foundations in the method of science.

A *citation index* enables efficient retrieval of documents from a large collection—a citation index consists of source items and their corresponding lists of bibliographic descriptions of citing works. The use of citation indexing of scientific articles was invented by Dr. Eugene Garfield in the 1950s as a result of studies on problems of medical information retrieval and indexing of biomedical literature. Dr. Garfield later founded the Institute for Scientific Information (ISI), whose Science Citation Index (Garfield, 1973) is now one of the most popular citation indexes.

Recently, with the advent of digital libraries, Web-based indexing systems have begun to appear (e.g., ISI's 'Web of Knowledge' (http://www.isinet.com), CiteSeer (Bollacker et al., 1999)).

In the biomedical field, we believe that the usefulness of automated citation classification in literature indexing can be found in both the larger context of managing entire databases of scientific articles or for specific information-extraction problems. On the larger scale, database curators need accurate and efficient methods for building new collections by retrieving articles on the same topic from huge general databases. Simple systems (e.g., Andrade and Valencia, 1988, Marcotte et al., 2001) consider only keyword frequencies in measuring article similarity. More-sophisticated systems, such as the Neighbors utility (Wilbur and Coffee, 1994), may be able to locate articles that appear to be related in *some* way (e.g., finding related Medline abstracts for a set of protein names (Blaschke et al., 1999), but the lack of specific information about the nature and validity of the relationship between articles may still make the resulting collection a less-than-ideal resource for subsequent analysis. Citation classification to indicate the nature of the relationships between articles in a database would make the task of building collections of related articles both easier and more accurate. And, the existence of additional knowledge about the nature of the linkages between articles would greatly enhance navigation among a space of documents to retrieve meaningful information about the related content.

A specific problem in information extraction that may benefit from the use of citation categorization involves mining the literature for protein-protein interactions (e.g., Blaschke et al., 1999, Marcotte et al., 2001, Thomas et al., 2000). Currently, even the most-sophisticated systems are not yet capable of dealing with all the difficult problems of resolving ambiguities and detecting hidden knowledge. For example, Blaschke et al.'s system (Blaschke et al., 1999) is able to handle fairly complex problems in detecting protein-protein interactions, including constructing the network of protein interactions in cell-cycle control, but important implicit knowledge is not recognized. In the case of cell-cycle analysis for *Drosophila*, their system is able to determine that relationships exist between **Cak**, **Cdk7**, **CycH**, and **Cdk2**: **Cak** inhibits/phosphorylates **Cdk7**, **Cak** activates/phosphorylates **Cdk2**, **Cdk7** phosphorylates **Cdk2**, **CycH** phosphorylates **Cak** and **CycH** phosphorylates **Cdk2**. However, the system is not able to detect that **Cak** is actually a complex formed by **Cdk7** and **CycH**, and that the **Cak** complex regulates **Cdk2**. While the earlier literature describes inter-relationships among these proteins, the recognition of the generalization in their structure, i.e., that these proteins are part of a complex, is contained only in more-recent articles: "There is an element of generalization implicit in later publications, embodying previous, more dispersed findings. A clear improvement here would be the generation of associated weights for texts according to their level of generality" (Blaschke et al., 1999). Citation categorization could provide just these kind of 'ancestral' relationships between articles—whether an article is foundational in the field or builds directly on closely related work—and, if automated, could be used in forming collections of articles for study that are labelled with explicit semantic and rhetorical links to one another. Such collections of semantically linked articles might then be used as 'thematic' document clusters (cf. (Wilbur, 2002)) to elicit much more meaningful information from documents known to be closely related.

An added benefit of having citation categories available in text corpora used for studies such as extracting protein-protein interactions is that more, and more-meaningful, information may be obtained. In a potential application, Blaschke et al. (1999) noted that they were able to discover many more protein-protein interactions when including in the corpus those articles found to be related by the Neighbors facility (Wilbur and Coffee, 1994) (285 versus only 28 when relevant protein names alone were used in building the corpus). Lastly, very difficult problems in scientific and biomedical information extraction that involve aspects of deep-linguistic meaning may be resolved through the availability of citation categorization in curated texts: synonym detection, for example, may be enhanced if different names for the same entity occur in articles that can be recognized as being closely related in the scientific research process.

5.1 Our Guiding Principles

The automated labelling of citations with a specific citation function requires an analysis of the linguistic features in the text surrounding the citation, coupled with a knowledge of the author's pragmatic intent in placing the citation at that point in the text. The author's purpose for including citations in a research article reflects the fact that researchers wish to communicate their results to their scientific community in such a way that their results, or *knowledge claims*, become accepted as part of the body of scientific knowledge. This persuasive nature of the scientific research article, how it contributes to making and justifying a knowledge claim, is recognized as the defining property of scientific writing by rhetoricians of science, (e.g., Gross, 1996, Gross et al., 2002, Hyland, 1998, Myers, 1991). Style (lexical and syntactic choice), presentation (organization of the text and display of the data), and argumentation structure are noted as the rhetorical means by which authors build a convincing case for their results.

Our approach to automated citation classification is based on the detection of fine-grained linguistics cues in scientific articles that help to communicate these rhetorical stances and thereby map to the pragmatic purpose of citations. As part of our overall research methodology, our goal is to map the various types of pragmatic cues in scientific articles to rhetorical meaning. Our previous work has described the importance of *discourse cues* in enhancing inter-article cohesion signalled by citation usage (Mercer and Di Marco, 2003, Di Marco and Mercer, 2003). We have also been investigating another class of pragmatic cues, *hedging cues*, (Mercer et al., 2004), that are deeply involved in creating the pragmatic effects that contribute to the author's knowledge claim by linking together a mutually supportive network of researchers within a scientific community.

5.2 Our Design Methodology

The indexing tool that we are designing is an enhanced citation index. The feature that we are adding to a standard citation index is the function of each citation, that is, given an agreed-upon set of citation functions, we want our tool to be able to automatically categorize a citation into one of these functional categories. To accomplish this automatic categorization we are using a decision tree—currently, we are building the decision tree by hand, but in future we intend to investigate machine learning techniques to induce a tree. Our aim is to have a working indexing tool whenever we add more knowledge to the categorization process. This goal appears very feasible given our design methodology choice of using a decision tree: adding more knowledge only refines the decision-making procedure of the previously working version.

Two factors influence the development of the tree as follows:

- the granularity of the categories determines the number of leaves in the decision tree
- the number of features used to categorize determines the potential depth of the tree.

We are using Garzone and Mercer's 35-category scheme (Garzone, 1996, Garzone and Mercer, 2000) in the citation classifier, but a finer or coarser granularity is obviously permitted. Concerning the features on which the decision tree makes its decisions, we have started with a simple, yet fully automatic prototype (Garzone, 1996) which takes journal articles as input and classifies every citation found therein into at least one of the 35 categories. Its decision tree is very shallow, using only sets of cue-words and polarity switching words (not, however, etc.), some simple knowledge about the IMRaD structure of the article together with some simple syntactic structure of the citation-containing sentence. In addition to having a design which allows for easy incorporation of more-sophisticated knowledge, it also gives flexibility to the tool: categories can be easily coalesced to give users a tool that can be tailored to a variety of uses.

Although we anticipate some small changes to the number of categories due to category refinement, the major modifications to the decision tree will be driven by a more-sophisticated set of features associated with each citation. When investigating a finer granularity of the IMRaD structure, we came to realize that the structure of scientific writing at all levels of granularity was founded on *rhetoric*, which involves both argumentation structure and stylistic choices of words and syntax. This was the motivation for choosing the rhetoric of science as our guiding principle.

We rely on the notion that rhetorical information is realized in linguistic 'cues' in the text, some of which, although not all, are evident in surface features (cf. Hyland, 1998) on surface hedging cues in scientific writing. Since we anticipate that many such cues will map to the same rhetorical features that give evidence of the text's argumentative and pragmatic meaning, and that the interaction of these cues will likely influence the text's overall rhetorical effect, the formal *rhetorical relation* (cf. (Mann and Thompson, 1988)) appears to be the appropriate feature for the basis of the decision tree. So, our long-term goal is to map between the textual cues and rhetorical relations. Having noted that many of the cue words in the prototype are discourse cues, and with two recent important works linking discourse cues and rhetorical relations (Knott, 1996, Marcu, 1997), we began our investigation of this mapping with these cues. We have some early results that show that discourse cues are used extensively with citations and that some cues appear much more frequently in the citation context than in the full text (Mercer and Di Marco, 2003). Another textual device is the hedging cue, which we are currently investigating (Mercer et al., 2004).

Although our current efforts focus on cue words which are connected to organizational effects (discourse cues), and writer intent (hedging cues), we are also interested in other types of cues that are associated more closely to the purpose and method of science. For example, the scientific method is, more or less, to establish a link to previous work, set up an experiment to test an hypothesis, perform the experiment, make observations, then finally compile and discuss the importance of the results of the experiment. Scientific writing reflects this scientific method and its purpose: one may find evidence even at the coarsest granularity of the IMRaD structure in scientific articles. At a finer granularity, we have many targetted words to convey the notions of procedure, observation, reporting, supporting, explaining, refining, contradicting, etc. More specifically, science categorizes into taxonomies or creates polarities. Scientific writing then tends to compare and contrast or refine. Not surprisingly, the morphology of scientific terminology exhibits comparison and contrasting features, for example, *exo-* and *endo-*. Science needs to measure, so scientific writing contains measurement cues by referring to scales (0–100), or using comparatives (larger, brighter, etc.). Experiments are described as a sequence of steps, so this is an implicit method cue.

Finally, as for our prototype system, we will continue to evaluate the classification accuracy of the citation-indexing tool by a combination of statistical testing and validation by human experts. In addition, we would like to assess the tool's utility in real-world applications such as database curation for studies in biomedical literature analysis. We have suggested earlier that there may be many uses of this tool, so a significant aspect of the value of our tool will be its ability to enhance other research projects.

6. Conclusions and Future Work

In this paper we have motivated our hypothesis that hedging cues should and can be exploited in the process of determining the nature of citation function, and our approach to developing a literature indexing tool that computes the functions of citations. The function of a citation is determined by analyzing the rhetorical intent of the text that surrounds it. This analysis is founded on the guiding principle that the scientific method is reflected in scientific writing. The purposeful nature of citation function is a feature of scientific writing which can be exploited in a variety of ways. We anticipate more-informative citation indexes as well as more-intelligent database curation. Additionally, sophisticated information extraction may be enhanced when better selection of the dataset is enabled. For example, synonym detection in a corpus of papers may be made more tractable when the corpus is comprised of related papers derived from navigating a space of linked citations. Our early investigations have determined that linguistic cues and citations are related in important ways. Our future work will be to map these linguistic cues to rhetorical relations and other pragmatic functions so that this information can then be used to determine the purpose of citations

7. Acknowledgements

Our research has been financially supported by the Natural Sciences and Engineering Research Council of Canada and by the Universities of Western Ontario and Waterloo.

8. Bibliography

Andrade, M. A., and Valencia, A. (1988) Automatic extraction of keywords from scientific text: Application to the knowledge domain of protein families. *Bioinformatics*, 14(7), 600-607.

Blaschke, C., Andrade, M. A., Ouzounis, C., and Valencia, A. (1999) Automatic extraction of biological information from scientific text: Protein-protein interactions. In *Int. Conf. on Intelligent Systems for Molecular Biology (ISMB)*, 60-67.

Bollacker, B., Lawrence, S., and Giles, C. L. (1999) A system for automatic personalized tracking of scientific literature on the Web. In *The Fourth ACM Conf. on Digital Libraries*, 105-113.

Cole, S. (1975) The growth of scientific knowledge: Theories of deviance as a case study. In *The Idea of Social Structure: Papers in Honor of Robert K. Merton*, Harcourt, New York, 175-220.

Di Marco, C., and Mercer, R. E. (2003) Toward a catalogue of citation-related rhetorical cues in scientific texts. In *Proc. of the Pacific Assoc. for Comp. Ling. Conf. (PACLING)*, 63-72.

Duncan, E. B., Anderson, F. D., and McAleese, R. (1981) Qualified citation indexing: its relevance to educational technology. In *Information retrieval in educational technology*, 70-79.

Fahnestock, J. (1999) *Rhetorical figures in science*. Oxford University Press.

Finney, B. (1979) The reference characteristics of scientific texts. Master's thesis, The City University of London.

Frost, C. (1979) The use of citations in literary research: a preliminary classification of citation functions. *Library Quarterly*, 49, 399-414.

Garfield, E. (1965) Can citation indexing be automated? In M. E. Stevens et al., editors, *Statistical Association Methods for Mechanical Documentation (NBS Misc. Pub. 269)*. National Bureau of Standards, Washington, DC.

Garfield, E. (1973) Information, power, and the *Science Citation Index*. In *Essays of an Information Scientist*, 1, 1962–1973, Institute for Scientific Information.

Garzone, M. (1996) *Automated classification of citations using linguistic semantic grammars.*, M.Sc. Thesis, The University of Western Ontario.

Garzone, M., and Mercer, R. E. (2000) Towards an automated citation classifier. In *Proc. of the Conf. of the Canadian Society for the Computational Studies of Intelligence (CSCSI)*, 337-346.

Gross, A. G. (1996) *The rhetoric of science.* Harvard University Press.

Gross, A. G., Harmon, J. E., and Reidy, M. (2002) *Communicating science: The scientific article from the 17th century to the present.* Oxford University Press.

Hyland, K. (1998) *Hedging in scientific research articles.* John Benjamins Publishing Company.

Knott, A. (1996) *A data-driven methodology for motivating a set of coherence relations.* Ph.D. thesis, University of Edinburgh.

Lakoff, R. (1972) The pragmatics of modality. In P. Peranteau, J. Levi, and G. Phares, editors, *Papers from the Eighth Regional Meeting*, Chicago Linguistics Society, 229-246.

Lipetz, B. A. (1965) Problems of citation analysis: Critical review. *Am. Doc.*, 16, 381-390.

Mann, W. C., and Thompson, S. A. (1988) Rhetorical structure theory: Toward a functional theory of text organization. *Text*, 8(3).

Marcotte, E. M., Xenarios, I., and Eisenberg, D. (2001) Mining literature for protein-protein interactions. *Bioinformatics*, 17(4), 359-363.

Marcu, D. (1997) *The rhetorical parsing, summarization, and generation of natural language texts.* Ph.D. thesis, University of Toronto.

Mercer, R. E., and Di Marco, C. (2003) The importance of fine-grained cue phrases in scientific citations. In *Proc. of the Conf. of the Can. Soc. for the Comp. Studies of Int. (CSCSI)*, 550-556.

Mercer, R. E., Di Marco, C., and Kroon, F. W. (2004) The frequency of hedging cues in citation contexts in scientific writing. In *Proc. of the Conf. of the Canadian Society for the Computational Studies of Intelligence (CSCSI)*, 75-88.

Miller, R. G. (1981) *Simultaneous statistical inference*, Springer Verlag.

Moravscik, M. J., and Murugesan, P. (1975) Some results on the function and quality of citations. *Social Studies of Science*, 5, 86–92.

Myers, G. (1989) The pragmatics of politeness in scientific articles. *Appl. Linguistics,* 10(1), 1-35.

Myers, G. (1991) *Writing biology*. University of Wisconsin Press.

Nanba, H. and Okumura, M. (1999) Towards multi-paper summarization using reference information. In *Proc. of the 16th Int. Joint Conf. on Artificial Intelligence (IJCAI)*, 926-931.

Nanba, H., Kando, N., and Okumura, M. (2000) Classification of research papers using citation links and citation types: Towards automatic review article generation. In *Proc. of the American Society for Information Science (ASIS)*, 117-134.

Peritz, B. C. (1983) A classification of citation roles for the social sciences and related fields. *Scientometrics*, 5, 303-312.

Small, H. (1982) Citation content analysis. *Progress in Communication Sciences*, 3, 287-310.

Spiegel-Rösing, I. (1977) Science studies: Bibliometric and content analysis. *Social Studies of Science*, 7, 97-113.

Teufel, S. (1999) *Argumentative zoning: Information extraction from scientific articles*. Ph.D. thesis, University of Edinburgh.

Thomas, J., Milward, D., Ouzounis, C., Pulman, S., and Carroll, M. (2000) Automatic extraction of protein interactions from scientific abstracts. In *Proc. of the 5th Pacific Symp. on Biocomputing (PSB)*, 538-549.

Weinstock, M. (1971) Citation indexes. In *Encycl. of Library and Information Science*, 5, 16-40.

Wilbur, W. J. (2002) A thematic analysis of the AIDS literature. In *Proc. of the 7th Pacific Symp. on Biocomputing (PSB)*, 386-397.

Wilbur, W. J., and Coffee., L. (1994) The effectiveness of document neighboring in search enhancement. *Information Processing Management*, 30, 253-266.

Chapter 20

Towards a Robust Metric of Polarity

Kamal Nigam and Matthew Hurst
Intelliseek Applied Research Center
5001 Baum Blvd, Suite 644
Pittsburgh, PA 15213, USA
{knigam, mhurst}@intelliseek.com

Abstract
This chapter describes an automated system for detecting polar expressions about a specified topic. The two elementary components of this approach are a shallow NLP polar language extraction system and a machine learning based topic classifier. These components are composed together by making a simple but accurate collocation assumption: if a topical sentence contains polar language, the polarity is associated with the topic. We evaluate our system, components and assumption on a corpus of online consumer messages.

Based on these components, we discuss how to measure the overall sentiment about a particular topic as expressed in online messages authored by many different people. We propose to use the fundamentals of Bayesian statistics to form an aggregate authorial opinion metric. This metric would propagate uncertainties introduced by the polarity and topic modules to facilitate statistically valid comparisons of opinion across multiple topics.

Keywords: natural language processing, text classification, sentiment analysis, text mining, metrics.

1. Introduction

In the field of market research, one largely untapped data source is unsolicited first-person commentary freely available on the internet through blogs, Usenet, and web sites with discussion boards. Traditional methods of market research include surveys and focus groups. With these methods it is relatively easy to collect a limited amount of data in a structured form amenable to statistical analysis. In contrast, the characteristics of unsolicited first-person commentary include (1) a huge volume of mostly irrelevant content that (2) is created by a non-random sample of consumers, and (3) is available as unstructured text instead of checkboxes or rankings on a survey form.

With the proper tools, these seeming disadvantages become advantages because each increases the richness of the data available. The huge volume of total data means that typically there is also a large amount of topical relevant data. Typically, the authors of this commentary are key targets for marketers—they are disproportionately influential, spreading their opinions in large public forums. Finally, the unstructured nature of the data allows a level of detail and unfiltered feedback that is not available by forcing everyone to have an opinion on a survey form.

The goal of our research is to create text analysis techniques that facilitate real-world market research over first-person commentary from the internet. An emerging field of research related to this is that of automatically identifying sentiment or polarity in unstructured text. For example, sentences such as *I hate the BrightScreen LCD's resolution* and *My BrightScreen LCD had many dead pixels* indicate negative authorial opinion and objective but negatively oriented description respectively.

In a previous paper (Hurst and Nigam, 2004) we demonstrated an algorithm for identifying subjective or polar sentences about a particular topic of interest, such as a product offering or corporate brand. The goal of that work was to identify sentences that could be efficiently scanned by a marketing analyst to identify salient quotes to use in support of positive or negative marketing conclusions. To this end, the work focused on achieving high-precision results without concern for the recall of the algorithm. Given the volume of text under consideration by an analyst, high recall was not necessary.

Our previous work enabled discovery of anecdotal evidence in support of a marketing finding, but it did not provide any technique for assessing the overall average opinion of the authorial public. In this paper, we take the first steps toward automated techniques that assess at an aggregate level the orientation of a corpus of unsolicited first-person commentary regarding a particular topic. That is, we seek text analysis techniques that result in a well-founded metric score that represents public opinion about a topic such as a product offering or corporate brand. If such an automated technique exists, it can be used to efficiently evaluate brands in the marketplace. For example, it could score different makes of automobiles based on unsolicited customer satisfaction feedback in blogs, Usenet, and message board discussions.

The general approach that we take is:

- Segment the corpus into individual expressions (sentences, in our case).
- Use a general-purpose polar language module and a topic classifier to identify individual polar expressions about the topic of interest.
- Aggregate these individual expressions into a single score, taking into account the known and measured performance characteristics of the polarity and topic modules as well as other properties of the corpus.

This paper describes and evaluates our techniques for the first two steps of this process and presents our thoughts and some initial empirical exploration detailing how we plan to proceed on the third step.

2. Related Work

Agrawal et al. (2003) describe an approach to opinion mining that relies on the link structure implied by citations in newsgroup postings. A subset of topical message is derived using a simple keyword filter and the graph described by the link structure is partitioned into 'for' and 'against' sub-graphs. An explicit assumption is made (and tested) that citations represent 'antagonistic' standpoints. An implicit assumption is made that there is a single topic per posting and a poster is either 'for' or 'against' that topic. Our own work suggests that the distribution of topical segments is not so trivially modeled. However, work is needed to clarify the nature of 'topics', their granularity (in terms of textual expression - do some topics require long tracts of text?) and their taxonomy.

Pang et al. (2002) describe a set of initial experiments using supervised text classification methods. The domain is movie reviews. An assumption is made that each review is about an individual movie (one that doesn't hold on inspecting the data). They evaluate a number of algorithms using a bag-of-words representation. Interestingly, the labeling of the data comes from user supplied star ratings common in the review genre. As these stars are part of the discourse, and consequently the context of the text, it is not clear what dependencies hold between the textual content of the documents and the stars. If I provide all my polar information by the star mechanism, I am free to use any language I choose to discuss the various aspects of the movie that I have strong feelings about. Dave et al. (2003) describe a similar approach applied to the domain of product reviews. Both of these papers report an exploration of the space of supervised learning algorithms and feature sets that improve performance. Interestingly, neither of them found any real benefit from linguistically motivated features including stemming and a simple transformation of tokens following a negating word.

The domain of movie reviews is certainly a popular one for work in the area of automated opinion mining. GoogleMovies provides an online classification mechanism for movie reviews. Again, as with Pang et al. (2002), there are issues in GoogleMovies to do with topic. Many of the 'reviews' encountered on the site are actually plot synopses.

It is notable that the literature to date refers to systems that make assumptions about the topicality of the texts being classified. Movie reviews are assumed to be restricted to one movie and about only that movie, work on consumer goods reviews makes similar assumptions and the network based methods described by Agrawal et al. (2003) use a simple method for selecting messages that contain content on a topic but which has no control for multi-topic messages or a notion of a 'main' topic.

The work described in this paper, and earlier work reported by Hurst and Nigam (2004), aims to explore the intersection of polar and topical language with the ultimate aim of deriving reliable models of attitudes toward predefined topics.

This work might be compared to Nasukawa and Yi (2003) which adopts a similar approach, but in which topicality is derived from the recognition of fixed terms in noun phrases as derived by shallow parsing. There are two aspects to comparing to the approach described in Nasukawa and Yi (2003), which relies wholly on shallow parsing methods, and that described here, which is a hybrid of shallow parsing and machine learning. Using shallow parsing for topic discovery limits the topics to those which are discovered by the shallow parser as noun chunks, and which can be mapped (i.e. interpreted) to appropriate semantic objects. The topics are limited to those that are captured in a certain grammatical relationship with the polar expression as determined by the grammatical patterns and the semantic lexicon. The advantage of this approach is that the associations have more precision as they are constrained grammatically. The machine learning approach admits a broader class of topic (no constraints on the topic being described by a single noun phrase) and a more robust interpretation (when we view the classification as the discovery of a semantic object). Our hybrid approach does not rely on grammatical constraints for association, other than the sentential proximity assumption. Consequently, what we lose on precision we gain in recall.

Recent work (Engstrom, 2004) has looked at the association problem from a trained classifier point of view. The results reported there emphasize the problem of topicality when adopting a machine learning approach and gives support to the intuition that there is a strong linguistic aspect to the solution.

3. Classes of Polar Expression

Defining the language of polarity is a challenging task. However, when creating labeled data for training and evaluation, a definition is vital to making judgments.

We focus on two general aspects of expression. The first we term *opinion*. Statements used by the author to communicate opinion reflect a personal state of the author (Wiebe et al., 2001). The second we term *evaluative factual*. Statements with this aspect are objective but describe what is generally held to be a desirable or undesirable state. In other words, the first class reflects the users' personal evaluation and the second reflects the assumption of a social evaluation.[1]

For example, *I love this car* reflects the authors personal state and is an opinion. However, *The screen is broken* is clearly an objective expression describing what is generally accepted to be an undesirable state of affairs and is thus an evaluative factual. The notion of generally accepted evaluation is an interesting one as it is to some degree context and time dependent. At some point, the phrase *it has a color screen* will be positive. However, at some point later in time when all devices have a color screen, this will not necessarily be a polar phrase.

Opinion may be communicated indirectly via the use of emotive language—an indirect form of polar statement. For instance *The screen is frickin' broken again!* contains both emotive language as well as an objective reflection of the state of the world. This example shows that any single statement can easily mix both opinion and evaluative factive aspects of expression.

It is tempting to refer to intuition when describing opinionated or subjective language. However, the subtlety of expression requires that some lines be drawn even if they only serve to help us tackle a simpler problem. The literature in this novel field is often lacking in definition.[2] We have identified four features of the language of opinion that will be useful taxonomically for creating labeled data as well as constructing model driven analysis of polar language.

The first dimension that we call out is that of explicit versus implicit language. Explicit expressions of opinion include:

---

[1] The term *sentiment* is often used in this field. As we are including both opinion (subjective) and factual (objective) expressions, we defer to the term *polarity* indicating the common feature of *orientation*.

[2] Wiebe *et al.* (2001), however, provide a useful definition of subjective language in terms of textual representations of *private states*: they are represented in text either directly or indirectly. The class of direct statements allows us to build up lexical items corresponding to states, for example concern, disgust, etc. Indirect textual representations of private states appear as *expressive subjective elements* (Banfield, 1982). Private states are by definition subjective. However, descriptions of these states may be objective, thus Wiebe's work on sources and nested sources to chain the mentioning and author attribution of descriptions.

- Direct statements: *I like it.*
- Subjective evaluative language: *It is good.*

Implicit expression, on the other hand, involves sarcasm, irony, idiom and other deeper cultural referents:

- *It's really jumped the shark.* (cultural referent)
- *It's great if you like dead batteries.* (irony/sarcasm)
- *I give this two thumbs up.*

Of course, one might argue that lexicalized idioms, sarcasm, etc. are not distinct classes of expression but exist on a continuum with the explicit expression.

The next dimension is that of the matter about which an opinion is being expressed. This may be an established 'real world' concept, or it may be a hypothetical 'possible worlds' concept. For example *I love my new car* is an expression regarding an established object, where as *I am searching for the best possible deal* describes something that may or may not exist.

A third aspect that concerns us is that of modality, conditionals and temporal aspects of the language used. Statements such as *I might enjoy it* have a clear evaluative element (*enjoy it*) but do not express a definite opinion. *If it were larger...* describes a condition that perhaps must be met before the author admits an opinion. Such expression may also involve language indicating time: *The version coming in May is going to rock!*.

Finally, there is the matter of attribution. *I think you will like it* suggests that the author has a model of my likes and dislikes. It might mean that the author likes it and assumes I have the same taste, and so on. Quite possibly nobody likes it!

The above is an attempt to describe the space of expressions and their relationship to the author's communicative intent. For purposes of this paper, we define polar language to include both explicit and implicit expressions, 'real world' concepts and not hypothetical concepts, reject modal, conditional and temporal language and accept expressions regardless of attribution. This definition is used in driving the algorithmic approach to polarity recognition, and is consistent with the labeling criteria in the evaluation section.

4. Recognizing Polar Language

Our system begins by identifying polar language in individual sentences. To that end, a polar phrase extraction system was implemented with the following steps.

In the set up phase, a lexicon is developed which is tuned to the domain being explored. For example, if we are looking at digital cameras, phrases like 'blurry' may be negative and 'crisp' may be positive. Care is taken not to add ambiguous terms where possible as we rely on assumptions about the distribution of the phrases that we can detect with high precision and its relationship to the distribution of all polar phrases. Each item in the lexicon is a pairing of a word and its part-of-speech. Note that our lexicon contains possibly 'incorrect' terms that reflect modern language usage as found in online messages. For example, there is an increasing lack of distinction between certain classes of adverbs and adjectives and so many adjectives are replicated as adverbs.

At run time, the input is tokenized. The tokenized input is then segmented into discrete chunks. The chunking phase consists of the following steps. The input is tagged with part of speech information. Semantic tagging adds polar orientation information to each token (positive or negative) where appropriate using the prepared polarity lexicon. Simple linear POS tag patterns are then applied to form the chunks. The chunk types that are derived are basic groups (noun, adjective, adverb and verb) as well as determiner groups and an 'other' type.

The chunked input is then further processed to form higher-order groupings of a limited set of syntactic patterns. These patterns are designed to cover expressions that associate polarity with some topic, and those expressions that toggle the logical orientation of polar phrases (*I have never liked it.*). This last step conflates simple syntactic rules with semantic rules for propagating the polarity information according to any logical toggles that may occur.

If the text *This car is really great* were to be processed, firstly the tokenization step would result in the sequence {this, car, is, really, great}. Part of speech tagging would provide {this_DT, car_NN, is_VB, really_RR, great_JJ}. Assuming the appropriate polarity lexicon, additional information would be added thus: {this_DT, car_NN, is_VB, really_RR, great_JJ;+} where '+' indicates a positive lexical item. Note that features are encoded in a simplified frame structure that is a tree. The standard operations of unification (merging), test for unifiability and subsumption are available on these structures.

The chunking phase would bracket the token sequence as follows: {(this_DT)_DET, (car_NN)_BNP, (is_VB)_BVP, (really_RR, great_JJ;+)_BADJP}. Note that the basic chunk categories are {DET, BNP, BADVP, BADJP, BVP, OTHER}.

The interpretation phase then carries out two tasks: the elevation of semantic information from lower constituents to higher, applying negation logic where appropriate, and assembling larger constituents from smaller. Rules are applied in a certain order. In this example, a rule combining DET and BNP chunks would work first over the sequence, followed by a rule that forms verb phrases from BNP BVP BADJP sequences whenever polar information is found in a BADJP.

Note that there is a restriction of the applicability of rules related to the presence of polar features in the frames of at least one constituent (be it a BNP, BADJP, BADVP or BVP).

The simple syntactic patterns used to combine semantic features are: Predicative modification (*it is good*), Attributive modification (*a good car*), Equality (*it is a good car*), and Polar clause (*it broke my car*). Negations of the following types are captured by the system: Verbal attachment (*it is not good, it isn't good*), Adverbial negatives (*I never really liked it, it is never any good*), Determiners (*it is no good*), and Superordinate scope (*I don't think they made their best offer*).

5. Topic Detection in Online Messages

In the previous section we approached the task of assessing the polarity of a sentence through a shallow NLP approach. In this section, we take a different approach for determining the topicality of a sentence. We treat the topicality judgment as a text classification problem. For some types of topics, a well-written hand-built rule can suffice to identify a topic. (For example, imagine writing a rule to match the topic *Toyota Corolla.*) However, it's often the case that a topic is more accurately recognized from a complex language expression that is not easily captured by a rule. Thus, we often approach topic classification with machine learning techniques.

In the standard text classification approach, representative training examples are provided along with human judgments of topicality. From these, a learning algorithm forms a generalization hypothesis that can be used to determine topicality of previously unseen examples. Typically, the types of text that form the training examples are the same type as those seen during the evaluation and application phases for the classifier. That is, the classifier assumes the example distribution remains constant before and after training.

Given our application of identifying topical polar sentences, the requisite distribution for training would be a distribution of hand-labeled sentences. However, hand-labeling individual sentences for building a classifier can be extremely expensive. For example, in our test domain fewer than 3% of all sentences were found to be topical. On the other hand, labeling entire messages provides much more labeled data with lower cost. Therefore, in our text mining system, a machine learning text classifier is trained to assess topicality on *whole messages*. We then use this classifier to accurately predict topicality at the sentence level, even though sentence distribution is quite different than whole message distribution.

5.1 Classifying Text with Winnow

The provided classifier is trained with machine learning techniques from a collection of documents that have been hand-labeled with the binary relation of topicality. The underlying classifier is a variant of the Winnow classifier (Littlestone, 1988; Blum, 1997; Dagan et al., 1997), an online learning algorithm that finds a linear separator between the class of documents that are topical and the class of documents that are irrelevant. Documents are modeled with the standard bag-of-words representation that discards the ordering of words and notices only whether or not a word occurs in a document. Winnow learns a linear classifier of the form

$$h(x) = \sum_{w \in V} f_w c_w(x)$$

where $c_w(x) = 1$ if word w occurs in document x and $c_w(x) = 0$ otherwise. f_w is the weight for feature w. If $h(x) > V$ then the classifier predicts topical, and otherwise predicts irrelevant. The basic Winnow algorithm proceeds as:

- Initialize all f_w to 1.
- For each labeled document x in the training set:
  - Calculate $h(x)$.
  - If the document is topical, but Winnow predicts irrelevant, update each weight f_w where $c_w(x) = 1$ by $f_w = f_w \times 2$
  - If the document is irrelevant, but Winnow predicts topical, update each weight f_w where $c_w(x) = 1$ by $f_w = f_w \div 2$

In a setting with many irrelevant features, no label noise and a linear separation of the classes, Winnow is theoretically guaranteed to quickly converge to a correct hypothesis. Empirically, we have found Winnow to be a very effective document classification algorithm, rivaling the performance of Support Vector Machines (Joachims, 1997) and k-Nearest Neighbor (Yang, 1999), two other state-of-the-art text classification algorithms. We use Winnow because it is more computationally efficient than SVMs at training time and more computationally efficient than kNN at application time.

5.2 Using a Whole-document Classifier on Sentences

We use a straightforward and ad-hoc technique of adapting a given document classifier into a high precision/low recall sentence classifier. If a document is judged by the classifier to be irrelevant, we predict that all sentences in that document are also irrelevant. If a document is judged to be topical, then we further examine each sentence in that document. Given each sentence and our text classifier, we simply form a bag-of-words representation of the sentence as if an entire document consisted of that single sentence. We then run the classifier on the derived pseudo-document. If the classifier predicts topical, then we label the sentence as topical, otherwise we label the sentence as irrelevant.

A machine learning classifier expects the training document distribution and the testing distribution to be similar, and any theoretical guarantees of performance are abandoned when this type of adaptation is performed. However, we have empirically observed quite good performance from this technique. We find that sentence-level classification tends to maintain high precision but have lower recall than the performance of the classifier over whole documents. For the class of linear separator document classifiers, this result is expected when the frequency of topical training documents is relatively small (significantly less than 50%). Since a sentence is substantially shorter than the average document, there will be many fewer features in a sentence bag-of-words than in a document bag-of-words. In the extreme case, a document with no words will always be classified as irrelevant, because the default always-on feature will predict irrelevant, since the topic is relatively rare. With just a very few features on for a sentence, the words in the sentence need to be very topical in order for the classifier to predict positive. Thus, many sentences that are truly topical will not be classified as such, because the strength of their word weights will not be enough to overcome the default feature's weight. This leads directly to a loss in recall. On the other hand, the sentences that are predicted positive tend to have a large frequency of topical words, making the prediction of positive sentences still have the high precision that the classifier had on the document level.

6. The Intersection of Topic and Polarity

In the previous two sections we described fairly general-purpose tools for identifying polar expressions and topical expressions within sentences. However, each of these modules does so without any knowledge of the other. If a sentence is assessed as having both a polar expression and a topical expression, the independence of these judgments does not obviously lead us to conclude that the polar expression was with reference to the topic in question.

However, our system does assert that a sentence judged to be polar and also judged to be topical is indeed expressing polarity about the topic. This relationship is asserted without any NLP-style evidence for a connection between the topic and the sentiment other than their apparent locality in the same sentence. It is an empirical question whether or not this is a reasonable assumption to make. Our empirical results presented later demonstrate that this assumption generally holds with high accuracy in our domain of online messages.

The system we have described to this point is a shallow NLP-based system that assesses polar orientation of sentences and a machine learning-based text classifier for assessing topicality of individual sentences. Sentences that are predicted as both topical and polar are then identified by the text analysis system as being polar about the topic. The next section evaluates the performance of the individual modules as well as the overall identification of topical polar sentences. The following section discusses how these results and algorithms might be combined to create a metric for aggregating these identified sentences into an overall score.

7. Empirical Analysis

In this section we describe a corpus for evaluating topical polarity and present experimental results showing that we can automatically identify topical sentences with positive or negative orientation.

7.1 Experimental Testbed

Using the Intelliseek message harvesting and text mining toolkit, we acquired about 34,000 messages from online resources (blogs, Usenet, and online message boards). Our message harvesting system collects messages in a particular domain (a vertical industry, such as 'automotive', or a specific set of products). From these messages, a trained topic classifier was built and a polarity lexicon was customized.

We hand-labeled a separate random sample of 822 messages for topicality, 88 (11%) which were topical. We hand-labeled all 1298 sentences in the 88 topical messages for topicality, polarity (positive and/or negative), and the correspondence between them. For the 7649 sentences in messages that were not topical, every sentence was automatically labeled as topically irrelevant, and thus containing no topical polarity either. Out of 8947 total sentences, just 147 (1.6%) have polar expression about the specified topic.

We evaluate the polarity module in isolation using the 1298 sentences with the complete polarity labels. We use the full dataset for evaluating topic and its combination with polarity. To evaluate the difficulty of the task for humans, we had a second labeler repeat the hand labeling on the 1298 sentences. Human agreement numbers are presented along with the algorithmic performance numbers in the next section.

7.2 Experimental Results

Below are several randomly selected examples of sentences predicted to be positive and negative about the topic of interest in our domain. This gives some idea for both the success of the algorithm, the types of errors it makes, and the sorts of marketing insights that can be gathered by quickly scanning topical polar sentences.

Sentences predicted as topical positive:

- The B&W display is great in the sun.
- Although I really don't care for a cover, I like what COMPANY-A has done with the rotating screen, or even better yet, the concept from COMPANY-B with the horizontally rotating screen and large foldable keyboard.
- At that time, superior screen.
- The screen is the same (both COMPANY-A & COMPANY-B decided to follow COMPANY-C), but multimedia is better and more stable on the PRODUCT.
- The screen is at 70 setting (255 max) which is for me the lowest comfortable setting.

	Algorithmic		Human Agreement	
	Precision	Recall	Precision	Recall
Positive	77%	43%	82%	78%
Negative	84%	16%	78%	74%

Table 1. Performance of the polarity analysis module compared to human agreement measured over messages relevant to a specific topic.

Sentences predicted as topical negative:

- Compared to the PRODUCT's screen this thing is very very poor.
- I never had a problem with the PRODUCT-A, but did encounter the "Dust/Glass Under The Screen Problem" associated with PRODUCT-B.
- broken PRODUCT screen
- It is very difficult to take a picture of a screen.
- In multimedia I think the winner is not that clear when you consider that PRODUCT-A has a higher resolution screen than PRODUCT-B and built in camera.

Table 1 shows the results of the polarity module in isolation. Note that the precision of identifying both positive and negative topical language is very similar to the precision given by human agreement. This is indicative both of the difficulty of the task given the vagaries of language and the success of the algorithm at identifying these expressions. The automated recall, though, is significantly lower than human performance. One of the main reasons for this is the grammatical distinction between explicit and implicit polar language (c.f. the definitions section). Our approach to polar language detection is grammatical, suitable for many explicit expressions. However, the grammatical approach is less appropriate for the indirect language of implicit polarity that is generally more semantic in nature and may be better modeled by sets of cue phrases.

Also note that the recall of negative polarity is quite a bit lower than the recall of positive polarity. This confirms our anecdotal observation that language used for negative commentary is much more varied than that used for positive commentary. This observation in part drives the Bayesian approach to metric generation outlined in the next section.

Table 2 shows the performance of the trained topic classifier when measured over whole messages as well as individual sentences. Note that the precisions of applying the topic classifier on the message-level and on the sentence-level are very similar, while the sentence-level classifier has lower recall. This result is expected as described in an earlier section. In future work, we are looking towards various anaphora resolution techniques to improve the recall of the topic classifier on the sentence level.

Topicality	Algorithmic		Human Agreement	
	Precision	Recall	Precision	Recall
Message	71%	88%	---	---
Sentence	71%	77%	88%	70%

Table 2. Performance of the topic classifier compared to human agreement when run on both whole messages and individual sentences.

	Algorithmic		Human Agreement	
	Precision	Recall	Precision	Recall
Positive Topical	65%	43%	76%	62%
Negative Topical	65%	23%	80%	62%

Table 3. The performance of algorithmically identifying polar sentences about a specific topic compared to human performance.

We used the ground truth data to test our basic assumption for correlating topic and polar language. Our system assumes that any expression of polarity in a topical sentence is expressing polarity about the topic itself. We examined topical sentences that also contained positive polarity. 91% (90/99) of the time, the polarity was about the topic. In topical sentences that contained negative polarity, 80% (60/75) of the negative expressions concerned the topic. These statistics validate our basic assumption as a light-weight mechanism for correlating topic and polarity and represent an upper bound on our precision measurements for the recognition of topical polar sentences.

Table 3 shows the end results of identifying polar topical sentences given a polarity extraction system and a topic classifier. Unsurprisingly, the precision for both positive and negative topical extraction is lower than for positive and negative extraction in isolation. The correlation assumption between topic and polarity does not always hold, and the topic classifier adds in additional error. However, it is encouraging to notice that the drop in precision is less than would be suggested if all three sources of error were independent. This suggests that a certain amount of salient locality exists, where sentences that are topical are easier to identify polarity in, and vice-versa.

8. Metrics for Topic and Polarity

In this section we discuss how to use the polarity and topic modules to compile an aggregate score for a topic based on expressions contained in the data. We envision an aggregate topical orientation metric to be a function of:

- The total number of topical expressions
- The underlying frequency of topical expressions
- The underlying frequency of positive topical expressions
- The underlying frequency of negative topical expressions

For example, one very simplistic metric might be just the ratio of positive to negative expressions about a topic. The actual functional form of the metric may be driven more by marketplace requirements, but certain properties are very desirable. Ideally, such a metric would be able to propagate any uncertainty in the estimates of the various true frequencies. That is, the metric should not only support a single estimation of orientation, but also include some confidence in its measure. This will allow us to compare two or more competing topics of interest and say with a quantifiable probability that one topic is more favorably received than another.

Given the functional form of a polarity metric, one naive way of calculating the metric would be to plug in the values of the empirically measured frequencies of topic and polarity. If we believed that every topic classifier had the same accuracy, and that our polarity module performed equally in all domains, this might be a reasonable first pass. However, we believe that the performance of these modules will vary from domain-to-domain and topic-to-topic. Thus it is necessary to have some idea of the accuracy of each of our components in order to estimate the true frequencies from the empirical ones.

We plan to treat the estimation of the true underlying frequencies of topic and polarity as an exercise in Bayesian statistics. That is, we posit a probabilistic model for how the data are generated and use the data to estimate the parameters of the model. The model we propose has a set of parameters that are fixed for each domain and topic:

- With probability p_{topic} any expression will be written about specified topic.
- With probability $p_{pos|topic}$ any topical expression will be positive about the topic
- With probability $p_{neg|topic}$ any topical expression will be negative about the topic.

In practice, we observe expressions by seeing the output of our topic and polarity modules. These are not perfect observers, and they cloud the data by the following process:

- With probability $p_{topic,falsePos}$ we observe a true irrelevant expression as a topical one.
- With probability $p_{topic,falseNeg}$ we miss observing a true topical expression.
- With probability $p_{pos,falsePos}$ we observe a positive expression when there is none.
- With probability $p_{pos,falseNeg}$ we miss observing a positive expression.
- With probability $p_{neg,falsePos}$ we observe a negative expression when there is none.
- With probability $p_{neg,falseNeg}$ we miss observing a negative expression.

Using this explicit generative process of the data, we can use our observed data with standard statistical techniques to estimate the true underlying parameters of interest, p_{topic}, $p_{pos|topic}$, and $p_{neg|topic}$. These parameters are exactly the inputs needed by our hypothesized metric. Because we are working in the world of Bayesian statistics, we also get variances on our estimates that can be propagated through our metric. One nice property of Bayesian statistics is that the more data available for the estimation process, the smaller the measured variances become.

One requirement for this estimation process is the reliance on prior probability distributions for each of the model's parameters. We expect that uninformative priors will not serve well in this role. The whole point of the explicit modeling process is to get beyond the empirical estimates to a more robust estimate of the true underlying model parameters—the frequencies of polar topical expressions. To this end we plan to build empirical priors for each of our model parameters. We will do this by hand-labeling sets of data for a variety of topics and build empirical priors based on the distribution of the measured precision, recall and frequencies of each of our modules. These informative priors will give us a more solid underpinning to our estimation process, resulting in more statistically valid metrics.

We have implemented a simplified version of the metric estimation described above. Our initial implementation assumes that the performance of polarity and topic is equivalent across topics, and thus has only a single set of estimation parameters. The metric is a 1-10 normalization of the ratios of the MAP estimates of the frequencies of positive and negative polarity for the topic. A 1.0 score indicates a very negative rating, a 10.0 indicates a very positive rating, and a 5.0 indicates a balanced rating of positive and negative. Table 4 shows the results of measuring polarity for location topics in a data set of messages about Caribbean destinations. Note that the

Location	Buzz %	Polarity
St. Lucia	2.3	10.0
Barbados	3.9	10.0
Aruba	6.9	8.0
Antigua	2.1	7.2
Grand Bahama	0.5	6.9
St. Bart's	0.7	6.4
Curacao	1.3	6.2
Jamaica	12.6	5.8
Grand Cayman	4.1	5.2
Belize	2.2	4.3
Cuba	6.3	4.1

Table 4. Example output of topical polarity scores. Buzz % shows the frequency of the topic, where the Polarity score is a 1-10 normalization of aggregate sentiment.

polarity score and the frequency of the topic are not correlated. By drilling down on these scores by reading the supporting positive and negative statements, an analyst can quickly determine that:

- Barbados and Aruba score well due to a good general opinion of dining out, snorkeling and beach activities.
- Cuba has a low score due to poor snorkeling and beach activities
- Grand Bahama's medium score comes from above average opinion of snorkeling, moderate opinion of dining out and a slightly lower opinion of beach activities.

9. Conclusions and Future Work

This paper has described continued work in the detection of topic and polarity. We have outlined a proposal for a metric relating the two that may be used as an aggregate measure of authorial sentiment on a particular topic drawn from online messages. We have described the components of a system working toward an implementation of this metric, and presented an evaluation of their performance with respect to a hand-labeled data set. In addition, we have tested the assumption that topical sentences that contain polar language are polar on that topic. We believe that our investigation supports this assumption.

There are a number of necessary steps required to complete the system and to improve the performance of its elements:

- Improve polarity recognition. Improvements can be made in both precision and recall. These issues may be addressed both by improvements and extensions to the underlying grammatical system and by the application of novel methods perhaps seeded by the results of this algorithm.
- Improve recall for topic. A number of assumptions regarding the collocation of topical sentences within paragraphs can be tested to improve the selection of topical sentences. For example, all the sentences in a paragraph starting with a topical sentence may be assumed to also be topical.
- Implement and test the full version of the metric described above.

10. References

Agrawal, R., Rajagopalan, S., Srikant, R., and Xu, Y. (2003) Mining newsgroups using networks arising from social behavior. In *Proceedings of the 12th World Wide Web Conference.*

Banfield, A. (1982) *Unspeakable Sentences.* Boston: Routledge and Kegan Paul.

Blum, A. (1997) Empirical support for Winnow and weighted-majority based algorithms: Results on a calendar scheduling domain. *Machine Learning* 26:5-23.

Dagan, I., Karov, Y, and Roth, D. (1997) Mistake-driven learning in text categorization. In *EMNLP '97, 2nd Conference on Empirical Methods in Natural Language Processing.*

Dave, K., Lawrence, S., and Pennock, D. M. (2003) Mining the peanut gallery: Opinion extraction and semantic classification of product reviews. In *Proceedings of the 12th World Wide Web Conference.*

Engstrom, C. (2004) *Topic Dependence in Sentiment Classification.* Master's thesis, Cambridge University.

GoogleMovies. http://24.60.188.10:8080/demos/googlemovies/googlemovies.cgi.

Hurst, M., and Nigam, K. (2004) Retrieving topical sentiment from online document collections. In *Proceedings of the 11th Conference on Document Recognition and Retrieval.*

Joachims, T. (1998) Text categorization with support vector machines: Learning with many relevant features. In *Machine Learning: ECML-98 Tenth European Conference on Machine Learning,* 137-142.

Littlestone, N. (1998). Learning quickly when irrelevant features abound: A new linear-threshold algorithm. *Machine Learning* 2:285-318.

Nasukawa, T., and Yi, J. (2003) Sentiment analysis: Capturing favorability using natural language processing. In *Proceedings of K-CAP '03.*

Pang, B., Lee, L., and Vaithyanathan, S. (2002) Thumbs up? Sentiment classification using machine learning techniques. In *Proceedings of EMNLP 2002.*

Wiebe, J., Wilson, T., and Bell, M. (2001) Identifying collocations for recognizing opinions. In *Proceedings of ACL/EACL '01 Workshop on Collocation.*

Yang, Y. (1999) An evaluation of statistical approaches to text categorization. *Information Retrieval* 1(1/2): 67-88.

Chapter 21

Characterizing Buzz and Sentiment in Internet Sources: Linguistic Summaries and Predictive Behaviors

Richard M. Tong
Tarragon Consulting Corporation
1563 Solano Avenue, #350
Berkeley, CA 94707, USA.
Email: rtong@tgncorp.com

Ronald R. Yager
Machine Intelligence Institute
Iona College
New Rochelle, NY 10801, USA
Email: yager@panix.com

Abstract

Internet sources, such as newsgroups, message boards, and blogs, are an under-exploited resource for developing analyses of community and market responses to everything from consumer products and services, to current events and politics. In this paper, we present an overview of our exploration of effective ways of characterizing this large volume of information. In our approach, we first create time-series that represent the subjects, opinions, and attitudes expressed in the Internet sources, and then generate "Linguistic Summaries" that provide natural and easily understood descriptions of the behaviors exhibited by these time-series.

Keywords: Internet buzz, sentiment, linguistic summaries, marketing research, intelligence analysis, data mining, text mining, fuzzy sets, time-series analysis.

1. Introduction and Motivation

An often-unrecognized feature of the Internet is that it provides an unlimited number of forums for individuals, groups of individuals, and organizations to express their opinions about anything that concerns them. These forums include those that are inherently Internet-based, such as message boards, listservs and blogs, as well as those that are online extensions of traditional media, such as newspapers, magazines and newsletters. This vast array of "conversations" is increasingly seen, by both Government and Industry, as rich, but mostly untapped, source of understanding of how communities and markets are responding to everything from current events, to political issues, to the latest consumer products, to cast changes on popular TV programs.

Several research groups, as well as a number of companies, have begun to explore the issues of mining these on-line sources for uses such as brand monitoring, new product feedback, assessing the impact of advertising, and image management. The recent AAAI Symposium on "Exploring Attitude and Affect in Text" (Qu et al., 2004) contains several papers on these problems and illustrates the broad range of challenges that work in this area entails. In this paper, we present the results of our own activities, with an emphasis on techniques for summarizing the aggregate behaviors and trends that emerge from the large-scale analysis of multiple on-line sources.

In the remainder of this paper, we first introduce the basic concept of a linguistic summary, in both its static and temporal forms. Then we illustrate the use of linguistic summaries in a variety of contexts using data taken from the Internet. We complete the paper with a brief overview of our data collection and analysis system, and with a short discussion of related work and open R&D issues.

2. Linguistic Summaries

A basic premise of our work is that much of the useful information in on-line sources is only apparent when we aggregate over time and across forums. This means that we are fundamentally interested in methods for combining information from disparate sources, and then with techniques for characterizing the dynamic behaviors of these sources.

In this paper, we focus on the latter, and specifically on ways to create summaries that are natural and easily understood by human intelligence analysts and decision-makers. We call such summaries "linguistic summaries" because we create them by using the mathematics of fuzzy set theory to map quantitative features of the underlying data into controlled language descriptions. We distinguish between static summaries that describe data independently of any time referent, and temporal summaries that focus on the change in data characteristics. We briefly describe each of these in the following sections.

2.1 Static Summaries

In Yager (1991) we introduced the idea of a (static) linguistic summary and described its role in summarizing information contained in a database. In this section we briefly summarize the basic ideas.

Assume V is some attribute in a database having as its domain the set X. Examples of V could be age, city of residence, years of education or amount of sales. Associated with V is a collection of elements drawn from X consisting of the values for V assumed by the objects in the database, we denote this as $D = [a_1, a_2, ..., a_n]$. A linguistic summary associated with V is a proposition containing meta-knowledge about the elements in D. If V is the attribute age then some examples of linguistic summaries are:

> "*Most* people in the database are *about 25 years old.*"
> "*Nearly a quarter* of the people in the database are *middle aged.*"

Formally, a linguistic summary is a statement of the form:

"*Q* objects in the database have *V* is *S*.*"

In the above, *S* is called the summarizer and *Q* is called the quantity in agreement. Associated with each linguistic summary is a value *T*, called the measure of validity of the summary. Given the dataset *D* the value *T* is used to indicate the truth of the statement that *Q* objects have the property that *V* is *S*.

A fundamental characteristic of this formulation is that the summarizer and quantity in agreement are expressed in linguistic terms. One advantage of using these linguistic summaries is that we can provide statements about the database in terms that are very natural for people to comprehend. A second advantage, which will be useful in database discovery, is that these types of propositions have large granularity.

With the aid of fuzzy subsets we are able to provide a formal semantics for the terms used in the linguistic summary. In a procedure to be subsequently described, we shall use this ability to formalize the summarizers and quantity in agreement to evaluate the validity of the linguistic summary. This validation process will be based upon a determination of the compatibility of the linguistic summary with the data set *D*. It should be pointed out that for a given attribute we can conjecture numerous different summaries, then with the aid of the data set *D* we can evaluate *T* to determine which are the valid summaries. In Yager (1991; 1996) we discuss methods for quantifying the amount of information contained in a linguistic summary.

In our approach use is made of the ability to represent a linguistic summarizer by a fuzzy subset over the domain of the attribute. If *V* is some attribute taking its value from the domain *X* and if *S* is some concept associated with this attribute we can represent *S* by a fuzzy subset *S* on *X* such that for each $x \in X$, $S(x) \in [0, 1]$ indicates the degree of compatibility of the value *x* with the concept *S*. If we are considering the attribute age and if *S* is the concept middle age then $S(40)$ would indicate the degree to which 40 years old is compatible with the idea of middle age. It should be noted that even in environments in which the underlying domain is non-numeric using this approach allows us to obtain numeric values for the membership grade in the fuzzy subset. For example if *V* is the attribute city of residence that takes as its domain the cities in the U.S. we can express the concept "lives near New York" as a fuzzy subset. The second component in our linguistic summary is the quantity in agreement *Q*. These objects belong to a class of concepts called linguistic quantifiers. Examples of these objects are terms such as *most, few, about half, all*. Essentially linguistic quantifiers are fuzzy proportions. We can represent these linguistic quantifiers as fuzzy subsets of the unit interval. In this representation the membership grade of any proportion $r \in [0, 1]$, $Q(r)$, is a measure of the compatibility of the proportion r with the linguistic quantifier we are representing by the fuzzy subset *Q*. For example if *Q* is the quantifier *most* then $Q(0.9)$ represents the degree to which 0.9 satisfies the concept most.

Having discussed the concepts of summarizer and quantity in agreement we are now in a position to describe the methodology used to calculate the validity *T* of a linguistic summary. Assume $D = [a_1, a_2, ..., a_n]$ is the collection of values that appear in the database for the attribute *V*. Consider the linguistic summary "*Q* items in the database have values for *V* that are *S*."

The basic or default procedure for obtaining the validity *T* of this summary in the face of the data is as follows:

(1) For each $a_i \in D$, calculate $S(a_i)$, the degree to which a_i satisfies the summarizer *S*

(2) Let $r = \dfrac{1}{n} \displaystyle\sum_{i=1}^{n} S(a_i)$ be the proportion of D that satisfy S

(3) $T = Q(r)$, the grade of membership of r in the proposed quantity in agreement.

As an example, assume we have a database consisting of 10 entries. Let D be the collection of ages associated with these entries: $D = [30, 25, 47, 33, 29, 50, 28, 52, 19, 21]$. Then:

(1) Consider the linguistic summary "*most* people are *at least 25*". In this case the summarizer *at least 25* can be expressed simply as $S(x) = 0$ if $x < 25$ and $S(x) = 1$ and $x \geq 25$. We define *most* by the fuzzy subset $Q(r) = 0$ if $r < 0.5$ and $Q(r) = (2r - 1)^{1/2}$ if $r \geq 0.5$. The first eight items in the data collection $S(x) = 1$ while for the remaining two items $S(x) = 0$. Thus in this case $r = 8/10$ and hence $T = Q(8/10) = \left(\dfrac{16}{10} - \dfrac{10}{10} \right)^{1/2} = \left(\dfrac{6}{10} \right)^{1/2} = 0.77$.

(2) Consider the proposition "*about half* the ages are *near 30*". We define *near 30* by:

$$S(x) = \exp^{-\left(\frac{x-30}{25} \right)^2}$$

and we define *about half* as:

$$Q(r) = \exp^{-\left(\frac{r-0.5}{0.25} \right)^2}$$

In this case $r = 3.94/10 = 0.394$ and $Q(0.394) = 0.95$.

(3) Consider the proposition "*most* of the people are *young*". We define *young* as:

$$S(x) = 1 \qquad \text{if } x < 20$$
$$S(x) = -\frac{1}{10}x + 3 \qquad \text{if } 20 \leq x \leq 30$$
$$S(x) = 0 \qquad \text{if } x > 30$$

In this case $r = 0.27$ and using our previous definition of most we get $T = Q(r) = 0$.

Thus far we have considered linguistic summaries involving only one attribute. The approach described above can be extended to the case of multiple attributes from a database. We first consider summaries of this form "*Most* people in the database are *tall* and *young*." Assume U and V are two attributes appearing in the database. Let R and S be concepts associated with each of these attributes respectively the generic form of the above linguistic summary is:

"Q people in the database have U is R and V is S."

In this case our data set D consists of the collection of pairs, $D = [(a_1, b_1), (a_2, b_2), ..., (a_n, b_n)]$ where a_i is the value of the V attribute and b_i is the value of the U attribute for the ith object in the database. Our procedure for evaluating the validity of the linguistic summary in this case is defined as follows:

(1) For each i calculate $R(a_i)$ and $S(b_i)$.

(2) Let $r = \dfrac{1}{n} \displaystyle\sum_{i=1}^{n} \left(R(a_i) S(a_i) \right)$

(3) $T = Q(r)$

We now consider another class of linguistic summaries manifested by statements like:

"*Most tall* people in the database are *young*."

In this case we have as our generic form:

"Q U is R objects in the database have V is S."

In the above we call R the qualifier of the summary. The procedure for calculating the validity of this type of linguistic summary has the same three-step process except that the calculation for r is as follows:

$$r = \frac{\displaystyle\sum_{i=1}^{n} R(a_i) S(a_i)}{\displaystyle\sum_{i=1}^{n} R(a_i)}$$

We note that we can naturally extend this procedure to handle summaries of the form "*Few well paid* and *young* people in the data base live in the *suburbs*."

2.2 Temporal Summaries

In our current work we are concerned with the extension of the preceding ideas to cover situations where the behavior of data over time is of primary interest. Such an extension will allow us to characterize time-series data, such as Internet buzz, in ways that lead to an understanding of the significance of the patterns the data exhibits.

In this context, a linguistic summary has the form, "In the last few weeks knowledgeable insiders have become strongly optimistic about the new operating system to be introduced by Apple." or, "Since his announcement in August the media coverage of Arnold Schwarzenegger's candidacy has been friendly." Each of these has a similar structure that involves a time interval over which the summary holds, a source (or set of sources) from which the data is derived, a variable that is the focus of the summary, and a characterization of the behavior.

We capture this idea by defining a temporal linguistic summary (TLS) as a 4-tuple:

$TLS := \{T, S, V, B\}$

where:

Time Extent (T): is the time interval over which the summary holds
Source (S): is the set of sources from which the data is derived
Variable (V): is the subject or concept that the data represents
Behavior (B): is the characterization of behavior of the data over T

and where each component is an independent facet that we can compute from our knowledge of the underlying time-series data.

So the first example above can be mapped (somewhat loosely) onto:

T: "In the last few weeks"
S: "knowledgeable insiders"
V: "opinion of the new operating system to be introduced by apple"
B: "have become strongly [optimistic]"

and the second example can be mapped onto:

T: "Since his announcement in August"
S: "the media"
V: "coverage of Arnold Schwarzenegger's candidacy"
B: "has been [friendly]"

In both cases note that the behavioral component is defined by a combination of a behavioral pattern and directionality (or polarity) that reflects the underlying sentiment - "optimism" in the first case, and "friendliness" in the second.

Given this framework, we view the summarization task as one of generating the most useful TLS over an underlying database of time-stamped data objects. That is, we treat the task as a data-mining exercise in which we pre-specify the set of elements from which we can construct the extracted information descriptions.

In the remainder of this section we briefly review the underlying concepts for each facet and discuss the issues we face in computing a summary from the data.

2.2.1 Time Extents

In our model, time extents are treated as fuzzy time intervals and often anchored at one end with respect to a date or an event. That is, we think of these intervals as being relative to a reference point that corresponds to a date around which a user is interested in exploring the behavior of the source.

So for example, an extent such as "Several days prior to the policy speech ... " uses a specific event (here a particular speech), and hence a specific date, to anchor the interval and then extends it backwards in time to some fuzzy end-point. Similarly, an extent such as "In the early part of the year ... " refers to an interval that begins on a specific date (here January 1st) and extend forwards in time.

Fuzzy time intervals are a well-understood mathematical concept (Dubois and Prade, 1989; Yager, 1997) so the challenge for our approach is to define the formal equivalents of descriptions like "several days" and "early part of the year." For now we are relying on a pre-defined set of parameterized intervals that correspond to prototypical extents.

2.2.2 Data Sources

In our approach, a data source is a general designator for any collection of documents that, when taken together, provide the basis for the kinds of behavioral analysis we want to perform. Note that in this definition, we use "document" as the generic term for any information-bearing object that uses written human language. This very general perspective allows us to create arbitrary "sources," although normally we expect that a user would be interested in a specific forum, or author, or publication.

Sources are then characterized using a set of meta-data that encodes information such as the type, the language, geo-location, as well as information that is specific to a type (e.g., whether a on-line news source is state controlled or independent), and also information about the reliability and authoritativeness of the source content.

The meta-data are then used to create sets of taxonomic organizations that we think of as hierarchical dimensions and that form a framework within which we can do the kinds of data analysis we envision. So, for example, we might organize on-line news sources according to their geo-location as shown in Figure 1 below.

This hierarchy provides a natural set of aggregates that we can use to perform "roll-up" and "drill-down" operations as we mine the underlying data for interesting behaviors. That is, we use source organizations of this kind to control the focus of our analysis. This in turn allows us to detect that, say, the behavior that has the highest informativeness emerges at the level of "Mid-East Sources" rather than at the level of a specific publication such as the Tehran Times.

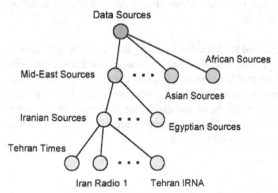

Figure 1. Taxonomy of Media Sources by Geo-Location.

2.2.3 Variables

The third element in our model is the concept of variable. By variable we mean any topic or subject that is mentioned in the documents we are analyzing. What constitutes an interesting set of topics is highly domain and application specific, but can range from such things as the particular characteristics of a consumer product to high-level political and economic concerns.

Whatever the domain, we organize the topics hierarchically to facilitate our data analysis. So, for example, Figure 2 shows a fragment of a current affairs taxonomy.

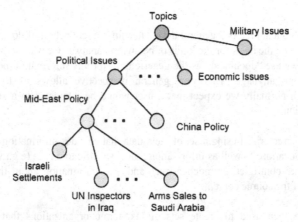

Figure 2. Taxonomy of Current Affairs Topics.

Other typical subject organizations would be by person or organization or event types, and multiple such hierarchies are likely to be in use within a single application context.

Determining that a particular document is "about" a particular subject is, of course, a significant challenge that researchers in the fields of Information Retrieval and Natural Language Processing have been investigating for many years. Our own techniques are evidentially based, and allow us to assert that a document is about a particular topic with some degree of confidence. Since in this paper our focus is on summaries of behaviors, we will not elaborate further, except to note that any technique that can make assertions of this form could be used to provide inputs to our summarization algorithms.

Once we have determined the topicality of a text, then in the general case we are also interested in the attitudes and opinions that are being expressed about the topic. Detecting and classifying opinions is also a hard problem, and we use a mix pattern-based and syntactic analysis tools within our evidential framework to extend our basic assertion model to include qualified statements about polarity. We make no special theoretical claims for these techniques since they are similar in spirit to those used by other groups, but in our application efforts we have focused on the questions of efficiency and cost-performance tradeoffs.

2.2.4 Behaviors

The final element of our TLS model is the idea of a behavior. This is the key element in the summary since it carries the information that is critical to the user in both understanding the historical characteristics of a source, and in alerting them to significant current changes.

Since each document is represented as a time-stamped data object with information about the source, the topical content, and polarity, our behavior detection algorithms work by attempting to match time-series segments to one of a number of canonical behavior classes. This is an active area of investigation for us, but currently we have classes that describe trends (e.g., up, down), level changes (e.g., higher than, same, lower than), and simple dynamic patterns (e.g., spike, oscillation). We use modified landmark detection techniques to identify inflection points in the time-series (Dunham, 2003) and fuzzy pattern matching techniques (Dubois et al., 1988) to map time-series sub-segments to the behavior class descriptors.

The output of this step is a candidate behavior descriptor that we then combine with the other elements of the TLS to produce the final formal summary. Creating the actual English language gloss is done using straightforward template-based techniques.

3. Example Applications

In this section we present two illustrative excerpts from a variety of projects in which we have explored techniques that analyze and then characterize buzz and sentiment in online sources. The first example is taken from a pilot project to track attitudes and opinions towards US foreign policy as expressed in state-controlled media. The second example is taken from a longer-term project in which the objective was to mine online discussions of movies for leading indicators of a movie's financial performance.

3.1 State Controlled Media

The State Controlled Media Project (SCMP) looked at the technical and operational challenges of using state-controlled media as a source of attitudes and opinions towards the US in general and towards US foreign policy initiatives specifically. The source data were taken from the Foreign Broadcast Information Service (FBIS) and organized based on geographic location. The topics of interest were taken from a predefined set of foreign policy themes and issues similar to the one shown in Figure 2 above.

To illustrate the processing concept, the following is a text taken from the Islamic Republic News Agency (IRNA), the official news agency of Iran:

```
<FBIS_DOC>
<ID>HZQ23000110</ID>
<DTG>23 May 02 1810 GMT</DTG>
<SOURCE> Tehran IRNA</SOURCE>
<TEXT>
Tehran, May 23, IRNA -- Iranian Foreign Minister Kamal Kharrazi here Thursday
described the ongoing situation in the Middle East &quot;convulsive and
critical&quot; and blamed &quot;repeated US mistakes&quot; for that.

Talking to IRNA, he said that the US policy line in the aftermath of the
September 11 attack on American landmarks was centered on meeting the
Zionists&apos; interests.

&quot;The US decision-making and its foreign policy line is based on  meeting
illegitimate goals of the Zionists and this should not be allowed to lead to
instability and collapse of the international community,&quot; Kharrazi said.

&quot;The new American policy has adopted use of pressure as a means to carry
other countries along its side, which has led to the spread of spite, hatred
and war,&quot; Kharrazi further said.
</TEXT>
</FBIS_DOC>
```

Using a set of topic classifiers and sentiment analysis tools, each message text is represented as an XML data object that records the assessment of the sentiment of the text with respect to the issues of interest. In this case we get something like:

```
<MSG_METADATA docid="HZQ23000110">
<DTG>23 May 02 1810 GMT</DTG>
<SOURCE>Tehran IRNA</SOURCE>
<ISSUE>
    <ISSUE_NAME>US Mid-East Policy</ISSUE_NAME>
    <ISSUE_SENTIMENT>-0.80</ISSUE_SENTIMENT>
</ISSUE>
</MSG_METADATA>
```

where the value of -0.80 in the `<ISSUE_SENTIMENT>` slot indicates that there is a significant degree of negative sentiment in this text. Sentiment values range over the interval [-1, +1], and, typically, a text would get multiple `<ISSUE>` tags.

Over a period of time, the set of such data objects allows us to create a time series that represents the changing state of attitudes in a specific source or an aggregation of sources with respect to a topic of interest.

Figure 3 shows an example time-series created by analyzing a set of Mid-East sources and aggregating all of the negative `<ISSUE_SENTIMENT>` scores.

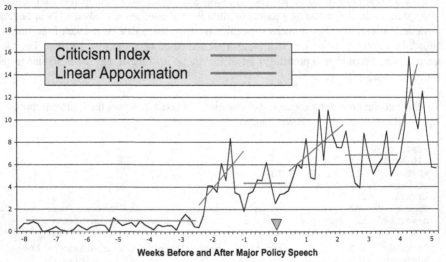

Figure 3. Mid-East Sources via FBIS (April 2002 through July 2002).

This time-series segment spans April 2002 through July 2002 and is centered on a date in late June 2002 when President Bush gave a speech on the need for new leadership in Palestine. The x-axis is labeled with major time divisions at weekly intervals and minor time-divisions at daily intervals. The y-axis is the aggregate amount of negative sentiment (i.e., the sum of the negative `<ISSUE_SENTIMENT>` scores) on a daily basis across all sources.

The piecewise linear approximation segments show (simplified for presentation purposes) the main sub-segments detected by our algorithms. In this example, the sub-segments get mapped onto either a trend or level-change behavior, and support generation of TLSs like, "In the weeks immediately preceding the speech, criticism reached new levels" and, "Since the speech, criticism has continued to rise."

3.2 Entertainment Forums

The second example is taken from a large-scale effort to analyze on-line discussion forums about movies to determine if patterns of conversations, and especially the sentiments expressed, can be used as indicators of such things as the response to advertising, or the likely box office receipts.

An edited example posting taken from the Usenet group rec.art.movies.current-films is shown below:

```
<ARTICLE>
<DOCID>tgn-2972</DOCID>
<BOARD>rec.arts.movies.current-films</BOARD>
<SUBJECT>Crouching Tiger, Hidden Dragon</SUBJECT>
<BODY> <TEXT>
I must say that the film blew me away. It&apos;s the best martial arts film
I&apos;ve ever seen, and probably the best action film I&apos;ve seen. The
direction by Lee makes all the difference. His camera moves with each blow.
There is an amazing fludity in the film that, comibined with the scenery,
makes the film easily the most ravishing of the year.
</TEXT> </BODY>
</ARTICLE>
```

As with the state-controlled media example, we process texts of this type to generate sets of structured representations, which include the sentiment about specific aspects of the movie (e.g., the camerawork, the acting, the production, etc.), and then perform our analysis at various levels of granularity.

Figure 4 shows the aggregated positive and negative sentiment for the movie "Crouching Tiger, Hidden Dragon" which was released on December 22, 2000. Positive sentiment is shown as a continuous curve with positive value. Negative sentiment is shown as a continuous curve with negative values. Overlaid on this are the figures for the weekly box office receipts in millions of US dollars (shown as columns).

As with Figure 3, the x-axis is labeled at weekly and daily intervals, but in this case the left y-axis measures aggregated daily sentiment in both directions.

We do not have the space, or the permissions, to discuss the details of our analysis of these kinds of time-series, but in general we have not found any significant correlation between sentiment and absolute box office receipts. We have found, however, that certain characteristics of the basic buzz time series allow us to make good predictions of what the movie industry calls the "longevity" of a movie (usually defined as the ratio of the total theatre receipts to the opening weekend receipts). We also found many cases in which national advertising campaigns had detectable effects on both the volume and content of the on-line conversations.

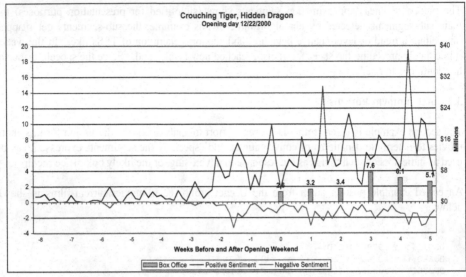

Figure 4. Usenet movie groups (October 2000 through February 2001).

4. TRENDS-2™ Infrastructure

In the work reported in this paper, we made use of Tarragon's TRENDS-2™ content acquisition system shown in Figure 5 below.

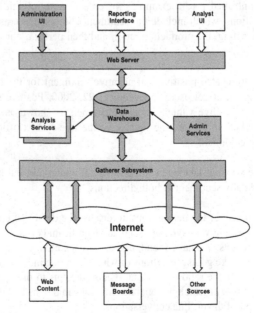

Figure 5. Basic TRENDS-2™ Architecture

TRENDS-2™ is a totally automated approach to Internet data gathering and analysis that combines smart web crawlers, data warehousing technology, fully configurable data processing and analysis workflows, and interactive report generation. In the standard configuration (shown shaded in Figure 5) the TRENDS-2™ infrastructure includes a set of standard "Analysis Services," namely: a generic query language and search capability; families of meta-data extractors and taggers; content analyzers that use fuzzy regular expression techniques; document deduplication algorithms; and, time series analysis tools. Specialized modules, such as advanced sentiment detection algorithms, can be inserted into the processing architecture as needed to meet specific application requirements.

5. Previous and Related Work

Our basic techniques for detecting and tracking opinions, as first reported by Tong (2001), rely on the use of custom lexicons that capture what we call speaker emotion, topic features, and language tone. The lexicons are developed using a mixture of handcrafted and automatic, corpus-derived patterns, and then used in various scoring algorithms to generate "sentiment scores" of the kinds we illustrate in Section 3. So in the case of the movie analysis, we model the way posters feel about the movie (e.g., "I really liked this movie", "I hated it"), the subjective comments they make on various aspects of the movie (e.g., "great acting", "wonderful visuals", "terrible score", "uneven editing"), and the overall use of vocabulary that indicates the general tone of their comments (e.g., "exhilarating", "go see it", "it sucks", "entertaining", "waste of money", "highly recommended").

Our original approach was influenced by the work of Wilson and Rayson (1993) on the analysis of transcripts of market research interviews, and by the work of Subasic and Huettner (2000) on the development and use of affect lexicons. This work also drew on earlier ideas by Hearst (1992) for looking at directionality in text, on the tools for generating lexicons developed by Spertus (1997) in her system for recognizing hostile messages, and on the methods used by Sack (2000) to characterize discussion themes in Usenet newsgroups. More recently, we have been encouraged by the work of Turney (Turney, 2002; Turney and Littman, 2003) and Wiebe (Wiebe, 2000; Wiebe et al., 2003) to explore more robust attitude and opinion detection techniques.

Our work on linguistic summaries is based on the original work by Yager (1991; 1996), together with the advances and applications of this work made by Kacprzyk, Yager and Zadrozny (2001). We drew from the extensive literature on time-series modeling to create our time-series segmentation and approximation algorithms.

6. Open R&D and Application Issues

There are a significant number of challenges that need to be addressed if we are to make effective, large-scale use of on-line, open-source material. In this final section, we review the key technical challenges and application concerns that we face in our own work.

The first technical issue is what we call "source characterization." In order to effectively aggregate data from multiple sources, we need a methodology for characterizing a source along a number of dimensions, including properties like reliability, coverage, bias and timeliness. These are all difficult concepts in their own right, but do need to be factored into the kinds of large-scale analysis we envision.

The second technical issue is sentiment detection and classification in text. The techniques we have used to date have worked well on sources in the consumer product spaces (e.g., movies, automobiles, and personal healthcare), but begin to lose their effectiveness when we look at sources that address current events and politics. Some of the reasons for this are the highly informal nature of language usage in politically oriented forums coupled with the often chaotic nature of the discourse, and the use of standard language constructs in state-controlled media that need to be calibrated to ascertain their real attitudinal value.

The third technical issue is how develop more effective techniques for generating linguistic summaries. These are technical concerns that are specific to our approach and include such questions as how to formally represent the information we discover in the data, how we test the validity of conjectured observations, and the kinds of measures we need to assess of value of the summaries we produce. We are also interested in trying to produce more complex linguistic summaries like, "Most Mid-East sources are critical of US policy on …" or even, "Sources that were united in their views … are now exhibiting a diversity of opinions."

As important as the technical challenges are, there is an equally important set of application issues that need to be addressed if this kind of technology is to be successfully deployed in end-use organizations.

The first application-related issue is the one of scalability. Given our premise that only when we look at large amounts of material do the important patterns emerge, then we need our processing algorithms to be able to work with large volumes of data that have a low "signal to noise" ratio. We also need to be able to handle very diverse sources that encompass multiple genre, languages and contexts, and we need to be able to do much of the processing in near real-time.

The second application issue is the need to develop appropriate metrics, both at the component level as well as at the system level. Although we have adopted an obvious numerical representation for sentiment, it is not clear exactly what it means to talk about the amount and directionality of sentiment, nor is it not obvious that the kinds of sentiment aggregation we do in our current implementation is justified. We also need metrics to help us understand the trade-off between the costs of achieving increased accuracy in text processing and summary generation, and the benefits that the ultimate end-user sees.

The final application issue is the fundamental need to demonstrate that the kinds of text data mining we are proposing do indeed provide significant added value for intelligence analysis and decision-making. In order for Government and Industry to invest substantial resources in this endeavor, it is important to have convincing evidence either that we can provide insights that were either not available before, or that we can provide them sooner and at a lower-cost than using existing techniques.

7. Bibliography

Dubois, D., Prade, H. and Testemale, C. (1988) Weighted fuzzy pattern matching. *Fuzzy Sets and Systems*, 28, 313-331.

Dubois, D. and Prade, H. (1989) Processing fuzzy temporal knowledge. *IEEE Transactions on Systems, Man and Cybernetics*, 19, 729-744.

Dunham, M. (2003) *Data Mining*. Prentice Hall, Upper Saddle River, NJ.

Hearst, M. (1992) Direction-Based Text Interpretation as an Information Access Refinement. In Jacobs, P. (Ed.) *Text Based Intelligent Systems*. Lawrence Erlbaum, Mahwah, NJ.

Kacprzyk, J. and Yager, R. (2001) Linguistic summaries of data using fuzzy logic. *International Journal of General Systems*, 30, 133-154.

Kacprzyk, J., Yager, R. and Zadrozny, S. (2001) Fuzzy linguistic summaries of databases for efficient business data analysis and decision support. In Abramowicz, W. and Zaruda, J. (eds.) *Knowledge Discovery for Business Information Systems*. Kluwer Academic Publishers, Hingham, MA.

Qu, Y., Shanahan, J. and Wiebe, J. (Co-chairs) (2004) *Exploring Attitude and Affect in Text: Theories and Applications*. AAAI Spring Symposium SS-04-07. AAAI Press, Menlo Park, CA.

Rasmussen, D. and Yager, R. (1997) A fuzzy SQL summary language for data discovery. In Dubois, D., Prade, H. and Yager, R. (Eds.) *Fuzzy Information Engineering: A Guided Tour of Applications*. 253-264. John Wiley & Sons, New York, NY.

Sack, W. (2000) Conversation Map: A Content-Based Usenet Newsgroup Browser. In *Proc. ACM International Conference on Intelligent User Interfaces*. New Orleans, LA.

Spertus, E. (1997) Smokey: Automatic Recognition of Hostile Messages. In *Proc. 9th Innovative Applications of Artificial Intelligence*. Providence, RI.

Subasic, P. and Huettner, A. (2000) Affect Analysis of Text Using Fuzzy Semantic Typing. In *Proc. 9th IEEE International Conference on Fuzzy Systems*. San Antonio, TX.
Tong, R. (2001) An Operational System for Detecting and Tracking Opinions in On-Line Discussions. In *ACM SIGIR 2001 Workshop on Operational Text Classification Systems*. New Orleans, LA.

Turney, P. (2002) Thumbs Up or Thumbs down? Semantic Orientation Applied to Unsupervised Classification of Reviews. In *Proc. 40th Annual Meeting of the Association for Computational Linguistics*. Philadelphia, PA.

Turney, P. and Littman, M. (2003) Measuring Praise and Criticism: Inference of Semantic Orientation from Association. *ACM Transactions on Information Systems*, 21 (4), 315-346.
Wiebe, J. (2000) Learning Subjective Adjectives from Corpora. In *Proc. 17th National Conference on Artificial Intelligence*. Austin, TX.

Wiebe, J., Breck, E., Buckley, C., Cardie, C., Davis, P., Fraser, B., Litman, D., Pierce, D., Riloff, E., Wilson, T., Day, D. and Maybury, M. (2003) Recognizing and Organizing Opinions Expressed in the World Press. In *New Directions in Question Answering*. AAAI Spring Symposium SS-03-07. AAAI Press, Menlo Park, CA.

Wilson, A. and Rayson, P. (1993) The Automatic Content Analysis of Spoken Discourse. In Souter, C. and Atwell, E. (Eds.) *Corpus-Based Computational Linguistics*. Rodopi, Amsterdam, The Netherlands.

Yager, R. (1991) On linguistic summaries of data. In Piatetsky-Shapiro, G. and Frawley, B. (Eds.) *Knowledge Discovery in Databases*. 347-363. MIT Press, Cambridge, MA.

Yager, R. (1996) Database discovery using fuzzy sets. *International Journal of Intelligent Systems*, 11, 691-712.

Yager, R. (1997) Fuzzy temporal methods for video multimedia information systems. *Journal of Advanced Computational Intelligence*, 1, 37-45.

Zadeh, L. (1975) The concept of a linguistic variable and its application to approximate reasoning: Part 1. *Information Sciences*, 8, 199-249.

Zadeh, L. (1999) From computing with numbers to computing with words - From manipulation of measurements to manipulations of perceptions. *IEEE Transactions on Circuits and Systems*, 45, 105-119.

Chapter 22

Good News or Bad News? Let the Market Decide

Moshe Koppel and Itai Shtrimberg
Dept. of Computer Science
Bar-Ilan University
Ramat-Gan, Israel
koppel@netvision.net.il, ishtrimberg@iai.co.il

Abstract

A simple and novel method for generating labeled examples for sentiment analysis is introduced: news stories about publicly traded companies are labeled positive or negative according to price changes of the company stock. It is shown that there are many lexical markers for bad news but none for good news. Overall, learned models based on lexical features can distinguish good news from bad news with accuracy of about 70%. Unfortunately, this result does not yield profits since it works only when stories are labeled according to cotemporaneous price changes but does not work when they are labeled according to subsequent price changes.

Keywords: sentiment analysis, financial analysis, automated labelling.

1. Introduction

The assessment of sentiment in written text is inevitably subjective and subject to considerable disagreement (Wiebe et al. 2001a). In some instances, such as starred movie (Turney 2002, Pang et al. 2002), restaurant (Finn and Kushmerick 2003) or product (Kushal et al. 2003) reviews, the author provides self-assessment. But in most cases, we require human judges to provide an assessment of a document's sentiment. As a result, one of the main research bottlenecks in sentiment analysis has been the procurement of large reliably labeled corpora.

The case of business news concerning a publicly-traded company is a special one, though, because price movements of the company's stock can serve as an objective measure of the valence of a news item (although, not every movement in price is a direct consequence of a given news story). The market effectively serves as judge. Thus the use of price movements correlated with the appearance of news items is a promising method for automatically generating a labeled corpus without directly invoking individual human judgments (though, of course, stock movements themselves are a product of collective human judgment).

In this paper, we classify news stories about a company according to its apparent impact on the performance of the company's stock. We will check the extent to which a learned model can be used to classify out-of-sample texts in accordance with market reaction. That is, we will determine how much of the information in a news story that drives market reaction can be gleaned from textual features alone. We will also test the degree to which such learned models can be used to turn a profit. (To prevent letdown, let us note already that our conclusions in this regard will be somewhat pessimistic.)

It is important to distinguish our approach from others (Das and Chen 2001, Seo et al. 2002) which directly judge whether a story is good news or bad news in the hopes of turning a profit based on the assumption that what human judges deem to be good (bad) news leads to exploitable price increases (decreases). In this work, we avoid such assumptions by making no judgment regarding a story itself. We are interested only in the market's reaction to the story. A similar approach was previously considered by Lavrenko et al. (2000).

2. Experiments

As our initial data set, we gathered news stories concerning each of the stocks in the Standard & Poor index of 500 leading stocks (S&P500) for the years 2000-2002. The stories were taken from the Multex Significant Developments corpus (which had been found at http://news.moneycentral.msn.com/ticker/sigdev.asp but has since been removed). The advantages of this particular corpus include that it covers only significant stories and eliminates redundancy. The total number of stories in our database is just over 12,000 – an average of 24 stories per stock. The average length of a story is just over 100 words – short enough to be focused but long enough to permit harvesting of statistics.

We used two approaches to labeling a story as having positive/negative impact on stock price. In the first approach, we matched each story with the change in price of the relevant stock from the market close the day preceding the publication of the story to the market open the day following the story. Thus for example if the news appeared on January 15, we compared the price of the stock at the close of January 14 and the open of January 16. This period is long enough to reflect market reaction to the news regardless of the particular hour of January 15 when the news became public but short enough to minimize the chances that other significant market or company news might mask the impact of this story.

A different approach, which we did not try, would be to assume that the time-stamp on the story accurately reflects the precise hour when the news became public and to check price changes during a narrower time band around that hour. Unfortunately, such an assumption would be unduly optimistic.

In the second approach, we matched each story with the change in price of the relevant stock from the market open the day *following* the publication of the story and the market open the day following that one. Thus for example if the news appeared on January 15, we compared the price of the stock at the open of January 16 and the open of January 17. Although, the first approach provides a more reliable assessment of the story's impact, the second offers a more exploitable one since, if the story is published after market close, the next day's open is the first price at which an investor might be able to purchase the stock.

In both cases, we defined a story as positive if the stock in question rose 10% or more and as negative if the stock declined 7.8% or more. We used these rather high thresholds because such dramatic price moves can be safely assumed to be reactions to news stories and not mere reflections of general market moves or random fluctuation. The lower threshold for downward moves was chosen so as to provide an equal number of negative examples as positive examples. Using our first approach, these thresholds resulted in 425 positive examples and 426 negative examples.

We also considered a subset of these stories that satisfied two additional conditions:

1.   The base price of the stock was at least $10.
2.   The percentage change in the stock price is in excess to the percentage change in the S&P.

Such stories can be more reliably linked to the price change of the stock than those that do not satisfy these conditions. Approximately half the stories satisfied both conditions.

We used as our feature set all words that appeared at least 60 times in the corpus, eliminating function words (with the exception of some obviously relevant words such as *above, below, up* and *down*). Since the texts are quite short, we represented each text as a binary vector reflecting whether or not a feature is present in the story, but ignoring frequency. Previous work (Pang et al. 2002) has indicated that presence information is superior to frequency information for sentiment categorization.

Our categorization methodology consisted of selecting the 100 features with highest information gain in the training corpus and then using a linear SVM (and other learners) to learn a model.

3. Results

Using our first labeling approach, 10-fold cross-validation experiments yielded accuracy of 70.3% using a linear SVM. Training on the entire 2000-2002 corpus, while testing on the 2003 corpus, yielded accuracy of 65.9%. Other learners, including Naïve Bayes and decision trees, yielded essentially the same results. Boosting and selection of other kernels for the SVM also had little effect on results. In addition, use of the narrower set of more reliable examples yielded essentially the same results despite the fact that the number of training examples was considerably smaller.

Closer analysis of the results offers some interesting insights. There are a number of features that are clear markers of negative documents. These include words such as *shortfall, negative* and *investigation*. Documents in which any of these words appear are almost always negative. However, unlike Tolstoy's happy families, every happy stock story is happy in its own way. There are no markers of positive stories; positive stories are characterized only by the absence of negative markers. In fact, of the twenty words in the corpus with highest information gain, all are negative markers. As a result, recall for positive stories is high (83.3%) but precision is much lower (66.0%); the misclassified documents are mostly those negative stories which fail to have any of the standard markers. This trend is evident regardless of which learner is used.

Since 77.5% of stories classified as negative really are negative, one might hope to develop a strategy which could leverage this information to make short investments based on such stories.

But recall that the labeling approach we have been using measures price moves from *before* the appearance of the story. To invest at that base price on the basis of a not-yet-published story would involve look-ahead unavailable to an investor not in possession of inside information. The honest investor interested in exploiting published news to select an investment vehicle, must use our second labeling approach which reflects price moves *subsequent* to the publication of the story. Unfortunately, 10-fold cross-validation experiments using this labeling approach yield much more modest results of just above 52% – probably too small a margin to overcome the cost of trading. This bears out the so-called Efficient Markets Hypothesis (Fama 1970): "prices fully reflect all available information".

4. Conclusions

The main contribution of this short paper is to suggest a new method for automatically collecting labeled data for sentiment analysis. The use of stock price movements offers several large advantages over hand-labeled corpora. First, the entire procedure is automatic and thus a large corpus can easily be generated. Second, the collective judgment of the market is a more reliable determiner of sentiment than that of a small number of judges. Finally, if the objective of the analysis is to maximize profit, the method of labeling directly matches the objective.

Having assembled a modest corpus in this way, w have found that we can learn to automatically characterize news stories about stocks according to their market impact with moderate success. At the very least, we can reliably identify certain stories as negative. More sophisticated features, such as word collocation (Wiebe et al. 2001b), might improve matters, but other learning methods are unlikely to improve results significantly.

However, our experiments leave little room for optimism that analysis of news stories might be successfully parlayed into an investment strategy. It is very likely, though, that labeling news stories according to their price impact in a period of several seconds or minutes following first publication of the story would yield more promising results. This should be the main direction of future research in this area.

5. References

Das, S. and Chen, M. (2001) Yahoo for Amazon: Extracting Market Sentiment from Stock Message Boards. In *Proceedings of the 8th Asia Pacific Finance Association Annual Conference (APFA 2001)*, Bangkok, Thailand.

Fama, E. (1970) Efficient Capital Markets: A Review of Theory and Empirical Work. *Journal of Finance 25*, 383-417.

Finn, A. and Kushmerick, N. (2003) Learning to classify documents according to genre. *In IJCAI-03 Workshop on Computational Approaches to Style Analysis and Synthesis*, Acapulco, Mexico.

Kushal D., Lawrence, S., and Pennock, D. M. (2003) Mining the peanut gallery: Opinion extraction and semantic classification of product reviews. In *Proceedings of the Twelfth International World Wide Web Conference (WWW-2003)*, 519-528, Budapest, Hungary.

Lavrenko, V., Schmill, M., Lawrie, D., Ogilvie, P., Jensen, D., and Allan, J. (2000) Mining of Concurrent Text and Time Series. In *Proceedings of Text Mining Workshop of the Sixth ACM*

SIGKDD International Conference on Knowledge Discovery and Data Mining, 37-44, Boston, MA.

Pang, B., Lee, L. and Vaithyanathan, S. (2002) Thumbs up? Sentiment Classification using Machine Learning Techniques. In *Proceedings of the 2002 Conference on Empirical Methods in Natural Language Processing (EMNLP)*, 79-86, Philadelphia, PA.

Seo, Y., Giampapa, J.A., and Sycara, K. (2002) *Text Classification for Intelligent Portfolio Management*. Technical report CMU-RI-TR-02-14, Robotics Institute, Carnegie Mellon University.

Turney, P. D. (2002) Thumbs Up or Thumbs Down? Semantic Orientation Applied to Unsupervised Classification of Reviews. In *Proceedings of ACL 2002*, 417-424, Philadelphia, PA.

Wiebe, J., Bruce, R., Bell, M., Martin, M., and Wilson, T. (2001) A Corpus Study of Evaluative and Speculative Language. In *Proceedings of 2nd ACL SIGdial Workshop on Discourse and Dialogue*. Aalborg, Denmark.

Wiebe, J., Wilson, T., and Bell, M. (2001) Identifying Collocations for Recognizing Opinions. In *Proceedings of ACL 01 Workshop on Collocation*. Toulouse, France.

Chapter 23

Opinion Polarity Identification of Movie Reviews

Franco Salvetti and Christoph Reichenbach
University of Colorado at Boulder
Dept. of Computer Science, University of Colorado at Boulder,
Campus Box 430
Boulder, CO 80309-430, U.S.A.
Email: {franco.salvetti, christoph.reichenbach}@colorado.edu

Stephen Lewis
University of Colorado at Boulder
Dept. of Linguistics, University of Colorado at Boulder,
Campus Box 295
Boulder, CO 80309-295, U.S.A.
Email: stephen.lewis@colorado.edu

Abstract
One approach to the assessment of overall opinion polarity (OvOP) of reviews, a concept defined in this paper, is the use of supervised machine learning mechanisms. In this paper, the impact of lexical feature selection and feature generalization, applied to reviews, on the precision of two probabilistic classifiers (Naïve Bayes and Markov Model) with respect to OvOP identification is observed. Feature generalization based on hypernymy as provided by WordNet, and feature selection based on part-of-speech (POS) tags are evaluated. A ranking criterion is introduced, based on a function of the probability of having positive or negative polarity, which makes it possible to achieve 100% precision with 10% recall. Movie reviews are used for training and testing the probabilistic classifiers, which achieve 80% precision.

Keywords: opinion polarity, sentiment identification, synonymy feature generalization, hypernymy feature generalization, POS feature selection, probabilistic classification.

1. Introduction

The dramatic increase in use of the Internet as a means of communication has been accompanied by an increase in freely available online reviews of products and services. Although such reviews are a valuable resource for customers who want to make well-informed shopping decisions, their abundance and the fact that they are mixed in terms of positive and negative overall opinion polarity are often obstacles. For instance, a customer who is already interested in a certain product may want to read some negative reviews just to pinpoint possible drawbacks, but may have no interest in spending time reading positive reviews. In contrast, customers interested in watching a good movie may want to read reviews that express a positive overall opinion polarity.

The overall opinion polarity of a review, with values expressed as positive or negative, can be represented through the classification that the author of a review would assign to it. Such a classification is here defined as the overall opinion polarity (OvOP) of a review, or simply, the polarity. The process of identifying the OvOP of a review will be referred to as Overall Opinion Polarity Identification (OvOPI).

A system that is capable of labelling a review with its polarity is valuable for at least two reasons. First, it allows the reader interested exclusively in positive (or negative) reviews to save time by reducing the number of reviews to be read. Second, since it is not uncommon for a review that starts with positive polarity to turn out to be negative, or vice versa, it avoids the risk of a reader erroneously discarding a review just because it appears at first to have the wrong polarity.

In this paper we frame a solution to OvOPI based on a supervised machine learning approach. In such a framework we observe the effects of lexical feature selection and generalization, applied to reviews, on the precision of two probabilistic classifiers. Feature generalization is based on hypernymy as provided by WordNet (Fellbaum, 1998), and feature selection is based on part-of-speech (POS) tags.

The results obtained by experiments based on movie reviews revealed that feature generalization based on synonymy and hypernymy produces less improvement than feature selection based on POS, and that for neither is there evidence of significantly improved performance over the system without neither such a selection nor such a generalization, although the overall performance of our system is comparable to that of systems in current research, achieving an precision of 80%.

In the domain of OvOPI of reviews it is often acceptable to sacrifice recall for precision. Here we also present a system whereby the reviews are ranked based on a function of the probability of being positive/negative. This ranking method achieves 100% precision when we accept a recall of 10%. This result is particularly interesting for applications that rely on web data, because the customer is not always interested in having all the possible reviews, but many times is interested in having just a few positive and a few negative. From this perspective precision is more important than recall.

2. Related Research

Research has demonstrated that there is a strong positive correlation between the presence of adjectives in a sentence and the presence of opinion (Wiebe et al., 1999). Hatzivassiloglou et al., (1997) combined a log-linear probabilistic model that examined the conjunctions between adjectives ("and", "but", "or") with a clustering algorithm that grouped the adjectives into two sets which were then labelled positive and negative. Their model predicted whether adjectives carried positive or negative polarity with 82% precision. However, because the model was unsupervised it required an immense, 21 million word corpus to function.

Turney (2002) extracted n-grams based on adjectives. In order to determine if an adjective had a positive/negative polarity he used AltaVista and its function, NEAR. He combined the number of co-occurrences of the adjective under investigation near the adjective "excellent" and near the adjective "poor", thinking that high occurrence near "poor" implies negative polarity and high occurrence near "excellent" implies positive polarity. He achieved an average of 74% precision in OvOPI across all domains. The performance on movie reviews, however, was especially poor at only 65.8%, indicating that OvOPI for movie reviews is a more difficult task than for other product reviews.

Pang et al., (2002) note that the task of polarity classification is not the same as that of topic classification; they point out that topic classification can often be performed by keyword identification, whereas sentiments tend to be expressed in more subtle ways. They applied Naïve Bayes, Maximum Entropy and Support Vector Machine classification techniques to the identification of the polarity of movie reviews. They reported that the Naïve Bayes method achieved 77.3% precision using bigrams. Their best results came using unigrams, calculated by the Support Vector Machine at 82.9% precision. Maximum Entropy performed best using both unigrams and bigrams at 80.8% precision, and Naïve Bayes performed best at 81.5% using unigrams with POS tags.

3. Probabilistic Approaches to Polarity Identification

There are many possible approaches to identifying the actual polarity of a document. Our analysis applies probabilistic methods, namely supervised machine learning, to identify the likelihood of reviews having "positive" or "negative" polarity using previously hand-classified training data. These methods are fairly standard and well understood; we list them below for the sake of completeness.

3.1 Naïve Bayes Classifier

The use of Naïve Bayes classifiers (Duda et al., 1973) is a well-known supervised machine learning technique. In this paper the "features" used to develop Naïve Bayes are referred to as "attributes" to avoid confusion with text "features".

In our approach, all word/POS-tag pairs that appear in the training data are collected and used as attributes. The formula of our Naïve Bayes classifier is defined as:

$$P(c|rv) = \prod_{w \in W} P(app_w|c) \cdot \prod_{w \notin W} P(\neg app_w|c)$$

$$\hat{c} = \arg\max P(c|rv)$$

where:

- rv is the review under consideration,
- w is a word/POS-tag pair that appears in the given document,
- $P(app_w|class)$ is the probability that a word/POS-tag pair appears in a document of the given class in training data, and
- $\hat{c}$ is an estimated class.

One interesting aspect of this particular application of Naïve Bayes is that most attributes do not appear in a test review, which means most factors in the product probability represent what is not written in a review. This is one major difference from the Markov Model classifier described in the next section.

3.2 Classifier Based on Markov Model

Because the Naïve Bayes classifier defined in the previous section builds probabilistic models based on individual occurrences of words, it is provided with relatively little information regarding the phrasal structure. Markov Model (Jurafsky et al., 2000) is a widely used probabilistic model that captures connectivity among words.

This Markov Model classifier develops two language models, one on positive reviews and the other on negative reviews. Any given unseen review rv is classified by computing the probability $P(+|rv)$ of this review having been generated with the language model for positive reviews, and a corresponding probability $P(-|rv)$ for the language model for negative reviews. If $P(+|rv) > P(-|rv)$, we consider rv to have been classified as a positive review, and classified as a negative review if $P(+|rv) < P(-|rv)$ (we did not observe reviews with equal probabilities arising in our tests). The following formula is used to compute the probability that a document could be generated with each language model.

$$P(rv) = \prod_{sn \in Reviews} P(sn)$$

$$P(sn) = P(w|<s>) \cdot \left(\prod_i P(w_{i+1}|w_i) \right) \cdot P(</s>)$$

where:

- rv is the review under consideration,
- sn is a sentence,
- $<s>$ is the start of a sentence, and
- $</s>$ is the end of a sentence.

4. Features for Analysis

Statistical analysis depends on a sequence of tokens that it uses as characteristic features of the objects which it attempts to analyze; the only necessary property of these features is that it must be possible to identify whether two features are equal.

The most straightforward way of dealing with the information found in reviews would be to use individual words from the review data as tokens. However, using just words discards semantic information about the remainder of the sentence; as such, it may be desirable first to perform some sort of semantic analysis to enrich the tokens with useful information, or even discard misleading or irrelevant information, in order to increase precision.

The following are three possible approaches to this kind of pre-processing:

- Leave the data as is; each word is represented by itself.

- Tag data as parts of speech (POS); each word is enriched by a POS tag, as determined by a standard tagging technique, such as Brill Tagger (Brill, 1995).
- Tag as POS and parse using, for instance, Penn Treebank (Marcus et al., 1994).

The third approach had severe performance issues during our early experiments, raising conceptual questions of how such data would be incorporated into a statistical analysis, whereas concentrating on POS-tagged data (sentences consisting of words enriched with their POS) was more promising because of the following:

1. As discussed by Losee (2001), information retrieval with POS-tagged data improves the quality of analysis in many cases.

2. It is a computationally efficient way of increasing the amount of (potentially) relevant information.

3. It gives rise to POS-based feature selection techniques for further refinement.

The following are assumptions about our test and training data:

1. All words are in upper case.

2. All words are stemmed.

3. All words are POS tagged; we denote (word, POS) pairs as "word/POS".

5. Part of Speech Feature Selection

Even the most positive reviews have portions with negative polarity or no clear polarity at all. Since the training data consists of complete classified reviews, the presence of parts with conflicting polarities or lack of polarity presents a major obstacle to accurate OvOPI. To illustrate this inconsistent polarity, the following were all taken from a single review of *Apollo 13* (Leeper, 1995):

- Positive polarity: *"Special effects are first-rate."*
- Negative polarity: *"The character is written thinly."*
- No clear polarity: *"The scenes were shot in short segments."*

Note that at different levels of granularity, individual phrases and words vary in their contribution to opinion polarity. Sometimes only part of the meaning of a word contributes to opinion polarity (section 7). Any portion that does not contribute to the OvOP is considered noise. To reduce such noise, feature selection was introduced by using POS tags to do the following:

1. Introduce custom parts of speech, e.g. NEG and COP, when the tagger does not provide desired specificity (Brill Tagger does not provide POS for "negation" and "copula").

2. Remove the words that are least likely to contribute to the polarity of a review (determiner, preposition, etc.).

3. Reduce only parts of speech that introduce unnecessary variance to POS. It may be useful, for instance, for the classifier to record the presence of a proper noun. However,

to include individual proper nouns would unnecessarily decrease the probability of finding the same n-grams in the test data.

Experimentation involved multiple combinations of such feature selection rules, yielding several separate results. An example of a specification of POS feature selection rules is shown in Figure 1.

	Rule	Example
Copula Conversion	is/* → */COP	be/VB → be/COP
Negation Conversion	not/* → /NEG	not/RB → /NEG
Noun Generalization	*/NN → /NN	food/NN → /NN
POS Tossing	*/CC → ∅	nor/CC → ∅

Figure 1. Abbreviated feature selection rule specification.

POS feature selection rules are not designed to reduce the effects of conflicting polarity, but to reduce the effect of lack of polarity. The effects of conflicting polarity have instead been addressed by careful preparation of the training data, as will be seen in the following section.

6. Experiments

For evaluation of their effects, feature selection rules were applied to a POS tagged corpus of movie reviews prior to training and classification. The experimental settings and results are given below.

6.1 Settings

The system and data used are as follows:

- Part-of-speech tagger: Brill (1995).
- WordNet: version 1.7.13 (Fellbaum, 1998).
- Data: Cornell Movie Reviews (Pang et al., 2002).

Movie reviews were used for training and evaluation of each probabilistic classifier. The decision to use only movie reviews for training and test data was based on the fact that OvOPI of movie reviews is particularly challenging as shown by Turney (2002), and therefore can be considered a good environment for testing any system designed for OvOPI. The other reason for using movie reviews is the availability of large bodies of free data on the web. Specifically we used the data available through Cornell University from the Internet Movie Database.

The Cornell data consists of 27,000 movie reviews in HTML form, using 35 different rating scales such as A to F or 1 to 10 in addition to the common 5 star system. We divided them into two classes (positive and negative) and took 100 reviews from each class as the test set. For training sets, we first identified the reviews most likely to be positive or negative. For instance, when reviews contained letter grade ratings, only the A and F reviews were selected. This was done in an attempt to minimize the effects of conflicting polarities and to maximize the likelihood that our positive and negative labels would match those that the authors would have assigned to the reviews. From these reviews, we took random samples from each class in set sizes ranging from 50 to 750 reviews (in increments of 50). These sets consisted of the reviews that remained after the test sets had been removed. This resulted in training set sizes of 100 to 1500 in increments of 100. HTML documents were converted to plain text, tagged using the Brill Tagger, and fed into feature selection modules and classifiers. The particular combinations of feature selection rules and classifiers and their results are described in the following sections.

The fact that as a training set we used data labelled by a reader and not directly by the writer poses a potential problem. We are learning a function that has to mimic the label identified by the writer, but we are using data labelled by the reader. We assume that this is an acceptable approximation because there is a strong practical relation between the label identified by the original writer and the reader. The authors themselves may not have made the polarity classifications, but we assume that language is an efficient form of communication. As such, variances between author and reader classification should be minimal.

6.2 Naïve Bayes

According to linguistic research, adjectives alone are good indicators of subjective expressions (Wiebe, 2000). Therefore, determining opinion polarity by analyzing occurrences of individual adjectives in a text should be an effective method. To identify the opinion polarity of movie reviews, a Naïve Bayes classifier using adjectives is a promising model. The effectiveness of adjectives compared to other parts of speech is evaluated by applying and comparing the results on data with only adjectives against data with all parts of speech. The impact of at-level generalization from adjectives to synsets, or "Sets of Synonyms" (section 7) is also measured. The Naïve Bayes classifier described above was applied to:

1. Tagged data.
2. Data containing only the adjectives.
3. Data containing only the synsets of the adjectives.

The adjectives in 3 were generalized to at-level synsets using a combination of the POS feature selection module and the feature generalization module. In Table 1 some of the most important POS tags used in this paper.

Tag	Description	Example
CC	Coordin. Conjunction	and, but, or
JJ	Adjective	Yellow
JJR	Adj., comparative	Bigger
JJS	Adj., superlative	Wildest
NN	Noun, sing. or mass	Llama
NNS	Noun, plural	Llamas
NNP	Proper noun, singular	IBM
NNPS	Proper noun, plural	Carolinas
RB	Adverb	quickly, never
RBR	Adverb, comparative	Faster
RBS	Adverb, superlative	Fastest
VB	Verb, base form	Eat
VBG	Verb, gerund	Eating
VBN	Verb, past participle	Eaten
VBZ	Verb, 3sg pres	Eats

Table 1. Some of the most important Penn Treebank part-of-speech tags (Jurafsky, et. al., 2000).

For each training data set, add-one smoothing (commonly known as Laplace smoothing) was applied to the Naïve Bayes classifier. Table 2 shows the resulting precisions of each data set type and size. The All-POS column describes the results when training and classifying on POS tagged data. The column tagged as JJ contains the results obtained after stripping away all words not tagged as adjectives, while the results listed in the JJ+WN column were generated after further generalization of all adjectives to their respective WordNet synsets.

Size	All-POS	JJ	JJ+WN
100	0.615	0.640	0.650
200	0.740	0.670	0.665
300	0.745	0.700	0.690
400	0.740	0.700	0.730
500	0.740	0.705	0.705
600	0.760	0.710	0.670
700	0.775	0.715	0.710
800	0.765	0.715	0.700
900	0.785	0.725	0.710
1000	0.765	0.755	0.720
1100	0.785	0.750	0.760
1200	0.765	0.735	0.750
1300	0.775	0.730	0.710
1400	0.775	0.735	0.745
1500	0.795	0.730	0.735

Table 2. Precisions of Naïve Bayes classifier trained on the results of different feature selections.

The results indicate that at-level generalization of adjectives is not effective and that extracting only adjectives degrades the classifier. However, this does not imply that feature selection does not work. Adjectives constitute 7.5% of the text in the data. The precision achieved on such a small portion of the data indicates that a significant portion of the opinion polarity information is carried in the adjectives alone. Although the resulting precisions are better in all-POS data, adjectives can still be considered good clues to opinion polarity.

6.3 Markov Model

Three types of data are applied to the Markov Model classifiers:

1.   Tagged data without feature selection.
2.   Tagged data with POS feature selection.
3.   Tagged data with both POS feature selection and feature generalization.

Witten-Bell (Jurafsky et al., 2000) smoothing is applied to these classifiers.

6.3.1 POS Feature Selection

One design principle of the feature selection rules is that they filter out parts of speech that should not contribute to the opinion polarity, and keep the parts of speech that do contribute such meaning. Based on analysis of movie review texts, we devised feature selection rules that take POS-tagged text as input and return less noisy, more concentrated sentences that have combinations of words and word/POS tag pairs removed from the originals. Table 3 is a summary of the feature selection rules defined in this experiment.

A new Part of Speech, "COP", was introduced to capture special verbs – is, was, am, are, were, be, been, like, liked, dislike, disliked, hate, hated, seem and seemed – which are here considered particularly relevant for capturing opinion polarities.

Parts of Speech	Rule 1	Rule 2	Rule 3	Rule 4	Rule 5
JJ/JJR/JJS	Keep	Keep	Keep	Keep	Keep
RB/RBS (without "not")	Drop	Keep	Keep	Keep	Keep
RBR (without "not")	Drop	Keep	Keep	Keep	Drop
VBG	Keep	Keep	Keep	Keep	Drop
NN/NNS (generalized to NN)	Gener.	Gener.	Gener.	Gener.	Gener.
NNP/NNPS (generalized to NNP)	Gener.	Gener.	Gener.	Gener.	Gener.
VBZ	Drop	Drop	Keep	Keep	Drop
CC	Drop	Drop	Drop	Keep	Keep
COP	Keep	Keep	Keep	Keep	Keep

Table 3. Summary of POS feature selection rules – "Gener." stands for "Generalize".

Wiebe et al., as well as other researchers, have shown that subjectivity is especially concentrated in adjectives (Wiebe et al., 1999; Hatzivassiloglou, 2000; Turney et al., 2003). Therefore, no adjectives or their tags were removed, nor were copula verbs or negative markers. However, noisy information, such as determiners, foreign words, prepositions, modal verbs, possessives, particles, interjections, etc., were removed from the text stream. Other parts of speech, such as nouns and verbs, were removed, but their POS-tags were retained.

The output returned from the feature selection module did not keep the original sentence structure. The concrete POS feature selection rules applied in this experiment are shown in Table 3. The following is an example of sentence preprocessing:

- "All Steve Martin fans should be impressed with this wonderful new comedy."
- /NNP /NNP /NN be/COP /VBN wonderful/JJ new/JJ /NN.

The resulting precisions for POS feature selection rules and different sizes of data sets are listed in Table 4.

Size	Rule 1	Rule 2	Rule 3	Rule 4	Rule 5	All-POS
100	0.555	0.625	0.625	0.630	0.630	0.575
300	0.660	0.635	0.655	0.655	0.655	0.675
500	0.640	0.665	0.665	0.680	0.680	0.720
700	0.705	0.700	0.700	0.690	0.690	0.735
900	0.700	0.740	0.740	0.765	0.765	0.760
1100	0.750	0.745	0.745	0.715	0.715	0.775
1300	0.715	0.695	0.695	0.705	0.705	0.805
1500	0.725	0.730	0.730	0.750	0.750	0.770

Table 4. Precisions on POS feature selection.

7. Synonymy and Hypernymy Feature Generalization

In non-technical written text repetition of identical words is not common, and is generally considered "bad style". As such, many authors attempt to use synonyms for words whose meanings they need often, propositions, and even generalizations. We attempted to address two of these perceived issues by identification of words with a set of likely synonyms, and by hypernymy generalization. For the implementation of these techniques, we took advantage of the WordNet system (Fellbaum, 1998), which provides the former by means of synsets for four separate classes of words (verbs, nouns, adjectives and adverbs), and the latter through hypernymy relations between synsets of the same class.

7.1 Synonyms

WordNet maps each of the words it supports into a synset, which is an abstract entity encompassing all words with a "reasonably" similar meaning. In the case of ambiguous words, multiple synsets may exist for a word; in these instances, we picked the first one. Note that synonyms (and general WordNet processing) are available only in instances where the word under consideration falls into one of the four classes of words outlined above. We determined the appropriate category for each word by using the assigned tag, and did not consider words which fell outside the classes supported by WordNet.

7.2 Hypernyms

For verbs and nouns WordNet provides a hypernymy relation which can be informally described as follows. If s_1 and s_2 are synsets, then s_1 is hypernym of s_2, notation $s_1 \vee s_2$, if and only if anything that can be described by a word in s_2 can also be described by a word in s_1, where $s_1 \gamma s_2$. For each of the hypernym categories, we determine a set of abstract synsets A such that, for any $a \chi A$, there does not exist any s such that $s \vee a$. We say that a synset h is a *level n hypernym* of a synset s if and only if $h \vee^* s$ and one of the following holds for some $a \chi A$:

1. $a \vee^n h$

2. $s = h$ and $a \vee^l s$, with $l < n$

For example, given the WordNet database, a generalization to a level 4 hypernym for the nouns "movie" and "performance" will generalize both of them to one common synset which can be characterized by the word "communication".

7.3 Analysis

In order to determine the effects of translating words to synsets and performing hypernym generalization on them, we ran a series of tests which quickly determined that the effects of pure synset translation were negligible. We thus experimented with the computation of level n hypernyms with $n \chi \{0,\ldots,10\}$, separately for nouns and verbs.

As we can see from Figure 2, applying hypernym generalization to information gathered from large data sets yielded little improvement; instead, we observed a decline in the quality of our classification caused by the loss of information.

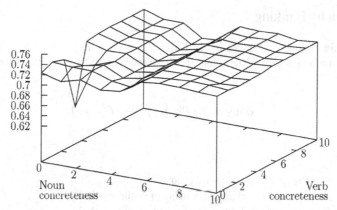

Figure 2. Hypernym generalization with 1500 reviews from each class.

The x and y axes describe the level of hypernym generalization for nouns and verbs, z the precision achieved. Maximum concreteness is reached at level 10, which indicates practically no generalization.

We assume that for larger data sets bigram classification is already able to make use of the more fine-grained data present. Shrinking the size of our training data, however, increased the impact of Wordnet simplification; for very small data sets (50 reviews and less) we observed an improvement of 2.5% (absolute) in comparison to both full generalization and no generalization. Increasing the size of the set of observable events by using trigram models resulted in a small gain (around 1%). The effect of verb generalization was relatively small in comparison to noun generalization for similar levels of hypernymy.

7.4 Discussion

Our results indicate that, except for very small data sets, the use of Word-Net hypernym generalization is not significantly beneficial to the classification process. We conjecture that the following reasons could explain such a phenomenon:

- WordNet is too general for our purposes. It considers many meanings and hypernymy relations which are rarely relevant to the field of Movie Reviews, but which potentially take precedence over other relations which might be more appropriate to our task.
- Choosing the first synset out of the set of choices is unlikely to yield the correct result, given the lack of WordNet specialization in our domain of focus.
- For reasonably large data sets supervised learning mechanisms gain sufficient confidence with related words to make this particular auxiliary technique less useful.

In light of these reasons, the use of a domain-specific database might improve the performance of this technique.

8. Selection by Ranking

The probabilistic models computed by the Naïve Bayes classifiers were sorted by log posterior odds on positive and negative orientations for the purpose of ranking, i.e. by a score computed as follows:

$$score = \log P(+|rv) - \log P(-|rv)$$

where:

- rv is the review under consideration.
- $P(+|rv)$ is the probability of rv being of positive polarity.
- $P(-|rv)$ is the probability of rv being of negative polarity.

We modified the classifier so that it:

1. sorts the reviews in the test data by log posterior odds,

2. returns the first N reviews from the sorted list as positive reviews,

3. returns the last N reviews from the sorted list as negative reviews.

The resulting precisions and recalls on different N are summarized in Table 5.

N	Precision	Recall
10	1.00	0.10
30	0.90	0.27
50	0.88	0.44
70	0.83	0.58
90	0.78	0.68

Table 5. Precisions and Recalls by Number of Inputs.

The classifier was trained on the same 1500-review data set and was used with ranking on a repository of 200 reviews which were identical to the test data set. The result is very positive and indicates that adjectives provide enough sentiment to detect extremely positive or negative reviews with good precision. While the number of reviews returned is specified in this particular example, it is also possible to use assurance as the cut-off criterion by giving log posterior odds.

This idea has already been applied in information retrieval tasks. Zhai et al. (1999) refer to it as *adaptive filtering* and identify two basic problems: *threshold setting*, which assigns initial threshold values, and *threshold updating*, which updates these thresholds based on feedback. Shanahan et al. (2003) apply Zhai's beta-gamma algorithm to SVM classification in order to improve recall.

9. Discussion

Taking all results into consideration, both the Naïve Bayes classifier and Bigram Markov Model classifier performed best when trained on sufficiently large data sets without feature selection. For both Bigram and Trigram Markov Models, we observed a noticeable improvement with our feature generalization when training on very small data sets; for trigram models, this improvement even extended to fairly large data sets (1500 reviews).

One explanation for this result is that the feature selection and generalization are unable to make use of the more fine-grained information provided to them. A likely reason for this is that the ratio between the size of the set of observable events and the size of the training data set is comparatively large in both cases. However, further research and testing will be required in order to establish a more concrete understanding of the usefulness of this technique. The learning curve of classifiers with the POS features selection and/or the feature generalization climbs at higher rates than those without, and results in lower precision with larger data sets. One possible explanation of the higher climbing rates is that the POS feature selection and the feature generalization compact the possible events in language models while respecting the underlying model by reducing the size of the vocabulary. This also explains why the plateau effect is observed with data sets of smaller size. The degraded results with feature selection and generalization also indicate that when information is removed from training and test data, the compacted language model loses resolution.

10. Conclusion

In a supervised machine learning framework a two-phased classification mechanism is introduced and implemented with a POS feature selection, a feature generalization, a Naïve Bayes classifier and a Markov Model classifier. Precisions of combinations of feature selection and generalization and classifiers are evaluated by experiments. Although the results from classifications without feature selection and generalization are generally better than the results from those with, the POS feature selection and feature generalization still have potential to improve overall opinion-polarity identification. Feature generalization using synonymy and hypernymy shows good precision for small data sets and warrants further research. Using the Naïve Bayes classifier with ranking on adjectives has confirmed that high precision can be achieved by dropping recalls. For the task of finding reviews of strong positive or negative polarity within a given data set, very high precision was observed for adequate recall.

11. Acknowledgements

The authors would like to thank Tomohiro Oda for his extensive help and support during the course of all stages of the project. We also wish to acknowledge Larry D. Blair, Francis I. Donahue, Assad Jarrahian, Helen Johnson, James H. Martin, Jim Glasscock, Jeff Rueppel and Philipp Wetzler for their valuable contributions.

12. Bibliography

Brill, E. (1995) *Transformation-Based Error-Driven Learning and Natural Language Processing: A Case Study in Part-of-Speech Tagging.* Computational Linguistics, 21(4):543-565.

Duda, R. O. and Hart, P. E. (1973) *Pattern Classification and Scene Anaylsis.* A Wiley Interscience Publication, New York.

Fellbaum, C. (1998) *Wordnet: An Electronic Lexical Database.* The MIT Press.

Hatzivassiloglou, V. and McKeown, K. R. (1997) *Predicting the Semantic Orientation of Adjectives*. In Cohen, P. R. and Wahlster. W. (Ed.) *Proceedings of the Thirty-Fifth Annual Meeting of the Association for Computational Linguistics and Eighth Conference of the European Chapter of the Association for Computational Linguistics*. 174-181. Association for Computational Linguistics.

Hatzivassiloglou, V., and Wiebe, J. (2000) *Effects of Adjective Orientation and Gradability on Sentence Subjectivity*. Proceedings of the 18th International Conference in Computational Linguistics.

Jurafsky, D. and Martin, J. H. (2000) *Speech and Language Processing*. Prenctice Hall.

Leeper, M. R. (1995) *Review of Apollo 13*, Usenet rec.arts.movies.reviews.

Losee, R. M. (2001) *Natural Language Processing in Support of Decision-making: Phrases and Part-of-Speech Tagging*. Information Processing and Management, 37(6):769-787.

Marcus, M. P., Santorini, B. and Marcinkiewicz, M. A. (1994) *Building a Large Annotated Corpus of English: The Penn Treebank*. Computational Linguistics, 19(2):313-330.

Pang, B., Lee, L. and Vaithyanathan, S. (2002) *Thumbs up? Sentiment Classification using Machine Learning Techniques*. Proceedings of the 2002 Conference on Empirical Methods in Natural Language Processing (EMNLP).

Shanahan, J. G., Roma, N. (2003) *Improving SVM Text Classification Performance through Threshold Adjustment*. European Conference on Machine Learning (ECML) 2003, 361-372.

Turney, P. (2002) *Thumbs up or Thumbs down? Semantic Orientation applied to Unsupervised Classification of Reviews*. Proceedings of the 40th Annual Meeting of the Association for Computational Linguistics (ACL02), 417-424.

Turney, P. and Littman, M. (2003) *Measuring Praise and Criticism: Inference of Semantic Orientation from Association*. ACM Transactions on Information Systems (TOIS), 21(4):315-346.

Wiebe, J., Bruce, R. F. and O'Hara, T. (1999) *Development and Use of a Gold-Standard Data Set for Subjectivity Classifications*. Proceedings of the 37th Annual Meeting of the Association for Computational Linguistics (ACL99), 223-287.

Wiebe, J. (2000) *Learning Subjective Adjectives from Corpora*. Proceedings of the 17th National Conference on Artificial Intelligence and 12th Conference on Innovative Application of Artificial Intelligence, 735-740. AAAI Press / The MIT Press.

Zhai, C., Jansen, P., Stoica, E., Grot, N., Evans, D.A. (1999) *Threshold Calibration in CLARIT Adaptive Filtering*. Seventh Text Retrieval Conference (TREC-7), 149-156.

Chapter 24

Multi-Document Viewpoint Summarization Focused on Facts, Opinion and Knowledge

Yohei Seki
Department of Informatics,
The Graduate University for Advanced Studies (Sokendai) / National Institute of Informatics
National Institute of Informatics, 2-1-2, Hitotsubashi,
Tokyo 101-8430, Japan.
Email: seki@grad.nii.ac.jp

Koji Eguchi and Noriko Kando
National Institute of Informatics / Department of Informatics,
The Graduate University for Advanced Studies (Sokendai)
Email: eguchi@nii.ac.jp, kando@nii.ac.jp

Abstract

An interactive information retrieval system that provides different types of summaries of retrieved documents according to each user's information needs, situation, or purpose of search can be effective for understanding document content. The purpose of this study is to build a multi-document summarizer, *"Viewpoint Summarizer With Interactive clustering on Multi-documents (v-SWIM)"*, which produces summaries according to such viewpoints. We tested its effectiveness on a new test collection, *ViewSumm30*, which contains human-made reference summaries of three different summary types for each of the 30 document sets. Once a set of documents on a topic (e.g., documents retrieved by a search engine) is provided to *v-SWIM*, it returns a list of topics discussed in the given document set, so that the user can select a topic or topics of interest as well as the summary type, such as fact-reporting, opinion-oriented or knowledge-focused, and produces a summary from the viewpoints of the topics and summary type selected by the user. We assume that sentence types and document genres are related to the types of information included in the source documents and are useful for selecting appropriate information for each of the summary types. "Sentence type" defines the type of information in a sentence. "Document genre" defines the type of information in a document. The results of the experiments showed that the proposed system using automatically identified sentence types and document genres of the source documents improved the coverage of the system-produced fact-reporting, opinion-oriented, and knowledge-focused summaries, 13.14%, 34.23%, and 15.89%, respectively, compared with our baseline system which did not differentiate sentence types or document genres.

Keywords: multi-document summarization, viewpoint, opinion, genre classification, sentence type.

1. Introduction

Our goal is to summarize multiple documents using specified viewpoints. We implemented *"Viewpoint Summarizer With Interactive clustering on Multi-documents (v-SWIM)"* to achieve this goal. In this system a topical classification methodology with clustering techniques was applied to identify topics discussed in a set of documents, and then identify the most representative topical words for each cluster. For the summary type, we used "fact-reporting", "opinion-oriented", or "knowledge-focused" summaries, where the discrimination is based on the types of information that the user requires.

Text summarization is a reduction process of mostly textual information to its most essential points. Mani (2001) stated that multiple-document summarization (MDS) was the extension of single-document summarization toward collections of related documents, and the goal of MDS was to present the most important content to the user in a condensed form and in a manner sensitive to the user's needs. In this chapter, we define summarization as an interactive process to present information according to each user's information needs.

These needs may be different for each user. Human-made reference summaries tend to differ among summary writers (Rath et al., 1961; Lin and Hovy, 2002; Harman and Over, 2004). This is a result of the differences in viewpoints of users when accessing information, because summary writers assume ideal users would read their summaries. "Viewpoint" is defined as *"a mental position or attitude from which subjects or questions are considered."* (Simpson and Weiner, 1991) Query-biased Summarization (SUMMAC, 1998) has been proposed as a method for generating summaries by focusing on the topics related to a query in the context of information retrieval. This is one aspect of summary viewpoints, because topics related to queries could give a mental position from which document sets are considered. Viewpoints, however, relate not only to the topics that the summary reader is focusing on but can also be extended to include other aspects such as the type of information. In the Document Understanding Conference (DUC) 2003, viewpoint summary was tested as one of the tasks, and viewpoint statements about each topic were given to participants to produce summaries. The viewpoints were not explicitly defined but these viewpoint statements included subjective descriptions such as "authority response" or "causal relation of flood". Angheluta et al. (2003) tried viewpoint summarization with topic segmentation, but its effectiveness was not fully investigated.

The purpose of this study is to build a multi-document summarizer that produces summaries according to viewpoints based on user's information needs. In this paper, "viewpoint" in the summarization is defined as the combination of "topic" and "summary type", such as "fact-reporting", "opinion-oriented", or "knowledge-focused".

The distinction of topics and information types can be found in *question taxonomies* (Pomerantz, 2002), which discriminates between subjects (main topics) of questions and functions of expected answers, or in *relevance dimensions*, as topical and situational relevance (Borlund, 2003). The above mentioned summary types are also related to Pomerantz (2002, p.70), which surveyed question types for long answers, e.g., definition, example, comparison, and causal antecedent:

1. Fact-reporting summary: event example, causal antecedent or consequence, object or resource
2. Opinion-oriented summary: expectation, judgment, motivation, goal orientation
3. Knowledge-focused summary: definition, comparison, interpretation, assertion

The second summary type, opinion-focused summarization for multi-perspective question-answering (Cardie et al., 2003), has attracted much interest. For the third summary type, an extraction-based approach for definitional questions has been proposed (Xu et al., 2004). This research focused on information extraction techniques based on surface linguistic features and question profiles. In contrast, we focus on information types and explicitly use sentence type and document genre information.

To produce summaries from multiple documents according to the point-of-view, we investigated the advantage of using document genre information. "Document genre" here means document type such as "personal diary" or "report", and is defined as a recognizable form of communization in a social activity (Bazerman, 2004). Document genre is also defined as "an abstraction based on a natural grouping of documents written in a similar style and is orthogonal to topic," as in (Finn et al., 2002). In this chapter, we use "document genre" as a concept that defines the information type described in a document. Researchers in summarization have focused on factual information and topics, but users might require subjective information such as opinions, evaluations, and prospects that are mentioned in the source documents. In this paper, we described the "genre feature" of each document by a combination of four dimensions based on Biber's multi-dimensional register analysis (Biber, 2002).

Spärck-Jones (1999) proposed a model of summary factors which are formulated as input factors, purpose factors, and output factors[1]. This chapter focuses on the associations between the purpose factors such as "user's situation in which the summary is used" or "user's intention in information", "the form of the source" as an input factor, and "the expression of the summary" as an output factor. Such association between a user's intention in retrieving information and output summary has not yet been surveyed or proposed clearly.

This chapter consists of six sections. In the next section, our experiment overview comparing several types of multi-document summaries is described. Then, our methods of sentence-type annotation and automatic genre classification are detailed in Sections 3 and 4. The experimental results then follow. Finally, we present our conclusions.

2. Experiment Overview: Multi-Document Viewpoint Summarization with Summary Types

To clarify viewpoints that are represented as combinations of topics and summary types, we investigated the effectiveness of using "information type" to discriminate summary types based on information needs for multi-document summarization. In this research, two kinds of information

---

[1] http://duc.nist.gov/RM0507/ksj/factors

types are defined: sentence type and document genre (text type). They are detailed in Sections 3 and 4. In this section, the experiment overview is described.

2.1 Experiment: Summary Types for Multi-Document Summarization

We suppose that users recognize information type from their own viewpoint for multi-document summarization. In order to test this hypothesis, we constructed a summary test collection called *ViewSumm30* and tested the effectiveness of the proposed summarization algorithm which differentiated summary types. The human-made reference summaries in *ViewSumm30* were produced with explicit instructions for summary writers to focus on each of the three summary types: fact-reporting, opinion-oriented, and knowledge-focused. This process is detailed in Section 2.2. On this test collection, we tested our baseline multi-document summarization algorithm without differentiating summary types, as well as our proposed algorithm with differentiating summary types using sentence-type annotation and genre classification of the source documents. For the three summary types, we changed the weighting parameters to extract sentences with genre features and sentence-type. Then, coverage and precision for human-made reference summaries was computed. "Coverage" and "precision" are proposed by (Hirao et al., 2004) as metrics to evaluate effectiveness of sentence extraction against reference summaries and were used in the NTCIR-4[2] Text Summarization Challenge (Kando, 2004; Hirao et al., 2004). Finally, the genre dimensions and sentence types effective for MDS of each of the summary types were discussed. The results are detailed in Section 5.

2.2 Summary Data with Three Summary types

In this experiment, the authors made a summary test collection, *ViewSumm30*. Like the test collections used in DUC[3] or the NTCIR Text Summarization Challenge (TSC), it consists of a set of document sets with particular topics and a set of human-made reference summaries for each of the document sets. As shown in Table 1, we selected 30 topics and retrieved Mainichi and Yomiuri newspaper articles published in 1998–1999 using an information retrieval system. Then, we manually selected 6–12 documents from the 60 top ranked retrieved documents, and composed 30 document sets. The topics resemble the queries input by the users of the information retrieval systems and the set of documents for each topic can be thought of as a set of retrieved documents for the query. Then human-made reference summaries were created discriminating the three summary types: fact-reporting summaries, opinion-oriented summaries and knowledge-focused summaries. Such differentiation was not included in any existing summary test collections such as those used in DUC or NTCIR. Three different types of reference summaries for a document set were created by the same professional editors. A reference summary was created for each summary type for a document set. In total, three professional editors were used as summary writers. Instructions for the summary writers as to which summary types to produce were given as follows:

1. Fact-reporting summary: Summaries focused on events, which happened in real time or in past times; that is, the summaries for users who want to know facts or to check back for events related to topics.

---

[2] http://research.nii.ac.jp/ntcir

[3] http://duc.nist.gov

2. Opinion-oriented summary: Summaries focused on the authors' opinions or experts' opinions by third parties; that is, the summaries for users who want advice, prospects, or evaluations related to topics.

3. Knowledge-focused summary: Summaries focused on definitional or encyclopedic knowledge; that is, the summaries for users who are interested in descriptive knowledge related to topics.

ID	Topic	Source Articles	
		# of Articles	# of Bytes
S010	European monetary union	10	41060
S020	Annual pension	10	43408
S030	Accounting fraud	9	42414
S040	Itoman fraud case	10	41294
S050	Removal of deposit insurance	11	38502
S060	Digital cellular phone	11	40706
S070	Guidelines for Japan-U.S. defense cooperation	9	41374
S080	Kosovo	11	41166
S090	Strategic arms reduction	8	30998
S100	Brain-death diagnosis	7	42104
S110	Juvenile proceedings	11	41934
S120	Freedom of Information Act	8	33906
S130	Donor card	10	31804
S140	Defined contribution pension plan	12	38262
S150	Genetically-engineered foods	12	40450
S160	Organized Crime Control Act	8	42850
S170	Criticality-caused nuclear accident	7	33870
S180	Financial Big Bang	8	38822
S190	Pluthermal	9	38184
S200	Theater Missile Defenses	8	34646
S210	Government-owned company in China	6	27058
S220	Conflict of Nothern Ireland	10	28482
S230	Russian economic and financial crises	7	31362
S240	Taepodong missile	8	40260
S250	International Convenants on Human Rights	7	41904
S260	Impeachment case	8	38340
S270	Sunshine Policy	7	33884
S280	Endocrine-disrupting Chemicals	10	36736
S290	International Space Station	8	30242
S300	Convention concering the Protection of the World Cultural and Natural Heritage	7	33624
	Max	12.0	43408.0
	Min	6.0	27058.0
	Average	8.9	37321.5
	Standard Deviation	1.6	4661.7

Table 1. Topics of the document sets in the ViewSumm30 test collection for multi-viewpoint document summarization.

The maximum length of the reference summaries was 1600 bytes. For some document sets, subtopics on which summaries focused were specified by summary writers.

2.3 Baseline Summarization Algorithm

The baseline is a multi-document summarizer using paragraph-based clustering with Ward's Method but without considering summary types. It was tested in the NTCIR-4 TSC and worked well among other participants. The goal of multi-document summarization (MDS) is usually defined as extracting content from a given set of related documents and presenting the most important content. The baseline system could extract important content sensitive to the user's needs by specifying subtopics in document sets.

Many clustering-based multi-document summarization frameworks (Stein et al., 2000; Hatzivassiloglou et al., 2001; Maña-López et al., 2004; Radev et al., 2004) have been proposed. Their research focused on making the topic structure explicit. By detecting similarities in topic structure, such systems could avoid redundant information in summaries. These methods have four principal aspects: (1) clustering algorithms, (2) cluster units, (3) sentence extraction strategy, and (4) cluster size.

For the clustering algorithm, we used Ward's after testing the clustering using complete link, group average, or Ward's method on the same document collection. For cluster unit, we used paragraphs rather than sentences. It was for the following reasons: (1) it allowed real-time interactivity, and (2) because of the sparseness of vector spaces when using sentence vectors. In addition, we did not cluster source documents by document units because source document counts (from 6 to 12 documents) were too small compared to summary sizes.

An algorithm is detailed below. The evaluation results in NTCIR-4 TSC3 using this algorithm are described in more detail in (Seki et al., 2004a).

[1] Paragraph Clustering Stage

    a)   Source documents were segmented to paragraphs, and then term frequencies were indexed for each paragraph.

    b)   Paragraphs were clustered based on Euclidean distance between feature vectors with term-frequency. The clustering algorithm was Ward's method. Cluster sizes varied according to the number of extracted sentences.

[2] Sentence Extraction Stage

    a)   The feature vectors for each cluster were computed with term frequencies and inverse cluster frequencies: TF * log (Total Clusters / Cluster Frequency).

    b)   *If* questions or subtopics focusing on a summary were given, clusters were ordered by the similarity between content words in the questions and the cluster feature vectors. Questions were used for expressing information needs for the original documents to produce summaries.

    c)   *Else* we computed the total term frequencies of all documents and ordered clusters based on similarities between total TF and cluster feature vectors.

    d)   *End*

    e)   Sentences in each cluster were weighted based on question words, heading words in the cluster, and TF values in the cluster.

    f)   One or two sentences were extracted from each cluster in cluster order to reach the maximum allowed number of characters or sentences.

In Chapter 5, this algorithm was compared to the extended algorithm with sentence-type annotation (Chapter 3) and genre classification (Chapter 4).

3. Sentence-type Annotation

In this section, sentence types, which represent information type effectively for finer-grained units than documents, are detailed. This information, along with document genres, which are elaborated in Section 4, is used to discriminate summary types in the proposed system.

3.1 Sentence Types for News Articles

Sentence types (Seki et al., 2004b; McKnight and Srinivasan, 2003; Teufel and Moens, 2002) were broadly used to discriminate information type with text structure. Kando (1996) has defined five sentence types for newspaper articles: *main description, elaboration, background, opinion,* and *prospect*. The intercoder consistency for these five sentence types was proved by experiments (Kando, 1996). The meanings of the five sentence types are as follows:

1. "Main description": the main contents in a document.
2. "Elaboration": the "main description" is detailed.
3. "Background": history or background is described.
4. "Opinion": author's opinion.
5. "Prospect": likely developments in the future are expressed.

In this experiment, a sixth type, "authority's opinion", was added to the above mentioned five sentence types, and then these six were used to discriminate the summary types.

6. "Authority's opinion": opinion reported by third parties such as experts, authorities, and so on.

3.2 Automatic Sentence-type Annotation

3.2.1 Manual annotation for training data

The training set consisted of 352 articles (5201 sentences total) from the 1994 Nikkei newspaper. All the sentences in the training set were annotated manually with sentence types. The number of sentences for each type was as follows: main description (1052), elaboration (3003), background (585), author's opinion (483), authority's opinion (391), and prospect (506).

3.2.2 Automatic sentence-type annotation with SVM

An automatic sentence type annotation was implemented using SVM. According to Joachims (2002), SVM is fairly robust to overfitting and can scale up to considerable dimensionalities. The feature set for automatic annotation was as follows:

1. Sentence position in document or paragraph
2. Paragraph position
3. Sentence length
4. The number of heading words in the sentence
5. The number of words with high TF/IDF value in the sentence
6. Voice, tense and modality information judged by auxiliary verb

7.   Eight kinds of named entity frequencies extracted with parsers[4]
8.   20–40 kinds of semantic primitives for predicates and subjects extracted using the thesaurus published by The National Institute for Japanese Language (2004)
9.   30–40 kinds of keyword frequencies for background, author's and authority's opinion, and prospect types
10.   Sentence type for pre-position sentences and post-position sentences

This classification technique was evaluated for three measures: *precision, recall,* and *accuracy* (Joachims, 2002; Sebastiani, 2002). *Precision* and *recall* are of widespread use in information retrieval. In Table 2, a convenient display of the prediction behavior is provided. We define *precision, recall* and *accuracy* based on this table. The diagonal cells count how often the prediction was correct. The off-diagonal cells show the frequency of prediction errors. The sum of all cells equals the total number of predictions.

- *Precision*: $f_{++} / (f_{++} + f_{+-})$
- *Recall*: $f_{++} / (f_{++} + f_{-+})$
- *Accuracy*: $(f_{++} + f_{--}) / (f_{++} + f_{--} + f_{-+} + f_{+-})$

	label = +1	label = -1
prediction = +1	f_{++}	f_{+-}
prediction = -1	f_{-+}	f_{--}

Table 2. Contingency table for accuracy, precision, and recall (Joachims, 2002).

In addition, we use *macro-averaging* and *micro-averaging* when averaging the precision, recall and accuracy, respectively, over the four-fold cross-validations that will be described below. *Macro-averaging* corresponds to the standard way of computing an (arithmetic) average, while *micro-averaging* averages each frequencies in Table 2 and computes the precision, recall, and accuracy.

Four-fold cross-validation was applied to 352 newspaper articles. Cross-validation was processed in the following steps. First, the 352 articles were divided into four groups by publishing dates. From the four training sample groups, the first group was removed. The resulting sample groups were used for training, leading to a classification rule. This classification rule was tested on the removed sample group. This process was repeated for all training sample groups. These results are summarized in Tables 3. They showed good accuracy, so we used this set as training data and the feature set for automatic annotation of sentence types in the summary test collections. Of the 11926 sentences in the summary test collections, 797 were annotated as main description, 1871 as elaboration, 189 as background, 1506 as authors' opinion, 1179 as authority's opinion, and 190 as prospects.

---

[4] http://chasen.org/~taku/software/cabocha

	Main Description (M)			Elaboration (E)			Background (B)		
	Accuracy	Precision	Recall	Accuracy	Precision	Recall	Accuracy	Precision	Recall
Group A	97.02	89.00	96.49	85.45	83.65	91.87	92.90	75.00	60.00
Group B	97.40	90.97	98.60	86.99	89.29	88.80	93.98	78.26	57.14
Group C	95.78	89.83	90.05	84.72	86.06	89.64	94.68	64.57	58.99
Group D	96.72	86.17	98.20	85.29	82.67	91.65	90.59	81.17	60.10
Macro Avg.	96.73	88.99	95.84	85.62	85.42	90.49	93.04	74.75	59.06
Micro Avg.	96.54	88.93	94.68	85.33	85.00	90.58	93.16	74.52	59.49

Table 3 (a). Results of 4-fold cross validation test of automatic sentence-type annotation on main description, elaboration, and background-type.

	Authors' Opinion (O1)			Authority's Opinion (O2)			Prospect (P)		
	Accuracy	Precision	Recall	Accuracy	Precision	Recall	Accuracy	Precision	Recall
Group A	91.61	69.51	60.64	95.13	64.20	54.74	91.00	78.95	39.89
Group B	96.91	82.61	55.88	94.96	83.33	49.02	93.98	62.50	44.44
Group C	93.01	73.29	52.97	92.70	63.64	50.84	93.90	66.82	75.00
Group D	96.39	63.79	62.71	96.89	71.01	74.24	94.37	71.43	35.29
Macro Avg.	94.48	72.30	58.05	94.92	70.55	57.21	93.31	69.93	48.66
Micro Avg.	93.85	70.84	57.35	94.62	67.18	55.50	93.19	70.00	52.57

Table 3 (b). Results of 4-fold cross validation test of automatic sentence-type annotation on authors' opinion, authority's opinion, and prospect-type.

4. Genre Classification

In this section, document genres, which represent document-level information types, are detailed. This information and the sentence types described in the previous section were used to determine summary types in the proposed system.

4.1 Genre Feature

To begin with, genre taxonomies for news articles were surveyed. International Press Telecommunications Council (here after, IPTC) defined a set of document genres[5] for news delivery. These, however, number more than 40 and are based on several different classification criteria, such as categories from "opinion" and "background" down to resource-type information, such as "music" and "raw sound", or type of news source, such as "press release". This framework is not appropriate for discriminating among document genres for the summary type because the categorizing criteria are complex and relate to the different attributes of the documents.

Therefore, in this research, document genres were represented by a combination of the values for each of the multiple dimensions representing different genre features. It is based on Douglas Biber's proposal (Biber, 2002). The merits of using this idea are as follows.

- The effectiveness of each dimension is explicit.
- New genre dimensions can be added easily without changing the entire framework.
- Annotation rules were expected to be simple for each of the dimensions.

---

[5] http://www.iptc.org/download/dliptc.php?fn=topicset/topicset.iptc-genre.xml

The five basic dimensions in Biber's framework were:

1. Elaborated vs Situation-Dependent Reference
2. Overt Expression of Argumentation
3. Impersonal vs Non-Impersonal Style
4. Narrative vs Non-Narrative Discourse
5. Involved vs Information Production

Of Biber's dimensions, the fifth could not be discriminated using *ViewSumm30* because all documents were categorized as "information production" in this dimension. We used the remaining four dimensions. The definitions are as following:

1. Situation-Dependency (G1): documents marked according to the degree of coincidence between their publishing time and the event time.
2. Argumentation (G2): documents marked according to the degree of persuasion and the author's point of view.
3. Impersonal Styles (G3): documents marked according to criteria such as frequent passive constructions.
4. Fact-Reporting (G4): documents marked that reported facts in the inverse-pyramid discourse structure of newspaper articles.

In this research, the "genre feature" of each document was described by the combination of these four dimensions.

4.2 Manual Annotation for Genre Feature

To begin with, we tested the inter-coder consistency of genre feature manual annotation. The corpus consists of 208 newspaper articles which are not included in *ViewSumm30*, but published in the same years as those in *ViewSumm30*. Three coders, a1, a2, and a3, annotated each of the 208 documents independently. The annotation instructions were prepared and updated through pretests with all three coders. As shown in Table 4, the kappa coefficient value showed good agreement between coders.

Genre Dimension	Pair of Assessors			Avg.
	(a1,a2)	(a1,a3)	(a2,a3)	
Situation-Dependency (G1)	0.618	0.595	0.665	0.626
Argumentation (G2)	0.41	0.536	0.678	0.541
Impersonal Styles (G3)	0.459	0.506	0.604	0.523
Fact-Reporting (G4)	0.604	0.566	0.657	0.609

Table 4. Kappa coefficients: inter-coder consistency.

These results suggest that manual annotation can be moderately or substantially consistent (Landis et al., 1977).

4.3 Automatic Genre Classification

Similar to the method used for automatic sentence type annotation, we applied SVM to automatic genre classification. In order to examine its effectiveness, we performed 4-fold cross validation using the 208 annotated documents mentioned in subsection 4.2. For automatic genre classification, we selected about 200 structural features as listed below:

- Five structural features: author signature, section, photo, figure, and news source.
- Nine statistical features ('#' is defined as "numbers"): # of characters, Type-to-Token Ratio, # of sentences, # of opinion sentences, # of prospect sentences, # of background sentences, # of conjunctions, # of quote parentheses, and average sentence length.
- Eight kinds of named entity frequencies extracted with parsers[6].
- 60 function phrases (which relate to opinion, prospect, and background information).
- 93 symbols (which include several punctuation-related symbols).
- 20–40 kinds of semantic primitives for predicates and subjects extracted using the thesaurus published by The National Institute for Japanese Language (2004).

It has been claimed that function phrases and punctuation mark counts (Kessler et al., 1997; Stamatatos et al., 2000) are effective for genre classification. Statistical features (Karlgren and Cutting, 1994) are also often used to classify texts in the corpus linguistics field. Function phrases and symbols were selected from the corpus used for sentence-type annotation clues. For 4-fold cross validation, the 208 documents were divided into four groups, each containing 52 documents. We used one group as a test set and the other three groups as training sets, and evaluated the effectiveness four times. The results are shown in Tables 5 below.

	Situation-Dependency (G1)			Argumentation (G2)		
	Accuracy	Precision	Recall	Accuracy	Precision	Recall
Group A	82.69	88.57	86.11	84.62	70.00	58.33
Group B	78.85	85.19	76.67	88.46	72.73	72.73
Group C	84.62	95.83	76.67	92.31	87.50	70.00
Group D	75.00	72.22	89.66	90.38	50.00	80.00
Macro Avg.	80.29	85.45	82.27	88.94	70.06	70.27
Micro Avg.	80.29	84.43	82.40	88.94	70.27	68.42

Table 5 (a). Results of 4-fold cross validation test of automatic genre classification for G1 and G2.

	Impersonal Styles (G3)			Fact-Reporting (G4)		
	Accuracy	Precision	Recall	Accuracy	Precision	Recall
Group A	88.46	93.33	93.33	90.38	93.18	95.35
Group B	78.85	83.33	93.02	92.31	95.35	95.35
Group C	90.38	97.67	91.30	90.38	100.00	89.36
Group D	96.15	95.83	100.00	92.31	95.65	95.65
Macro Avg.	88.46	92.54	94.42	91.35	96.05	93.93
Micro Avg.	88.46	92.39	94.44	91.35	96.00	93.85

Table 5 (b). Results of 4-fold cross validation test of automatic genre classification for G3 and G4.

Table 5 shows that G1, G2, G3, and G4 could be classified properly.

---

[6] http://chasen.org/~taku/software/cabocha

5. Experiment Results

In the experiment, the *v-SWIM* using sentence types and document genres was tested on the test collection *ViewSumm30*, and its effectiveness over the baseline algorithm was evaluated for the *coverage* and *precision* of the human-made reference summaries. The extended algorithm with the genre classification and the sentence-type annotation algorithm were also evaluated. Hirao et al. (2004) defined *precision* as the ratio of how many sentences in the system output are included in the set of sentences that correspond to sentences in the human-made reference summaries. *Coverage* was defined in (Hirao et al., 2004) as an evaluation metric for measuring how close the system output is to the reference summary, taking into account the redundancy found in the set of sentences in the output.

There are two aspects for evaluation. The first aspect is: 1. Genre classification effect, 2. Sentence-type annotation effect, and 3. Combination of both effects. The second aspect is: A. fact-reporting summary, B. opinion-oriented summary, and C. knowledge-focused summary. These effects are described in this section.

5.1 Summarization based on Genre Classification

We first surveyed the *coverage* and *precision* for the extended algorithm with genre feature for baseline sentence extraction, as stated in Section 2.3. Sentences in each article were annotated with genre feature in the article. With this genre information, sentence weights were multiplied by variables ranging from 0 to 4 with 0.1 intervals. For example, when the G1 (G2, G3, or G4) dimension for an article was annotated as positive, sentence weights in the article were multiplied by a variable to extract in the summary. When the dimension was annotated as negative, sentence weights remained unchanged. Then, coverage and precision values for extracting sentences were computed as the variables changed. The results are shown in Figures 1, 2, and 3.

5.1.1 Fact-reporting Summaries

In Figure 1, the coverage changes for multiplying weighting parameters varied from 0 to 4 with 0.1 intervals for genre feature (G1, G2, G3, and G4) are shown. For "sentence weighting = 1" on the *x*-axis, sentence weights with positive genre features were multiplied by one, so the sentence weights to extract were unchanged. The points at this *x*-axis position were common for G1, G2, G3, and G4. They represent the points evaluated for the baseline system without genre feature. The coverage for the baseline system was 0.175. Compared to this value, the coverage values for G3 were higher than the baseline coverage with variables greater than one. This means that **positive values** for the *impersonal styles* (G3) feature had a positive effect when producing a fact-reporting summary. Overall, the genre feature effect was stable for fact reporting summaries. This result shows that the baseline algorithm is well suited to fact-reporting summary production.

5.1.2 Opinion-oriented summaries

For opinion-oriented summaries, the coverage changed drastically according to the weighting parameter using the genre feature. This result is shown in Figure 2. This result was totally different from the result in Figure 1 for the change in slope. The coverage for the baseline system was 0.111. Compared to this value, **negative values** for the *impersonal styles* (G3) and *fact* (G4) feature had positive effects on producing opinion-oriented summaries. This effect was shown more explicitly than the effects of the genre feature for fact-reporting summaries. In contrast,

positive values for the *argumentation* (G2) feature had a positive effect in producing opinion-oriented summaries.

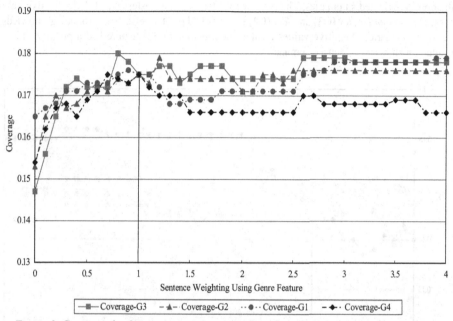

Figure 1. Coverage for fact-reporting summaries based on sentence weighting using genre feature.

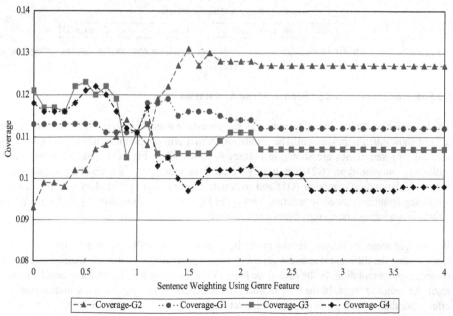

Figure 2. Coverage for opinion-oriented summary based on sentence weighting using genre feature.

5.1.3 Knowledge-focused summaries

The coverage and precision for knowledge-focused summaries did not change as drastically as for the opinion-oriented summaries. The coverage for the baseline system was 0.151. **Positive values** for the *impersonal styles* (G3) and *fact* (G4) features had positive effects in producing knowledge-focused summaries. **Negative values** for the *argumentation* (G2) feature had a positive effect in producing knowledge-focused summaries.

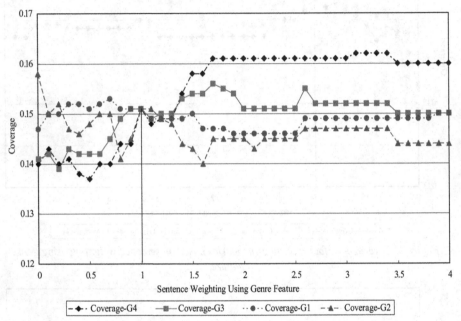

Figure 3. Coverage for knowledge-focused summary based on sentence weighting using genre feature.

5.2 Summarization based on Sentence-type Annotation

The extension of the baseline algorithm with sentence-type annotation across all source documents did not show much improvement. The results for fact-reporting, opinion-oriented, and knowledge-focused type summaries are shown in Figures 4, 5, and 6. In Figure 4, positive values for the *authority's opinion*-type (O2) had positive effects in producing fact-reporting summaries. In Figure 5, the *author's opinion* (O1) and *authority's opinion*-types (O2) had positive effects in producing opinion-oriented summaries. Finally, in Figure 6, the *elaboration*-type (E) had positive effects in producing knowledge-focused summaries.

We thought some ineffective results might be caused by the different distributions of sentence types among the different document genres. Another possibility was the low quality of automatic sentence-type annotation. In the future, we hope to compare this result with the manual annotation result for sentence types. In the next subsection, the experiment results for the sentence-annotation effects peculiar to each genre dimension are detailed.

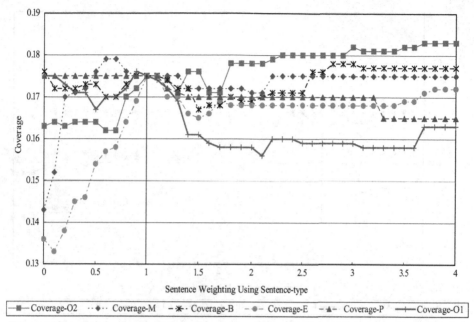

Figure 4. Coverage for fact-reporting summary based on sentence weighting using sentence type.

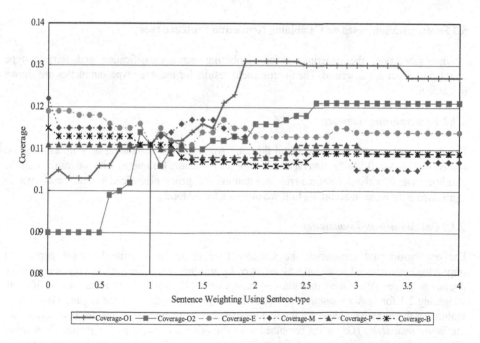

Figure 5. Coverage for opinion-oriented summary based on sentence weighting using sentence type.

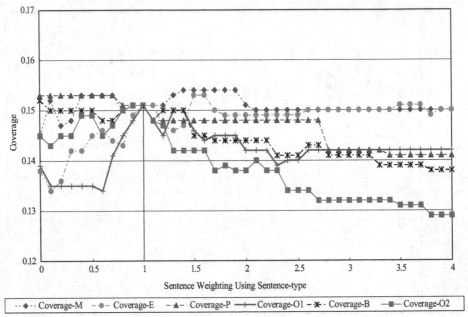

Figure 6. Coverage for knowledge-focused summary based on sentence weighting using sentence type.

5.3 Summarization based on Combining Genre and Sentence-type

In this subsection, the experiments for combining genre classification and sentence-type annotation effect are described. The improvement results for the three type summaries are shown in Table 6.

5.3.1 Fact-reporting summaries

For fact-reporting summaries, we found the improvement from combining only information on sentence types was 0.198 for coverage and 0.189 for precision. Compared with the result from the baseline system without sentence-type annotation and genre classification, this result was a significant improvement according to *Wilcoxon* tests for 30 topics.

5.3.2 Opinion-oriented summaries

For opinion-oriented summaries, the sentence type effect in specific document genres for improving coverage and precision was surveyed by weighting specific sentence-types in specific document genres. We found that the coverage was 0.149 and the precision was 0.136 with weighting 2.3 for *author's opinion*-type (O1) in the **positive values** for the *argumentation* (G2) feature, in the **negative values** for the *fact-reporting* (G4) feature, or in the **negative values** for the *impersonal styles* (G3) when combined with the other sentence-type weightings. This result was a significant improvement according to *Wilcoxon* tests for 30 topics, compared with the result from the baseline system.

Summary Type	Baseline		v-SWIM		Improvement (percent)	Weighting parameter		
	coverage	precision	coverage	precision		Sentence-type	Genre	Weighting
Fact-reporting	0.175	0.166	0.198*	0.189	13.14	Main Description	G4 positive	2
						Elaboration & Background & not Reported Opinion	G3 positive	5
						Background	G1 positive	4
							G3 positive	4
						Reported opinion & not Prospective	All	5
						Author's opinion	All	0.9
						Prospective	All	0
Opinion-oriented	0.111	0.104	0.149*	0.136	34.23	All	G2 positive	1.5
						Author's opinion	G2 positive G3 negative G4 negative	2.3
						Reported opinion	G1 negative	3
						not Author's Opinon & not Reported Opinion	G1 positive	0.4
						Elaboration & not Author's Opinon & not Reported Opinion	G3 positive	0.5
						Main Description & not Author's Opinion & not Reported Opinion	All	0
						Background & not Author's Opinion & not Reported Opinion	All	0
Knowledge-focused	0.151	0.156	0.175	0.170	15.89	Elaboration	G4 positive	3.2
						Author's opinion		3.2
						Elaboration & not Author's Opinion	G1 negative & G4 positive	2.3
						Main Description	All	1.7
						Reported opinion && not Elaboration	G2 negative	0
						Background	All	0
						Prospective	All	0

*: statistically significant with *Wilcoxon* tests: p < 0.05

Table 6. Coverage and precision improvement effect for three type summaries based on sentence weighting in the specific document genre.

5.3.3 Knowledge-focused summaries

For knowledge-focused summaries, the improvement effect of *elaboration*-type sentences was not significant but the improvement can be observed in Figure 6. We surveyed the association between *elaboration*-type (E) and document genre and found the detailed weighting rule that combined with **negative values** for the *author's opinion*-type (O1). This weighting was applied only to **negative values** for the *situation-dependency* (G1) and **positive values** for the *fact-reporting* (G4) features. This result was not a significant improvement according to *Wicoxon* tests for 30 topics, compared with the result from the baseline system.

6. Conclusion

In this chapter, we considered multi-viewpoint document summarization that is focused on topics and summary types to suit users' information needs. We found significant improvements in summary coverage by combining sentence type and genre classification information to discriminate among fact-reporting, opinion-oriented, and knowledge-focused summaries in experiments with our new test collection.

7. Acknowledgement

This work was partially supported by the Grants-in-Aid for Exploratory Research (#16650053) and Scientific Research in Priority Areas of "Informatics" (#13224087) from the Ministry of Education, Culture, Sports, Science and Technology, Japan. This research was also partially supported by the Kayamori Foundation of Informational Science Advancement.

8. Bibliography

Angheluta, R., Moens, M. F., and De Busser, R. (2003) K. U. Leuven Summarization System - DUC 2003. In *Proceedings of the Workshop on Text Summarization (DUC 2003) at the 2003 Human Language Technology Conference (HLT/NAACL 2003)*, Edmonton, Canada.

Bazerman, C. (2004) Speech Acts, Genres, and Activity Systems: How Texts Organize Activity and People. In Bazerman, C. and Prior, P. (Eds.) *What Writing Does and How It Does It – An Introduction to Analyzing Texts and Textual Practices*. 309-339. Lawrence Erlbaum Associates, Mahwah, NJ.

Biber, D., Conrad, S., and Reppen, R. (1998) Corpus Linguistics - Investigating Language Structure and Use (Reprinted, 2002). Cambridge Approaches to Linguistics. Cambridge University Press.

Borlund, P. (2003) The Concept of Relevance in IR. *Journal of the American Society for Information Science and Technology*, 54(10), 913-925.

Cardie, C., Wiebe, J., Wilson, T., and Litman, D. (2003) Combining Low-level and Summary Representations of Opinions for Multi-Perspective Question Answering. In *AAAI Spring Symposium on New Directions in Question Answering*, 20-27.

Finn, A., Kushmerick, N., and Smyth, B. (2002) Genre Classification and Domain Transfer for Information Filtering. In Crestani, F., Girolami, M., and van Rijsbergen, C. J. (Eds.) *Proceedings of ECIR 2002 Advances in Information Retrieval, 24th BCS-IRSG European Colloquium on IR Research*, Glasgow, UK, 353-362. Published in *Lecture Notes in Computer Science 2291*, Springer-Verlag, Heidelberg, Germany.

Harman, D. and Over, P. (2004) The Effects of Human Variation in DUC Summarization Evaluation. In *Proceedings of Text Summarization Branches Out, Workshop at the 42nd ACL 2004*, Barcelona, Spain, 10-17.

Hatzivassiloglou, V., Klavans, J. L., Holcombe, M. L., Barzilay, R., Kan, M. Y., and McKeown, K. R. (2001) Simfinder: A Flexible Clustering Tool for Summarization. In *Proceedings of the Workshop on Automatic Summarization at the Second Meeting of the North American Chapter of the Association for Computational Linguistics (NAACL 2001)*, Pittsburgh, PA, 41-49.

Hirao, T., Okumura, M., Fukushima, T. and Nanba, H. (2004) Text Summarization Challenge 3: Text summarization evaluation at NTCIR Workshop 4. In *Proceedings of the Fourth NTCIR Workshop on Research in Evaluation of Information Access Technologies: Information Retrieval, Question Answering, and Summarization*. National Institute of Informatics, Japan. Available from: <http://research.nii.ac.jp/ntcir>.

Joachims, T. (2002) Learning to Classify Text Using Support Vector Machines: Methods, Theory, and Algorithms. Kluwer Academic Publishers.

Kando, N. (2004) Overview of the Fourth NTCIR Workshop. In *Proceedings of the Fourth NTCIR Workshop on Research in Evaluation of Information Access Technologies: Information Retrieval, Question Answering, and Summarization.* National Institute of Informatics, Japan. Available from: <http://research.nii.ac.jp/ntcir>.

Kando, N. (1996) Text Structure Analysis Based on Human Recognition: Cases of Japanese Newspaper Articles and English Newspaper Articles (in Japanese). In *Research Bulletin of National Center for Science Information Systems,* 8, 107-126.

Karlgren, J. and Cutting, D. (1994) Recognizing Text Genres with Simple Metrics Using Discriminant Analysis. In *Proceedings of the 15th International Conference on Computational Linguistics (COLING 1994),* Kyoto, Japan, 1071-1075.

Kessler, B., Nunberg, G., Schuetze, H. (1997) Automatic Detection of Text Genre. In *Proceedings of the 35th ACL/8th EACL 1997,* Madrid, Spain, 32-38.

Landis, J. R. and Koch, G. G. (1977) The Measurement of Observer Agreement for Categorical Data. *Biometrics,* 33, 159-74.

Lin, C-Y., and Hovy, E. (2002) Manual and Automatic Evaluation of Summaries. In *Proceedings of the Workshop on Automatic Summarization at the 40th ACL 2002,* University of Pennsylvania, PA.

Maña-López, M. J., Buenaga, M. D., and Gómez-Hidalgo, J. M. (2004) Multidocument Summarization: An Added Value to Clustering in Interactive Retrieval. *ACM Transactions on Information Systems (TOIS),* 22(2), 215-241.

Mani, I. (2001) Automatic Summarization. Volume 3 of Natural Language Processing, John Benjamins Pub, Amsterdam, Netherlands.

McKnight, L. and Srinivasan, P. (2003) Categorization of Sentence Types in Medical Abstracts. In *Proceedings of the American Medical Informatics Association (AMIA) Symposium,* Ottawa, Canada, 440-444.

Pomerantz, J. (2002) Question Taxonomies for Digital Reference. Ph. D. thesis, Syracuse University.

Radev, D. R., Jing, H., Styś, M., and Tam, D. (2004) Centroid-based Summarization of Multiple Documents. *Information Processing and Management,* 40(6), 919-938.

Rath, G. J., Resnick, A., and Savage, T. R. (1961) The Formation of Abstracts by the Selection of Sentences. *American Documentation,* 2(12), 139-208.

Sebastiani, F. (2002) Machine Learning in Automated Text Categorization. *ACM Computing Surveys,* 34(1), 1-47.

Seki, Y., Eguchi, K., and Kando, N. (2004a) User-focused Multi-Document Summarization with Paragraph Clustering and Sentence-type Filtering. In *Proceedings of the Fourth NTCIR Workshop on Research in Evaluation of Information Access Technologies: Information Retrieval, Question Answering, and Summarization*. National Institute of Informatics, Japan. Available from: <http://research.nii.ac.jp/ntcir>.

Seki, Y., Eguchi, K., and Kando, N. (2004b) Compact Summarization for Mobile Phones. In Crestani, F., Dunlop, M. and Mizzaro, S. (Eds.) *Mobile and Ubiquitous Information Access*. 172-186. Published in *Lecture Notes in Computer Science 2954,* Springer-Verlag, Heidelberg, Germany.

Simpson, J. A. and Weiner, E. S. C. (1991) The Oxford English Dictionary (second edition). Clarendon Press, New York.

Spärck-Jones, K. (1999) Automatic Summarizing: Factors and Directions. In Mani, I., and Maybury, M. T. (Eds.) *Advances in Automatic Text Summarization*. 1-12. MIT Press, Cambridge, MA.

Stamatatos, E., Fakotakis, N., and Kokkinakis, G. (2000) Text Genre Detection Using Common Word Frequencies. In *Proceedings of the 18th International Conference on Computational Linguistics (COLING2000),* Saarbrücken, Germany, 808-814.

Stein G. C., Strzalkowski, T., and Wise, G. B. (2000) Evaluating Summaries for Multiple Documents in an Interactive Environment. In *Proceedings of the Second International Conference on Language Resources & Evaluation (LREC2000)*, Athens, Greece, 1651-1657.

Teufel, S. and Moens, M. (2002) Summarizing Scientific Articles: Experiments with Relevance and Rhetorical Status. *Computational Linguistics*, 28(4), 409-445.

The National Institute for Japanese Language (2004) Bunruigoihyo – enlarged and revised edition. Dainippon-Tosho.

Xu, J. Weischedel, R., and Licuanan, A. (2004) Evaluation of an Extraction-Based Approach to Answering Definitional Questions. In *Proceedings of the 27th ACM SIGIR 2004*, Sheffield, UK, 418-424.

INDEX

A

academic writing, 233, 234, 243, 244
accuracy, 95, 140, 144, 152, 153, 154, 155, 156, 167, 211, 215, 222, 223, 235, 240, 243, 260, 273, 276, 294, 297, 299, 324
affect
  class centrality, 104
  classes, 94, 95, 96, 104, 106
  expression, 49
  lexicon, 93, 95, 97, 98, 100, 101, 104, 293
  patterns, 103, 105
  tool, 143
animacy, 23, 28
animate agent, 23, 24, 25
annotating opinions, 61, 78, 80, 91
antonymy, 42, 109, 111, 112, 118
argumentation, 159, 164, 169, 173, 219, 246, 247, 248, 252, 259, 260, 329, 330, 332
argumentative structure, 11, 12, 233, 248
argumentative zoning, 159, 161, 162, 163, 167, 233, 236, 237, 244
arguments selection, 113
arguments structure, 113
attitude, 1, 2, 3, 4, 6, 7, 9, 23, 25, 26, 27, 28, 29, 35, 36, 41, 44, 63, 64, 79, 81, 82, 88, 115, 118, 143, 144, 146, 187, 188, 189, 190, 191, 192, 195, 199, 203, 217, 221, 249, 293, 318
  assessment, 1
  expressions, 23, 25, 28, 29
  extraction, 23
attitudinal loading, 23, 25, 29
attribution, 11, 13, 17, 19, 20, 125, 162, 164, 216, 229, 230, 231, 237, 268, 269
automated labeling, 129
automatic citation analysis, 247
automatic dialogue summarization, 172, 181, 182
automatic genre classification, 319, 326, 327
automatic sentence-type annotation, 325, 330
automatic summarization, 172
automatic tagging, 143, 144, 146, 158

B

backchannel, 152
base attitudinal valence, 1, 2
base valence, 3, 4, 5, 7, 9
belief space, 11, 19, 21
bias, 84, 162, 172, 173, 175, 177, 179, 181, 182, 219, 293
bigrams, 136, 138, 145, 146, 147, 150, 151, 156, 305
biomedical literature, 247, 256, 257, 260

C

calculation of local interactions, 9
CATS, 156, 157
centrality of a word, 95
certainty expressions, 61, 63, 74
citation, 159, 160, 161, 163, 165, 166, 167, 168, 237, 247, 248, 250, 251, 252, 253, 254, 255, 256, 257, 258, 259, 260, 261, 262, 263, 266
citation analysis, 159, 248, 250, 251, 262
classification scheme, 132, 162, 251
  probabilistic, 303
clinical genetics, 33, 35, 38
clustering-based multi-document summarization frameworks, 322
computational lexicon, 109, 188
computational stylistics, 215, 216
Computerized Referential Activity, 51
  CRA, 49, 51, 52, 53, 58
conjunction, 234
connotative force, 2
contextual shifters, 1, 2, 4, 5

D

data mining, 281, 294
database, 46, 109, 116, 117, 118, 121, 123,
    140, 150, 151, 152, 258, 260, 261, 282,
    283, 284, 285, 286, 298, 312, 313
decision tree, 211, 259, 260, 299
discourse, 1, 3, 6, 7, 9, 23, 24,
    25, 30, 31, 42, 46, 51, 62, 63, 76, 143,
    144, 145, 157, 161, 163, 164, 167, 169,
    203, 212, 213, 216, 217, 218, 220, 221,
    229, 235, 240, 246, 248, 249, 251, 252,
    253, 257, 259, 260, 267, 294, 326
    cues, 251, 252, 253, 259, 260
    Discourse Attributes Analysis Program
        (DAAP), 49, 52
    referent, 24
    structure, 3, 6, 9, 42, 157, 248, 252,
        326
Discourse Attributes Analysis Program
    (DAAP), 49, 52
document classification, 8, 199, 200, 201,
    207, 272
dynamic attitudinal loading, 23

E

elaborations, 6, 7
emotion, 23, 51, 52, 73, 78, 79, 93,
    94, 95, 98, 99, 106, 109, 110, 112, 113,
    121, 143, 144, 145, 146, 158, 172, 293
emotive patterns, 98, 99, 100, 101, 105
enhancement, 217, 227, 228, 263
entropy, 151, 153, 154, 155, 196
epistemic comments, 61, 63, 64, 65
experiencer, 35, 36, 37, 67, 78, 110, 113,
    114, 115, 117, 120
experimental science, 215, 216, 217, 218,
    219, 224, 229
explanatory reasoning, 218
extension, 19, 104, 105, 121, 125, 127, 130,
    196, 206, 217, 221, 227, 285, 318, 330

F

fact-reporting summary, 328, 331
feature
    hypernymy generalization, 303

representation, 199, 203, 206, 207, 208,
    211
selection, 209, 303, 304, 307, 308, 309,
    310, 311, 314, 315
structure, 109, 121
synonymy generalization, 303
feeling, 28, 97, 109, 110, 111, 112, 113,
    114, 115, 116, 117, 118, 119, 120, 121,
    122, 123, 172
financial analysis, 297
fuzzy sets, 281, 296

G

General Inquirer, 94, 95, 98, 99, 100, 101,
    107, 188, 189, 198
genetic, 33, 34, 35, 36, 37, 38
genre, 1, 3, 7, 8, 9, 14, 17, 33, 34,
    63, 74, 139, 167, 213, 215, 216, 234, 244,
    247, 267, 294, 300, 317, 318, 319, 320, 322,
    325, 326, 327, 328, 329, 330, 332, 333
    classification, 74, 216, 318, 320, 322,
        327, 328, 332, 333
    contraints, 9
    feature, 319, 320, 325, 326, 328, 329, 330
    structure, 1
gold standard evaluation, 98
graph, 111, 112, 121, 267

H

hedging
    cues, 248, 252, 253, 254, 255, 256, 257,
        259, 260, 261, 262
    hedge, 61, 64, 65, 161, 247, 249, 250,
        252, 253, 254, 255, 256
historical science, 216, 218, 219, 225, 229
hypernymy feature generalization, 303

I

information retrieval, 81, 83, 144, 257, 307,
    314, 317, 318, 320, 324
informational role, 25
inheritance, 35, 38, 109, 116
insults, 97
intelligence analysis, 281, 294
intensifier, 4, 65, 114, 116, 118, 121

intensity, 95, 96, 105, 106, 109, 111,
114, 118, 120, 121, 122, 123, 218
Internet buzz, 281, 285
interpersonal distance, 199, 200, 201,
203, 204, 205, 209, 210, 211, 212
interpretation, 2, 14, 17, 18, 19, 20, 34,
73, 109, 116, 119, 123, 126, 172, 219,
227, 228, 268, 270, 319
inter-subject agreement, 41
Inverse Document Frequency
IDF, 150, 151, 153, 154, 155, 163, 323
irony, 5, 190, 269

K

kappa coefficient, 326
knowledge-focused summary, 328, 330, 332

L

Lasswell Value Dictionary, 94, 106
lexical
choice, 1, 10, 24, 189, 193, 196, 197, 210,
248, 252
cohesion, 42, 43, 45
nuances, 187, 189, 191, 193
semantic relations, 41, 42, 43, 45
lexicon
discovery, 93
linguistic
properties, 113, 118
style, 49, 50
summaries, 281, 282, 283, 284, 285,
293, 294, 295, 296

M

machine learning, 10, 74, 107, 126, 140,
141, 159, 161, 162, 168, 197, 199, 200,
205, 209, 211, 214, 218, 219, 228, 230,
231, 233, 239, 245, 246, 259, 265, 267,
268, 271, 272, 273, 278, 279, 301, 303,
304, 305, 315, 316, 335
manual tagging, 61, 73
marketing research, 281
medical documentation, 33, 38

metaphor, 113
metonymy, 115, 116, 117
metrics, 151, 153, 157, 265, 277, 294, 320
modal context, 4
modal operators, 5
modality, 63, 65, 203, 209, 220, 221,
224, 262, 269, 323
modalization, 227
mode, 202, 217
modulation, 227, 228, 249
movie reviews, 8, 196, 267, 304, 305,
308, 309
multi-entity evaluation
multi-perspective question answering, 77,
78, 88, 90
multiple code theory, 49, 60
multiple constraints, 1
multiple-document summarization
MDS, 318, 320, 321

N

narrative analysis, 49
narrative mode, 50
natural language generation, 33, 34, 172,
188, 191, 197
natural language processing, 23, 41, 61, 78,
125, 143, 172, 265, 278
NEAR operator, 95, 101, 104
near-synonyms, 187, 188, 189, 190,
191, 193, 195, 196, 197
negatives, 4
n-grams, 145, 146, 147, 150, 151, 152, 153,
154, 155, 156, 157, 304, 308
nominalization, 113, 114, 118, 120, 203, 204
NTCIR Text Summarization Challenge
(TSC), 320

O

opinion
user, 94
opinion polarity, 303, 304, 307, 309, 310
opinion-holders, 125, 127, 129, 130, 135,
137, 140
opinion-oriented summary, 328, 329, 331

P

paradigm words, 95, 101, 102, 103, 104,
    105, 106
    positive-negative, 101
paraphrases, 11, 109, 116, 117, 118, 119,
    197
perlocutionary force, 3
perspective, 23, 33, 34, 35, 36, 37,
    38, 46, 51, 61, 62, 65, 67, 69, 70, 71, 72,
    73, 77, 78, 79, 80, 82, 83, 84, 86, 88, 89,
    123, 125, 203, 213, 214, 287, 304, 319,
    334
point of view, 3, 8, 9, 16, 33, 35, 38, 45,
    61, 67, 70, 71, 73, 74, 75, 111, 169, 171,
    173, 175, 176, 177, 178, 179, 180, 181,
    182, 188, 196, 268, 326
pointwise mutual information
    PMI, 103, 105, 107
polarity
    negative, 95, 111, 274, 275, 277, 303,
        304, 307, 314, 315
    positive, 105, 111, 274, 275, 304, 305,
        314
politeness, 73, 171, 172, 173, 174, 175,
    177, 178, 179, 180, 181, 182, 183, 184,
    248, 263
precision, 14, 99, 100, 123, 131, 136,
    137, 138, 139, 167, 240, 242, 266, 267,
    269, 272, 274, 275, 277, 278, 299, 303,
    304, 305, 306, 310, 313, 314, 315, 320,
    324, 328, 330, 332, 333
predicative clause, 25
predictive comment, 227
presuppositions, 5
product review, 7, 12, 16, 20, 267, 278, 300,
    305
profile structure, 11, 14, 15, 17, 18, 20
propositions, 63, 125, 126, 127, 132, 135,
    136, 137, 138, 140, 215, 217, 221, 224,
    227, 283, 312
prototype, 17, 18, 109, 116, 118, 251, 260
psychiatric, 51, 59, 143
psychoanalytic sessions, 53, 58
psychological
    models, 143
    state, 109, 110, 121, 122
    verb, 109, 110, 113, 114, 115, 123
    verbs, 109, 110, 113, 114, 115

psychology, 42, 43, 116, 156

Q

question answering, 77, 78, 80, 90,
    125, 127
    corpus, 77

R

recall, 14, 99, 131, 136, 138, 139, 167,
    240, 242, 266, 268, 272, 274, 277, 278,
    299, 300, 303, 304, 314, 315, 324
referential activity
    RA, 49, 50, 59, 60
referential process, 23, 51
register, 11, 94, 199, 201, 202, 203, 204,
    206, 207, 209, 210, 213, 216, 217, 228,
    244, 319
reported speech, 11, 12, 13, 14, 16, 17,
    18, 20
rhetoric of science, 247, 252, 256, 260, 262
rhetorical organization, 224, 228
rhetorical parsing, 228, 262
rhetorical structure, 14, 94, 216, 224,
    244, 245, 247, 252, 253, 256

S

science writing, 247
scientific method, 215, 228, 257, 260, 261
semantic
    axes, 93, 94, 105, 106
    category, 63, 117
    classe, 104, 105, 109, 110, 111, 113,
        116
    classification, 109, 278, 300
    database, 116
    fields, 94
    knowledge, 116
    lexicon, 109, 116, 267
    orientation, 106, 107, 140, 187, 188,
        189, 190, 192, 193, 195, 196, 203
    parsing, 125, 127, 129, 133
    polarity, 117
    representation, 77, 121, 122, 123, 191,
        196
    scales, 104

sentence type, 253, 254, 256, 317, 318, 319, 320, 323, 324, 325, 326, 328, 330, 331, 332, 333
   vectors, 146, 322
sentence-type annotation, 319, 320, 322, 323, 327, 328, 330, 332
sentence-type annotation effect, 332
sentiment, 10, 77, 78, 118, 120, 121, 122, 159, 168, 265, 266, 268, 272, 277, 278, 281, 286, 289, 290, 291, 293, 294, 297, 299, 300, 303, 314
   analysis, 77, 265, 290, 297, 300
   identification, 303
situational reference, 26, 27
spam, 93, 94
stochastic affect, 143
story line, 224
style, 13, 18, 28, 33, 34, 49, 50, 52, 74, 78, 83, 134, 188, 191, 216, 217, 247, 248, 251, 253, 257, 260, 272, 312, 319
   analysis, 33
subjectivity, 41, 42, 44, 45, 63, 65, 67, 80, 83, 89, 130, 140, 141, 168, 200, 228, 239, 252, 311
subjectivity collocations, 228
subtopics, 8, 321, 322
summarization
   knowledge-focused, 319, 321
   linguistic, 281, 282, 283, 284, 285, 293, 294, 295, 296
   multi-document, 318, 319, 320, 321
   opinion-oriented, 328, 329, 331
   viewpoint, 318, 321, 333
Summarizer With Interactive-Clustering from Multiple viewpoints SWIM, 317, 318, 328
support vector machines (SVM), 133, 134, 211, 222, 278, 299, 314, 316, 323, 326
SWIM
   Summarizer With Interactive-Clustering from Multiple viewpoints, 317, 318, 328
syntactic analysis, 13, 23, 24, 288
synthetic thinking, 218, 224
systemic features, 199, 203, 206, 209, 210, 212
systemic functional linguistics, 199, 215, 216

T

tenor, 202, 204, 210, 212, 217
term-document matrix, 150
text
   classification, 167, 206, 210, 211, 265, 267, 270, 271, 272
   generation, 187, 213
   mining, 11, 20, 265, 271, 273, 281
Thematic Apperception Test (TAT), 52, 53
thesaurus generation, 95
thought unit, 145, 146, 147, 148, 151, 152, 154, 155, 156
time-series analysis, 281
topicality, 24, 267, 268, 270, 271, 273, 288
transcription rules, 54, 58
transitivity, 23, 30, 31
trigrams, 136, 138, 146, 147, 150

U

uncertainty, 3, 38, 61, 64, 73, 249, 276
unigrams, 145, 146, 147, 149, 150, 151, 152, 156, 305

V

valence
   calculation, 1, 9
   negative, 4, 7, 8
   positive, 4, 5, 7
   shifters, 1, 196, 197
validative comment, 227, 228
vectors, 150, 151, 152, 322
viewpoint, 164, 177, 179, 180, 317, 318, 319, 320

W

weighted approach, 156
weighted dictionary, 49, 52, 57
Weighted Referential Activity Dictionary (WRAD), 49, 52
window, 95, 156, 185, 253, 254, 255, 256